Environmental Resources and Constraints in the Former Soviet Republics

Environmental Resources and Constraints in the Former Soviet Republics

edited by
Philip R. Pryde

Westview Press

BOULDER • SAN FRANCISCO • OXFORD

Copyright © 1995 by Westview Press, Inc.

Published in 1995 in the United States of America by Westview Press, Inc., 5500 Central Avenue, Boulder, Colorado 80301-2877, and in the United Kingdom by Westview Press, 12 Hid's Copse Road, Cumnor Hill, Oxford OX2 9JJ

Library of Congress Cataloging-in-Publication Data
Pryde, Philip R.
   Environmental resources and constraints in the former Soviet
Republics / Philip R. Pryde.
      p.   cm.
   Includes bibliographical references and index.
   ISBN 0-8133-1742-8 —0-8133-2965-5 (pbk.)
   1. Former Soviet republics—Environmental conditions.
2. Environmental policy—Former Soviet republics.   I. Title.
GE160.F6P79   1995
363.7'00947—dc20   94-33120
                                                                                        CIP

Printed and bound in the United States of America

 The paper used in this publication meets the requirements of the American National Standard for Permanence of Paper for Printed Library Materials Z39.48-1984.

10   9   8   7   6   5   4   3

Contents

Preface

This book represents one of the many international responses to the 1991 dissolution of the Soviet Union. Previously, most writers on topics dealing with the USSR chose to present their material in a topical fashion, describing a particular situation across the whole of the vast Soviet nation. After December 1991, the approach of examining the entire USSR in a topical manner was no longer feasible. Fifteen new countries had emerged from the womb of the dying Soviet Union and now had to be treated as individual entities. Very few previous books on the Soviet Union, whether textbooks or thematic works, had adopted this type of regional approach, and indeed, the editor's own 1991 work, *Environmental Management in the Soviet Union,* is unfortunately also now out of date in this regard. It seemed timely, therefore, to examine the environmental situation in the former USSR in the format of a regional analysis, to see how each new republic's environmental situation appeared when viewed in a discrete spatial context, shorn of the unifying umbrella of central Soviet planning and control.

Accordingly, most of the book's chapters are devoted to an examination of the environmental situation in a particular former Soviet republic. There are four exceptions. Chapter 1 examines the changed environmental situation in the context of the former USSR as a whole. Chapter 2 summarizes the situation over the vast breadth of the Russian Federation. The last chapter endeavors to present some conclusions that seem pertinent to the new conditions as these republics look ahead to the twenty-first century.

One portion of the book, Chapter 10, embraces a different format than the other republic-oriented chapters. It looks at the administrative structure for managing environmental affairs in some detail for one key republic, Ukraine, and in so doing provides considerable insight into environmental management in this important new nation. However, given that all the newly independent republics have inherited the same environmental legacy from the antecedent Soviet bureaucracy, what is said in Chapter 10 for Ukraine is equally applicable in a general sense for virtually all of the other former Soviet republics as well.

Chapters 3 through 20 have been prepared by highly knowledgeable authorities on each former republic. They were asked to include in each chapter, in addition to a discussion and analysis of environmental problems, background information on the history, physical geography, natural resources, and economic advantages and disadvantages of each republic. Since the goal was to present a view of the republic as seen through the author's eyes, no attempt was made to be sure that each chapter author gave exactly the same weight, or number of pages, to each of the requested topics. As a result, some chapters will contain more about the republic's history or physical geography than others. In some cases, the editor added small amounts of additional information he felt was important to an understanding of the region under discussion, but in general the approach and style of the individual chapter authors were honored to the maximum extent feasible. The editor is most grateful for the diligent effort taken by the various authors in the preparation of their respective chapters.

The transliteration style used is generally that of the U.S. Board on Geographic Names, with four exceptions. First, place-names that are commonly used in English in a non-transliterated form (e.g., Moscow instead of Moskva, Georgia, etc.) are accepted here in the common form. As with "Moscow," there appears to be a tendency in English-language works to retain the name "Kiev," rather than the Ukrainian form "Kyyiv." Second, the apostrophe that represents the Cyrillic soft sign is omitted from place-names in the text for ease of reading (e.g., Guryev instead of Gur'yev); however, for accuracy it is retained in transliterated titles in the bibliographies and in the names of individuals. Third, to assist readers not familiar with Russian to pronounce certain place-names correctly, "ai" is used rather than "ay" (e.g., Baikal, krai, Altai). Fourth, some chapter authors prepared their bibliographies using the Library of Congress system, and these have been retained in the style submitted. It should also be noted that in the bibliographies for certain chapters (such as Belarus and Ukraine), some of the works have been transliterated from languages other than Russian.

A problem for virtually everyone is the massive re-naming (or re-spelling) of cities and other place-names that has taken place since 1991. In general, the new names of cities are used in the text, immediately followed by the old name (in parentheses) the first time it appears, with the new name only generally used thereafter; an exception is made for certain Central Asian republics where many of the new names are so unfamiliar (e.g., Ququon instead of Kokand) that the old name has been used (with the new in parentheses) to avoid confusion.

Photographs taken by chapter authors or others are acknowledged in the photo captions. All photos without acknowledgment were taken by the editor of the volume. All republic maps, unless otherwise indicated, were prepared by Derrick Mar of the cartographic staff of the Department of Geography at San Diego State University, whose cheerful willingness to endlessly re-draft them is greatly appreciated.

The editor wishes to thank all those who helped make this work possible. The foremost expression of appreciation is extended to the National Council for Soviet and East European Research, whose generous support transformed this volume from concept into reality. Equal appreciation goes to the many chapter authors, whose expertise and research and writing skills have resulted in a coherent presentation of the current problems and potentials of each of the newly independent states. The assistance and guidance of Rebecca Ritke and Shena Redmond at Westview Press are likewise gratefully acknowledged. Other organizations that have assisted in the preparation of the work include the San Diego State University (SDSU) Foundation, the Center for Earth Systems Analysis Research (CESAR) of the Department of Geography at SDSU, the East European Programme of the IUCN (World Conservation Union), ISAR (formerly the Institute for Soviet-American Relations), the Institute of Geography of the Russian Academy of Sciences, the Center for Russian and Soviet Studies of the Monterey Institute for International Studies, and the editors of the magazine *Nature* and the publishing company V. H. Winston & Son, who graciously permitted certain tables and maps to be reprinted. The editor's thanks are extended to all of these organizations for their assistance.

Sincere appreciation is also extended to all those individuals who helped with the processing and preparation of the chapter manuscripts: Diane Huston, Lisa Chaddock, Derrick Mar, David McKinsey, Paul Lebowitz, Vicki Parker, Rebecca Ritke, Meg Streif, and Jillian Swope; also to Julie Marini at the SDSU Foundation; and to those individuals (chapter authors and others) who made their photographs available for use in the book and who are acknowledged by name in the text. Thanks are also extended for the help of all those (many of whom may not be known by name to the volume editor) who assisted the various chapter authors in preparing the individual manuscripts. A volume of this magnitude cannot come about without the cooperation of a great many persons, and the editor's indebtedness to them all is gratefully acknowledged.

Philip R. Pryde

1

The Environmental Implications of Republic Sovereignty

Philip R. Pryde

December 1991 was a month perhaps without precedence in the history of the world. For during that month, one of the two most powerful countries on the planet simply disappeared from the face of the earth virtually overnight, without a shot being fired. Other countries, generally much smaller ones, have been greatly transformed or diminished as a result of war, but usually at least the name remained. But by December 31, 1991, the Union of Soviet Socialist Republics (USSR), which had been the largest and most militarily powerful country on earth at the start of the month, was no longer extant in either form or name. It was superseded by fifteen independent countries, most (but not all) of them joined together in a loose confederation termed the Commonwealth of Independent States (CIS), created to address the common interests and problems of these newly independent republics (Figure 1.1).

These fifteen new countries vary tremendously, both in size and in population characteristics (Table 1.1). Some, such as Russia, Ukraine, and Kazakhstan, are large and rich in natural resources, while others, such as Armenia, Moldova, and Latvia, have relatively few mineral deposits. Some of the more interior republics are landlocked and lack any direct access to the ocean. Almost all have severe environmental problems that have been well studied and reported upon in recent years, in works such as those listed in the bibliography. However, the new political reality requires that the contemporary environmental situation be examined in a regional manner, that is, in the specific context of each of these fifteen new nation-states. Some of the new nations will have an economic foundation that will permit a modest amount of financial resources to be devoted to environmental enhancement, and some, unfortunately, will not.

The process of national independence typically constitutes a period of

2

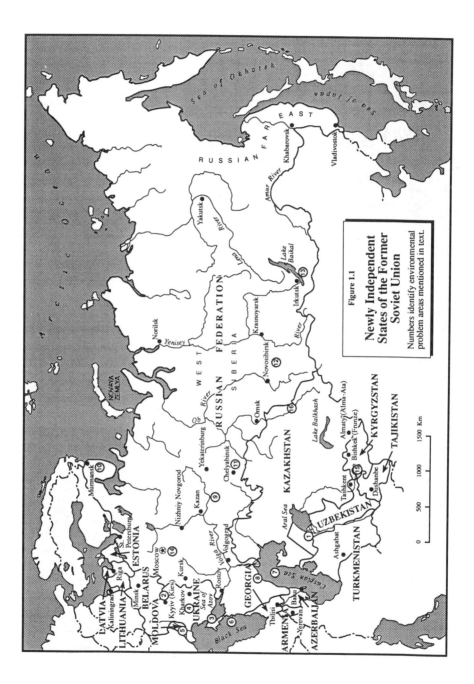

Figure 1.1

Newly Independent States of the Former Soviet Union

Numbers identify environmental problem areas mentioned in text.

Table 1.1 Population Characteristics of the Former Soviet Republics

Republic	1989 Population	Area (Sq. Km.)	Popu- lation per Sq. Km.	Titular Group as % of Pop'n	Russians as a % of Pop'n	Birth- rate, 1987	% Natural Population Increase 1989
Russia	147386000	17075400	8.63	81.5	81.5	19.8	0.20
Ukraine	51704000	603700	85.65	72.6	22.1	14.8	0.10
Uzbekistan	19906000	447400	44.49	71.3	8.3	37.0	2.70
Kazakhstan	16538000	2717300	6.09	39.7	37.8	25.5	1.40
Belarus	10200000	207600	49.13	77.8	13.2	16.1	0.30
Azerbaijan	7029000	86600	81.17	82.6	5.6	26.9	2.00
Georgia	5449000	69700	78.18	70.2	6.3	17.9	0.90
Tajikistan	5112000	143100	35.72	62.2	7.6	41.8	3.20
Moldova	4341000	33700	128.80	64.4	12.9	21.8	0.80
Kyrgyzstan	4291000	198500	21.62	52.3	21.5	32.6	2.20
Lithuania	3690000	65200	56.60	79.6	9.4	16.2	0.40
Turkmenistan	3534000	488100	7.24	71.9	9.5	37.2	2.70
Armenia	3283000	29800	110.17	93.3	1.6	22.9	1.80
Latvia	2631000	63700	42.09	52.1	34.1	15.8	0.10
Estonia	1573000	45100	34.88	61.5	30.3	16.0	0.20

Sources: Schwartz (1991); and Population Reference Bureau, "1992 World Population Data Sheet".

great euphoria followed by a long period of increasing realization that severe economic hardships (and sometimes political instability) are frequently the price of independence. In the case of the former Soviet republics, the second phase has already been encountered, and a number of sobering implications of independence are already apparent. The goal of this book is to examine one key set of challenges these new countries face, those relating to natural resources and environmental problems, and to examine how they relate to each country's larger economic and geographic setting. This first chapter will look at the general environmental situation that existed in 1992–93 following the dissolution of the Soviet Union as a national entity and some of the more important ways in which the fifteen new nations differ from one another.

Economic Implications of Independence for the Environment

In the short run, the independence of the former Soviet republics will tend to have generally unfavorable implications for environmental improvement. The reasons are mainly economic and relate to the potential for underemployment, lack of investment capital, and a tendency to give highest priority to rapid economic advancement. In difficult economic times, it is easy for environmental issues to be seen as a "frill" and to be relegated to a future agenda. The nature of the economic problem in most of the former Soviet republics can be appreciated by the following example from the Baltic states.

There are many factories in the Baltic republics that make good consumer products, though not quite up to U.S./EEC/Japanese standards. Thus, their market has been limited in the past to the USSR and Eastern Europe. They could still sell in these regions today, but Russians and most other peoples of eastern Europe have no money to buy expensive durable goods, and the Baltic countries aren't particularly desirous of acquiring rubles anyway. A further complication is that Russia may also be the major supplier of raw materials or parts for these factories, but Russia doesn't currently view the Baltic states as a favored trading partner and may delay shipment or increase the prices of these materials. The Baltic factories do not have the economic ability to acquire these materials from western Europe or other outside sources; and as a result, many of these factories have had to decrease production, sometimes greatly. If privately owned, they might become bankrupt and be forced out of business. But at present they are government owned and are now kept operating on a part-time basis so that people will still have jobs. This situation, however, places severe economic strains on the governments of the Baltic countries, which formerly derived operating incomes from value-added taxes levied on these firms' products. As a result, there is presently little money for many worthwhile government programs, and among these is environmental enhancement. Much of this scenario applies to all the other former republics as well.

Further, a focus on environmental health has caused many factories and mines to shut down, at least temporarily. When coal miners in Ukraine or West Siberia go out on strikes, steel mills may be forced to cut back production, as well as the enterprises that use the steel.

For the above and other reasons, careful allocation and redirection of economic resources will be needed in most of the newly independent countries (McAuley, 1991). Each new country will now be responsible for funding not only its own environmental improvements but all of its other social needs as well. During the Soviet period, republics created a network of protected areas to help conserve biotic resources, and each new nation must now find funding for all of its parks and nature preserves, too (see Appendixes 1.1 and 1.2). In many of the former republics, economic development may well be given a short-term priority over environmental enhancement, echoing a philosophy found both in numerous developing nations, as well as in developed ones during hard economic times. In many republics, environmental conditions have deteriorated still further from 1991 levels. To achieve environmental improvements, outside economic help will be needed in many cases.

The availability of natural resources will also be an important variable, resulting from the inherently uneven distribution of such resources throughout the territory of the former Soviet Union (Table 1.2). Many of the new nations may find themselves cut off from easy access to key natural resources that exist mainly in other republics, or at least find them to be more expensive. For example, many southern republics will now have to import much of their timber needs, their metallurgical resources, and in some cases petroleum products from Russia or other foreign countries on less favorable terms than they enjoyed under the economic umbrella of the USSR.

Energy resources are central to the economy of all nations and will be a critical factor for many of the new republics. The vast majority of the nations of the world are not self-sufficient in energy resources, and the same will be true for most of the former Soviet republics. Russia, Kazakhstan, Azerbaijan, Turkmenistan, and Ukraine have reserves of one or more fossil fuels in abundance, but other republics will become net importers of energy products. Table 1.3 indicates the relative advantages or disadvantages of each republic with regard to internal fossil fuel resources. Trade agreements regarding these energy resources are emerging but may be different from those that existed under the USSR. For example, Ukraine has indicated an interest in acquiring fossil fuels from Iran, and Turkmenistan may sell its surplus natural gas to Turkey, Pakistan, and other non-CIS countries (as well as to some former USSR republics).

Some republics will have valuable resources to export to improve their foreign trade balance. As noted, Turkmenistan has natural gas, and Ukraine has iron ore, Azerbaijan has oil, and Kazakhstan possesses a wealth of mineral resources of many types. In certain of these cases, however, the countries are geographically remote, and gaining access to world trade routes may be a problem. Also, some republics, in the interest of gaining foreign income, may have to pursue economic activities that they might prefer to curtail for environmental reasons. As examples, Armenia, Ukraine, and Lithuania might have to continue to operate their Soviet-built nuclear power stations, and Estonia may have to mine at least a small portion of its phosphate deposits in the interest of both its internal economy and its international trade balance.

Among the environmental consequences of the former Soviet system with which the new countries will have to deal are those relating to public health,

Table 1.2   Economic Resources of the Former Soviet Republics

Republic	Soil for Agriculture	Fossil Fuel Resources(a)	Commercial Nuclear Reactor Units	Non-Fuel Mineral Resources	Electrical Energy Production 1990(b)
Armenia	Fair*	Few	2	Some	3.17(b)
Azerbaijan	Good*	Moderate O, Some NG	0	Some	3.30
Belarus	Good	Some NG	0	Few	3.87
Estonia	Fair	Sizable OS	0	Some	10.93
Georgia	Good	Few	0	Moderate	2.61
Kazakhstan	Very good	Sizable C, O, Some NG	1	Abundant	5.28
Kyrgyzstan	Good*	Some C	0	Some	3.12
Latvia	Good	Few	0	Few	2.46
Lithuania	Good	Few	2	Few	7.70
Moldova	Very good	Few	0	Few	3.62
Russia	Fair- Very good	Abundant C, O, NG	28	Abundant	7.34
Tajikistan	Good*	Some NG	0	Some	3.54
Turkmenistan	Good*	Abundant NG, Some O	0	Some	4.13
Ukraine	Very good	Sizable C, NG, Some O	15	Sizable	5.77
Uzbekistan	Good*	Sizable NG, Some C	0	Some	2.83

*   If irrigated.
(a) C = coal;   O = oil;   NG = natural gas;   OS = oil shale.
(b) In 1000 kWh per capita;   in 1990 the average for the USSR as a whole was 6,020 kWh/per capita.

Sources: *Atlas SSSR* , 1983;   Shabad, 1969;   Jensen *et al.*, 1983;   *Post-Soviet Geography*,   vol. 32, no. 4 (April 1991), and vol. 33, No. 4 (April 1992).

Table 1.3   Fossil Fuel Production by Republic, 1990

Republic	1989 population (millions)	1990 oil output mmt/yr	Tons of output, per capita	1990 natural gas output, bill. cu. m./yr	1000 cubic meters, per capita	1990 coal output, mmt/yr	Tons of output per capita
Russia	147.4	516.4	3.50	640.4	4.34	395	2.68
Ukraine	51.7	5.0	0.09	29.0	0.56	165	3.19
Belarus	10.2	2.0	0.19	0.2	0.02	0	0
Kazakhstan	16.5	25.1	1.52	7.1	0.43	131	7.94
Uzbekistan	19.9	2.8	0.14	40.8	2.05	6	0.30
Turkmenistan	3.5	5.6	1.60	87.8	25.08	0	0
Kyrgyzstan	4.3	0.2	0.05	0.1	0.02	4	0.93
Tajikistan	5.1	0.2	0.04	0.2	0.04	1	0.20
Azerbaijan	7.0	12.2	1.74	9.0	1.29	0	0
Georgia	5.4	0.2	0.04	0	0	1	0.18
Armenia	3.3	0	0	0	0	0	0
Moldova	4.3	0	0	0	0	0	0
Lithuania	3.7	0	0	0	0	0	0
Latvia	2.7	0	0	0	0	0	0
Estonia	1.6	0	0	0	0	0	0
Ex-USSR:	286.7	569.7	1.99	814.7	2.84	703	2.45

Source: M. Sagers, "Review of Soviet Energy Industries in 1990", *Soviet Geography*, vol. 32, no. 4 (April 1991), pp. 251-280.

especially among workers. The generally adverse state of the natural environment in the former Soviet Union has been well known for over two decades (Goldman, 1972; Pryde, 1972). More recently, detailed information has appeared on the disastrous effects on human health resulting from the Stalinist insistence on industrial development at any cost, most notably in the recent volume by Feshbach and Friendly and the article by Cole (see Table 1.4).

Another potential reason for future environmental neglect relates to inter-republic competition. Will all these new republics tend to compete for foreign economic investments, using relaxed environmental regulations as "bait," in order to entice new employment opportunities to locate there, rather than in a neighboring republic? This is a common tactic among states in the United States and could appear in the republics of the former Soviet Union as well.

Finally, an odd paradox exists in the former USSR's economy-environment equation. Indices of environmental pollution have shown "improvement" in recent years, but most of this improvement merely reflects that many factories are operating at less than full capacity (or have been shut down), for the reasons outlined above. Worse, it has been noted that the decreases in harmful emissions over the past four years have been generally less than the decrease in levels of economic production, implying that per-unit-of-produc-

Table 1.4   Quality of Life Variables in Soviet Republics
as Percentage of Most Favorable Republic Score (= 100)

	(1) Urban	(2) Life exp.	(3) Nat. incr.	(4) Inf. mort.	(5) Fer-tility	(6) Ind. empt.	(7) Women in work	(8) Cap. inv.	(9) High inc.	(10) Ret. sale	(11) Serv.	(12) Tele.
RSFSR	100	97	53	58	95	97	94	100	65	72	76	45
Estonia	97	98	68	90	95	92	100	87	100	100	100	78
Latvia	96	98	85	100	95	95	100	79	84	94	91	100
Lithuania	92	100	55	96	95	95	96	92	71	82	77	84
Belorussia (Belarus)	88	99	47	84	100	92	98	80	58	72	68	62
Moldova	64	94	25	48	75	87	96	57	33	60	57	41
Ukraine	91	98	100	77	100	90	96	61	42	62	68	53
Georgia	76	100	34	50	91	95	85	59	49	59	72	57
Armenia	92	95	25	43	81	100	89	52	28	53	54	79
Azerbaijan	73	97	14	41	72	80	80	53	19	39	40	39
Turkmenia	61	91	10	21	44	66	78	61	15	45	45	26
Uzbekistan	55	95	10	25	46	70	80	41	8	39	36	29
Tadzhikistan	45	96	8	22	37	70	72	36	4	35	31	18
Kyrgyzstan	51	94	12	30	50	80	91	40	14	45	44	27
Kazakhstan	77	96	17	38	66	98	91	84	39	55	60	43
USSR	89	96	32	45	84	93	94	81	51	65	68	50

	(13) High ed.	(14) Sci. wkrs.	(15) Doc-tors	(16) Hosp. beds	(17) Hous. space	(18) Alco-hol	(19) Crime	(20) Pollu-tion	(21) Grand total	(22) Ave.	(23) USSR = 100
RSFSR	100	100	81	99	74	6	18	9	1439	72.0	110.6
Estonia	81	63	83	87	100	13	16	8	1556	77.8	119.5
Latvia	86	74	86	100	91	7	18	37	1616	80.8	124.1
Lithuania	94	60	78	91	89	10	23	19	1499	75.0	115.2
Belorussia (Belarus)	92	61	69	97	81	9	31	19	1407	70.4	108.1
Moldova	66	34	69	93	82	7	22	24	1134	56.7	87.1
Ukraine	87	60	74	96	82	7	32	11	1387	69.4	106.6
Georgia	85	77	100	80	89	67	58	27	1410	70.5	108.3
Armenia	87	94	69	63	65	100	64	48	1381	69.1	106.1
Azerbaijan	74	46	67	71	57	71	100	24	1157	57.9	88.9
Turkmenia	59	23	60	78	50	26	39	15	913	45.6	70.0
Uzbekistan	81	29	60	87	55	28	48	34	956	47.8	73.4
Tadzhikistan	60	26	48	75	43	31	64	100	921	46.1	70.8
Kyrgyzstan	69	33	62	84	55	16	34	56	987	49.4	75.9
Kazakhstan	87	36	69	96	64	9	25	9	1159	58.0	89.1
USSR	92	76	76	94	73	8	23	11	1301	65.1	100.0

[a] For variables (4) - (6) and (19) - (21) low has been taken as "favorable" and the values reversed.

[b] Underlined values represent the highest- or lowest-ranking republic(s) on each variable, standardized in relation to the most favorable republic score (= 100).

Source: Cole, J. P. (1991), p. 594. Reprinted by permission V.H.Winston & Son.

tion pollution levels have actually been *increasing* in recent years. Therefore, if the economy improves, large increases in industrial emissions can be expected, with a corresponding increase in human health problems.

Decentralization Considerations

Under the previous system, only one nation was involved in environmental management, but today fifteen independent countries are involved in a vast array of environmental decision-making processes. Under the structure of the Union of Soviet Socialist Republics, decisions concerning natural resources conservation and environmental protection were made by what were termed all-Union, or Union-republic, ministries and state committees. With the dismemberment of the USSR, a new process will be needed to fulfill these functions. The new Commonwealth of Independent States, although a possible vehicle, will probably be limited to a coordinating role due to the minority republics' distrust of any supra-national authority. Also, the three Baltic republics do not belong to the CIS. Independent control by agencies within each of the new nations seems a far more likely course of action. In 1993, a new trend appeared to be emerging: regional associations. In addition to the Baltic states' commonality of interests, the Central Asian republics have created an economic association with neighboring Islamic nations; Russia and Belarus in 1994 formed a close economic association; and Russia, Ukraine and Belarus have begun looking at a possible "slavic economic union."

With regard to environmental protection, in all probability fifteen different structures will emerge. Some republics may divide responsibilities among a number of regulatory agencies, while others may opt for a "super-agency" concept. Given that no form of governmental structure is perfect, leadership priorities will become an important factor. Each republic will have to create its own mechanisms for ensuring a high level of environmental quality and find the resources to carry them out in practice. Well-worded laws that have meaning only on paper, a long-standing Soviet stock-in-trade, will no longer suffice.

One of the most critical regulatory concerns will involve nuclear energy. Most commercial nuclear reactors are located in Russia and Ukraine (see Table 1.2), and sufficient expertise may exist in these large and diverse nations to satisfactorily carry out their own nuclear control programs. But commercial nuclear facilities also exist in Lithuania, Armenia, and Kazakhstan (the latter including a breeder reactor). Both Lithuania and Armenia had earlier talked about creating a nuclear-free energy base, but economic realities will probably require both of their nuclear facilities to be operated for some years to come, suggesting a continuation of nuclear safety uncertainties (Potter, 1993). Thus, political decentralization engenders a host of questions. Will these reactors be operated by local nationals or by Russians? What arrangements will be made for disposing of radioactive wastes? Will waste repositories be required in the republic containing the nuclear facility, or will Russia accept them? Will the smaller states ask for Russian assistance in dismantling the reactors at the end of their active life? And at that time, what form of energy facility will replace them? One question along these lines has already been answered: Russia has virtually ceased providing any cash assistance to Belarus and Ukraine to aid in correcting the problems resulting from the Chernobyl accident.

The example of nuclear energy outlined above can be transferred to a number of other industries that are inherently "dirty": iron and steel, petroleum refining, chemicals, fossil fuel power plants, etc. Lacking centralized control from Moscow, each republic will need an effective mechanism to control emissions and toxic wastes from every category of polluting industry. This has major funding implications. Nor will the environmental situation be helped by the probable necessity of retaining in their jobs many of the middle-management personnel that were a part of the ineffective regulatory process under the former Soviet governmental system.

Geographic and Political Implications

The environmental implications of independence also have a spatial dimension. As suggested, many new trade partnerships will have to be developed. The geographic and political implications of this are immense. For example, a great many new bilateral and multilateral treaties will be required both among the fifteen new nations themselves and with outside powers.

As one prime example, consider the water problems of Central Asia. Formerly, a decision on any Central Asian water issue, wise or unwise, would have been made in Moscow and would have been binding on all republics concerned. Today, however, five separate countries are involved, and the experience in the American West suggests that self-interest could quickly divide these new nations into upstream (supplier) and downstream (consumer) negotiating blocks. A multilateral basin compact is essential if these water supplies are to be efficiently shared in the future. Further, it should be noted that parts of the upper basin of some Central Asian rivers lie in China or Afghanistan. These Central Asian problems will be examined in more detail in Chapters 16 through 20.

Another important geographic consideration is that many of these new nations are landlocked (Table 1.5). When they existed as merely a constituent republic of the USSR, this was not a particularly limiting constraint; a nationwide system of railroads and waterways existed to move goods in and out of these republics. Today, with independence, the right to move goods over these transportation lifelines will probably have to be negotiated with adjacent states and will also require maintaining good relations with their neighbors.

A key portion of this transport system is the Volga River and associated canal systems, all of which lie in the Russian Republic. The Azerbaijan, Turkmenistan, and Kazakhstan Republics all front on the Caspian Sea and could benefit from the continued accessibility to this system. It is always an inconvenience for a country to not have a port city accessible to the world ocean as many key economic items are best shipped by bulk cargo vessels over water.

Table 1.5   Geographic Situation of the Former USSR Republics

Republic	Area (sq. km.)	Latitude (of capital city)	Access to Ocean? Direct	Access to Ocean? Via river or Canal	Neighboring Countries Ex-USSR	Neighboring Countries Other
Russia (Rus)	17,075,400	55° 45'	yes	yes	(a)	(b)
Kazakhstan (Kaz)	2,717,300	43° 19'	no	yes	Rus, Tur, Uzb, Kyr	China
Ukraine (Ukr)	603,700	50° 27'	yes	yes	Rus, Bel, Mol	(c)
Turkmenistan (Tur)	488,100	39° 45'	no	yes	Kaz, Uzb	Iran, Afghanistan
Uzbekistan (Uzb)	447,400	41° 23'	no	no	Kaz, Tur, Kyr, Tad	Afghanistan
Belarus (Bel)	207,600	53° 54'	no	yes	Rus, Ukr, Lit, Lat	Poland
Kyrgyzstan (Kyr)	198,500	42° 49'	no	no	Kaz, Uzb, Tad	China
Tajikistan (Tad)	143,100	38° 41'	no	no	Uzb, Kyr	China, Afghanistan
Azerbaijan (Azr)	86,000	40° 28'	no	yes	Rus, Arm, Geor	Iran
Georgia (Geor)	69,700	41° 40'	yes	yes	Rus, Azr, Arm	Turkey
Lithuania (Lit)	65,200	54° 40'	yes	yes	Bel, Lat, Rus (d)	Poland
Latvia (Lat)	63,700	56° 55'	yes	yes	Rus, Est, Lit, Bel	(none)
Estonia (Est)	45,100	59° 26'	yes	yes	Rus, Lat	(none)
Moldova (Mol)	33,700	47° 02'	no	yes	Ukr	Romania
Armenia (Arm)	29,800	40° 10'	no	no	Geor, Azr	Iran, Turkey

(a) Russia borders on Estonia, Latvia, Belarus, Ukraine, Georgia, Azerbaijan, and Kazakhstan.
(b) Russia borders on Norway, Finland, China, Mongolia, and North Korea.
(c) Ukraine borders on Poland, Slovakia, Hungary, and Romania.
(d) Lithuania borders on Kaliningrad Oblast, an exclave of the Russian Republic.

Source: *Atlas SSSR*, 1983.

Landlocked republics may also find fish products to be more expensive because the former Soviet fishing fleet was largely based in the Russian Republic and fish catches from the Caspian Sea have declined (and those from the Aral are almost totally extirpated).

Another important environmental consideration having a strong spatial element is the movement of transboundary pollutants. This issue has at least four main components: (1) airborne pollutants, including not only smokestack and exhaust emissions but also windblown pesticides, salts, and other harmful particulates; (2) pollutants transmitted by international river systems or across international lakes; (3) the pollution of seas (Baltic, Black, etc.) whose coastlines are shared by two or more nations; and (4) deliberately conveyed pollutants, that is, those that are legally contracted for movement, or in some cases illegally smuggled, across international borders. Because many of the countries in eastern Europe are relatively small, transboundary pollution has become a significant international issue. Attempts to control this problem are embodied in such accords as the Convention on Long-Range Transboundary Air Pollution of 1979. The signing of an accord, however, does not mean that effective steps will be quickly taken to resolve the problem.

Political problems may also inhibit the pace of economic and environmental improvement. Not every republic has moved quickly to decentralize and reform the old USSR-era ministerial system, the cause of so many environmental problems. In some republics, such as Uzbekistan, the "new" system is as yet little changed from the old. Likewise, privatization, which might provide some competitive motivations to clean up old, inefficient industrial and agricultural procedures, is lurching along at greatly different speeds among the various republics.

The interests of minority populations also have environmental implications. This is particularly true in the Russian Federation, which is itself a patchwork of minority "autonomous" regions. Here, the largest individual political sub-unit, the Yakut Autonomous Republic (now known as Sakha), has asked for greater local control over its vast wealth of natural resources. The Tatar Republic (Tatarstan) for a while in the early 1990s voiced its desire for greater political sovereignty, implying that (if other ethnic areas were to follow suit) much of the extensive oil deposits within the Russian Federation could eventually be controlled locally, rather than from Moscow. Tatarstan will probably not be granted sovereignty, but it might gain more economic independence. If ethnic regions such as Tatarstan do gain control over their natural resources, various possible subsequent scenarios exist. The local area, feeling that it was previously exploited, might opt to decrease or halt production from one or more mineral deposits, creating a demand for increased production elsewhere. Or, needing income, the local area might increase production, with potentially greater environmental damage. The most favorable outcome, that the local area might force production to take place in a more environmentally benign manner, while possible, is unlikely to be the most widely implemented option, mainly for economic reasons.

One manifestation of ethnic identity has been the widespread renaming of cities, especially those that were given new names during the Soviet period to honor revolutionary figures. A short guide to some of the larger cities that have been renamed since 1991 is given in Appendix 1.3.

Mapping the Patterns of Soviet Environmental Deterioration

The former Soviet Union is a land of great ecological diversity. Even a generalized map of its landscape regions will show at least ten broad natural zones, ranging from Arctic tundra to the deserts of Central Asia (Figure 1.2). Unfortunately, almost all of these natural zones have undergone severe ecological deterioration.

At the start of the 1990s, a new way of looking at the severity of the Soviet environmental situation was emerging, that being the preparation of maps of critical ecological zones (Kochurov, 1991). The earliest of these maps showed general patterns and locations of environmental problems across the expanse of the USSR at a fairly small scale, as well as noting the location of the more critical regional problem areas (see Figure 1.1). Sixteen highly critical areas were identified, those being denoted on Figure 1.1 as: (1) the Aral Sea, (2) the Chernobyl fall-out region, (3) the Sea of Azov, (4) the Donbass region of Ukraine, (5) Moldavia, (6) the Black Sea coast, (7) the Caspian Sea, (8) the Kalmyk republic, (9) the Volga River, (10) the Kola Peninsula, (11) the Ural Mountains industrial region, (12) the Kuzbass coal mining region, (13) Lake

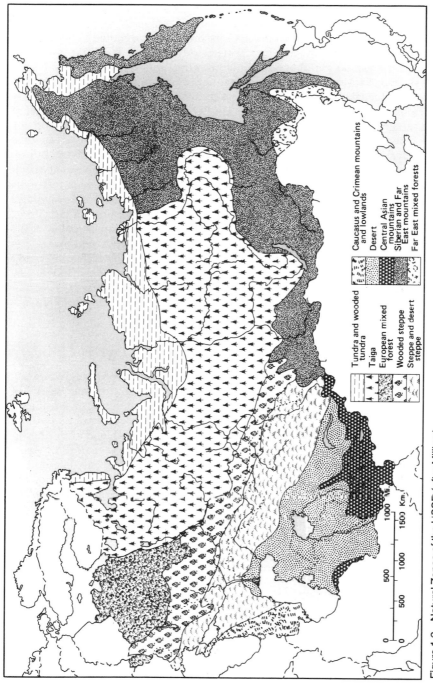

Figure 1.2 Natural Zones of the USSR (after Mil'kov)

Baikal, (14) the Moscow region, (15) the Fergana Valley, and (16) the Semi-palatinsk region of eastern Kazakhstan.

Later refinements produced much more precise and detailed regional environmental maps at a much larger scale (Kotlyakov et al., 1991), as well as maps of particular republics, such as Ukraine, and specific oblasts (provinces), such as Moscow and St. Petersburg. An example of the larger-scale mapping, focusing on European Russia, is shown in Figure 3.3. The severity of regional environmental disruption is often described as falling into one of five categories: provisionally favorable, satisfactory, stressed, critical (crisis), and catastrophic. In the USSR at the beginning of the 1990s, two areas were generally considered to fall into the catastrophic category: the Chernobyl region and the Aral Sea region. Many might place the area of the Kyshtym disaster, near the Urals city of Chelyabinsk, into this category as well (see Chapter 4). Recent information suggests that perhaps Novaya Zemlya and the Kara Sea should also be accorded this dubious distinction (Broad, 1993). More recent efforts (1993) have produced a larger scale map, in color, of the entire former USSR, showing over 100 critical environmental regions.

These maps are an instructive, visually compelling way of summarizing regional environmental situations for public education purposes. Today they are being prepared in many other portions of the world besides the former Soviet Union, with the effort being coordinated by the International Geographical Union.

Military Conflict and the Environment

It has been frequently observed that the greatest of environmental disasters is war, a point that was vividly driven home during, and after, the 1991 Gulf War in Kuwait and Iraq. Unfortunately, during the time this book was being prepared, at least four armed conflicts were taking place in various parts of the former Soviet Union, specifically in Nagorno-Karabakh and surrounding portions of Azerbaijan, in the South Ossetian and Abkhazia regions of Georgia, in Tajikistan, and in Checheniya in southern Russia. Not only is the environment in these areas directly harmed by the destructive activities of the conflict, but the economic cost of the military activities often hampers effective environmental cleanup once the hostilities cease. Substantial levels of foreign capital are often necessary for environmental restoration in such situations (as in the case of Kuwait), which may not be readily available, especially if there are several claimants for this aid.

In the Soviet Union, normal military manufacturing, training, and testing programs were routinely conducted in ways that frequently imperiled both civilian populations and the natural environment. The nuclear weapons testing program near Semipalatinsk, particularly during the 1950s era of atmospheric testing, is one of the most graphic examples. It remains to be seen whether the demise of the USSR will necessarily change the conduct of military practices and lead to a cleanup of radioactive waste sites, either in the Russian Federation or in the minority republics (Table 1.6).

Table 1.6   Sources of Radioactive Wastes

Republic	Nuclear Power Plants	ICBM Missile Sites	Surface Bomb or Accident Residue*	Under-ground Atomic Tests	Mining, Milling or Processing Sites	Nuclear Research Center	Radio-active Waste Burial Sites
Armenia	X					X	X
Azerbaijan							X
Belarus		X	X			X	X
Estonia					X		X
Georgia						X	X
Kazakhstan	X	X	X	X	X	X	X
Kyrgyzstan					X		X
Latvia						X	
Lithuania	X						X
Moldova							X
Russia	X	X	X	X	X	X	X
Tajikistan					X		X
Turkmenistan				X	X		X
Ukraine	X	X	X	X	X	X	X
Uzbekistan				X	X	X	X

*Residual contamination from either atmospheric nuclear tests or major accident.

Sources: Derived from material in Bradley, 1992, and Potter, 1993.

Another critical example involves the nuclear weapons themselves, a continuing legacy of the cold war. For decades, the United States and the USSR were able to negotiate between themselves the possibility of a nuclear arms reduction. Suddenly, in 1991, the number of nations possessing strategic nuclear weapons and delivery systems increased by three as Belarus, Ukraine, and Kazakhstan, all containing former Soviet missile sites, became independent nations. Thus, in 1992, the United States had to expand the scope of its START (Strategic Arms Reduction Treaty) negotiations to deal with four countries, rather than one. The fact that some of these new nations may view the temporary retention of these weapons as an important political bargaining chip does not help the cause of nuclear non-proliferation.

This leads immediately to another military-related environmental legacy of the cold war. Although the vast improvements in U.S.–USSR/Russian relations over the past few years led to a significant level of mutual disarmament, even this came at an environmental price. The frequently cited adage of ecologists that "everything has to go somewhere" takes on appreciable significance here. How will both sides dispose of the conventional explosives, bomb-grade nuclear materials, rocket propellants, nuclear submarine reactors, chemical weapons, biological agents, etc., that will still exist even after their conveyance systems are dismantled? Has either side even provided a complete list of what it possesses? These wastes are now known to be causing widespread environmental harm over vast areas of the former USSR (Bradley 1992; Feshbach and Friendly, 1992), and there is also a great fear that some of these items may be clandestinely sold to parties in other countries. Disposing of all this military "detritus" may become one of the major environmental challenges of the 1990s.

Other Considerations

The fifteen new countries will be facing other new problems and challenges related to environmental management as well. One group of such problems relates to demographic factors.

One of the most pressing of these concerns is birthrates. Among the former Soviet republics, birthrates tend to be lowest in the Slavic and Baltic regions and highest in the Islamic republics. Birthrates in Georgia and Armenia, formerly high, dropped off somewhat during the 1980s. In Central Asia and Azerbaijan, the unfortunate combination of high birthrates and limited employment opportunities could lead to a philosophy of subordinating environmental concerns to an overriding effort to create jobs. This would be particularly unfortunate since these are portions of the former Soviet Union already known to have severe problems of air and water pollution and toxic pesticide contamination (Pryde, 1991; Feshbach and Friendly, 1992; *Nats. doklad*, 1991). On the other hand, in the Russian Republic for the first time since World War II, the birthrate lagged behind the death rate in 1992 and 1993.

A related consideration is the large number of ethnic Russians in many of the former Union republics (see Table 1.1). They vary in numbers from 52,000 in Armenia to over 11 million in Ukraine (Harris, 1993, p. 5). Some republics (such as Estonia) wish to see these Russian residents return to the Russian Federation, a stance that is creating considerable friction. With time, many of the more recent of these transplanted Russians may opt to return to the more familiar countryside of their forebears, though those who have lived in the host republic all their lives may wish to stay. Of those Russians who return, some will be professional people, including environmental professionals, and in the short run their expertise may be greatly missed. A large scale movement of this nature has apparently already begun in Uzbekistan (Feshbach and Friendly, 1992, p. 87). Other displaced persons, however, are less fortunate as they are refugees from the wars in Azerbaijan and Tajikistan. In 1994, they numbered in the tens of thousands.

The factor of financial resources can hardly be overemphasized. Environmental cleanup requires capital, huge amounts of it, and none of the republics has such a luxury. In 1993, Russia and other new nations were eagerly seeking foreign financial aid to assist their struggling economies, and environmental cleanup was not at the top of the needs list. Perhaps the most optimistic scenario is that the new nations will simply shut down the worst polluting industries, and the foreign aid can help to build newer factories that use inherently cleaner technologies. There is no guarantee this will happen, however, and foreign industrial aid can often be environmentally unfriendly. In the short run, there is little question that much pollution will simply continue to flow.

Another factor relating to foreign countries involves natural resource exploitation. Many republics have a variety of mineral resources that they could make available for world trade (Jensen et al., 1983). As noted earlier, however, many of the republics have poor access to the world ocean and may have to utilize harbor facilities in cities in other new nations (see Appendix 1.4). There are also environmental considerations. In their quest for economic development, will the former Soviet republics exercise sufficient control over the development of their natural resources by foreign companies? U.S. firms, for example, presently don't have to prepare environmental impact analyses for projects in foreign countries. Will each of the fifteen former USSR republics have the internal organization (and political will) to adequately supervise this outside development of their natural resources? Chapter 5 will note that at least in the area of timber resources, the early answer to this question was "no."

Within the territory of the former Soviet Union, these are both exciting and troublesome times. While some might wish to argue that most of these new nations have more urgent problems than environmental improvement, this would be an unfortunate and misleading conclusion. In many of these new countries (especially in Central Asia), the state of the environment is so deteriorated that other problems, such as public health, agriculture, and even the ability to site new industry, are being severely impacted by the ecological crisis itself (see Table 1.4). The proper way to view the situation, it would seem, is not that environmental improvement is in fourth or sixth place on a shopping list of national priorities and capital needs, but rather that it is an essential component of all items on that shopping list. It must be understood that there is no such thing as a healthy economy built on top of a polluted environment and that environmental degradation is merely the postponement of necessary costs of production, often at the expense of public health. Future generations will thus have to pay twice, once to cover the (inflated) cost of the cleanup and a second time to cure health problems. This neglect constitutes political irresponsibility and should be rejected by both the citizenry and political leaders of all countries. The only responsible approach is to internalize the costs of a healthy environment into the production and pricing procedures of today. Only in this way can the countries of the former Soviet Union, like all the other nations of the world, avoid inflicting the environmental misjudgments of the present onto their own future generations.

Appendix 1.1   Preserved Land in the Former Soviet Republics

Republic	Sq. Kilometers Preserved	% of Republic Preserved
Armenia	3070	10.30
Estonia	3311	7.34
Tajikistan	8862	6.19
Lithuania	3391	5.20
Azerbaijan	4407	5.09
Belarus	8436	4.06
Russia	656557	3.85
Latvia	2274	3.57
Turkmenistan	17184	3.52
Georgia	1987	2.85
Kyrgyzstan	5600	2.82
Ukraine	8111	1.34
Uzbekistan	3264	0.73
Kazakhstan	12648	0.47
Moldova	149	0.44
Former USSR	739251	3.30

Source: Pryde, 1991, pp. 153-8 and 210 (data as of mid-to-late 1980s).

Appendix 1.2   Types of Preserved Lands in the Former Soviet Republics

1. Zapovedniki (nature reserves).   These are the primary type of nature conservation territories in all of the former Soviet republics.   They are primarily scientific study areas;   most have very restricted public access (usually only for educational purposes), and very few serve a recreation function.   Most are composed of undisturbed landscapes, but portions of them can be used for active (that is, ecosystem altering) scientific research.   In most, biotic preservation is a major goal, and some are quite active in managing endangered species.   There are about 160 zapovedniki altogether in the fifteen republics.   About twenty of them are also designated as biosphere reserves under the United Nations' "Man and the Biosphere" program.

2. National parks.   National parks are a relatively new feature in the fifteen former republics, the first one having been created only in 1971.   Like national parks elsewhere, they are intended to serve a major tourism and recreation function, but portions of them are usually set aside as strictly preserved areas as well.   They are modelled after the English concept of a national park (that is, the preservation of traditional and typical landscapes, including villages, traditional economic activities, and historic sites), rather than the American model (spectacular natural features).   In 1992 there were 27 national parks in the 15 republics.

3. Zakazniki (natural preserves).   These are a type of semi-preserved area in which either temporary or permanent restrictions are placed on all or some economic activities, so as to assist the preservation of local flora or fauna.   Different categories of zakazniki exist, including botanical, zoological (the most common), landscape, hydrological, and geological.   A typical function that they might perform is to protect the breeding grounds of a particular species of wildlife.   In the mid-1980s, there were almost 3,000 of these preserves distributed across the Soviet Union.

4. Hunting preserves (zapovedno-okhotnich'ye khozyaystvo).   These are wildlife protection areas on which hunting is allowed.   They bear some similarity to those national wildlife refuges in the United States on which hunting is a major function.   They are not widely used, however;   in 1992 there were only 7 of them, and they were found in only three of the republics.

5. Monuments of nature (pamyatniki prirody).   This category of preserve is used in many republics to give protection to unusual, rare, or scientifically valuable geological, paleological, or botanical features of the landscape.   They are generally small in area, and usually do not protect more than the immediate area around the particular feature of interest.

6. Forest parks, protected riparian woodlands, shelterbelts, and urban greenbelts.   These and similar categories of protected vegetation (which may be secondary growth) serve primarily to protect other natural resources (watersheds, erodable soils, etc.) and to provide for human amenities and enjoyment.

Sources: Pryde, 1991;   Braden, 1987;   and Isakov and Krinitskiy,1986.

Appendix 1.3   Major Cities That Have Been Re-named or Significantly Re-spelled (a)

Soviet name	New Name	New name	Soviet name
Aktyubinsk	Aqtobe	Almaty	Alma-Ata
Alma-Ata	Almaty	Aqmola	Tselinograd
Ashkhabad	Ashgabat	Aqtobe	Aktyubinsk
Bendery	Tighina	Ashgabat	Ashkhabad
Frunze	Bishkek	Atyrau	Guryev
Gorkiy	Nizhny Novgorod	Bishkek	Frunze
Guryev	Atyrau	Chisinau	Kishinev
Kalinin	Tver	Ganca	Kirovabad
Karaganda	Qaraghandy	Gyumri	Leninakan
Kiev	Kyyiv	Khudzhand	Leninabad
Kirovabad	Ganca	Kryvyy Rih	Krivoy Rog
Kirovakan	Vanadzor	Kyyiv	Kiev
Kishinev	Chisinau	Mykolayiv	Nikolayev
Kokand	Quqon	Nizhniy Novgorod	Gorkiy
Krivoy Rog	Kryvyy Rih	Oral	Uralsk
Kustanay	Qostanay	Oskemen	Ust-Kamenogorsk
Kuybyshev	Samara	Petropavl	Petropavlovsk
Leninabad	Khudzhand	Qaraghandy	Karaganda
Leninakan	Gyumri	Qostanay	Kustanay
Leningrad	St. Petersburg	Quqon	Kokand
Nikolayev	Mykolayiv	Samara	Kuybyshev
Petropavlovsk	Petropavl	Semey	Semipalatinsk
Semipalatinsk	Semey	St. Petersburg	Leningrad
Sverdlovsk	Yekaterinburg	Tighina	Bendery
Tselinograd	Aqmola	Tver	Kalinin
Uralsk	Oral	Vanadzor	Kirovakan
Ust-Kamenogorsk	Oskemen	Yekaterinburg	Sverdlovsk

(a)   Those cities whose new spelling differs by only a letter or two (e.g., Odessa, Odesa; Dzhambul, Zhambyl; Samarkand, Samarqand) are not included in the above list.   Refer to the maps that accompany each chapter, as well as Appendix 16.2.

Appendix 1.4   Largest Seaports of the Former Soviet Union

Port City	Liquid Cargoes	Dry Cargoes	Total Traffic	Port is in Republic of	Port is located on
1 Novorossiysk	34.0	9.0	43.0	Russia	Black Sea
2 Ventspils	26.2	5.0	31.2	Latvia	Baltic Sea
3 Odessa	16.8	9.3	26.1	Ukraine	Black Sea
4 Klaipeda	7.0	8.2	15.2	Lithuania	Baltic Sea
5 Tuapse	11.8	2.6	14.4	Russia	Black Sea
6 Il'yichevsk(a)	0.0	14.3	14.3	Ukraine	Black Sea
7 Nakhodka	4.5	7.4	11.9	Russia	Pacific Ocean
8 Vostochnyy(b)	0.0	11.4	11.4	Russia	Pacific Ocean
9 St. Petersburg	0.0	10.8	10.8	Russia	Baltic Sea
1 0 Mariupol'	0.0	10.8	10.8	Ukraine	Sea of Azov
1 1 Baku	7.3	3.3	10.6	Azerbaijan	Caspian Sea
1 2 Yuzhnyy(a)	0.0	10.2	10.2	Ukraine	Black Sea
1 3 Reni	0.0	8.4	8.4	Ukraine	Danube River
1 4 Tallinn(c)	0.0	8.3	8.3	Estonia	Baltic Sea
1 5 Krasnovodsk	3.3	4.9	8.2	Turkmenistan	Caspian Sea
1 6 Murmansk	0.0	7.8	7.8	Russia	Barents Sea
1 7 Kholmsk(d)	0.0	6.6	6.6	Russia	Pacific Ocean
1 8 Izmail	0.0	6.4	6.4	Ukraine	Danube River
1 9 Riga	0.0	6.0	6.0	Latvia	Baltic Sea
2 0 Batumi	4.5	1.4	5.9	Georgia	Black Sea

All figures are in million metric tons.

(a) Near Odessa; could be considered part of the Odessa port complex.

(b) Located east of Nakhodka; could be considered part of port of Nakhodka.

(c) Includes the twin ports of Tallinn and Novo-Tallinn.

(d) Located on Sakhalin Island.

Source: Post-Soviet Geography, Feb. 1992, p. 120.

Bibliography

Atlas SSSR. (1983). Moscow: Glavnoye upravleniye geodezii i kartografii pri Sovete Ministrov SSSR.

Batalden, S.K., and Batalden, S.L. (1993). *The Newly Independent States of Eurasia.* Phoenix: The Oryx Press.

Braden, K. (1987). "The Function of Nature Reserves in the Soviet Union," In F. Singleton (ed.), *Environmental Problems in the Soviet Union and Eastern Europe.* Boulder: Lynne Rienner.

Bradley, D. J. (1992). *Radioactive Waste Management in the Former USSR.* (3 vols.). Richland, WA: Pacific Northwest Laboratories (for the U.S. Dept. of Energy), June.

Broad, W. J. (1993). "Radioactive Wastes Dumped by Soviets," *New York Times,* April 27.

Cole, J. (1991). "Republics of the Former USSR in the Context of a United Europe and New World Order." *Soviet Geography,* vol. 32, no. 9, pp. 587–603.

DeBardeleben, J. (ed.) (1994). *Environmental Quality and Security After Communism.* Boulder: Westview Press.

Dienes, L. (1993). "Economic Geographic Relations in the Post-Soviet Republics." *Post-Soviet Geography,* vol. 34, no. 8, pp. 497–529.

Dodd, C. K. (1994). *Industrial Decision-Making and High-Risk Technology: Siting Nuclear Power Facilities in the USSR.* London: Rowman & Littlefield.

Dunlop, J. et al. (1993). "Profiles of the Newly Independent States: Economic, Social and Demographic Conditions." In *The Former Soviet Union in Transition.* Washington, D.C.: Joint Economic Committee of Congress, vol. 2, pp. 1019–1187.

Feshbach, M., and Friendly, A. (1992). *Ecocide in the USSR.* New York: Basic Books.

The First Book of Demographics for the Republics of the Former Soviet Union (1992). Shady Side, MD: New World Demographics.

The Former Soviet Union in Transition (1993). (2 vols.). Washington, DC: Joint Economic Committee of Congress, especially pp. 461–609.

Goldman, M. (1972). *Spoils of Progress.* Cambridge, MA: MIT Press.

Harris, C.D. (1993). "The New Russian Minorities: A Statistical Overview." *Post-Soviet Geography,* vol. 34, no. 1, pp. 1–27.

———. (1994). "Ethnic Tensions in the Successor Republics in 1993 and Early 1994." *Post-Soviet Geography,* vol. 35, no. 4, pp. 185–203.

Isakov, Yu, and Krinitsky, V. (1986). "The System of Protected Natural Areas in the USSR and Prospects for Its Development." *Soviet Geography,* vol. 27, no. 2, pp. 102–114.

IUCN East European Programme (1991). *Environmental Status Reports: 1990.* Vol. 3, USSR. Norwich, UK: Page Brothers.

Jancar, B. (1987). *Environmental Management in the Soviet Union and Yugoslavia.* Durham, NC: Duke University Press.

Jensen, R., Shabad, T., and Wright, A. (1983). *Soviet Natural Resources in the World Economy.* Chicago: University of Chicago Press.

Kochurov, B. (1991). "Methodological Approaches to the Creation of a Map of Critical Environmental Situations," In T. C. Meredith et al. (eds.), *Defining and Mapping Critical Environmental Zones for Policy Formulation and Public Awareness.* Montreal: McGill University.

Komarov, B. (1980). *The Destruction of Nature in the Soviet Union.* New York: M. E. Sharpe.

Kotlyakov, V. M. et al. (1991). "An Approach to Compiling Ecological Maps of the USSR." *Mapping Sciences and Remote Sensing,* vol. 28, no. 1, pp. 3–14.

Massey Stewart, J. (1992). *The Soviet Environment: Problems, Policies, and Politics.* Cambridge: Cambridge University Press.

McAuley, A. (1991). "The Economic Consequences of Soviet Disintegration." *Soviet Economy,* vol. 7, no. 3, pp. 189–214.

Milkov, F. N. (1977). *Prirodnyye zony SSSR.* Moscow: Mysl'.

Mnatsakanian, R. A. (1992). *Environmental Legacy of the Former Soviet Republics.* Edinburgh: Centre for Human Ecology, University of Edinburgh.

Natsional'nyy doklad SSSR k konferentsii OON 1992 goda po okruzhayushchey srede i razvitiyu (1991). Moscow: MinPriroda.

Peterson, D. J. (1993). *Troubled Lands: The Legacy of Soviet Environmental Destruction.* Boulder: Westview Press.

Population Reference Bureau (1992). *1992 World Population Data Sheet.* Washington, D.C.: Population Reference Bureau, Inc.

Potter, W. C. (1993). "The Future of Nuclear Power and Nuclear Safety in the Former Soviet Union." *Nuclear News,* March, pp. 61–67.

———. (1993). *Nuclear Profiles of the Soviet Successor States.* Monterey: Monterey Institute of International Studies.

Pryde, P. R. (1972). *Conservation in the Soviet Union.* Cambridge: Cambridge Univ. Press.

———. (1991). *Environmental Management in the Soviet Union.* Cambridge: Cambridge University Press.

Sagers, M. J. (1992a). "Regional Industrial Structures and Economic Prospects in the Former USSR." *Post-Soviet Geography,* vol. 33, no. 8, pp. 487–515.

———. (1992b). "Review of the Energy Industries in the Former USSR in 1991," *Post-Soviet Geography,* vol. 33, no. 4, pp. 237–268.

Schwartz, L. (1991). "USSR Nationality Redistribution by Republic, 1979–89," *Post-Soviet Geography,* vol. 32, no. 4, pp. 209–248.

Shabad, T. (1969). *Basic Industrial Resources of the USSR.* New York: Columbia University Press.

Singleton, F. (ed.) (1987). *Environmental Problems in the Soviet Union and Eastern Europe.* Boulder: Lynne Rienner.

Statistical Handbook 1993: States of the Former USSR (1993). Washington, DC: The World Bank.

Stran-chleny SNG: Statisticheskiy ezhegodnik (1992). Moscow: Statkomitet SNG.

Turnbull, M. (1991). *Soviet Environmental Policies and Practices.* Aldershot, UK: Dartmouth Publishing Co.

USSR Energy Atlas (1985). Washington, DC: Central Intelligence Agency.

Wolfson, Z. (1993). *The Geography of Survival: Ecology in the Post-Soviet Era.* Armonk, NY: M. E. Sharpe.

Young, S. W., Bee, R. J., and Seymore, B. (1992). *One Nation Becomes Many.* Washington, DC: ACCESS.

Ziegler, C.E. (1987). *Environmental Policy in the USSR.* Amherst: University of Massachusetts Press.

2

Russia: An Overview
of the Federation

Philip R. Pryde

The view from the Moscow State University cartographic laboratory, located on the 22nd floor of the university's main skyscraper building, was spectacular, affording a sweeping panorama to the north across all of Moscow. Inside, staff cartographers were hard at work on new maps similar to the detailed ones of the Soviet Union that had been prepared on many subjects in the past. The large map we were observing detailed the environmental situation over the full expanse of the country, from the Gulf of Finland to the Kamchatka Peninsula. But something was strangely unfamiliar about the map. The shape of the country was not the same; indeed, it was markedly different. The reason was obvious—this was not a map of the Soviet Union; it was a map of Russia. Gone were the republics of Central Asia and the Transcaucasus; gone were the Baltic republics, Belarus, Moldova, and Ukraine. These are all now separate countries and must therefore map their own environmental situations. The "state" in Moscow State University now refers only to Russia and has no bearing on the other fourteen republics of the former Soviet Union.

This chapter, and the three that follow, will examine the environmental situation in what is now the world's largest country, Russia (properly referred to as the Russian Federation). In this chapter, a brief overview of the country, its resources, and its environmental situation will be presented. The following three chapters will break up its 17.1 million square kilometers (6.6 million square miles) into three somewhat more easily discussed sub-regions: the European portion, the Urals-Baikal portion, and the Russian Far East.

Ethnic Aspects of the Russian Federation

When the USSR ceased to exist, Russia represented by far its largest constituent republic both in area and population. As noted, the Russian Federation has taken over the Soviet Union's old position as the largest country in area on earth. From east to west, it stretches over 7,000 kilometers and 11 time zones and takes in an area almost as large as the United States and Canada combined (Figure 2.1). However, compared to the former Soviet Union, its position in the ranks of the world's most populous nations has dropped several places. It is now smaller in population than Brazil and has only twenty percent more people than Japan (Table 2.1).

Like the old Soviet Union that preceded it, the Russian Federation is a complex association of numerous ethnic groups, linguistic stocks, and national territories. Russians, of course, dominate, while the largest ethnic minority group is the Tatars, of whom over five million reside in the Russian Republic (but less than two million of whom reside in Tatarstan). Other ethnic groups within Russia numbering over one million are Ukrainians, Chuvash, Bashkirs, Belarusians, and Mordvinians. A large and very diverse assortment of ethnic groups live in the North Caucasus region of Russia (see Figure 3.2 in the following chapter). Several smaller groups reside in the Russian arctic. A more inclusive listing of the largest of these groups (those with over, or close to, 100,000 population) is given in Appendix 2.1. Significantly, no less than 40 ethnic groups meet this criterion.

An agreement was signed on March 31, 1992, by eighteen of the twenty main ethnic groups to respect and preserve the existing form and territorial integrity of the Russian Federation (Table 2.2). The two groups that did not sign were Tatarstan and the Chechen-Ingush Autonomous Republic, although Tatarstan subsequently signed a separate treaty with Russia in 1994. Although the accord gave the minority republics control over their own natural resources, the right to make economic agreements directly with foreign nations, and a few other attributes of autonomy, some of these national groups are nevertheless demanding a still greater degree of independence from Moscow. Among the more outspoken of these national groups are the Tatars, Chechens, Yakuts, Bashkirs, and Ossetians, as well as certain of the indigenous peoples in the Russian Arctic. Helpful information about these numerous ethnic groups can be found in the volume by Wixman (1984) cited in the references.

In 1993, however, the situation became even more complex as some nonethnic areas within the Russian Federation also suggested that they wished to have a certain degree of "autonomy." The regions that were making these kinds of statements included the Maritime Province in the Far East (Primorskiy Krai), Yekaterinburg (Sverdlovsk) Province, Vologda Province, and Krasnoyarsk Krai. Their goal appeared similar to that of the autonomous republics: to put pressure on Moscow to grant them more economic autonomy. None of these areas professed a desire to break up the fundamental concept of a Russian federation. The issue may have been quieted in November of 1993 when Yeltsin obtained an agreement that none of the political sub-units would be referred to as "sovereign states" in the new Russian Federation constitution.

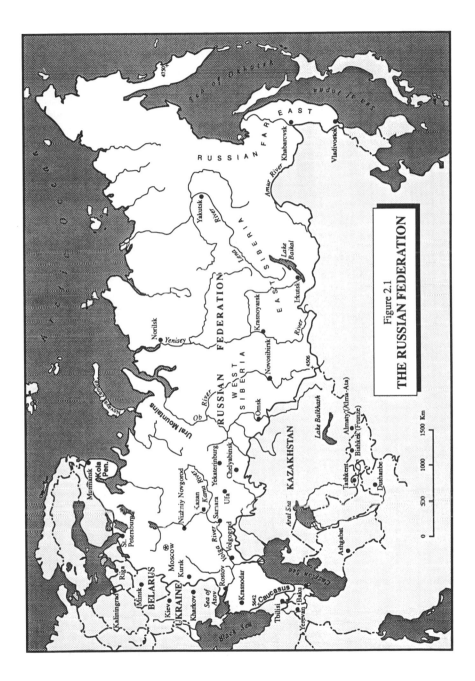

Figure 2.1
THE RUSSIAN FEDERATION

Table 2.1   The World's Largest Countries

	Country	1989/1990 Population
1.	China	1,069,628,000
2.	India	833,422,000
[3]	[former USSR]	[287,015,000]
3.	U.S.A.	249,220,000
4.	Indonesia	187,726,000
5.	Brazil	153,992,000
6.	Russian Federation	147,386,000
7.	Japan	123,231,000

Physical Geographic Overview

Within Russia's 1.7 billion hectares are found a vast assortment of physical landscapes and natural resources. Most of European Russia is made up of the vast East European Plain, which stretches from the Arctic to the Black Sea. It includes the small, non-contiguous Kaliningrad Oblast (Province), west of Lithuania. Its eastern limit is the Ural Mountain range, except on the south where it blends almost imperceptibly into the treeless steppe of Kazakhstan. Beyond the Urals lies the oil-rich West Siberian lowland, drained by the Ob River system and bounded on the east by the Yenisey River.

Still farther east are the huge expanses of East Siberia and the Russian Far East, which together make up an area as large as the United States. Rich in both mineral and biotic resources, but with generally poor access and bitter cold in winter, this vast area is partially mountainous and partially a plateau dissected or bordered by such major rivers as the Lena, Aldan, Amur, and their tributaries. Russia has important outlets to the world ocean at Murmansk, St. Petersburg, the eastern end of the Black Sea, the entire eastern coastline fronting on the Pacific and, less importantly, the entire Arctic Ocean coastline. A more complete description of the country's physical characteristics will be given in Chapters 3, 4, and 5.

Not unexpectedly, the Russian Federation contains the majority of the former Soviet Union's natural resource base. With about 51.6 percent of the former USSR's total population, the Russian Republic produced in 1990 56.2% of its coal, 62.6% of its electricity, 78.6% of its natural gas, and fully 90.6% of its petroleum. It also produced 58.4% of its steel, but only 45.3% of its iron ore, so that the Russian Federation may now have to import iron ore from other republics, most likely Kazakhstan and Ukraine (or, alternatively, downsize its steelmaking capacity). In addition, the Russian Federation produces at least some of almost every other important industrial resource, many of them in large amounts. Its natural resource base will serve it well in the years ahead, assuming that it learns to utilize these resources with much more thrift and in a more environmentally responsible manner than did the previous Soviet ministries.

Table 2.2   Autonomous Republics Within the Russian Federation

Republic	USSR Designation(a)	1989 Pop'n (1000's)	Linguistic Group	Dominant Religion	% Russian 1989
Adygea	Adyge AO	432	Circassian	Sunni Moslem	68
Bashkortostan	Bashkir ASSR	3952	Turkic	Sunni Moslem	39
Buryatia	Buryat ASSR	1042	Mongolic	Buddhist	70
Checheno-	Chechen-	(c)	Caucasic	Sunni Moslem	(c)
Ingushetia(b)	Ingush ASSR	1277	Caucasic	Sunni Moslem	23
Chuvashia	Chuvash ASSR	1336	Turkic	Eastern Orthodox	27
Dagestan	Dagestan ASSR	1792	Various(d)	Various(d)	9
Gorno-Altai	Gorno-Altai AO	192	Turkic	(e)	60
Kabardino-	Kabardino-	(c)	Circassian	Sunni Moslem	(c)
Balkaria	Balkar ASSR	760	Turkic	Sunni Moslem	32
Kalmykia	Kalmyk ASSR	322	Mongolic	Buddhist	38
Karachai-	Karachai-	(c)	Turkic	Sunni Moslem	(c)
Cherkessia	Cherkess AO	418	Circassian	Sunni Moslem	42
Karelia	Karelian ASSR	792	Finnic	Eastern Orthodox	74
Khakassia	Khakass AO	569	Turkic	(e)	79
Komi	Komi ASSR	1263	Uralian	(e)	58
Mari-el	Mari ASSR	750	Uralian	(e)	48
Mordvinia	Mordov ASSR	964	Uralian	Eastern Orthodox	61
North Ossetia	North Ossetian ASSR	634	Ossetian	Eastern Orthodox	30
Tatarstan	Tatar ASSR	3640	Turkic	Sunni Moslem	43
Tuva	Tuva ASSR	309	Turkic	Buddhist	32
Udmurtia	Udmurt ASSR	1609	Finnic	(e)	59
Yakut-Sakha	Yakut ASSR	1081	Turkic	(e)	50

(a) AO = Autonomous Oblast; ASSR = Autonomous Soviet Socialist Republic.
(b) There was an ongoing movement in 1993 to divide this region into separate Chechen and Ingush republics.
(c) Figure immediately below reflects entire former ASSR or AO in 1989.
(d) Dagestan is composed of several ethnic groups; see Appendix 2.1.
(e) Combination of animist-shaminist and Eastern Orthodox.

Sources: *Soviet Geography*, May 1989, pp. 413-6; Wixman, 1984; U.S. State Department map, "Administrative Divisions of Russia", January 1993; *Current Digest of the Soviet Press*, vol. 43, no. 21, p. 8.

Russia's resource base is arguably the most generous in the world. In 1990, the Russian Republic (not the entire USSR) had the largest reserves of natural gas in the world, the third largest reserves of coal, and probably the largest reserves of petroleum outside the Middle East. Russia was the world's largest producer of mercury and nickel; the third largest producer of hydropower, lead, and gold; and among the five largest producers of iron ore, zinc, and copper. Indeed, there is virtually no industrial natural resource that is not in reserve somewhere beneath the republic's surface. In addition to minerals, Russia also possesses huge hydroelectric power potential on its very large rivers, much of which has already been developed. Overall, Russia is the most self-sufficient country in the world in terms of natural resources.

It is equally blessed in biotic resources. Russia extends through seven biogeographical zones, from polar ice cap and tundra in the Arctic to dry steppe and semi-desert areas near the Caspian Sea. It has the most extensive forest in the world, the famous taiga, which consists (where undisturbed) mainly of pine, larch, and other coniferous species. It is also blessed with excellent agricultural resources, most notably over one million square kilometers of fertile chernozem (black earth) soil beneath the Russian steppe. Within its several biogeographic zones is an abundance of plant and animal species, including many that are threatened or endangered. To protect these biotic resources, a network of over 70 nature reserves, as well as twelve national parks, has been created (see Table 2.3). In 1993, it was announced that a huge new "Great Arctic Reserve" had been established, whose 4 million hectares (not included in Table 2.3) makes it the largest in the Russian Federation.

Table 2.3   Preserved Areas in Russia

Type of Preserve(a)	Number(b)	Total area(c)	Average size(c)	% of Re-public(d)
Zapovedniki	75	198,194	2,642.6	1.16
Above that are Biosphere Reserves	14	47,121	3,365.8	0.28
National Parks(e)	12	18,497	1,541.4	0.11
Zakazniki	1203	439,866	365.6	2.58
Total	1290	656,557	509.0	3.85

National Parks (date created) (e)	Hectares
Bashkir (1986)	98,134
Kurshskaya Kosa (1987)	6,100
Losiniy Ostrov (1983)	10,058
Mariy Chodra (1985)	36,600
Pereslavskiy (1990)	21,700
Pribaikalskiy (1986)	412,750
Priel'brus (1986)	101,000
Samarskaya Luka (1984)	128,000
Shorskiy (1989)	418,200
Sochi (1983)	189,400
Valdai (1990)	158,500
Zabaikalskiy (1986)	269,300
Total	1,849,742

(a) For the definition of each type of preserve, see Appendix 1.2.
(b) As of 1/1/91; a 1994 report by the World Wildlife Fund lists 85 zapovedniki, 16 biosphere reserves, and 26 national parks.
(c) In square kilometers.
(d) Area of Russia equals 17,075,400 sq. kilometers
(e) New national parks have been created since 1991, but details are unavailable.

Sources: Pryde (1991); Okhrana ... (1991); Krever et al. (1994).

Environmental Problem Areas

The Soviet-era mandate of industrialization at virtually any cost has left a mosaic of environmental deterioration across the Russian Federation. The main discussion of these environmental problem areas will be presented in the next three chapters; only a few summary comments need be made here.

Numerous "critical environmental zones" have been identified throughout the federation (see Chapter 1 for a discussion of this concept). Some of the larger of these critical zones within the Russian Federation include the area on the eastern slopes of the Ural Mountains near Chelyabinsk that was contaminated by the Kyshtym disaster (see Chapter 4), the central Volga region, the Kara and Barents Seas (particularly around the islands of Novaya Zemlya), the portions of Bryansk Oblast that were contaminated by Chernobyl fallout, the oil producing regions of West Siberia, and coal producing regions such as the Kansk-Achinsk and Kuznets basins.

Urban areas with deteriorated environmental conditions exist in or around such industrial cities as St. Petersburg, Moscow, and Krasnoyarsk. Additionally, air pollution is notably bad in such specific industrial cities as Nizhniy Tagil, Angarsk, Omsk, Lipetsk, Cherepovets, Magnitogorsk, Ufa, Novokuznetsk, Monchegorsk, Sterlitamak, and Norilsk (Table 2.4). A 1992 document lists 84 cities in the Russian Federation with at least three pollutants that exceed the permitted norms by ten times or more (Yablokov, 1992).

In addition to Bryansk, portions of Kaluga, Tula, Ryazan, and Orel Provinces have been contaminated by radioactive fallout from the Chernobyl explosion. Other serious areas of nuclear contamination exist in the Urals, in East Siberia, and around Novaya Zemlya in the Arctic. The latter area suffers in part from the disposal of radioactive military wastes; it has been estimated that by the year 2000 Russia will have more than 150 obsolete nuclear submarines to dispose of (Litovkin, 1993). Nor can the fate of scientifically important Lake Baikal be considered secure from pollution by logging and pulp mills as yet. A host of lesser but still highly significant problems also confronts the environmental management leadership of the Russian Federation, including deteriorating and frequently leaking oil pipelines (Baiduzhy, 1993). More details on all of these environmental problem areas will be provided in the ensuing three chapters.

Unfortunately, in 1994, the declining state of the Russian economy served as a very restrictive brake on both capital investment and environmental improvement. Ironically, however, it also indirectly resulted in short-term improvements in air and water pollution indices, as many enterprises were either operating at less than full capacity or had been closed altogether. As a result, many Russian cities showed statistical improvements in air quality and other environmental indices between 1987 and 1992 (see Table 2.4). For example, of 53 major Russian cities whose air quality was listed as poor in a 1991 volume of environmental statistics, all but three showed an improvement during the 1987–90 period. These data are probably misleading, however. This "improvement" may well dissipate with improved economic conditions, and in the interim, the drive to open up new industrial and em-

Table 2.4   Twenty Russian Cities with Highest Air Pollution

City	Location(a)	1000 tons* 1987	1000 tons* 1991	
Norilsk	SI	2400.1	2486.1	
Novokuznetsk	SI	892.9	674.1	
Magnitogorsk	SI	871.4	665.6	
Cherepovets	ER	671.7	547.8	
Lipetsk	ER	722.1	511.3	
Nizhniy Tagil	SI	685.2	468.5	
Omsk	SI	479.4	408.9	
Angarsk	SI	466.8	375.8	
Orsk	SI	n.a.	364.6	
Chelyabinsk	SI	446.7	341.0	
Moscow	ER	369.1	297.8	
Ufa	ER	349.1	246.3	
Novokuybyshevsk	ER	n.a.	240.0	
Monchegorsk	ER	n.a.	220.8	
Krasnoyarsk	SI	291.0	217.1	
Grozniy	ER	308.5	197.5	
Nikel	ER	n.a.	194.3	
St. Petersburg	ER	254.1	191.5	(1990)
Novotroitsk	SI	290.9	188.2	
Volgograd	ER	280.0	185.2	

(a) ER = European Russia; SI = Siberia.

  * Stationary sources only. Some large cities such as Moscow and St. Petersburg would rank higher if mobile sources (automotive, etc.) were included.

Sources: 1987 data: *Okhrana ...*(1991), pp. 43-45;   1991 data: Yablokov and Danilov-Danil'yan (1992), p. 4 of appendix.

ployment opportunities with as little delay and inconvenience as possible may result in additional environmental compromises. Indeed, the percentage "improvement" in atmospheric emissions has been less than the percentage decline in industrial output, suggesting that an upturn in the economy may render air quality worse than before. Neither the short nor the intermediate run looks promising in this regard.

Environmental Management

To safeguard environmental values in the course of developing its natural resource base, Russia in 1992 created the Ministry of Ecology and Natural

Resources (MinEkologia). This agency replaces the earlier USSR State Committee for the Environment (Goskompriroda), which itself had been upgraded to a ministry just before the climactic events of December 1991. But, as with Goskompriroda, the question must be asked as to whether, at this early point in its history, MinEkologia has any real power, or resources, to enforce existing environmental laws. MinEkologia and other governmental environmental agencies are discussed further in Chapter 3.

The most important of these new laws is the 1991 Russian Law on Environmental Protection ("Ob okhrane," 1992). It was signed and went into force on December 19, 1991, but for some reason was not printed in the mass media until the government paper *Rossiyskaya gazeta* published its text on March 3, 1992. It is a massive document, containing fifteen sections and 94 articles. Among its many provisions are articles requiring environmental impact analyses, prohibiting the importation of nuclear wastes, defining "ecological disaster zones," granting broader rights to citizens in the area of environmental protection, establishing means of financing environmental improvements, and defining who is responsible for establishing MPC (maximum permissible concentration) norms.

This new law gives somewhat more authority in the environmental field to the Russian Republic government and to autonomous republics within Russia than it does to oblasts and local governments. For more information on this new law, see the referenced article by Bond and Sagers (1992). On May 5, 1992, *Rossiyskaya gazeta* also published a newly passed Russian Federation "Law on Underground [i.e., mineral] Resources." A new statute on forest resources was similarly passed in March of 1993.

The section of the law that authorizes the establishment of "environmental emergency zones" was utilized initially in 1993 when the northern Urals city of Nizhniy Tagil applied for this dubious distinction. The law (Article 58) requires that the activity producing the adverse effect, in this case steel mills, be terminated; presumedly this could mean either closing the mills (creating huge unemployment) or installing greatly improved technologies to minimize the pollution. The high cost of either option is to be picked up by the responsible ministries and from "special funds"; but whether an adequate amount of such funding is available in the mid-1990s is extremely doubtful. It will be interesting to observe whether Article 58 will prove to be an effective device for environmental improvement or simply one more well-intentioned but ultimately ineffective legal document.

The difficulties of implementing environmental legislation in Russia are many and complex. These complexities are looked at and analyzed in some detail in Chapter 10 in the context of a highly analogous republic, Ukraine. Much of what is said in that chapter is likewise directly applicable to conditions in the Russian Federation.

As the legal successor state to the Soviet Union, Russia automatically became a signatory to all of the treaties and international agreements on the environment that the USSR had signed over the years. It likewise assumed the responsibility for complying with them, including picking up whatever costs might be involved. For a discussion of these international agreements, see Pryde (1991, Chap. 15).

Domestic problems, however, are of the most contemporary concern. One step that Russia appears set to take to provide needed power supplies without increasing air pollution is apt to be particularly controversial. That step is a stated commitment, made public in early 1993, to resume a vigorous program of building new nuclear power stations. The plan calls for the construction of 31 new nuclear reactors by the year 2010, which would double Russia's nuclear power capability. One of the reactors (to be built at the existing Kursk nuclear complex) would be of the Chernobyl (RBMK) type; the rest would be of the pressurized water design used in the United States and elsewhere. The latter are proposed for the existing complexes at Balakova and Kalinin and for new sites at Komsomolsk and Vladivostok. The plan was opposed by Yeltsin's environmental adviser, Alexei Yablokov, but was approved nevertheless.

Whether such an ambitious plan can be realized is questionable. Not only will there be public opposition (one industry official said that no plants would be built in areas where the public didn't want them), but the financial implications of the plan and relatively short completion horizon seem of dubious practicality. One alternative approach would be to increase the efficiency of the energy currently being used in Russia. Soviet industry required twice as much energy per unit of output as was needed in the West or in Japan. Improving on this unfortunate situation would both eliminate the need for some new power plants and reduce the output of pollution.

The huge gulf between "wishing" and "doing" in Russia today is well illustrated by a 1993 Gallup poll that queried environmental attitudes in a number of both developed and developing countries (with Russia being included among the latter). Among the respondents to the poll in the Russian Federation, 62% felt that environmental problems were a "very serious issue" in their country (Dunlap et al., 1993, p. 10). This was very close to the highest percentage in any developing country. More revealingly, 88% rated environmental problems in Russia as "very" or "fairly" bad, and this was tied (with Poland) as the highest negative response from any of the 24 countries included in the survey. Similarly, 89% of Russian respondents said that environmental problems affected their own health either "a great deal" or "a fair amount," and this was the highest negative response among all the countries in the survey (Dunlap et al., 1993, p. 14).

But as soon as restorative reality was injected into the questioning, environmental enthusiasm started to wane rapidly. For example, only 56% of respondents said that the environment should be given priority even if this meant slowing down economic growth somewhat, a response rate below that of most other developing countries and below almost all developed ones. And, reflecting the 1993 state of the Russian economy, only 39% said they would be willing to pay higher prices to protect the environment, ranking Russia 21st lowest out of the 24 countries surveyed (Dunlap et al., 1993, p. 35). Although this response is understandable, it also reflects a lack of understanding of the reality of environmental cleanup. Perhaps even more discouraging, only 9% of Russians (the lowest percentage in the world) said that citizens should have primary responsibility for environmental protection, and only 17% said citizens could have a great deal of effect on solving environmental problems. Again, given Soviet history, this response rate is predictable, but it suggests a probably misplaced confidence in Russia's environmental bureaucracy, as well as a hard fight for Russia's new environmental nongovernmental organizations (NGOs).

Future Prospects

The overwhelming problem facing the Russian Federation in 1994, and unquestionably for some years to come, is its economic situation. As noted in Chapter 1, the unfortunate state of the Russian economy will serve to limit expenditures on environmental improvements. However, factors other than industrial modernization, labor productivity, and capital formation will also affect, for better or worse, Russia's economic and environmental options.

One of these is Russia's physical setting. The physical environment of Russia places some very practical constraints on its economic development. European Russia has a relatively livable environment but is not without regionally important problems. The northern portion of European Russia is hampered by bitter cold in winter, and the southernmost portion near the Caucasus Mountains is subject to major earthquakes. In the vast fertile plains of both European Russia and southern West Siberia, periodic drought and desiccating winds make large areas subject to wind erosion (deflation).

In East Siberia and the Russian Far East, winter temperatures are even more extreme, and in all but the southernmost portions, permafrost underlies the surface, and ice doesn't leave the rivers until after the first of May (Rodgers, 1990, Chap. 3). In addition, large sections of these eastern regions are subject to strong seismic events, especially around Lake Baikal and on the Kamchatka Peninsula, and the latter region (together with the Kurile Islands) is one of the world's most active volcanic areas. The Pacific coastal zone is also subject to strong storm systems moving inland from the ocean.

Another factor hampering both economic and environmental improvement is the current level of political uncertainty. This involves in part the ongoing power struggle for control of the Russian government, but it also takes in organizational confusion resulting from the dissolution of the USSR. In the summer of 1992, the author spoke with several mid-level governmental regulators who professed uncertainty as to where their agency stood in the new Russian Federation organization, how much funding it would get, and consequently how many of its assigned goals they would be able to implement. In addition, it must be remembered that most of the high positions in the production ministries are still held by persons who came up through, and were rewarded by, the previous USSR and Communist Party organizational systems (and in many cases are still loyal to them). This creates a tremendous problem for the new pro-environmental health personnel appointed by the Yeltsin government to regulate these polluting industries (Figure 2.2).

Many hard questions remain to be answered. One has already been mentioned (and presumedly decided): the future role of the nuclear power industry. An equally important question concerns the role that foreign industrial

Figure 2.2   Air pollution emanating from the Shelekhov aluminum plant, southwest of Irkutsk; an example of obsolete industrial technology.

firms will play and how much environmental control over their activities will be exercised by the Russian government. A case study in the forests of the Russian Far East will be presented in Chapter 5. The new comprehensive environmental law reads well, but will it be enforced, and will sufficient funds be diverted from other programs to pay for the improvements it mandates?

The foregoing questions cannot be easily answered, and the short-run environmental picture for Russia has to be viewed as cloudy. Many problems abound, and far too little financial resources are at hand to begin to address them. If there is any thought on the part of the Russian leadership that simply converting to private enterprise and to a market economy will necessarily correct these problems, the pre-1970 history of the United States needs to be studied in considerably more detail. The current thrust of the Russian government to decentralize and give more authority to the provinces often works against the environment, as local officials are generally pro-development and local environmental groups are typically weak (Kotov and Nikitina, 1993).

Ultimately, citizen activist organizations, such as "green parties" or the Socio-Ecological Union, may have to assume a major role in "making the system work," just as their counterpart organizations do in the West. At present, they are still too weak to make a major difference, although the first-ever lawsuit against a Russian government by a private environmental organization was filed in 1993, perhaps a harbinger of things to come.

Overall, however, increased public awareness and environmental education are needed. One effort along these lines was the opening in 1992 of an "International Independent Environmental Political Science University" in Moscow. Another interesting development was that one environmental political party, the "Constructive Ecology Movement of Russia" (whose initials in Cyrillic spell out the Russian word for "cedar"), was an approved party in the Russian Federation parliamentary election of December 12, 1993. Unfortunately, the party was not able to elect any representatives to the new parliament, and it was later identified as being made up and run largely by self-serving bureaucrats, not grass-roots environmentalists.

In the long run, if the regulators and overseers, both public and private, accept the magnitude of the problem that faces them and can find successful mechanisms for steering the Russian economic machine along an environmentally benign highway, instead of being bulldozed onto the polluted shoulders by it, then a healthier and more prosperous future for the peoples of the Russian Federation may be realizable. No one, however, is suggesting that achieving this will be easy, quick, or cheap. Given the high level of political uncertainty, public disenchantment, and economic expediency that characterized the Russian Federation at the time of this writing in 1994, the short-run environmental prognosis unfortunately has to be very pessimistic.

Appendix 2.1 **Minorities within the Russian Federation**

Ethnic group	1989 Population within Russia	Total population in their region(a)	Ethnic population in their region(b)	Percent of their region	% Russians in their region
Russians	119,866,000	147,022,000	119,866,000	81.5	81.5
Tatars	5,522,000	3,640,000	1,765,000	48.5	43.3
Ukrainians	4,363,000	n/a	n/a	n/a	n/a
Chuvash	1,774,000	1,336,000	906,000	67.8	26.7
Bashkir	1,345,000	3,952,000	864,000	21.9	39.3
Belorussians	1,206,000	n/a	n/a	n/a	n/a
Mordvinians	1,073,000	964,000	313,000	32.5	60.8
Chechen	899,000	1,277,000	735,000	57.8	23.1
Germans	842,000	n/a	n/a	n/a	n/a
Udmurts	715,000	1,609,000	497,000	30.9	58.9
Mari	644,000	750,000	324,000	43.3	7.5
Kazakhs	636,000	n/a	n/a	n/a	n/a
Avars (c)	544,000	1,792,000	496,000	27.6	9.2
Jews	537,000	216,000	9,000	4.2	83.2
Armenians	532,000	n/a	n/a	n/a	n/a
Buryats	417,000	1,042,000	250,000	24.0	70.0
Ossetians	402,000	634,000	335,000	53.0	29.9
Kabards	386,000	760,000	363,000	48.2	32.0
Yakuts	380,000	1,081,000	365,000	33.4	50.3
Dargins (c)	353,000	1,792,000	280,000	15.6	9.2
Azeris	336,000	n/a	n/a	n/a	n/a
Komi	336,000	1,263,000	292,000	23.3	57.7
Kumyks (c)	277,000	1,792,000	232,000	12.9	9.2
Lezgins (c)	257,000	1,792,000	204,000	11.3	9.2
Ingush	215,000	1,277,000	164,000	12.9	23.1
Tuvans	206,000	309,000	198,000	64.3	32.0
Moldovans	173,000	n/a	n/a	n/a	n/a
Kalmyks	166,000	322,000	146,000	45.4	37.7
Gypsies	153,000	n/a	n/a	n/a	n/a
Karachay	150,000	418,000	129,000	31.2	42.4
Komi-permyaks	147,000	159,000	95,000	60.2	36.1
Georgians	131,000	n/a	n/a	n/a	n/a
Uzbeks	127,000	n/a	n/a	n/a	n/a
Karelians	125,000	792,000	9,000	10.0	73.6
Adygey	123,000	432,000	95,000	22.1	68.0
Koreans	107,000	n/a	n/a	n/a	n/a
Laktsy (c)	106,000	1,792,000	92,000	5.1	9.2
Poles	95,000	n/a	n/a	n/a	n/a
Tabasarans (c)	94,000	1,792,000	8,000	4.3	9.2
Greeks	92,000	n/a	n/a	n/a	n/a

(a) This column shows the total population in 1989 within the borders of the autonomous republic or oblast that has been set aside in the name of these people.

(b) Indicates the number of people of this nationality that reside within their own autonomous republic or oblast.

(c) These ethnic groups reside mainly within Dagestan, which is anomalous in being made up of several different ethnic peoples.

Sources: *Rossiyskaya Federatsiya v tsifrakh*, 1992, pp. 47-51; *Current Digest of the Soviet Press*, Vol. 53, No. 21 (June 26, 1991), p. 8; Bond, 1989; Schwartz, 1991; Wixman, 1984.

Bibliography

Atlas SSSR (1983). Moscow: Glav. Uprav. Geodezii i Kartografii.

Baiduzhy, A. (1993). "Prediction: The End of the Century in Russia Will Be a Time of Catastrophes." *Nezavisimaya gazeta*, July 7 1993, p. 6, as translated in *Current Digest of the Post-Soviet Press*, vol. 45, no. 27, pp. 17–18.

Bond, A. R. (1989). "Preliminary Results of the 1989 Census Released." *Soviet Geography*, vol. 30, no. 5, pp. 410–431.

Bond, A. R., and Sagers, M. J. (1992). "Some Observations on the Russian Federation Environmental Protection Law." *Post-Soviet Geography*, vol. 33, no. 7, pp. 463–474.

Borodin, A. M. (ed.) (1985). *Krasnaya kniga SSSR*. Moscow: Lesnaya Promyshlennost'.

Dienes, L. (1993). "Prospects for Russian Oil in the 1990s: Reserves and Costs." *Post-Soviet Geography*, vol. 34, no. 2, pp. 79–110.

Dunlap, R., Gallup, G., and Gallup, A. (1993). "Of Global Concern: Results of the Health of the Planet Survey." *Environment*, vol. 35, no. 9, pp. 7–15 and 33–39.

Harris, C. D. (1993). "The New Russian Minorities: A Statistical Overview." *Post-Soviet Geography*, vol. 34, no. 1, pp. 1–27; see also vol. 34, no. 9, pp. 543–597.

IUCN List of Nature Preserves and National Parks in the Former Soviet Republics (1992). Untitled computer listing. Cambridge, UK: IUCN Protected areas Data Unit.

Knystautas, A. (1987). *The Natural History of the USSR*. New York: McGraw-Hill.

Kotov, V.. and Nikitina, E. (1993). "Russia in Transition: Obstacles to Environmental Protection." *Environment*, vol. 35, no. 10, pp. 10–20.

Krever, V. et al. (1994). *Conserving Russia's Biological Diversity: An Analytical Framework and Initial Investment Portfolio*. Washington, DC: World Wildlife Fund, January.

Litovkin, V. (1993). "93 Nuclear-Powered Submarines Are Waiting to Be Scrapped in Russia." *Izvestiya*, July 9, 1993, p. 6, as translated in *Current Digest of the Post-Soviet Press*, vol. 45, no. 27, pp. 18–19.

Marples, D. R. (1993). "The Post-Soviet Nuclear Power Program." *Post-Soviet Geography*, vol. 34, no. 3, pp. 172–184.

Narodnoye khozyaystvo RSFSR v 1990 g., statisticheskiy ezhegodnik (1991). Moscow: Respublikanskiy Inform.-izdat. Tsentr.

"Ob okhrane okruzhayushchey prirodnoy sredy" (1992). *Rossiyskaya gazeta*, March 3, pp. 3–6; as translated in JPRS-TEN-92-007, April 15, pp. 57–79.

Okhrana okruzhayushchey sredy i ratsional'noye ispol'zovaniye prirodnykh resursov (1991). Mosow: Informtsentr Goskomstat SSSR. (1991).

Pryde, P. R. (1991). *Environmental Management in the Soviet Union*. Cambridge: Cambridge University Press.

———. (1994). "Observations on the Mapping of Critical Environmental Zones in the Former Soviet Union." *Post-Soviet Geography*. vol. 35, no. 1, pp. 38–49.

Rodgers, A. (ed.) (1990). *The Soviet Far East: Geographical Perspectives on Development*. London: Routledge.

Rossiyskaya Federatsiya v tsifrakh, 1992 (1992). Moscow: Goskomstat Rossii.

Schwartz, L. (1991). "USSR Nationality Redistribution by Republic, 1979–1989." *Soviet Geography*, vol. 32, no. 4, pp. 209–248.

Wixman, R. (1984). *The Peoples of the USSR: An Ethnographic Handbook*. Armonk, NY: M. E. Sharpe.

Yablokov, A. V. (1992). "Notes on the Environmental Situation in Russia."*Environmental Policy Review*, vol. 6, no. 2, pp. 1–20.

Yablokov, A. V., and Danilov-Danil'yan, V. I. (eds.) (1992). *Gosudarstvennyy doklad: O sostoyanii okruzhayushcheyy sredy Rossiyskoy Federatsii v 1991 godu*. Moscow: Goskompriroda.

"Zakon RSFSR ob okhrane okruzhayushchey prirodnoy sredy" (1992). *Rossiyskaya gazeta*, March 3, pp. 3–6; as translated in JPRS-TEN-92-007, April 15, pp. 57–79.

3

European Russia

Boris I. Kochurov

The European territory of the Russian Federation, with an area of almost five million square kilometers, enjoys a wide range of natural conditions and resources. The territory contains Russia's highest population density, most of its industry, and its most intensive agriculture. Nearly four-fifths of the entire population of the Russian Federation live in its European portion, mainly around such principal economic centers as Moscow, St. Petersburg, Nizhniy Novgorod (Gorkiy), Samara (Kuybyshev), Volgograd, and Kazan (Figure 3.1). Compared with Asiatic Russia, European Russia is less endowed with resources, in particular with energy resources, forests, and water resources. However, the main deposits of iron ore, bauxite, phosphate, and calcium compounds, as well as the most arable land, are here. The territory maintains an extensive transportation network, great scientific and cultural potential, and a large number of highly trained specialists in all branches of science and technology.

Ethnographic Characteristics and History

Many tribal groups of Slavic origin comprised the original population of the ancient Rus. Over the ensuing centuries, many other ethnic groups settled within European Russia, particularly various groups of people who spoke either Turkic or Finno-Ugric languages. Presently, about one hundred different ethnic groups live on the territory of European Russia (see Appendix 2.1); they differ significantly from one another in language, culture, religious attributes, patterns of settlement and other characteristics.

The text for Chapter 3 was prepared in Moscow by Dr. Kochurov; it was translated by Holly Strand and edited by Philip Pryde. The bibliography for this chapter was compiled by Philip Pryde.

Figure 3.1
European Russia

△ Nature Reserves
(see Figure 3.2 for names
of North Caucasus reserves)

1 Galichya Gora
2 Central Chernozem
3 Les-na-Vorskle
4 Voronezh
5 Central Forest
6 Volga-Kama
7 Kostomuksh
8 Lapland

According to the 1989 census, 105 million people live in European Russia, over 70% of the total for the Russian Federation. They represent several linguistic families and subgroups. The vast majority of ethnic groups in the European part of Russia belong to the Indo-European, Altaic, Caucasus, and Uralic linguistic families.

The Russian nationality is the largest (about 80% of the population) and is part of the eastern Slavic group of the Indo-European language family, along with Ukrainians and Belarusians. Although Russians are the dominant ethnic group throughout European Russia, over time migrations and intermarriage with other nationalities resulted in the appearance of new ethnographic groups, such as the Pomors on the banks of the White and Barents Seas and the Don, Kuban and Ural Cossacks. Ossetians and Jews are two other major ethnic groups within the Indo-European family that are found in the region.

Another important language family of European Russia is the Altaic, which includes the Turkic dialects. The Bashkirs are a Turkic group of ancient and complex origin who live just south of the Urals; their republic is now named Bashkortostan. The Chuvash and Kazan Tatars who live in the central Volga region belong to the same Turkic group, but their languages differ substantially.

The Uralic language family is primarily represented by Finnish groups, which include the Karelians, Saami/Lopari, Komi, Komi-Permyaks, Udmurts, Mari, and Mordvins. The Karelians are settled in the extreme northwest, along the border of Finland, and are closely related to the Finns in both origin and language. The other major groups, including the Mordvins, Mari, and Udmurts, all live in the basin of the middle and lower Volga.

Three groups represent the Caucasus linguistic family in European Russia: the Adygeo-Abkhazian group, the Dagestan group, and the Nakh group. Kabards, Cherkess, Abkhazians and Adygeis belong to the first group. Avars, Lezgins, Laks, Dargins and other nationalities of Dagestan belong to the second, which takes in over thirty separate groups in all. The Chechens and Ingush belong to the Nakh group.

Accessible from the steppe, the North Caucasus has always attracted immigrants. Thus, in the 16th century, Russian Cossacks formed on the Terek, and in the 1700s, the czarist government sent the Zaporozhye Cossacks to settle the Kuban region east of the Sea of Azov. Before this, Iranian-speaking nomadic tribes of Scythian origin lived here. Scholars consider the Ossetians to be descendants of Iranian-speaking Alans who date back to the first few centuries A.D.

The post-1991 period has seen a rise in nationalism among some of the North Caucasus peoples. Thus, the Chechens and the Ingush wish to split into two separate republics, and the North Ossetians have expressed a desire to be independent of Russia.

The various ethnic groups that live in European Russia also have differing religious heritages. The majority of peoples are of the Orthodox Christian faith. Introduced at the end of the 10th century, it remained the official state religion prior to the 1917 revolution. The Komi, Komi-Permyaks, Mordvins, Mari and other Finno-Ugric groups were also converted to Christianity.

During the 10th to 12th centuries, the ancestors of the present-day Tatars became Islamic. Islam became widely accepted among the Chuvash and Bashkirs due to Tatar influence. Several of the ethnic groups in the Caucasus region also adopted Islam.

Buddhism was officially recognized within Russia in 1741. Buddhism is intertwined with the ancient traditions of the Kalmyk people near the lower Volga and is a part of their national culture.

Physical Characteristics and Natural Hazards

European Russia is characterized by numerous natural zones, including tundra, forest (both taiga and broadleaf forests), forest-steppe, steppe, and semi-desert. To the north, the islands of the Arctic Ocean lie in the arctic desert zone. Winter here is long and severe, while summer is cold and short. Many of the islands are largely ice covered; soils and vegetation are practically absent.

The tundra zone lies along the coast of the Arctic Ocean. Summer is cool and short; winter is long and cold. There is relatively little precipitation, but evaporation is also very low. Permafrost is found almost everywhere, melting in the summer down to 10–50 centimeters. The soil is quite poor; in the summer the tundra becomes pasture for reindeer. A transitional tundra–scrub forest zone borders the area on the south; taller forests stretch along the river valleys.

The taiga zone (conifer forest) occupies a fairly wide belt of the Eastern European Plain, as well as a majority of the Kola Peninsula and Karelia. A moderately warm summer and cold winter with snow are characteristic of the taiga. Coniferous tree species (pine and fir) predominate on podzolic soils, and in low-lying areas (such as West Siberia) marshes cover a significant amount of the land. Birch forests replace conifers when the latter are removed.

The next zone to the south, consisting of mixed and broadleaf forests, is fairly narrow, although in the west it extends from St. Petersburg to the Ukrainian border. Here, summers are warmer than in the taiga, and annual precipitation ranges from 500 to 800 mm. Mixed conifer-broadleaf forests in the north are progressively replaced by broadleaf trees in the south. The vegetation has been altered significantly by human activity, particularly agriculture, and forests now cover less than 30% of the area.

In the forest-steppe belt, broadleaf forests alternate with mixed grass steppe. The balance between warmth and moisture is close to optimal here, but precipitation is variable. Droughts and hot dry winds are a frequent occurrence. The soils are very productive; as a result, 80% of the land has been cultivated.

The steppe zone occupies southern European Russia. Summers here are hot and dry; evaporation often exceeds precipitation. The native vegetation is mixed grasses on chernozem and chestnut soils, and today about 60–80% of the land has been cultivated. Frequent downpours cause erosion and remove topsoil, and dry winds periodically turn plowed fields into dust storms.

Semi-arid desert conditions occur in the northwestern section of the Caspian lowlands. Evaporation occurs at 4 to 5 times the rate of precipitation and can cause salinization of the soils. The semi-desert zone's vegetation cover of sagebrush and grasses can offer good pasture for sheep, camels and horses. Cultivation here must be irrigated.

The majority of European Russia is located in the cool continental (humid) and steppe (semi-arid) climatic zones, but there is also a small region with a subtropical climate on the Black Sea coast. Interior Russia is noted for its marked continentality, with moderately cold winters and warm summers. Cyclonic air masses from the Atlantic Ocean bring in the moisture that falls as rain and snow. Arctic air masses from the north cause sudden cold spells in winter and frosts in spring, early summer, and fall.

The cold period in most of European Russia lasts from 4 to 6 months. The average January temperature in the central region is from −7.3°C to 13.8°C. An Arctic anticyclone can lower the temperature to −40. Snow cover is greatest at the end of February and early March and in Moscow averages 46 cm annually. July is the warmest month, when the average air temperature in the central region is from 16.7 to 19.6°C.

The rivers of European Russia are historically important transportation routes but are typically locked in ice all winter. The Volga is the largest river in European Russia and is joined with the Baltic, White, Azov, and Black Seas by canals. The Volga's largest tributary is the Kama, which gets its water from numerous, often polluted rivers that drain from the Ural Mountains' western slope.

There are many lakes in northwestern Russia. These are usually not very large, except for Lake Ladoga, the largest lake in Europe, and Lake Onega. Ladoga and Onega are parts of the Volga-Baltic waterway.

Floods, karsts, mud flows, soil erosion, drought, extreme cold, and erosion along coastlines are examples of natural hazards in European Russia. Soil erosion, drought, and temperature extremes have already been mentioned. Damage to slopes from landslides affects more than 50% of the region. Flooding occurs mostly in the northern and central parts of the region. During the past 20 years, high waters have flooded towns on the Northern Dvina, upper Kama, Vyatka, Vetlugi, and other rivers.

The city of St. Petersburg is often a victim of flooding, as the water from the Gulf of Finland will sometimes push into the city when major storms coincide with high tides. In the past 20 years, there have been 17 floods when the waters of the Neva River rose from 180 to 281 cm above normal; four of the floods were in 1983 alone. In 1982, construction began on a controversial dike in the Gulf of Finland to protect the city from floods.

After several decades of a drop in surface level, the Caspian Sea has risen 1.5 meters in the last 10 years. On some sections of Russia's Caspian coast there is noticeable submergence due to the rise in groundwater levels.

Regions and Resources of European Russia

Eight main economic regions can be identified within European Russia: the Central, Northern, Northwestern, Central Chernozem, Volga-Vyatka, Volga, North Caucasus, and western slopes of the Urals. The western portion of the Urals region (Perm and Orenburg Provinces, and Udmurtia and Bashkortostan) also lies in European Russia.

Of these regions, the most important is the *Central Economic Region*, which takes in 12 oblasts (provinces) centered around Moscow. The population is mostly urban, reflecting a high degree of industrial development. Cities beyond the region are linked to Moscow via numerous railroads leading into the capital and also via canal systems that link Moscow to the Volga and Dnepr Rivers and the Baltic Sea. The major cities in European Russia, and their relative rates of growth, are listed in Table 3.1.

The major natural resource in the center is a brown coal deposit south of

Table 3.1   Largest cities in European Russia

City	Date founded	Capital of	Population (thousands) 1989	Population (thousands) 1959	% gain	On "most polluted" list?
Moscow	1147	Oblast	8,769	6,009	46	Yes
St. Petersburg (Leningrad)	1703	Oblast	4,456	3,003	48	Yes
Nizhniy Novgorod (Gorkiy)	1221	Oblast	1,438	941	53	Yes
Samara (Kuybyshev)	1586	Oblast	1,257	806	56	Yes
Kazan	13th c.	Tatarstan	1,094	667	64	
Perm	1568	Oblast	1,091	629	73	Yes
Ufa	1574	Bashkortostan	1,083	547	98	Yes
Rostov	1761	Oblast	1,020	600	70	Yes
Volgograd	1589	Oblast	1,000	591	69	Yes
Saratov	1590	Oblast	905	579	56	Yes
Voronezh	1586	Oblast	887	407	118	
Izhevsk	1760	Udmurtia	635	285	123	
Yaroslavl	1010	Oblast	633	407	56	
Tolyatti (Togliatti)	?	not a capital	630	72	775	Yes
Ulyanovsk (Simbirsk)	1648	Oblast	625	206	203	Yes
Krasnodar	ca. 1795	Krasnodar Krai	620	310	100	
Orenburg	ca. 1735	Oblast	547	267	105	Yes
Penza	1666	Oblast	543	255	113	
Tula	1146	Oblast	540	351	54	
Ryazan	1095	Oblast	515	214	141	Yes
Astrakhan	1558	Oblast	509	305	67	Yes
Naberezhnyye Chelny	?	not a capital	501	16	3031	
Ivanovo	ca. 1100	Oblast	481	335	44	
Murmansk	1915	Oblast	468	222	111	
Bryansk	ca. 1146	Oblast	452	207	118	
Tver (Kalinin)	1180	Oblast	451	261	73	
Lipetsk	ca. 1779	Oblast	450	157	187	Yes
Kirov	1174	Oblast	441	252	75	
Kursk	ca. 1095	Oblast	424	205	107	
Cheboksary	ca. 1371	Chuvashia	420	104	304	
Arkhangelsk	1584	Oblast	416	258	61	Yes
Groznyy	1869	Checheno-Ingushia	401	250	60	

Source: 1989 census of the USSR

Moscow. This central region specializes in machine building, transportation, and chemical industries and in its long-established cotton and linen textile industries. A large, polluting steel mill complex operates at Cherepovets. There are major nuclear power complexes at Smolensk and Tver (Kalinin), but a proposed new complex in Kostroma Province may not be built due to public opposition.

The *Northern Economic Region* includes Arkhangelsk, Vologda and Murmansk Oblasts, and the Karelian and Komi Republics. The northern region is noted for its forest products, mining, and fishing industries and the production of metals such as aluminum. Highly polluting copper-nickel smelters use ores from the Kola Peninsula, and superphosphates are produced near apatite concentrations. There are sizable coal deposits in the northeastern part of the region, and a nuclear power complex is located on the Kola Peninsula. A major oil spill occurred on the Pechora River in 1994.

At these northern latitudes, agriculture is of secondary importance and is limited to rye, barley, and dairy farming. The local fishing industry, centered in Murmansk, is important to the national economy. The Northern Economic Region is distinguished by low population density (4 persons/sq km) and a high degree of urbanization (76%).

The *Northwestern Economic Region* includes Leningrad, Novgorod and Pskov Oblasts and enjoys a convenient position for international trade via the Baltic Sea. It contains several ancient Russian settlements and historical towns, such as Novgorod, Pskov, and Velikie Luki.

Local mineral resources include bauxite, phosphorous, and slate, as well as peat, building materials, forests, and ample water supplies. The main industries, found mostly in and around St. Petersburg (Leningrad), include turbines and other energy machinery, electrical and radio instruments, shipbuilding, and the production of other technical tools and equipment. The region operates mostly on imported fuels, but the giant Sosnovy Bor nuclear energy facility (west of St. Petersburg) has a capacity of 4 million kilowatts. Flax and dairy farming are the main agricultural activities.

The *Central Chernozem Economic Region* includes Voronezh, Lipetsk, Kursk, Belgorod, and Tambov Oblasts. The fertile chernozem (black earth) soils of the region permit intensive agriculture and food production with an emphasis on grains, potatoes, sunflowers, and sugar beets.

Iron ore resources from the vast Kursk Magnetic Anomaly (KMA) are the basis for a major metallurgical center at Lipetsk. Industry in other large cities includes agricultural machinery, aircraft, chemical equipment, machine tools, radio equipment, and measuring instruments. Large nuclear power complexes are located near Kursk and Voronezh.

The *Volga-Vyatka Economic Region* includes Nizhniy Novgorod (Gorkiy) and Kirov Oblasts and the Chuvash, Mari-el and Mordvinian Republics. Automobile manufacturing and shipbuilding in Nizhniy Novgorod (Gorkiy) play a leading economic role, as do instrument, electronic, and machine manufacturing plants there and in Kirov and Cheboksary. There is a chemical industry in Dzerzhinsk, where synthetic resins and plastics are produced.

Industrial resources here are few (peat, building materials, phosphorous), but there is a timber industry concentrated along river corridors and cellulose-paper factories in Pravdinsk, Balakhin, and Volzhsk. Agricultural products include livestock farming, grains, and potatoes.

The *Volga Economic Region* includes Penza, Samara (Kuybyshev), Ulyanov, Saratov, Volgograd, and Astrakhan Oblasts, as well as Tatarstan and Kalmykia. It stretches almost 1,500 km along the Volga River, from the Kama to the Caspian Sea. Canals and railroads connect the Volga with the Caspian, Black, Azov, Baltic and White Seas. Natural zones become drier as one moves south: forests transition into steppe and steppe into semideserts.

The extensive Volga-Ural oil and gas fields along the Volga and Kama Rivers were the most important in the USSR until the 1970s but today are well past their peak. There are major oil refineries at Saratov and near Samara (Kuybyshev). Electricity is produced from large thermal power plants, from huge hydroelectric stations on the Volga River, and from the Balakova nuclear energy facility. Additional reactors have been proposed for the Balakova complex, for a site near Volgograd, and at a site under construction in Tatarstan, but these have all met with strong public opposition and may not be completed. The huge automobile factory VAZ at Togliatti is Russia's largest producer of private cars, and the largest truck plant is at Naberezhnyye Chelny.

Grains, such as rye and winter wheat, are grown in the north, where there are also cattle and dairy farming. Farther south, agriculture includes spring wheat and corn, some industrial crops, and livestock. Sheep farms are common south of Volgograd.

The *North Caucasus Economic Region* includes Krasnodar and Stavropol Krais (territories), Rostov Oblast, and six autonomous republics (Figure 3.2). The natural landscapes of the North Caucasus are extremely varied, extending from mountain ranges in the south to dry plains in the east, plus a small moist subtropical area along the Black Sea coast.

The foothills of the Greater Caucasus are rich in mineral and energy resources, including oil, gas, coal, ferrous and rare metals, hydroelectric resources, and geothermal springs. Electricity is produced mainly at thermal power stations that burn natural gas. The North Caucasus oil deposits were important prior to World War II but are now becoming depleted. Construction work on a nuclear power complex near Rostov has been suspended, and a proposed plant at Krasnodar has been canceled.

Many different crops are grown in the North Caucasus, including winter wheat, corn, rice, sunflowers, and small amounts of grapes, tobacco, citrus, and tea. The latter three are grown only in the moist subtropics along the Black Sea coast. Sheep are the main livestock in the region.

Resorts have been developed around the mineral springs at Pyatigorsk, Kislovodsk, Yessentuki, Nalchik, Sochi, and other smaller towns. The area around Sochi is the largest resort region within the Russian Federation.

The western portion of the *Urals Economic Region*, which includes Perm and Orenburg Oblasts, as well as Bashkortostan and Udmurtia, is dominated by oil extraction and petrochemical industries. There are major oil refineries at Perm and Ufa and chemical complexes at smaller cities such as Ster-

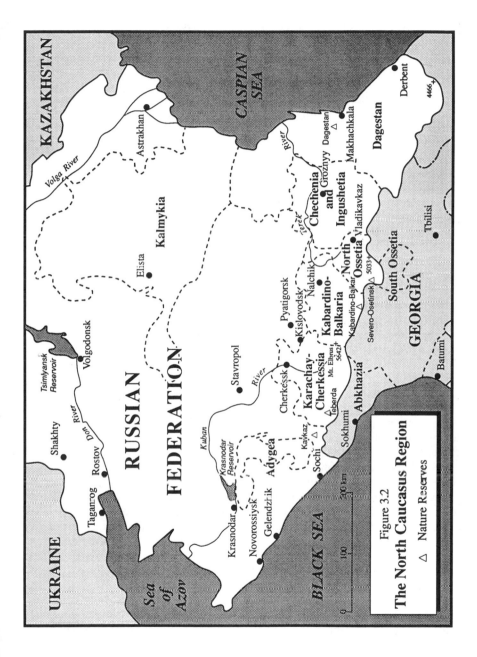

Figure 3.2
The North Caucasus Region
△ Nature Reserves

litamak, Salavat, Berezniki, and Solikamsk. A proposed nuclear power complex in Bashkortostan has been canceled due to public opposition. South of Ufa, wheat production is important; north of Ufa, agriculture is limited to dairying and hardier grains.

Primary Ecological Problems

Many severe ecological problems have developed in European Russia, including pollution of the atmosphere, water and soil; destruction of forests; exhaustion of fish resources; degradation of pastures; erosion; deflation and salinization of soils; and despoliation of land by mining operations.

According to the map of critical environmental regions of the former USSR described in Chapter 1, European Russia is an area with some of the most serious ecological conditions. This is where the bulk of industrial enterprises are concentrated, equipped with instruments and technology that are not capable of purifying emissions into air and water. Overall, the most critical zones include the area affected by the Chernobyl accident, Novaya Zemlya and the Barents Sea, the Kola Peninsula, the Moscow region, the St. Petersburg region, the central and lower Volga regions, and Kalmykia and Bashkortostan.

Environmental conditions are poor in many Russian cities. Only 15% of urban residents live within areas that meet permissible levels of atmospheric pollution. Air quality is especially bad around metallurgical, chemical, petrochemical, fertilizer, and timber processing centers, such as Lipetsk, Moscow, Saratov, Volgograd, Perm, Ufa, Sterlitamak, Cherepovets, and others (see Table 2.4). In most cities, the majority of pollution is caused by industrial emissions, but in Moscow 65% comes from automobiles. Many smaller but highly industrial cities have especially bad conditions for human health; these include Monchegorsk, Sterlitamak, Novokuybyshevsk, Chapayevsk, Nikel, and many others (Feshbach and Friendly, 1992). In many of these towns, the effects on public health have been disastrous; in Sterlitamak, for example, only 16% of births are considered completely normal.

The historic city of St. Petersburg suffers from two serious (and related) water quality problems. First, the Neva River, which flows through the city, is polluted by upstream timber processing factories around Lake Ladoga. This in turn causes the city's water supply to be unhealthy and at times undrinkable. Second, the large dike built across the Gulf of Finland, referred to earlier, has blocked normal water circulation in the section of the Gulf near St. Petersburg; the stagnant water, constantly receiving impurities from the large metropolitan area, is becoming eutrophic and highly polluted. There are many calls to tear down the dike.

Greater Moscow's high concentration of population, together with intensive industrial development and a highly polluting automotive transport system, had led to high levels of atmospheric pollution and the exhaustion and degradation of surface and ground water. There are 111 unauthorized trash dumps in Moscow, and in 1992, 50,000 trees were felled in its greenbelt. From 1990 to 1992 there was a 750% increase in Moscow's diphtheria rate

(Baiduzhy, 1993). Previously buried radioactive wastes have been discovered at numerous locations within Moscow, some in areas of recent residential construction.

Areas with excessive radioactive contamination are a particular concern. Fourteen oblasts (Bryansk, Belgorod, Voronezh, Kaluga, Kursk, Lipetsk, St. Petersburg, Orel, Ryazan, Tambov, Tula, Penza, Smolensk, Ulyanovsk) and the Mordvinian Republic contain zones where cesium-137 is higher than 1 cu/km². Areas with cesium-137 levels above 5 cu/km² are located in Bryansk, Tula, Kaluga, and Orel Oblasts, covering a total area of about 7,900 km². There are two locations in Bryansk Oblast that register 15 and 40 cu/km² (2,130 and 310 km², respectively); these are areas that received heavy fallout from the Chernobyl explosion. Those areas heavily impacted by Chernobyl fallout are shown on Figure 3.3.

Nuclear weapons testing, as well as careless disposal of radioactive wastes, reactors, and other materials, has created a zone perilous to human and other life forms on Novaya Zemlya island and in the adjacent Kara Sea. The average level of surface pollution by radionucleides in Novaya Zemlya is higher than any other location in the polar region. The problem of radioactive pollution will be discussed further in the next chapter on Siberia.

Mining and non-ferrous metallurgy in the fragile natural landscape of the Kola Peninsula have disturbed natural processes and reduced environmental quality. Acid rain, some of which is associated with pollution in western Europe, is also a matter of concern here. The nickel smelters at Monchegorsk and Nikel are especially critical polluters and require immediate remedial measures.

The ecological condition of Volga, Kama, Oka and other rivers of central European Russia have suffered due to increased extraction of water, an increase in unrecycled water consumption, the dumping of industrial effluents into rivers, the seepage of fertilizers and pesticides from agricultural fields, and pollution from urban areas. The ability of these rivers to purify or reconstitute their normal ecosystems has been significantly reduced.

Critical environmental situations have arisen in the lower Volga region and the areas north of the Caspian Sea in connection with irrigation and the development of the oil and gas industry. This has led to the appearance of such problems as soil, air and water pollution; loss of fish stocks; and the transformation of the Volga-Akhtubinsk floodplain and its water regime. The rate of illness of the local population increased significantly after the construction of the Astrakhan gas complex. For additional discussion of the Caspian Sea problem, see Chapter 15 on Azerbaijan.

The Kalmykia landscape, just to the east of the lower Volga, is especially sensitive to anthropogenic influences. The main problem here involves degradation of pastures due to excessive and non-systematic pasturing, as well as secondary salinization of soils in irrigated regions. This has led to wind erosion and general desertification over the past five years. In Kalmykia alone, 47,000 hectares have been taken over by sand (see Figure 16.2).

The agricultural development of the extensive, fertile soils in the Central Chernozem Region has led to their degradation and destruction. Breakdown

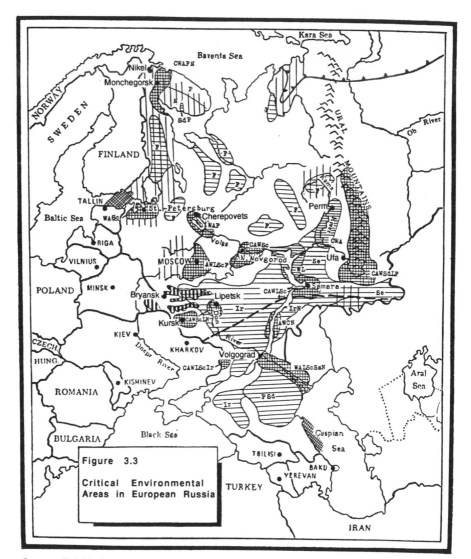

Figure 3.3

Critical Environmental Areas in European Russia

Source: B. I. Kochurov, N. I. Koronkevich, A. V. Antipova, T. B. Denisova, N. A. Zherevtsova, and O. Yu Bykova; Institute of Geography of the Russian Academy of Sciences Laboratory of Complex Geographical Forecasts.

EXPLANATION

1. **AREAS OF THE MOST CRITICAL ENVIRONMENTAL SITUATIONS**
   (according to the degree to which human impact exceeds the landscape's potential and sustainability)

   1.1 Very complicated situations (areas where many environmental protection problems are combined)

   1.2 Complicated situations (areas where two-three environmental protection problems are combined)

   Simple environmental situations (areas where one environmental problem prevails)

   Areas of severe marine pollution

2. **INDICES OF ENVIRONMENTAL PROBLEMS**
   (their sequence in a given area reflects the degree of the problems' criticality and consequences)

A	- 2.1	Air pollution (chemical, particulate, thermal)
W	- 2.2	Depletion and pollution of fresh water resources
F	- 2.3	Deforestation (over-cutting of forests)
Fd	- 2.4	Forest degradation as a result of human impact
P	- 2.5	Degradation of natural pastures
Se	- 2.6	Soil erosion by water
Sd	- 2.7	Soil wind erosion (deflation)
Ss	- 2.8	Soil secondary salination
Sc	- 2.9	Chemical soil pollution
Ir	- 2.10	Intensive growth of ravines
C	- 2.11	Complex land destruction and mineral resources depletion (in the areas with mineral resources extraction)
L	- 2.12	Loss of productive lands (use of agricultural lands and forests for development, reservoirs, etc.)
O	- 2.13	Deterioration and loss of recreational potential
N	- 2.14	Destruction of ecological regime of nature reserves and protected natural territories

3. **DISTRIBUTION OF BROAD-SCALE DESTRUCTIVE FORCES**
   (exceeding environmental standards and norms)

   3.1 Areas of radioactive pollution (from Cesium 137)

   3.2 Acid rain (on the basis of snow cover in 1988)

4. **TERRITORIES WITH ENVIRONMENTALLY DESTRUCTIVE PROCESSES**

   4.1 Northern border of dust storms

   4.2 Southern border of permafrost (of both continuous and isolated permafrost)

5. **LOCALES WITH A DANGEROUS DEGREE OF ENVIRONMENTAL POLLUTION**

   ● Ufa 5.1 Cities with the highest air pollution levels

of soil structure and loss in soil productivity are most detrimental to chernozems, along with erosion and pollution, which lead to a loss in organic
material (humus). In the past 20 years, the amount of humus in chernozems
has declined by 10–30%. Irrigation and the excessive application of pesticides and fertilizers have also damaged the chernozem soils. In areas such as
the Kursk Magnetic Anomaly, industry, mining, and expanding cities have
eliminated much productive farmland, lowered the water table, destroyed
wildlife habitat, and contributed to local air and water pollution (Figure 3.4).

Bashkortostan (formerly the Bashkir ASSR) and the Belaya River have
severe pollution problems, due mainly to the cities of Ufa, Sterlitamak, and
Salavat being centers of the chemical and petrochemical industries (refer to
Figure 4.3). The Yuzhny River, a water source for the capital city of Ufa, is
polluted by upstream oil refineries and synthetic chemical plants. In 1990 it
was revealed that herbicides produced by one of these factories was releasing
highly toxic dioxin into Ufa's water supply. Infant abnormalities and mortality in the republic are reported as very high (*Izvestiya*, August 31, 1993).

Forests should be looked at not only as providing industrial resources, but
as performing regulatory and protective functions for the environment as
well. Despite this, the overcutting of forests is common in the more accessible
areas of the north. In the past few decades, coniferous forests have been replaced by deciduous forests in a number of areas. The forest has been logged
completely in some parts of Arkhangelsk, Vologda, and Kirov Oblasts and
in the Karelian and Komi Republics. Forest cover in the Northwest, Volga-

Figure 3.4   View across the main pit of the huge Kursk Magnetic Anomaly iron ore mine,
situated 70 km northwest of the city of Kursk.

Vyatka, and Central regions has decreased by up to half, and in the Central Chernozem, Volga, and North Caucasus regions forests make up only 9–10% of the land cover. In forests located near populated regions and transportation corridors, the maximum permissible cut is fully realized and sometimes surpassed. Because forest regeneration in these areas lags behind the pace of logging, forest resources are becoming exhausted. This results in adverse changes in local water regimes and accelerates erosion. Floating and processing the logs further damage rivers and lakes, and pulp-and-paper mills are universally among the worst sources of air pollution.

The surface and groundwater resources that are needed to satisfy industrial, agricultural and municipal demands are becoming less and less sufficient. The waters of Lake Ladoga and Lake Onega and of the Sukhona, Vychegda, northern Dvina, Pechora, Kama, Volga, and other rivers are already significantly polluted by nutrients or industrial wastes. In 1994, a major break in an oil pipeline severely polluted the Pechora and several other streams in the Komi Republic.

Wildlife resources have been heavily depleted by industrial development, as well as by decreases in critical habitat associated with widespread cultivation of the steppe and meadows, replacement of primary forests with secondary forests, and draining of marshes. Fish resources have been degraded because of deteriorated conditions for reproduction caused by dam construction, regulated water flow, pollution of water bodies and sea coasts, etc. Although several large nature reserves *(zapovedniki)* exist in European Russia, including several major biosphere reserves (Table 3.2), in total they represent less than 1% of the land area. There are also seven national parks in European Russia, all created since 1983.

Environmental Monitoring and Public Involvement

Currently, there is no single government agency for monitoring the natural environment, natural resources development, and effects of environmental contamination on human health in the Russian Federation. Instead, there are a number of networks in place to measure various types of pollution.

The Committee on Hydrometeorology and Environmental Monitoring gathers data on atmospheric pollution in 334 Russian cities, 225 of which are measured regularly. In the various cities, concentrations of 5 to 25 substances are measured. Pollution of surface waters is determined for 1,194 flowing rivers and streams and 147 lakes or reservoirs. Hydrobiological observations are carried out in 156 water bodies. Marine pollution is measured at 623 different marine stations. There are 3 stations and 35 posts to measure transnational pollution. They examine atmospheric aerosols, sulphur dioxide, and nitrogen levels, as well as performing more complex monitoring tasks. One hundred twenty-one stations determine chemical concentrations, while 116 sites measure acid rain deposition. The system for monitoring snow cover includes 645 stations covering 17 million km^2.

Measurements of radioactivity are taken daily. The six stations that measure background radiation are located in biosphere reserves (see Table 3.2).

Table 3.2   Largest Nature Reserves in European Russia

Name	Area (ha)	Natural Zone	Biosphere Reserve?
Pechoro-Ilych	721,322	taiga	yes
Lapland	278,436	wooded tundra	yes
Kavkaz (Caucasus)	263,277	Caucasus Mtns	yes
Zavidov	125,442	mixed forest	no
Darwin	112,630	water, forest	no
Teberda	84,996	Caucasus Mtns	no
Kabardino-Balkar	74,099	Caucasus Mtns	no
Bashkir	72,140	Ural foothills	no
Astrakhan	63,400	Volga wetlands	yes
Kandalaksha	58,100	Arctic islands	no
Kostomuksh	47,457	Karelian taiga	no
Pinega	41,436	taiga	no
Nizhne-Svir	41,244	wetlands, taiga	no

Other Biosphere Reserves Located in European Russia

Voronezh	31,053	forest-steppe	yes
Oka	22,911	river forests	yes
Central Forest	21,348	mixed forest	yes
Prioksko-Terrasny	4,945	wet woodlands	yes
Central Chernozem	4,847	steppe	yes

Source: Pryde, 1991.

More than 1,300 posts determine the level of local radiation and radioactive fallout at 300 monitoring locations. All population centers (including the area affected by Chernobyl) where pollution is greater than 5 cu/km^2 are monitored regularly.

The State Committee for Sanitary Epidemiological Inspection collects information annually on the effects of the environment on public health. Water supply, surface water, soil, air, food products, noise levels, vibrations, and electromagnetic and other types of radiation are measured. Since 1982, the government information system Zdorov'ye (Health) has operated within Russia; it looks for links between illness and pollution problems. In 1986, a universal sanitary-hygienic inspection system for detecting residual quantities of pesticides in food products and other sources was created.

The Russian Ministry of Justice has registered the charters of 12 public ecological unions, with branches in 150 cities. Unofficial organizations often aggressively tackle local problems; activists in 1993 used sit-in and obstructionism techniques to try to block continued rock quarrying in Samara Bend National Park (*Izvestiya*, July 22, 1993). Currently there is considerable political activism, and in 1991 the Green Party of Russia was formed. Non-governmental domestic ecological organizations have increased their contact with foreign and international counterparts. They were involved in preparations for the 1992 U.N. Conference on Environment and Development in Rio de Janeiro. The Green Party ran candidates in the December 1993 national elections but did not garner adequate votes to seat any representatives.

Because Moscow is the capital of the federation, many environmental organizations are headquartered there. The largest and best organized is the Socio-Ecological Union (SEU), which has nationwide affiliates. Formed in 1988, the SEU serves both as an activist association and as an "umbrella organization" that coordinates the activities of scores of local environmental groups.

A change in public ecological consciousness is reflected in the number of written and verbal appeals by citizens to government organs in response to proposed activities of the government and other public organizations. A recent poll showed that about 86% of the population believe that conservation should not be sacrificed for a quick fix of current economic and social problems. From 45 to 65% think that full information about the state of the environment is either insufficient or non-existent. Fifty percent do not believe official information at all. The majority do not know anything at all about the work of public environmental groups. Thirty percent of the people do not take part in conservation activities; 50% participate occasionally.

Public opinion polls show that 90% of the population experience ecological discomfort. When evaluating the state of their health, 80% of those polled associate a decline in their health with local pollution problems. Over 68% consider that environmental pollution has affected the health of their children, and 20% wish to change their place of residence. Clearly, public awareness is high, but relatively few people consider themselves environmental activists.

Future Prospects

Russia's changing economic geography has implications for local environmental conditions. Commerce and transport routes have experienced dislocations since 1991 as a result of political realignments. Russia now has Novorossiisk as its only major port on the Black Sea, and only St. Petersburg, which freezes over in the winter, remains on the Baltic. In 1993, the primary land route to western Europe was through Belarus, and the major pipelines to Europe ran through Ukraine. The importance of Arkhangelsk and Murmansk, of the White Sea–Baltic and Northern Dvina water transport systems, and of parallel railroad lines should increase. These realignments will have significant environmental ramifications in the areas where commerce will increase.

In general, if the "late USSR" was characterized by attempts to have equal rights with the developed countries, then the "early CIS" is characterized by developing connections with newly industrialized countries of the Third World. Currently, Germany, Finland, Turkey, Iran, China and both Koreas are among those countries enjoying the closest ties, replacing the previous strong ties to eastern Europe.

European Russia has a tremendous potential for international trade. It has retained the lion's share of the Soviet fuel/energy complex and hydroelectric potential. A potential for foreign trade also remains for light industry, electronics, and military technology, especially pure metals and alloys. The forests are still a significant resource, although they are not being managed satisfactorily and are in danger of being badly exploited.

The dilemma of power production and use must be solved. The previous chapter noted that Russia intended to resume building more nuclear power plants. The alternative would be to build fossil fuel plants, which would have serious atmospheric quality repercussions. Yet much energy is wasted or poorly used; increases in the efficiency of energy use would be a way out of this dilemma.

The breakup of the USSR greatly decreased access to many of the popular resort regions in other republics. Together with the increase in the cost of recreational services, this has produced many problems for the Russian recreational system. There is a tendency for areas of recreational development to become overcrowded, to become concentrated near population centers, and often to become sites for permanent residence. Some of the area's nature reserves and all of its national parks could become points of controlled tourism (see Table 2.3).

International tourism could also become a growth industry in European Russia, with the vast market of western Europe so close by. Potential spots for tourism include historic destinations, especially along the "Golden Ring" of the Russian north and along ancient routes where unique monuments to the past remain. The mineral spas of the North Caucasus are scenically located near impressive montane landscapes and could be a popular destination, assuming a resolution of current ethnic unrest in such areas as the Chechen and Ossetian Republics (Figure 3.2). Other remaining resources for recreational tourism include ecologically clean areas (Valdai, Seliger and the European north), unique geologic and geographic monuments, and areas of ethnographic interest.

Russia's primary challenge in the mid-1990s is to strengthen both its economy and its political systems to the point where, among other things, they can satisfactorily respond to the environmental crisis presently facing the country. Too little financial capital and too many competing political priorities are presently at hand to permit a resolution of Russia's serious environmental problems. Green groups are presently not strong enough to be a catalyst for significant change, nor is it likely that foreign investors will be. Thus, for the immediate future, the pace of environmental improvement in Russia is apt to be slow.

Bibliography

Baiduzhy, A. (1993). "Moscow as a Mirror of Russia's Ecological Crisis." *Nezavisimaya gazeta,* August 1, 2, 1993, pp. 1, 25, as translated in *Current Digest of the Post-Soviet Press,* vol. 45, no. 34, pp. 15–16.

Bond, A.R., and Sagers, M. J. (1992). "Some Observations on the Russian Federation Environmental Protection Law," *Post-Soviet Geography,* vol. 33, no. 7, 463–474.

Bradley, D. J. (1992). *Radioactive Waste Management in the Former USSR.* (3 vols.). Richland, WA: Pacific Northwest Laboratory (for the U.S. Dept. of Energy), June.

Dienes, L. (1993). "Prospects for Russian Oil in the 1990s: Reserves and Costs." *Post-Soviet Geography,* vol. 34, no. 2, pp. 79–110.

Feshbach, M., and Friendly, A. (1992). *Ecocide in the USSR.* New York: Basic Books.

Harris, C. D. (1993). "The New Russian Minorities: A Statistical Overview." *Post-Soviet Geography,* vol. 34, no. 1, pp. 1–27.

IUCN East European Programme (1991). *Environmental Status Reports: 1990.* Vol. 3, USSR. Norwich, UK: Page Brothers.

Komarov, B. (1980). *The Destruction of the Soviet Union.* New York: M. E. Sharpe.

Marples, D. R. (1993). "The Post-Soviet Nuclear Power Progam," *Post-Soviet Geography,* vol. 34, no. 3, pp. 172–184.

Massey Stewart, J. (1992). *The Soviet Environment: Problems, Policies, and Politics.* Cambridge: Cambridge University Press.

Mnatsakanian, R. A. (1992). *Environmental Legacy of the Former Soviet Republics.* Edinburgh: Centre for Human Ecology, University of Edinburgh.

Natsional'nyy doklad SSSR k konferentsii OON 1992 goda po okruzhayushchey srede i razvitiyu (1991). Moscow: MinPriroda.

Nilsson, S. et al. (1992). *The Forest Resources of the Former European USSR.* Carnforth, UK: The Parthenon Publishing Group.

Okhrana okruzhayushchey sredy i ratsional'noye ispol'zovaniye prirodnykh resursov v SSSR (1989). Moscow: Goskomstat.

Peterson, D. J. (1993). *Troubled Lands: The Legacy of Soviet Environmental Destruction.* Boulder: Westview Press.

Pryde, P. R. (1991). *Environmental Management in the Soviet Union.* Cambridge: Cambridge University Press.

———. (1992). "Current Status of the St. Petersburg (Leningrad) Flood Barrier." *Post-Soviet Geography,* vol. 33, no. 9, pp. 612–616.

Rossiyskaya Federatsiya v tsifrakh, 1992. (1992). Goskomstat Rossii.

Sagers, M. J. "Review of the Energy Industries in the Former USSR in 1991." *Post-Soviet Geography,* vol. 33, no. 4, pp. 237–268.

Wixman, R. (1984). *The Peoples of the USSR: An Ethnographic Handbook.* Armonk, NY: M. E. Sharpe.

Wolfson, Ze'ev (1993). *The Geography of Survival: Ecology in the Post-Soviet Era.* Armonk, NY: M. E. Sharpe.

4

The Urals and Siberia

Anna Scherbakova and Scott Monroe

This chapter examines the vast region of Russia that takes in the eastern slopes of the Ural Mountains and West and East Siberia. This huge territory occupies ten million square kilometers of northern Asia, from the Urals in the west to Yakutia (Sakha) in the east, and from the shores of the Arctic Ocean in the north to the steppes of Kazakhstan and the Chinese and Mongolian borders in the south (Figure 4.1). In addition to the Urals, the principal regions are the West Siberian plain, the mid-Siberian plateau, the mountains of southern Siberia, and the mountain system of northeastern Siberia. Within Siberia's borders are the republics of Buryatia and Tuva, the Altai and Krasnoyarsk territories, and the Chelyabinsk, Yekaterinburg (Sverdlovsk), Tyumen, Kurgan, Omsk, Novosibirsk, Tomsk, Kemerovo, Irkutsk, and Chita Provinces (Oblasts). According to the 1989 census, 33,620,000 people lived in this region.

Physical Characteristics and Settlement

Siberia is situated in the middle and high latitudes of the Northern Hemisphere, in the temperate and arctic climatic belts. The climate in most of Siberia is continental and seasonally arid; average annual air temperature is less than 0 degrees C, and in northeastern Siberia it drops below −18 degrees C. Winters are long and cold. Most precipitation (up to 75–80 percent of the annual total) occurs during the warm period of the year, and thus snowfall during the remaining portion generally is not substantial, averaging 30–40 cm.

Siberia's arid climate contributes to the freezing of the soil and the formation of permafrost. Over six million square kilometers of Siberian territory are under permafrost, which in northern areas reaches a depth of 200–500 m. This permafrost is one of the major obstacles to expansion into Siberia and to the completion of construction projects of any size and scope.

Figure 4.1
West and East Siberia
● Cities
△ Nature Reserves
1. Kuznetskiy Alatau
2. Sayan Shushenskoye
3. Barguzin
4. Sokhonda

The majority of Siberian rivers, including the most voluminous (the Ob-Irtysh system and the Yenisey and Lena), empty into the Arctic basin (Figure 4.1). Rivers are blocked with ice from five months a year in the south to eight months a year in the north, which limits navigation on the extensive river systems. Nevertheless, due to their immense volume (they account for over fifty percent of the former USSR's hydroelectric potential), Siberian rivers play a significant role in the Russian economy.

The soil and plant cover of Siberia vary primarily with latitude, forming sharply defined zones from north to south: arctic desert, tundra, forested tundra, taiga, and, in southern West Siberia and southeastern Chita Province, forested steppe and steppe. Siberia's most typical landscape is the taiga, with dense, pine-dominated forests and more open, larch-dominated conifer forests being most common in the western and eastern portions, respectively. Except in the southernmost steppe regions, soils are generally poor.

Until the end of the sixteenth century the population of Siberia was quite sparse, but the following century saw the rapid settlement of its interior regions by Russians. Tomsk was settled in 1604, Krasnoyarsk in 1628, and Yakutsk in 1632. Expansion into Siberia was characterized by three factors: speed, due to the abundance of rivers made accessible by the virtual absence of resistance from indigenous peoples; relatively low financial costs; and the stability and cohesion of settled lands.

The stream of settlers grew after the emancipation of serfs in 1861 and especially following the construction in 1891–1905 of the Trans-Siberian Railroad. As a result of the expansion of Russians into Siberia, indigenous peoples were pushed away from their traditional places of residence, and their ancient ways of life suffered irreparable damage. In economic terms native Siberian peoples (about four percent of the total population) mainly belong to one of two groups: agrarian cattle-raisers and farmers (most Yakuts, Buryats, Tuvans, and other peoples of southern Siberia) and the so-called small peoples of the north, who engage in deer-raising, hunting, and fishing. The northern peoples are related in the west to the Laplanders of northern Europe and in the east to the Inuits and Aleuts of North America. The Tuvans and Yakuts are Turkic, and the Buryats are closely related to the people of Mongolia. Some of the interior indigenous groups, such as the Nenets, belong to the Uralo-Altaic linguistic family.

Natural Resources Development

Siberia is famed for its wealth of natural resources, from the oil fields of Tyumen to the gold mines of Kolyma. Although the harsh climate and sheer enormity of the Siberian territory present natural barriers to development, industry was well developed in the Urals in tsarist times, and Soviet planners have subsequently built many important industrial centers throughout Siberia.

Post-revolutionary heavy industry development in this region was first emphasized in the Urals by Stalin and then spread ever-farther eastward along the Trans-Siberian Railroad as the need for coal, steel, and timber grew. By the start of the Second World War, Siberia stood alongside the Urals, Ukraine, and Volga regions as one of the USSR's most important industrial centers.

Between 1950 and 1960 the enormous hydroelectric potential of the Angara, Yenisei, and Ob Rivers began to be developed. Hydroelectric power plants were constructed near Novosibirsk, Irkutsk, Bratsk, and Krasnoyarsk. Two of the largest hydroelectric plants in the world, Sayano-Shushenskoye and Krasnoyarsk, are located on the Yenisey and together have a capacity of twelve million kilowatts. Power plants such as these were used as the energy sources for enormous complexes that produce aluminum and steel, chemicals, and pulp and paper.

Huge stores of oil and natural gas are present in western and eastern Siberia. Oil pipelines were laid down from the Urals to Angarsk, which became a major oil-refining and petrochemical center, and from Surgut to Omsk and Anzhero-Sudzhensk. A gas pipeline was built that ran from northern West Siberia to the center of the country. Cities such as Norilsk, Bratsk, Krasnoyarsk, and Novokuznetsk became centers of non-ferrous metallurgy, while Novosibirsk, Irkutsk, and other cities developed machine-building and woodworking industries.

In addition, timber-processing facilities were developed in Bratsk, Ust-Ilimsk, Lesosibirsk, Igarka, and Krasnoyarsk in order to exploit the most extensive forest resources in the world. Russia possesses one-third of the world's remaining old-growth forest and about twenty percent of its total forested area. Known as the taiga, Russia's forest stretches 2.3 million square miles from Yakutia to European Russia, and its crucial role in atmospheric issues such as global warming is being increasingly recognized. The taiga absorbs 60 billion tons of atmospheric carbon annually; Amazonian rain forests absorb 80 billion tons a year.

Though lip service was paid to the notion of preserving the inviolability of Russia's natural wealth, in reality environmental impacts were never a serious consideration for the central government as it tapped the vast resources of Siberia. Not surprisingly, the remarkable productivity of Siberian industrial cities came at a great cost to the environment, and by extension, to public health (Pryde, 1991a, pp. 403f; and Feshbach and Friendly, 1992). In essence, the very industries on which the Soviet Union based much of its economic and military might ultimately undercut the integrity of the natural resources that allowed the creation of those industries in the first place.

An excellent example of this ironic situation is the hydroelectric industry. Central planners emphasized the low cost of energy to be generated at hydroelectric plants without any regard for the substantial environmental impact of damming. Huge reservoirs with a surface area of hundreds of square kilometers were formed on both the Yenisey and Angara Rivers, flooding arable land and forests and forcing the evacuation of entire villages.

Reservoirs were visualized as man-made lakes teeming with fish and shore-side resorts, but the poor water quality forestalled such ambitions. Some trees were felled before flooding, but most were left standing. As a result, the total volume of timber left under water in the Sayano-Shushenskoye and Krasnoyarsk Reservoirs was three million cubic meters. The timber decomposed and contaminated the water with phenols, phosphorous, nitrogen, and other organic substances, which led to oxygen depletion. This also defeated efforts to introduce various types of fish to the reservoirs (see Pryde, 1991b, pp. 56–61).

However, the "project of the century" mind-set that is blamed for such oversights did not disappear entirely with the regime that fomented it. Support still exists among officials of the Gorno-Altai region for the construction of a dam 200 meters (650 ft.) high and a 1,900 MW hydroelectric power plant on the Katun River. Work on the project began in 1983 but was soon halted by public protest. Three studies by government-appointed commissions found that mercury deposits in the area of the dam would contaminate the reservoir and the Katun and Ob rivers, and the dam would operate at only 25 percent for four months of the year due to winter freezing. Many Russian environmentalists believe that there is no environmentally acceptable version of the project. Nevertheless, some officials are seeking private financing of the dam as long as state-controlled funds are on hold, and President Yeltsin has indicated that he would support the project.

Siberian forests are sorely threatened by a combination of irresponsible logging methods, forest fires, and industrial pollution. The remaining area of taiga is steadily decreasing at a rate of five million acres a year (*CIS Environmental Watch*, Spring 1992, p. 3). According to official statistics, between 1970 and 1990 annual losses due to forest fires ranged from 72,000 to 2.1 million hectares. Very little money or effort is expended on fire control; only forty percent of the total forested area is monitored by air patrol. Official statistics, however, do not tell the full story. Actual damage in the area east of Lake Baikal due to fires, for example, is double the official figure, and forest losses in the Krasnoyarsk territory exceed the official figure by a factor of five.

Forests are being adversely affected by air pollution as well. East Siberia is the major source region for atmospheric sulfuric acids, producing 51 percent of the former USSR total (Nilsson, 1992, p. 120). The total area of forest damaged by the Norilsk nickel-smelting combine is 740,000 ha (*Ekologicheskii vestnik*, 1992). This figure does not include hundreds of hectares of damaged reindeer pastures around the combine. In other instances, 140,000 ha of forest have been damaged in the vicinity of the Bratsk aluminum-smelting plant, as well as 70,000 ha in the Irkutsk region.

Lake Baikal

Even Lake Baikal, which is the world's deepest freshwater lake and is regarded by Russians as a national treasure, has not been spared the harmful impact of industry. Baikal, 650 km long and reaching 1,620 m in depth, is one of the world's most abundant sources of freshwater (Figure 4.2). It also is home to over 2,500 species, two-thirds of which are endemic; these include the omul fish and the nerpa (a freshwater seal). Over the past decade, a ten percent decrease has been observed in the nerpa population, and at one spot in the lake the number of indigenous benthic species was found to have decreased from 27 to 10. In some omul spawning grounds less than two percent of the roe are living; the marked decrease in omul catches has adversely affected the local fishing industry. The quality of the lake's water, particularly in its southern portion, has declined considerably in only a few decades.

The degradation of Baikal originates from numerous sources, including waste disposal into the lake and its tributaries, air pollution, and deforestation. One of the most notorious polluters is the Baikalsk Pulp and Paper Mill, which annually releases nearly 400,000 cubic meters of wastewater into the lake. As a result of the mill's operation, an area of up to 30 sq km is considered permanently contaminated; levels of phenols, sulfates, chlorides, and petroleum products register at several times permissible levels (*Natsional'nyi doklad*, 1991).

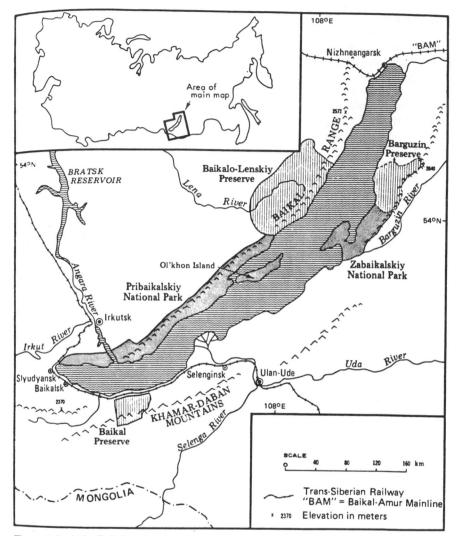

Figure 4.2   Lake Baikal and environs

The lake also is contaminated by waste products emptied into the Selenga River by the Selenginsk Cellulose Combine and a number of industrial enterprises in the Buryat city of Ulan-Ude. Although these wastes supposedly are treated before being returned to the river, independent tests by scientists have shown that they retain mutagenic properties. The Selenginsk mill empties its wastewater into one of the river's most fertile shoals, with disastrous consequences for the organisms living there. Pollutants in Baikal from the Selenga River have been traced up to 130 km from the river's estuary.

Each year up to 70,000 tons of organic substances are released into the lake by enormous amounts of rotting timber lost during river transport, which upsets Baikal's aquatic ecosystem. This ecosystem is further damaged by petroleum products (as much as 20–30 times permissible levels in some ports) from the hundreds of ships that traverse Baikal daily and by airborne pollutants from industry. No less than 770,000 tons of airborne emissions from enterprises in Irkutsk and Angarsk reach the lake each year, and the Baikalsk mill alone emits 100 tons a day into the atmosphere of substances such as sulfur oxides (Yanshin and Melua, 1991). In addition, the logging of millions of cubic meters of forest around Baikal have contributed to the desiccation of many of the small rivers and streams that once fed the lake (Galaziy, 1991). Although many resolutions have been passed over a twenty-year period aimed at protecting the lake, the mills continue to pollute it, and there is still widespread concern for Baikal's future (Pryde, 1991b, pp. 84–87).

Water and Air Pollution

Freshwater is at risk throughout the Siberian territory. As in the case of the Selenga River and Lake Baikal, most of the wastes poured into Siberian rivers and freshwater bodies receive little or no treatment. Up to eighty percent of wastewaters in Omsk and Tyumen Oblasts reach the river systems without any treatment. The Yenisey River annually receives 600 million cubic meters of partially treated and 200 million cubic meters of untreated wastes, as well as 130 tons of such substances as phenols, metals, and petroleum products (*Ekologicheskaya*, 1990). Timber-processing factories in Bratsk, Ust-Ilimsk, and Krasnoyarsk regularly produce over 300 chemicals as waste products; Russia lacks both the equipment and the methodology necessary for tracking the whole range of pollutants. Concentrations of hydrogen sulfide and methylmercaptans, for example, have reached levels 300–600 times permissible in reservoirs of the Angara River due to years of dumping by the Bratsk and Ust-Ilimsk timber-processing facilities (*Gidrokhimicheskii ezhegodnik*, 1992).

Much of the water supply in the Urals region contains excessive amounts of chemical fertilizers and dioxins. Drinking water in the city of Ufa was contaminated with phenol in 1991, when several hundred tons of the chemical were spilled by the Khimprom Production Association. Ufa's water supplies have also been reported as being heavily contaminated by dioxin (*Surviving Together*, Spring 1993, p. 46). Rivers that flow in the Urals, where 95 percent of water consumption goes to industry, contain oil, ammonia, zinc, chromium, phenols, and other chemicals that are dozens, even hundreds, of times in excess of permissible limits set by the government. The same may be said for the rivers of western Siberia. For example, near Novosibirsk the Ob River contains phenols at levels up to 120 times the maximum allowable concentration.

Reports released by the Soviet State Committee for the Protection of the Environment and Natural Resources in the late 1980s revealed that many of Siberia's cities were among the worst in terms of air pollution in the former Soviet Union. That situation has not changed and in some places has even worsened. Cities such as Bratsk, Angarsk, Chelyabinsk, and Ufa still are among the most ecologically dangerous in Russia, according to the Russian Ministry of Ecology. There is virtually no industrial city in Siberia in which levels of contaminants in the atmosphere correspond to established norms. The most heavily polluted cities are shown in Table 4.1.

Fewer than eighteen percent of industrial enterprises in the Siberian regions of Tyumen and Yakutia could claim that their air emissions received any treatment. Metallurgical plants in Magnitogorsk fail to capture fifty percent or more of their emissions of ammonia, phenols, and sulfuric compounds. Fewer than half of the thousands of sources of air pollution in Kemerovo Oblast have emissions treatment facilities. In this oblast, lung cancer exceeds the Russian average by 47 percent and bronchial asthma by 38 percent.

Table 4.1   Siberian Cities with High per Capita Emissions in 1987

City	1989 population	Total emissions	Per capita emissions (tons/1000 residents)
1. Noril'sk	174,000	2,426.0	13,943
2. Novotroitsk	106,000	297.7	2,808
3. Magnitogorsk	440,000	899.9	2,045
4. Angarsk	266,000	482.0	1,812
5. Nizhniy Tagil	440,000	711.9	1,618
6. Novokuznetsk	600,000	948.7	1,581
7. Shelekhov	<50,000	70.2	>1,400
8. Usol'ye-Sibirskoye	107,000	103.9	906
9. Bratsk	255,000	210.1	824
10. Kamensk-Uralskiy	209,000	142.8	683
11. Omsk	1,148,000	622.8	543
12. Chelyabinsk	1,143,000	533.2	466
13. Barnaul	602,000	264.0	439
14. Krasnoyarsk	912,000	399.5	438
15. Kurgan	356,000	146.4	411
16. Kemerovo	520,000	206.9	398
17. Khabarovsk	601,000	231.4	385
18. Komsomol'sk	315,000	102.4	325
19. Yuzhno-Sakhalinsk	157,000	47.3	301
20. Tyumen	477,000	126.8	266
21. Chita[a]	366,000	>103.0	>250
22. Novosibirsk	1,436,000	356.2	248
23. Irkutsk	626,000	151.6	242
24. Ulan-Ude[a]	353,000	>72.0	>200
25. Prokop'yevsk	274,000	>43.3	>158
26. Sverdlovsk	1,367,000	183.9	135

[a] Data for Chita and Ulan-Ude calculated by the author,   Population data
from *Soviet Geography*, May 1989, pp. 423-431.
Source: Okhrana, 1989.

The Norilsk Metallurgical Combine in 1991 released nearly 2.4 million tons of pollutants into the atmosphere, exceeding by 187,000 tons the figure for the previous year. The sulfur oxide content of the air in Norilsk is at least forty times the level considered permissible. In September 1992 the combine was fined 1.8 billion rubles by a court of the Krasnoyarsk territory in order to generate money for forest protection. The combine refused to pay and has done nothing toward improving the city's environmental crisis. Of the 82 million rubles planned for installing filtering equipment at the plant, only 31 million were spent (*Ekologiya*, 1992). Sulfur pollution also is a problem in Magnitogorsk, where the Lenin Steel Works is blamed for widespread cases of respiratory diseases and asthma among the city's inhabitants.

In the city of Krasnoyarsk atmospheric pollutants reached a level of 366,000 tons in 1989; in 1991 they were measured at 412,000 tons. No less than fifty percent of the contaminants were released by one factory, the Krasnoyarsk Aluminum Factory, which the newspaper *Ekologicheskii vestnik* (1992) nominated as one of the worst 100 companies in the world regarding pollution. Each year the plant releases onto a stretch of 30 km more than 86,000 kg of aluminum, 6,000 kg of fluorine, 5 kg of beryllium, 95 kg of nickel, 21 kg of lead, 27 kg of mercury, and 531 tons of dust. Rates of stomach and lung cancer among workers at the aluminum factory are 3–5 and 4–9 times higher, respectively, than for the city as a whole.

Both air pollution and fossil fuel exploration and transport are wreaking havoc on fragile northern territories in Siberia. Emissions from Norilsk and other cities are decimating nearby reindeer pastures. Tens of thousands of hectares on the Yamal Peninsula were destroyed by the development of gas fields and the construction of roads in the late 1980s. The thin layer of vegetation requires decades to recover from damage, but even this slow pace is halted by oil and gas spills; as much as one-fifth of all oil extracted in East Siberia may be lost during transport. Such spills also take place with disastrous frequency in the oil and gas fields and pipelines of West Siberia, where poor maintenance and inefficient drilling techniques lead to huge losses of fuel and even deadly accidents. For example, breaks in pipelines of the Tyumen region lost over 1 million tons of oil in 1988, and a gas leak in 1989 in the Urals caused an explosion and the deaths of 300 people when a passing train ignited the fumes. The vast scale of the oil and gas extraction industries in West Siberia has done great damage to the land, with widespread oil pollution being commonplace, as well as severe damage to taiga and tundra soils and ecosystems caused by heavy equipment and drilling.

Another serious environmental accident occurred in the Urals region in 1979, in the large city of Yekaterinburg (Sverdlovsk). A serious outbreak of anthrax claimed at least 64 lives and has been widely attributed to biological warfare research, though this was strenuously denied by Soviet officials. Local (or perhaps military) authorities have never permitted a full investigation, and some believe that such research still goes on. Such lingering uncertainties could act as a serious brake on foreign investment in the Yekaterinburg area.

Nuclear Contamination

While the environmental impact of most Russian industries has been documented for many years, the nuclear weapons and fuels industry managed to avoid public scrutiny until recently. Now public interest groups such as the Socio-Ecological Union are struggling to expose the enormous environmental damage caused by military activities, particularly those involving nuclear materials. Many areas of radioactive contamination dot the vast area between the Ural Mountains and Lake Baikal, created by irresponsible waste disposal, nuclear weapons production and testing, and the use of nuclear explosives for natural resource extraction.

One of Siberia's, indeed the world's, most urgent ecological crises centers in Chelyabinsk Oblast in the southern Urals (Figure 4.3). An area famed for its industrial output, Chelyabinsk Oblast was significant for another, far more classified reason—the production of plutonium for nuclear weapons. Built in 1945 and located approximately seventy km north of Chelyabinsk at a closed site called Chelyabinsk-40 (or Chelyabinsk-65 or Sorokovka), the Mayak chemical production complex generated the material for the first Soviet nuclear weapon and for scores of successive bombs. The unforeseen consequence of the operation of this facility, however, was three major radiological disasters and an alarmingly large accumulation of radioactive wastes in the environment (Monroe, 1992; Bradley, 1992).

The first of the disasters occurred over several years, as the slow-moving Techa River, which passes through the territory of Mayak, was poisoned by radioactive wastes. From 1947 until 1951–1952 over 2 million curies of radioactive waste from Mayak accumulated in the Techa, and no effort was made to inform the villagers who used its waters. Radiation sickness and death among these villagers forced authorities to raze dwellings, evacuate their residents, and deny access to the river (Figures 4.4 and 4.5).

The second disaster was the September 1957 explosion of an underground liquid waste container at Mayak (commonly referred to as the "Kyshtym accident"), which released twenty million curies and sent a cloud of radioactivity over 20,000 sq km. The event was the single worst nuclear accident in the world before the Chernobyl meltdown in 1986. In the years following the blast, nearly two dozen villages were destroyed and over 10,000 people relocated, without ever being told the reason (Monroe, 1992; Bradley, 1992). Inexplicably, the residents of the largest village on the Techa, Muslyumovo, where the average lifespan is 46 years, were not evacuated (*CIS Environmental Watch*, Fall 1993, pp. 6–15). Soviet officials did not admit the explosion until 1989.

The response of Mayak authorities to the Techa emergency was to begin dumping wastes into natural and artificial reservoirs. About 8 lakes and reservoirs in all were radioactively contaminated, the largest of which is about 44 sq km in size (Bradley, 1992, p. 12.9). This practice led to the third disaster, when drought conditions in 1967 gave rise to the aerial dispersion of contaminated sediment on the dried-out shore of one of these reservoirs, Lake Karachai (see Figure 4.3). These particles were spread over 2,700 sq km and reached over 40,000 people. At least 400,000 people were exposed to radia-

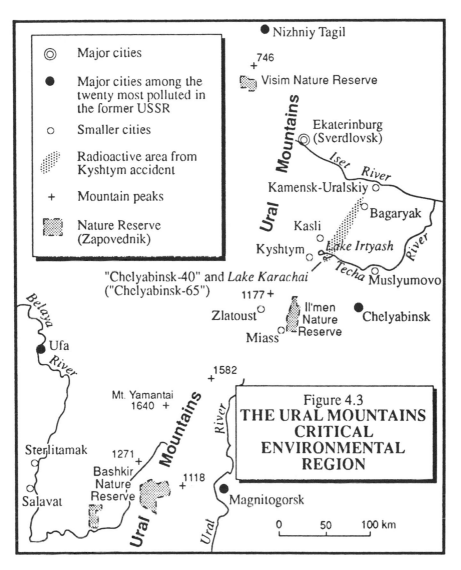

Figure 4.3
THE URAL MOUNTAINS CRITICAL ENVIRONMENTAL REGION

tion derived from all three nuclear disasters, and of these 935 people (officially) have developed radiation sickness.

Currently more than one billion curies of radioactive waste are said to be stored in either underground containers or reservoirs controlled by Mayak. Lake Karachai alone still contains an estimated 120 million curies; this is about 50 times the remaining radiation produced by Chernobyl. Exposure to the 600 roentgens that are given off at the lake's shore in one hour is fatal to human beings (Feshbach and Friendly, 1992, p. 175). The hermetic quality of

Figure 4.4   A church of the deserted village of Metlino, which was evacuated in the early 1950s after being contaminated by radiation in the Techa River. At right is one of the contaminated reservoirs of the Mayak Production Association.

all types of radioactive waste storage used by the USSR is highly question-able. In addition, residents of Muslyumovo and other settlements along the Techa continue to be exposed to elevated background radiation and to com-plain almost universally of health problems.

In addition to the military complex near Chelyabinsk, secret facilities were constructed near the major Siberian cities of Yekaterinburg (formerly Sverd-lovsk), Krasnoyarsk, and Tomsk. Chemical combines at Tomsk-7 and Krasno-yarsk-26, in particular, were involved in plutonium production, uranium enrichment, and waste treatment and storage. The effects of radioactive con-tamination created by the activities of these facilities on the rivers Tom and Yenisey are only recently coming under investigation by independent re-search teams. According to *Komsomol'skaya pravda*, French scientists sampled air, water, and sediment near the discharge site into the Tom River and found levels of radiation some twenty times normal (Chelnokov, 1992, p. 61). In April 1993, an explosion at the Tomsk-7 plant released a significant amount of radiation into the atmosphere and the surrounding environment.

The Yenisey has been polluted both by direct discharges and the practice of injecting liquid radioactive waste into subterranean crevices that then leaked into the river. About 150 centers of radioactive contamination are reported to exist along a 500 km stretch of the Yenisey, covering a total of 1,500 sq km,

Figure 4.5 A barrier on a bridge over the Techa River warns, "Attention! Radiation! The river is contaminated!!! 1150 microroentgen/hour." From ten to twenty microroentgens per hour is considered normal.

with excessively high levels of plutonium, strontium, cesium, and phosphorous, among others.

No region within West Siberia appears to be untouched by radioactive pollution. While a link between radiation and illnesses such as cancer has not been proven conclusively, many Russian citizens nevertheless feel endangered by exposure to abnormally high radiation in their surroundings. The continued discovery of radiation anomalies and forgotten waste storage sites does nothing to assuage their fears.

For instance, the village of Ozernyi in Sverdlovsk Oblast was evacuated when it was realized that homes and buildings were radioactive. By-products of uranium mining had been buried in thinly covered pits in the 1960s, a fact of which residents had not been informed. People digging a house foundation in Omsk discovered a cache of military instruments containing radium-226 and measuring 8,000 microroentgens per hour. The site was decontaminated, but the city reportedly still has over 200 sites of radioactive contamination. Storehouses near a railroad track in Krasnoufimsk that contain 82,000 tons of radioactive sand have been blamed for a "mysterious disease" that afflicts university students participating in farm work in the area.

Along the Trans-Siberian railroad in southern East Siberia is found the Kansk-Achinsk coal basin, the largest deposit of brown coal in the world

(Pryde, 1991b, pp. 238–240). Concern has arisen over the possible environmental effects of radioactive lignite from this deposit. Coal from this deposit has been found to contain between 0.005 and 0.01 percent uranium, with gamma emissions of 100–300 microroentgens per hour. Radioactivity within a radius of 15–20 km around thermal power plants that burn the coal is 20–30 times normal. It is estimated that each year the ash dumps of the Nazarovskiy regional power plant alone release 3–4 tons of natural uranium into the surrounding environment.

Nuclear explosions in the atmosphere have also generated considerable concern about health risks for the Siberian populace. Weapons testing at the Semipalatinsk nuclear test site in Kazakhstan affected not only that republic but the neighboring Altai region in Russia as well (see Chapter 16). Of the dozens of surface and air tests that were conducted at Semipalatinsk in the years before an international ban on aboveground testing was instituted, 24 produced fallout that spread beyond the confines of the testing range. Following the surface explosion of the Soviet Union's first nuclear bomb in 1949, radioactive dust reached all the way to the Kuzbass region, resulting in an exposure dosage of at least seven rems (0.5 rem per year is considered acceptable for humans). In the path of the dust was the town of Talmenka, where recently 42 of 59 children born in one month displayed yellow coloring and evidence of congenital defects (Dahlburg, 1992). In 1954, an atmospheric bomb test west of Orenburg exposed thousands of close-in military troops to high levels of radiation.

Nuclear explosions, 115 in all, were employed across the former USSR for various "peaceful" reasons. In the Urals region they were used for oil and gas exploration and the development of mineral deposits; in the far north they enabled seismologists to explore the crust and mantle. In other areas nuclear devices created underground caverns for the storage of industrial wastes. Ten such explosions took place in the Yenisey basin, while another twelve occurred in Yakutia. At least two of the underground experiment sites in Yakutia are known to be leaking radiation to the surface (Yemelyanenkov and Popov, 1992, p. 61).

The area that has captured the most international attention since the Chernobyl accident is the Novaya Zemlya region in the far north. An archipelago flanked by the Barents and Kara Seas, Novaya Zemlya was both one of the Soviet Union's two nuclear weapons test sites and a dumping ground for enormous amounts of radioactive and mixed waste. Approximately eighty nuclear tests were conducted on or near the archipelago; these tests may resume in the future if the Russian government decides to end its moratorium on nuclear tests. Given the site's military significance, independent parties have not been allowed to determine the effects that the tests have had on its fragile Arctic environment.

In addition, the Soviet Navy and the Murmansk Shipping Company engaged in the unreported disposal of radioactive and other wastes in shallow waters (60 to 300 m) around Novaya Zemlya. The dumping continued over the past three decades, in violation of the 1972 London Convention, which set restrictions on ocean dumping of radioactive wastes. The illegal practice was first brought to light by Andrei Zolotkov, a Soviet people's deputy, in the fall of 1991, when he shared information about dumpsites with journalists. The inventory of dumped materials is enormous: between 10,000 and 17,000 containers of radioactive and mixed waste; as many as fifteen retired or damaged nuclear reactors, five of which still contain fuel; two barges; and at least 150,000 cubic meters of liquid radioactive waste. It is also likely that the Kara Sea serves as a repository for radioactive and chemical contaminants carried from the mainland by the Ob and Yenisey Rivers.

Neither the current nor the future environmental danger posed by the wastes has been determined as yet. Nevertheless, the combination of nuclear tests and dumpsites has been blamed for the mass death of seals and starfish in the White Sea in 1990; the seals spend much of the year in the vicinity of Novaya Zemlya.

Future Prospects

In many respects Siberia is a microcosm of the former Soviet Union, illustrative of both its vast economic potential and its long-standing environmental neglect. Perhaps more than anywhere else in the former Soviet Union, Siberia was perceived by the central government as a land of inexhaustible resources, to be consumed without a thought of the inevitable consequences. Even Baikal, the world's deepest and most spectacular freshwater lake, was not immune to the all-inclusive five-year plan, nor was the largest forest in the Northern Hemisphere impervious to the encroachment of Soviet planners. Time has shown the unfortunate results of this approach.

It is true that the Soviet Union created a great many large nature reserves in Siberia. Indeed, eleven of the 20 largest are found in the regions covered by this chapter, and 19 of the 20 largest are included if the Russian Far East (Chapter 5) is added (see Table 4.2). Two national parks were created on the shores of Lake Baikal (see Figure 4.2). In 1993, the largest nature preserve in what is now the former Soviet Union, the Great Arctic Reserve of around 4 million hectares, was reportedly created on the Taimyr Peninsula. But many of these parks and reserves are threatened by some form of adverse outside influence, such as acid rain or poaching. Almost all of them are understaffed and underfunded.

Siberia also paid a huge price for its role as the cradle of the Soviet military-industrial complex. Although Siberia's plants for the production of plutonium and enriched uranium enabled the Soviet Union to claim its status as a military superpower, they simultaneously undermined the health of the workers and the economy that supported them, leaving a tragic environmental legacy that will persist long into the post–cold war era. Chelyabinsk, Krasnoyarsk, Magnitogorsk, Norilsk, and many other cities serve as grim reminders that pollutants do not follow class principles.

The long-term future of this region will hold promise only if in the near future post-Soviet planners and managers are diligently devoted to cleaning up the numerous environmental crisis areas that were created here during the Soviet period. Unfortunately, no source of the huge amount of funds

Table 4.2   **Twenty Largest Nature Reserves of the Former Soviet Union**

Reserve name	Created	Area (ha)	Location
Ust-Lenskiy	1986	1,433,000	East Siberia, in Lena delta
Taimyr	1979	1,348,316	*East Siberia, on Taimyr Peninsila
Tsentralno-Sibir	1985	972,017	*near mouth of Pod. Tunguska River
Kronotskiy	1967	964,000	eastern Kamchatka Peninsula
Magadan	1982	869,200	Far East, near city of Magadan
Altai	1968	863,728	*West Siberia, upper Ob River basin
Olekminsk	1984	847,102	East Siberia, on Olekma River
Dzhugdzhur	1990	806,300	in Far East, near town of Ayan
Wrangel Island	1976	795,650	Far East, in Chukot Sea
Pechora-Ilych	1930	721,322	*in northern Ural Mountains
Baikalo-Lena	1986	659,919	*west shore of Lake Baikal
Yugan	1982	648,636	*West Siberia, south of Surgut
Verkhne-Taz	1986	631,308	*West Siberia, upper Taz River
Vitim	1982	585,021	*East Siberia, north-east of Lake Baikal
Kaplankyr	1979	570,000	Turkmenistan
Kuznetskiy Alatau	1989	453,524	*West Siberia, east of Tomsk
Sayan-Shushenskoye	1976	389,750	*East Siberia, on upper Yenisey River
Bureya	1985	350,000	Far East, on Bureya River
Sikhote-Alin	1935	347,532	Far East, in Primorskiy Krai
Azas	1985	337,300	*Sayan Mtns, near source of Yenisey

* Indicates the reserve is located in the Ural Mountains, or in West or East Siberia

Source: Pryde, 1991.

needed to accomplish this is available either in the Russian Federation budget or in the spending plans of newly created joint ventures or other private sources. In the interim, large portions of the Urals and Siberia will continue to be unsafe for human occupation.

Acknowledgments

The authors would like to thank Dr. Alexander Bolsunovsky, vice-chairman of the Ecological Movement of Krasnoyarsk, for his help in the preparation of portions of this chapter.

Bibliography

Bolsunovsky, A. (1993). "Broken Swords: Military Pollution in Krasnoyarsk," *CIS Environmental Watch*, 4 (Summer 1993), pp. 4–10.

Bond, Andrew (1984). "Air Pollution in Norilsk: A Soviet Worst Case?" *Soviet Geography*, vol. 25, no. 9, pp. 665–680.

Bradley, D. J. (1992). *Radioactive Waste Management in the Former USSR* (Vol. 3). Richland, WA: Pacific Northwest Laboratory, June.

Chelnokov, A. (1992). "Tomsk-7, What the Film 'The Resident's Mistake' Did Not Tell About." *Komsomol'skaya pravda*, as translated in JPRS-TEN-92-016.

CIS Environmental Watch, 2 (Spring 1992), p. 3.

Dahlburg, John-Thor (1992). "The Atom Sows Crop of Sadness." *Los Angeles Times,* 2 September, p. A1.

Dienes, Leslie (1993). "Prospects for Russian Oil in the 1990s: Reserves and Costs," *Post-Soviet Geography,* vol. 34, no. 2, pp. 79–110.

Ekologicheskaya programma Krasnoyarskogo kraya (1990). Krasnoyarsk.

Ekologicheskii vestnik, 15 (Krasnoyarsk, 1992), p. 3.

Ekologiya Krasnoyar'ya, 9 (October-November 1992), p. 3.

Escalona, M. C. (1993). "Russia's Far Eastern and Northern Waters: Nuclear Waste Bins?" *CIS Environmental Watch 5* (Fall), pp. 16–39.

Feshbach, Murray, and Alfred Friendly Jr. (1992). *Ecocide in the USSR.* New York: Basic Books.

Galaziy, G. I. (1991). "Baikal Law: An Analysis of the Existing Primary Sources of Pollution," *Environmental Policy Review,* vol. 5, no. 1, pp. 47–55.

Kotkin, S. (1992). *Steeltown, USSR.* Berkeley and Los Angeles: University of California Press.

The Lake Baikal Region in the Twenty-First Century (1993). Report prepared by the Center for Citizens Initiatives, the Center for Socio-Ecological Issues of the Baikal Region, Davis Associates, and the Russian Academy of Sciences, 1993.

Mnatsakanian, R. (1992). *Environmental Legacy of the Former Soviet Republics.* Edinburgh. University of Edinburgh Press.

Monroe, Scott (1992). "Chelyabinsk: The Evolution of Disaster," *Post-Soviet Geography,* vol. 33, no. 8, pp. 533–545.

Natsional'nyi doklad SSSR k konferentsii OON 1992 goda po okruzhayushchei srede i razvitiyu (1991). Moscow: Ministerstvo Prirodopol'zovaniya i Okhrani Okruzhayushchei Sredy SSSR.

Nilsson, S. et al. (1992). *The Forest Resources of the Former European USSR.* New York: Parthenon Publ.

Okhrana okruzhayushchey sredy i ratsional'noye ispol'zovaniye prirodnykh resursov v SSSR: statisticheskiy sbornik (1989). Moscow: Goskomstat.

Pryde, Philip R. (1991a). "The Environmental Costs of Eastern Resources: Air Pollution in Siberian Cities." *Soviet Geography,* vol. 32, no. 6 pp. 403–411.

———. (1991b). *Environmental Management in the Soviet Union.* Cambridge: Cambridge University Press.

Scherbakova, A. and W. Wallace (1993). "The Environmental Legacy of Soviet Peaceful Nuclear Explosions," *CIS Environmental Watch,* 4 (Summer 1993), pp. 33–56.

Wood, Alan (ed.) (1987). *Siberia: Problems and Prospects for Regional Development.* London: Croon Helm.

"Yadernii sled Yeniseya" (1992). *Ekologicheskii vestnik,* 15.

Yanshin, A., and A. Melua (1991). *Uroki ekologicheskikh proschetov.* Moscow: Mysl', p. 90.

Yemelyanenkov, Aleksandr, and Vladimir Popov (1992). *Atom bez grifa 'sekretno:' tochki zreniya.* Berlin: International Physicians for the Prevention of Nuclear War.

5

The Russian Far East

Holly Strand

The Russian Far East is a vast and varied region forming the northeastern frontier of the Eurasian continent. Although the entire Russian territory east of the Urals is often labeled "Siberia,"the Far East is actually a separate geographic unit whose territorial size is almost equal to that of West and East Siberia. Furthermore, there are striking differences in both natural conditions and the economy of the two regions, as the Far East is heavily influenced by its proximity to the Pacific Ocean.

In this chapter, the Russian Far East will be defined as the former Soviet Union's Far Eastern economic planning region. Its area is 6,215,900 km^2, or 36% of the total area of the Russian Federation; this is roughly three-quarters the size of the coterminous United States. The region is divided into the following administrative sub-units: Primorskiy Krai (or territory, also called Primorye or the Maritime Province); Khabarovsk Krai; Kamchatka, Amur, Sakhalin, and Magadan Oblasts; the Republic of Sakha (sometimes given as Yakut-Sakha, formerly the Yakut Autonomous Republic); and the Jewish, Koryak, and Chukotsk Autonomous Regions. The 1990 population of the Russian Far East was only about eight million.

Physical Setting

Because of its vast size and latitudinal distribution, the Far Eastern landscape is tremendously varied. The southernmost tip of Primorskiy Krai lies at about 42° north latitude, similar to Chicago in the United States. The northernmost point is Wrangel Island at around 72°, slightly higher than Point Barrow, Alaska. In the Diomede Islands of the Bering Sea, Russia comes within 4 miles of the United States. The disputed southern Kurile Islands are similarly close to Hokkaido, Japan.[1] The Amur River forms a large portion of the southern border with China.

Much of the region is covered with medium to low elevation mountains, no more than 3,000 meters in height. The more significant ranges are the Stanovoy range on the northern border of Amur Oblast, the Verkhoyansk and Chersk ranges in Sakha, the Kolyma and Koryak Uplands in the northeast, and the volcanic ranges on Kamchatka. The Dzhugdzhur and Sikhote Alin are coastal ranges on the Okhotsk Sea and Sea of Japan, respectively. The Kamchatka Peninsula and the Kuriles are located at the eastern edge of the Asian continental plate and the western edge of the Pacific plate; tectonic interaction between these two plates produces an extremely active seismic zone.

Soviet geologists have delineated about two fifths of the Far East as susceptible to earthquakes destructive enough to cause large cracks in the ground, rockfalls, landslides, and mud eruptions and to deform groundwater and surface water regimes (Medvedev, 1976). Earthquakes with epicenters off the Pacific coast are capable of generating powerful tsunamis. The area surrounding eastern Kamchatka and the Kuriles is one of the most seismically active places on earth, as it coincides with a subduction zone where the Pacific plate dives under the Eurasian continent. Lively geological processes result in high mountains, volcanoes, and occasional valleys of hot springs and geysers. The Kuriles have forty active volcanoes and Kamchatka, twenty-two. Asian Russia's highest peak, Mount Kluchevskaya, is a Kamchatka volcano that rises to 4,750 meters.

The largest rivers are the Amur and the Lena, ninth and tenth longest in the world (4,416 km and 4,400 km, respectively). Among other Russian rivers, only the Ob is longer. The Lena, Indigirka, and Kolyma all flow north into the arctic seas, while the Amur flows mainly eastward and empties into the Tatar Strait, near Sakhalin Island (see Figure 5.1).

Over six thousand miles of coastline give Russia a considerable strategic presence in the Pacific. With the secession of the Baltic republics and Ukraine and therefore reduced access to the Atlantic, the importance of this presence has intensified. There are some excellent natural harbors, such as Vladivostok and Nakhodka, but icebreakers must operate to keep many of them open (Figure 5.2). The Sea of Okhotsk is frozen for much of the year, and even the northern Sea of Japan is completely free of ice for only a few months.

Climatic conditions in the Far East are highly variable. The precipitation regime is complicated by great fluctuations, and both flooding and droughts are not uncommon. Much of the coast is under the influence of a variable monsoon climate regime. Summers are humid and foggy, and winters are very dry with strong winds. Snow usually occurs in just two or three heavy storms but evaporates quickly, leaving the soil without insulation and consequently encouraging the formation of permafrost. Typhoons and heavy downpours occur in August to September, causing flood damage on the extensive number of small rivers in the south.

The northern location of the region produces long, extremely cold winters with temperatures dipping to as low as −70°C in the interior. Except for the southern and coastal portions, most of the territory has an average January

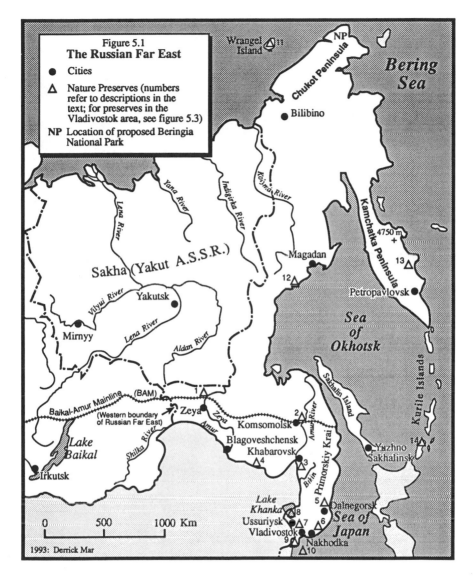

Figure 5.1
The Russian Far East

● Cities

▲ Nature Preserves (numbers refer to descriptions in the text; for preserves in the Vladivostok area, see figure 5.3)

NP Location of proposed Beringia National Park

1993: Derrick Mar

temperature of −28°C or lower. Cold sea currents refrigerate the Far East coastline, resulting in much colder temperatures than those that occur at North American latitudinal analogues. Over 90% of the territory is subject to permafrost of various depths and extent. In summer, swamps and frost-heaved soils create an unstable surface for building foundations and roads. Together with distance, the above factors escalate building costs three to five times above what they would be in European Russia.

Figure 5.2   The harbor at Nakhodka, with an oil tanker at center; the tanker symbolizes the increased environmental jeopardy that will come to the region as it becomes more involved in the Pacific Rim economy.

Demographic Profile

Perhaps the most striking feature of Far East settlement is the relative lack of it. Density is low; in 1991 there were only 1.3 persons per square kilometer, compared to the national average of 8.7. Understandably, the vast majority of this population is heavily concentrated in the south where the land and the climate are more hospitable, especially along transportation corridors such as the Trans-Siberian Railroad, the Baikal-Amur Mainline (BAM) and the Amur River. The southern administrative units (Amur Oblast, Khabarovsk Krai, Primorskiy Krai) hold 65% of the population while comprising only 28% of the total area. In 1991, 76% of the Far East population of 8.06 million was classified as urban. The 10 largest cities along with their respective growth rates are listed in Table 5.1.

The Soviet government (and the Imperial Russian government before 1917) sought to increase population in the Far East, both to secure the presence of Soviet/Russian power and to supply more labor resources to the region. In the Soviet period, Far East workers were paid wage coefficients of up to twice the normal European wage rates. Supplements were added according to region, and prices for consumer goods were often lower than in Europe. Migration was facilitated by various Soviet institutions, such as the Komsomol, obligatory post-graduate assignments, and colonization by convicts. The official media extolled the area for its beauty, Asian mystique, financial advantages, and the opportunity to demonstrate one's patriotism by settling there.

In spite of these efforts, the desired population growth was never achieved. Wage and price incentives to relocate there could not compensate for the lack of housing, schools, day care, consumer goods, communications, cultural amenities, and other problems of social infrastructure. The resulting labor

Table 5.1   Largest Cities in the Russian Far East

City	Population on January 1st 1979	Population on January 1st 1991	Percent Increase
Vladivostok	550,000	648,000	18
Khabarovsk	528,000	613,000	16
Komsomolsk-na-Amure	264,000	319,000	21
Petropavlovsk-Kamchatskiy	215,000	273,000	27
Blagoveshchensk	172,000	211,000	23
Yakutsk	182,000	193,000	6
Nakhodka	133,000	165,000	24
Yuzhno-Sakhalinsk	140,000	164,000	17
Ussuriysk	147,000	160,000	8
Magadan	121,000	155,000	28

Source: Narodnoye khozyaistvo RSFSR v 1990 g., Moscow: Respub. Info-Izdat. Tsentr, 1991, pp. 81-84.

turnover and transience have always canceled out the impressive in-migration rates. In a recent sociological study, only 20% of recent migrants indicated that they intended to stay in the Far East (Motrich and Shurkin, 1990).

The original inhabitants of the Far East were traditionally trappers, hunters, fishermen and nomadic reindeer herders. Starting in the 1800's, assimilation, epidemics and collectivization decreased their numbers precipitously; now only 6–8% of the population is aboriginal (see Table 5.2). Most of the languages were oral only, so many ethnic groups adopted the Cyrillic alphabet. Russian is spoken to some degree by many and is often used as a medium for literature. The religion of these peoples is a mix of Eastern Orthodox and shamanist-animist beliefs, often influenced by Chinese culture as well. The Chukchi, Yakuts and Koryaks control their own administrative territories.

The present ethnic composition of the Far East is primarily composed of Russian and Ukrainian migrants and their offspring. Historically, large numbers of Koreans, Chinese, and Japanese also inhabited the area, but these groups were resettled by one method or another in the 1930s to disperse any alternative political activism. Geographic names of Asian origin were changed to Russian ones to further emphasize Russian dominance.

The coming decades are likely to bring significant restructuring to the demographic profile of the Far East. If Russia continues to incorporate itself into global capitalism, the Far East's store of resources and location on the

Table 5.2   Native Peoples of the Russian Far East

Indigenous Group		Population (1989 census)	Linguistic Family
Yakuts		380,000	Uralo-Altaic
Evenki		30,000	Uralo-Altaic
Eveni		17,000	Uralo-Altaic
Chukchi		15,000	Paleoasiatic
Nanaitsy		12,000	Uralo-Altaic
Nivkhis		4,600	Paleoasiatic
Koryaki		8,900	Paleoasiatic
Ul'chi		3,200	Uralo-Altaic
Itel'mens		2,400	Paleoasiatic
Udeghetsy		1,900	Uralo-Altaic
Eskimos		1,700	Paleoasiatic
Chuvans		1,400	Paleoasiatic
Yukagirs		1,100	Paleoasiatic
Orochi		900	Uralo-Altaic
Aleuts		600	Paleoasiatic
Negidal'ts		600	Uralo-Altaic
Oroki		200	Uralo-Altaic
	Total:	481,500	

Source: Wixman, 1984; Narodnoye Khozyaistvo RSFSR, 1990. Figures are approximate since a small part of the population might live in Russian territory other than the Far East.

Pacific Rim will attract many immigrants and foreign workers. An Asian presence is readily perceptible in Khabarovsk and Primorye as Chinese and Korean workers, traders, farmers, and investors set up joint ventures and speculate on real estate. Asian goods have already heavily penetrated both official and unofficial markets.

Natural Resources and the Environment

The Far East has traditionally functioned as a resource colony for the rest of the Soviet Union. Raw materials are extracted, minimally processed and sent to the west for further processing and production. Should Russia continue on the path of economic integration with the West, extraction rates will increase, and more and more of these resources will be exported for hard currency. Industrial development is mostly limited to the southern edge along the railroads and southern Primorskiy Krai. The following is a description of the major Far Eastern natural resources, their distribution, and some of the contemporary factors affecting their exploitation.

Energy Resources

In 1990, the Soviet Union was the largest oil and gas producer in the world. The East Siberian gas fields in Yakutia around the upper and middle reaches of the Lena River and the oil and gas fields of Sakhalin Island contributed to this production. High grade hard coal is mined in southern Yakutia in the Neyrungi basin. There are still massive amounts of both hard and brown coal in the Lena basin.

A large hydroelectric dam has been built on the Zeya River, smaller ones exist on the Kolyma and Vilyui Rivers, and a large one is under construction on the Bureya. The single nuclear energy plant is a small (48 megawatt) graphite reactor located in the far north, near Bilibino. Construction of additional nuclear facilities was planned for Primorskiy and Khabarovsk Krais, but economic difficulties may prevent this from happening.

Other natural energy resoures are limited. Wind energy is problematic, since the winds in the Far East are seasonal (monsoonal). Although not yet exploited, tidal power could be harnessed on the Okhotsk coast, which has an unusually high tidal amplitude. The abundant geothermal resources on Kamchatka have been utilized to date only on a very limited scale. Solar energy is not feasible given the short winter days and foggy summers.

Although there are more than enough resources to produce energy for the relatively small population of the Far East, shortages have occurred and are becoming more and more frequent. Gas, oil, and coal production has declined since 1990, though mainly due to economic disorder rather than depletion of reserves. Vladivostok has already experienced rationing of electricity, and most Khabarovsk residents were without heat for an entire month in the winter of 1992.[2]

International agreements allow Russia to receive modern management expertise and extraction technology in exchange for limited development rights. A Japanese-American consortium (Marathon, McDermott and Mitsui) is planning further development of the Sakhalin oil reserves. Many developed countries, including Japan, have their sights set on the Sakha (Yakut) reserves. Foreign investment will almost certainly speed up production, but this does not guarantee that Russia's fuel problems will be solved; the adequacy of the reserves will partly depend on how much will be exported for foreign currency. Neither does foreign investment guarantee more environmentally sound methods of extraction, unless the Russian government is able to generate and enforce effective environmental regulation.

Minerals

The Far East is a treasure trove of mineral resources, often undeveloped because of poor accessibility and extreme climatic conditions. Nevertheless, in 1990 the Far East was producing 15% of Russia's mining output and 12.7% of its non-ferrous metals. In the Republic of Sakha and in Magadan Oblast, non-ferrous metals account for over 50% of the value of industrial production.

Gold is mined in the Kolyma and Zeya River basins and in scattered mines in Chukhotka. Sakha is the sole source of natural diamonds. The Sikhote Alin Mountains, the Komsomolsk area, and Sakha produce high quality and fairly accessible tin. Magnesium is mined in the Lesser Khingan Mountains. Near Udokan is one of the world's largest copper deposits. Other minerals of significance include tungsten, uranium, molybdenum, graphite, aluminum, mica, and mercury.

Because of this mineral wealth, mining activity has become one of the most serious disturbances to the Far Eastern landscape. It destroys relief through quarrying, pits, and tailing heaps. Mine water becomes a source of acidification and adds suspended materials to streams and rivers. Tailing ponds become a source of local dust in the atmosphere and contaminate drainage basins with heavy metals.

The Russian national environment report projects that environmental degradation due to mining will increase since the "system for mineral extraction is poorly conceived and there is a tradition of destructive forms of development," such as open pit mining and the use of few or no mitigation measures (Ministerstvo Ekologii, 1992, p. 26). As mineral and metal raw materials can bring in badly needed hard currency, exploitation of the Far Eastern reserves will undoubtedly increase.

Forests

The forests of Siberia and the Far East together cover 5.9 million square kilometers, contain 57% of the world's volume of coniferous forest and 25% of the world inventory of wood (Barr and Braden, 1988). Species include larch, spruce, fir, Korean and Siberian stone pine, Manchurian oak, ash, elm and walnut. The Okhotsk taiga is primarily composed of larch and other dark conifers. Broadleaf species predominate in the south.

The Siberian–Far Eastern boreal forest is the largest forest in the world. Significant alteration would have unpredictable, negative consequences on the global environment, especially since the Siberian forest may contain as much as 40,000 million tons of stored carbon, or half the amount of the Amazon (Rosencranz and Scott, 1992). Other forest benefits include the provision of a wildlife habitat, the filtering of air pollution, the protection of watersheds, the reduction of soil erosion, and a source of recreation. Many Russians look to the forest as a source of mushrooms, berries, firewood and medicinal plants.

Increased radiation in deforested regions can alter the pattern and structure of permafrost, creating waterlogged areas that are incapable of supporting the original flora. If regeneration of disturbed areas occurs at all, it is at a rate two to three times slower than in warmer climates.

Up until now, the absolute rate of forest clearing has never been particularly alarming in the Far East. Lack of modern logging infrastructure, the inaccessibility of the majority of the forest resources due to distance and climate, internal political and economic chaos, and alternative timber sources in the Pacific region provided some checks on forest devastation. But the forestry methods that are used now (extensive clear-cuts without systematic replanting and wasteful processing of timber) are not sustainable at a larger scale. The southern territories of Primorskiy and Khabarovsk Krais, and Amur Oblast, with their exotic Manchurian broadleaf species and proximity to rail and boat facilities, are already in need of stricter environmental practices.

At present, multinational logging activity presents a disturbing trend. An example is a resource conflict centered in the Bikin River basin in the Sikhote Alin Mountains, the home of the indigenous Udeghe minority. A Russian joint venture Svetloe (with the South Korean firm Hyundai as the foreign partner) has claimed this area for logging. Udeghe leaders have tried to stop the activity through legal channels, claiming that the logging has interfered with their local economy. Studies have produced two negative environmental evaluations, and according to Russian law, the Udeghe should have the right to make land use decisions in this area. Nevertheless, the local courts of Primorskiy Krai are supporting the forest developers' cause. In Moscow, Yeltsin's environmental adviser, A.V. Yablokov, has denounced the local court decision and openly supports the Udeghe. As the case moves to the Russian Supreme Court, the arguing continues and the logging continues, crossing over into the western Sikhote Alin Mountains, an area not even sanctioned by the Primorskiy officials.

Animals and Agriculture

The Far East is the chief reserve of marine resources in Russia. Kamchatka crab, shrimp, shellfish, salmon, cod, and seaweed are gathered commercially. Sea kale and trepang are Primorskiy specialties, but they have been under tight quota restrictions since they were almost decimated by irresponsible harvesting.

Agricultural production is mostly for regional consumption. Grains, potatoes, sugar beets, hemp and flax can be grown only in the south. Raising livestock and dairy farming occur as far north as Yakutia. Soy is produced exclusively in the Far East. Rice, an unusual crop for Russia, is grown in the floodplain surrounding Lake Khanka.

In the far north, indigenous peoples in collectives herd reindeer for their meat and hides. In the taiga, sable, mink, arctic fox and other fur-bearing animals are raised.

Areas of Environmental Concern

The Russian Far East has relatively fewer environmental problems than the rest of the Russian Federation and the other republics of the former Soviet Union. The Ministry of Ecology's 1992 national environmental report ranks the Far East as the economic region of the USSR having the lowest releases of hazardous substances into the atmosphere, having the least degradation to waters and soils, and in general having the least amount of harmful anthropogenic impact. A map of critical environmental zones, produced by the Academy of Sciences' Institute of Geography, does not identify any such sites in the Far Eastern region (Figure 1.1). Nevertheless, there still exist several environmental "hot spots" and industrial areas of extreme degradation.

Amur Industrial Belt

Much of the region's population, industry and agriculture are located somewhere along the Amur River; it has become an energy, water, and transportation resource, as well as a waste repository. The health of the river progressively deteriorates in the downstream direction. It is especially polluted with phenols, heavy metals and oil near the industrial cities of Blagoveshchensk, Komsomolsk-na-Amure, Khabarovsk, and Amursk (TIG, 1989). Komsomolsk-na-Amure and Khabarovsk were both included in the 1991 list of 85 Soviet cities cited for poor air quality.

According to recent studies, the Komsomolsk production center is the worst blight in the Khabarovsk territory. An outdated steel mill, built in 1943, is located in Komsomolsk. Nearby tin mining and enrichment of the sulfate-rich deposits pollute water bodies and create dust in the atmosphere. The health of certain groups of the population is already threatened by environmental factors. The Svobodnyy industrial complex in Amur Oblast (north of Blagoveshchensk) supports construction-related industries and open pit mining. It is also the most agricultural and most heavily populated region of Amur Oblast. Extraction and processing of hard coal and non-ferrous metals at the Urgal industrial area west of Komsomolsk have already done considerable damage to water and forests in the western part of the Khabarovsk Krai (TIG, 1989).

The natural area around the BAM is easily damaged and difficult to restore. The Ministry of Ecology estimates that 120 to 130 years will be needed to restore the BAM area permafrost. Damage was caused at first by the construction of the railroad but now results from the industrial and resource extraction centers that the railway serves. In 1993, a nationwide fiscal crisis was preventing improvements needed to complete the line from being carried out.

Primorskiy Krai

The Dalnegorsk region, near the Sea of Japan, is one of the oldest and most developed areas in the Far East. Non-ferrous metals, minerals for the chemical industry, and lead and tin are mined or processed here; the 1989 TIG environmental report described land and water resources as already in a state of extreme degradation. Soils around Dalnegorsk were found to contain lead concentrations over 10 times the acceptable maximum concentration. The health of the region's population is already at considerable risk. Typical of mining-industrial regions in the Far East, economic activity and population are highly concentrated in a relatively small area, while the rest of the territory remains vacant.

Soils near the port city of Rudnaya Pristan were also found to have lead concentrations at ten times the acceptable maximum permissible concentration (MPC), as well as mercury and cadmium (TIG, 1989). Traces have been found in agricultural products and even in people who live near the non-ferrous metallurgical plants such as Dalnometall. The Rudnaya River is contaminated with boronic substances and metal compounds. Concentrations of copper, zinc, and boron can reach 30, 60, or even 800 MPC.

Vladivostok is the largest city in the Far East. Marine pollution here results from heavy navigational use and occasional fuel spills. Radioactive contamination is suspected from the presence of nuclear submarines docked here as well as in nearby Nakhodka. Air quality is rapidly deteriorating as the number of cars on the road has doubled in the past 5–6 years; they are now brought in by the boatload from Japan. The air will continue to deteriorate unless mitigation measures are developed.

Lake Khanka is in critical condition because of surrounding agricultural practices. Khanka is the main source of irrigation water for nearby rice fields and loses .27 km^3 every year. Considering the total volume is only 18.7 km^3, the lake is losing about 1.5% of its water annually. Furthermore, agricultural chemicals such as nitrates, phosphates, and potash fertilizers have been directly discharged into the water or feeder rivers. Khanka fish have shown traces of Saturn, an herbicide, and even mercury. Khanka's status as a wetland of international importance under the Ramsar Convention, and its new protected status as a *zapovednik,* has not helped much. A buffer zone is needed around its shores; China's cooperation is absolutely necessary as part of the lake lies beyond the Russian border.

Sakhalin

The southern rivers of Sakhalin are often polluted with by-products from the oil and gas industries. In the south, cellulose/paper mills and other logging-related industries have serious effects on the environment. The capital, Yuzhno-Sakhalinsk, is rated 37th in poor air quality (Goskomstat SSSR, 1991).

Mining Areas of the North

In general, health problems in the north are due to both natural and anthropogenic causes. Neither the freshwater supply nor the system for dealing with solid and liquid wastes is satisfactory. Permafrost and weak solar activity complicate self-cleaning and mineralization problems. Human susceptibility to disease and sickness increases. Rivers of the north often carry an increased load of suspended substances because of mining, especially near the Kolyma gold fields.

Protected Areas

Because of its position at the conjunction of the Siberian taiga, Okhotsk taiga, and Manchurian broadleaf forest regions, the Far East has a number of ecosystems that it tries to represent and protect within the all-Russian natural reserve system. Habitat protection is especially important in southern Primorskiy Krai, which is the area with the highest concentration of endangered species in Russia (Pryde, 1987; Figure 5.3). At the end of 1992, 3,643,100 hectares of the Far East were protected as nature reserves (*zapovedniki*). Other types of protected areas are *zakazniki*, natural monuments, and the proposed Beringia International Park between Russia and the United States (see Appendix 1.2). Another category of protected vegetation are Group I forests. These forests are protected as greenbelts and recreational areas or to fulfill shelterbelt, water conservation, or soil management functions.

There are four nature reserves in the territories of Amur and Khabarovsk. They are mostly forested land—broadleaf, Okhotsk spruce, and Siberian

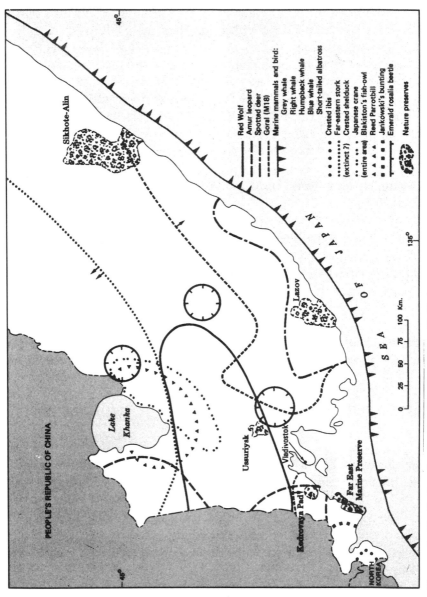

Figure 5.3   Distribution of endangered species, Primorskiy Krai

stone pine. (The numbers that follow relate to Figure 5.1.) (1) Zeya represents the northeastern outpost of Far Eastern monsoon vegetation, transitioning into Siberian larch forest. (2) Komsomolsk is composed of moist meadows and broadleaf forest on the Mid-Amur Plain. (3) Bolshe-Khekhtsir is at the junction of the Amur and Ussuri Rivers, a small mountain massif with steep slopes surrounded by marshy valleys. (4) Khingin is Far Eastern prairie with tall grass meadows on an Amur River terrace.

The Primorskiy Krai reserves protect a mixture of taiga, Manchurian forest, and marine ecosystems (see Figure 5.3). (5) Sikhote Alin, at the northern end of the Sikhote Alin Mountains, is a United Nations Biosphere Reserve. It is composed of transitional Okhotsk taiga, bald mountains, and the coast of the Japanese Sea. (6) The Lazov Reserve, on the southern end of the Sikhote Alin Range, has Manchurian oak, walnut, pine and relic yews and an intricate shoreline of rocky cliffs and bays. (7) Ussuriysk is an inland counterpart to Lazov, with Manchurian broadleaf forest, ferns, ginseng, interesting insects, and Amur tigers (which are also at Lazov and Sikhote Alin). (8) A new reserve protects Lake Khanka. Khanka is one of the largest lakes in Asia at 44,000 km², but it is very shallow, nowhere more than 10 meters deep. Reed-covered flats and grassy swamps create a magnificent bird habitat recognized by the Ramsar Convention on wetlands. (9) Kedrovaya Pad preserves a rich variety of broadleaf species, lianas, and many rare plants including ginseng. It provides the habitat for the endangered Amur leopard. (10) Dalnevostochniy (Far East) Marine Reserve is located south of Vladivostok and protects three groups of islands and the surrounding waters of the Japanese Sea.

The northern reserves are larger and more varied. (11) Wrangel Island preserves a unique island of arctic tundra in the Chukchi Sea. Walrus, polar bear, snow goose, musk ox, and reindeer are among the animals that inhabit the island. (12) Magadan is a large multi-parcel area of dark coniferous taiga of Dahurian larch and Siberian stone pine on the coast of the Sea of Okhotsk. (13) Kronotskiy encompasses a wondrous area of volcanoes, geysers, and hot springs on the Kamchatka Peninsula. Some areas support lush tall grass, but for the most part vegetation consists of creeping stone pine and larch stunted by the harsh climate. (14) Kurile Reserve protects flora and fauna on the disputed Kunashir Island. It is of volcanic origin, with Japanese-Korean vegetation, including bamboo.

The only national park currently proposed in the Far East, Beringia National Park, would be created at the tip of the Chukot Peninsula. The goal of this park is to protect the area of the ancient land bridge between Asia and North America. Efforts center on the conservation of sea mammals and bird colonies, as well as preserving the cultural heritage of the indigenous peoples of this area.

The shift in the Russian economy is causing Far Eastern *zapovedniki* to face new difficulties. The customary management services, such as fire protection and pest control, can no longer be provided to the same degree as they were prior to 1991. Negligible salaries prompt rangers to augment their income with bribes from poachers; sometimes they themselves become poachers.

Chinese demand for tiger and bear skins, deer antlers and wild ginseng make poaching particularly lucrative in the Far Eastern reserves (Zatz, 1993). In general, the reserves are noticeably rich in berries, mushrooms, and other food plants. Therefore, people who are no longer able to support themselves on the broken economy sometimes make forays into nearby *zapovedniki*.

Some of the nature reserve managers are trying to attract tourist dollars to their areas. Unless very carefully managed, even ecotourists could fundamentally alter the integrity of the *zapovedniki* and threaten the original designation as a region completely removed from human economic activity. A post-USSR development of some significance was the creation, with international assistance, of the first non-governmental nature preserve in Russia, the Muriovka preserve on the Amur River west of Khabarovsk.

Future Prospects

The immediate future of the Russian Far East is hard to predict. There are many unanswered questions as Russia struggles to stabilize itself under difficult economic conditions. Among other factors, much will depend on the eventual mix of socialism/capitalism, forms of private property, environmental regulation, foreign investment, immigration laws, the economic well-being of individual citizens, and the position of the entire Russian Federation within the world economy.

The role that free economic zones take is one indicator of development in the Far East. These fledgling experiments in capitalism may either facilitate the continued role of the Far East as a resource colony by expediting the export of raw materials, or they could attract the investment moneys necessary to encourage domestic industry. At the end of 1991, Vladivostok, Nakhodka, Sakhalin, and the Jewish Autonomous Region had been declared free economic zones (Bradshaw and Shaw, 1992).

The Tumen River Area Project is an international project with a potentially significant impact on Far Eastern development. This project, sponsored by the United Nations Development Program, envisions a cooperative economic zone where the borders of Russia, China, and North Korea meet. The project is meant to provide a marine outlet for mainland China and Mongolia while encouraging economic cooperation and development in the entire region. It could have seriously negative environmental consequences, however, due to the biological importance of the coastal and forest resources of this region.

A new economic element may appear in the Russian Far East: the creation of large new nuclear power stations. At present, there is only the complex of four very small reactors at Bilibino, but in 1993 there was discussion of building a pair of pressurized water reactors at Komsomolsk, at least one near Vladivostok, and possibly a nuclear-powered municipal heating station at Khabarovsk. As noted earlier, cost considerations may delay these projects, unless foreign investors take an interest.

Nature has provided the Far East with great beauty, an abundance of wealth in resources, and many challenges to intelligent human exploitation.

In a world of dwindling resources, more and more of these challenges will have to be addressed. It is already inevitable that the importance of both the economy and the environment of the Russian Far East will grow in national and global perception.

Notes

1. Iturup, Kunashir, Shikotan, and the Habomais are the four southernmost islands. They have been claimed by Russia since the 1945 Potsdam Declaration but are now under renewed dispute.

2. Conversations with local citizens revealed that many interpreted the blackout as a political ploy to overcome local fear of the construction of a nuclear energy facility.

Bibliography

Barr, Brenton M., and Kathleen E. Braden. 1988. *Disappearing Russian Forest: A Dilemma in Soviet Resource Management.* London: Rowman and Littlefield.

Berg, L. S. 1950. *Natural Regions of the USSR.* New York: Macmillan Co.

"Bol'shoi lesopoval na zemle malochislennykh narodov." 1992. *Izvestiya,* Oct. 29.

Bradshaw, Michael J. 1994. "Economic Relations of the Russian Far East with the Asian-Pacific States," *Post-Soviet Geography,* vol. 35, no. 4, pp. 234–246.

Bradshaw, Michael, and Denis Shaw. 1992. "Free Economic Zones in the Russian Republic." *Post-Soviet Geography,* vol. 33, no. 6, pp. 409–414.

CIA. 1985. *USSR Energy Atlas.* Washington DC: GPO.

Goskomstat RFSFR. 1991. *Narodnoe Khozyaistvo RFSFR v 1990 godu.* Moscow.

Goskomstat SSSR. 1991. *Okhrana Okruzhayushchei Sredy i Ratsional'noe Ispol'zovaniye Prirodnykh Resursov.* Moscow.

Kirkow, Peter, and Hanson, Philip. 1994. "The Potential for Autonomous Regional Development in Russia: The Case of Primorskiy Kray," *Post-Soviet Geography,* vol. 35, no. 2, pp. 63–88.

Kolarz, Walter. 1954. *Peoples of the Soviet Far East.* New York: Praeger.

Matyushkin, E. N., and Yu. V. Shubaev. 1992. "Mezhdunarodnye prigranichnye zapovedniki." *Priroda,* no. 1, pp. 34–42.

Medvedev, S. V., 1976. *Seismic Zoning of the USSR.* Jerusalem: Keterpress Enterprises.

Ministerstvo Ekologii i Prirodnykh Resursov Rossiiskoi Federatsii. 1992. *Gosudarstvennyi Doklad o sostoyanii okruzhayushchei Prirodnoi Sredy Rossiiskoi Federatsii v 1991 godu.* Moscow.

Motrich, E. L., and Skurkin A. M. 1990. "Demograficheskaya politika na Dal'nem Vostoke i yevo otrazhenie v dolgovremennoi gosudarstvennoi programme." *Vestnik Dal'nevostochnovo Otdeleniya Akademii Nauk SSSR,* no. 3, pp. 41–44.

Myagkov, Sergei M. 1992. "Otnositel'naya Veroyatnost' vosniknoveniya chrezvychainykh situatsii prirodnovo i tekhnogennovo kharaktera na territorii byvshevo SSSR." Moscow State University, Laboratory of Complex Cartography. Unpublished ms.

Narodnoye Khozyaistvo RSFSR. 1992. *Natsional'nii Doklad Rossiiskoi Federatsii.* Moscow: Goskomstat.

Pryde, Philip. 1987. "The Distribution of Endangered Fauna in the USSR." *Biological Conservation,* vol. 42, pp. 19–37.

Rodgers, Allan, ed. 1990. *The Soviet Far East: Geographical Perspectives on Development.* New York: Routledge.

Rosencranz, Armin, and Antony Scott. 1992. "Siberia's Threatened Forests." *Nature,* vol. 355, pp. 293–295.

Sagers, Mathew. 1992. "Review of the Energy Industries in the Former USSR in 1991." *Post-Soviet Geography,* vol. 33, no. 4, pp. 237–268.

Shabad, Theodore, and V. Mote. 1977. *Gateway to Siberian Resources (The BAM).* New York: Halsted Press Division, John Wiley.

Sokolova V. E., and Syroechdovskii, E. E. 1985. *Zapovedniki Dal'nevo Vostoka.* Moscow: Mysl'.

Suslov, S. P. 1961. *Physical Geography of Asiatic Russia.* San Francisco: Wm. Freeman.

Swearingen, Rodger, ed. 1987. *Siberia and the Soviet Far East.* Stanford, CA: Hoover Institution Press.

Tikhookeanskiy Institut Geografii (TIG). 1989. *Environmental Report on the Far East.* Vladivostok: TIG.

Wixman, Ronald. 1984. *The Peoples of the USSR: An Ethnographic Handbook.* Armonk, NY: M. E. Sharpe.

Zatz, Daniel. 1993. "Last Favor for a Missing Tiger."*International Wildlife* (July/August), pp. 19–22.

6

Estonia

Siim Sööt

The Estonian people have inhabited the shores of the Gulf of Finland and the Baltic Sea for thousands of years. Distinctly different from their Latvian neighbors to the south and the Russians to the east, Estonians have maintained a strong ethnic identity. For decades they have looked north to Finland as an economic and social model, which helped develop an early concern for environmental issues. In the 1970s an open letter was written decrying the ecological deterioration in the country, and in the 1980s the public protested against phosphorite mining proposed by Moscow. Over time the opposition grew larger and more vocal. With the lack of a sympathetic response from the USSR government, the population increasingly demanded more independence, and ultimately in November of 1988 Estonia became the first republic to declare its sovereignty from Moscow. This action shook the socialist world and contributed to the dissolution of the Soviet Union. Estonia's own name for itself is Eesti.

History and Ethnicity

The earliest records of inhabitants in what is now Estonia date back approximately 10,000 years; had the Ice Age not removed vestiges of previous activity, the period might have been longer. Regrettably, Estonia was not able to flourish as an independent entity throughout much of the last thousand years of this period. Occupying forces from Germany, Sweden, Denmark and Russia controlled the land. To the Germans, Swedes, and Danes, Estonia was a distant outpost from which wealth could be extracted, but to the Russians it was an important window to the West.

Estonia's fate can be attributed to its strategic location. The irregular rocky coastline affords numerous natural harbors, providing protection from the ravages of storms and an ideal sailing venue (Figure 6.1). The 1980 Olympic

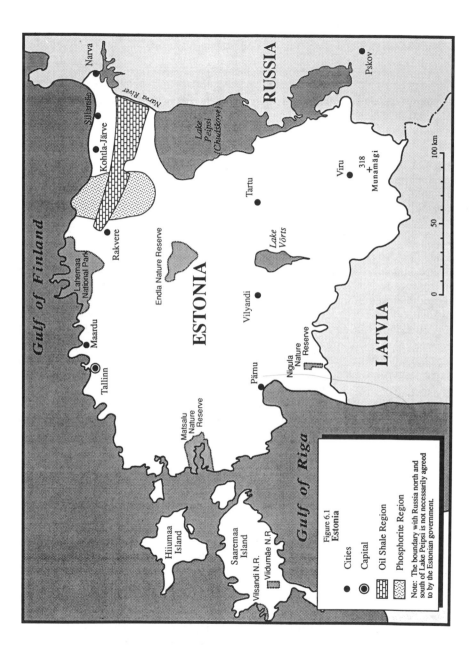

Figure 6.1
Estonia

sailing events were held here. Even more important, the warm currents provide a much longer shipping season than at St. Petersburg. Having lost its dominance over Finland at the beginning of the century, the Soviet Union was reluctant to relinquish its presence on the southern shores of the Gulf of Finland in Estonia.

During much of this century the population of Estonia has increased largely due to in-migration of people from the east. The number of ethnic Estonians has changed very little. In 1934 Estonians constituted 88.2% of the population, with the Russians constituting the largest minority group at 8.2%. Germans and Swedes were the next largest groups. By 1989 the Estonian percentage was down to 61.5, while the Russian proportion was up to 30.3%. Ukrainians and Belarusians replaced Germans and Swedes as the third and fourth largest groups. Although the total population since 1934 has increased from 1.1 million to 1.6 million, the number of Estonians has actually declined, from approximately 992,500 to 963,000 today. There are few ethnic groups worldwide that have diminished in numbers during the last half-century. Ethnic Estonians have consequently experienced the unenviable dilemma of seeing their own numbers declining while the number of in-migrants has grown.

Estonians are primarily an urban people (72% in 1989). The primary cities are Tallinn (482,000) and Tartu (114,000); no other cities in 1989 exceeded 100,000. Estonians are generally an educated people with high literacy rates, as reflected by very high per capita book and newspaper publishing figures. Estonia was the first Soviet republic to publish the complete works of Shakespeare in its native language.

As is common elsewhere, native Estonians tend to be more concerned with their natural environment than newer immigrants. This is noted also in the United Nations Conference on Environment and Development report (*National Report*, 1992, p. 9), which states, "The sparing attitude towards nature is weaker with newcomers than with the native population, [and] has led to problems of abuse, wasting or mismanagement of resources."

Physical Environment and Natural Resources

With its location between 57°N and 59°N, Estonia is truly a Nordic country. It was the northernmost minority republic of the former USSR. Tallinn is at the same latitude as Stockholm and is between that of Juneau and Anchorage, Alaska. The moderating effects of the Gulf Stream and its proximity to the Baltic Sea provide Tallinn with a climate approximating Chicago in the winter but with much cooler summers. February is generally the coldest month, averaging −6°C (21°F), and July is the warmest, with 17°C (62°F). There are typically 175 cloudy days during the year, and approximately one day in three will have rain during the summer. The long-term trend over the past four hundred years shows a general warming of approximately two degrees centigrade since the early 1700's (*National Report*, 1992, p. 8). Still, it is not the winter cold that represents the greatest challenge but rather the length of winter nights. Winter days are frequently overcast, which keeps the temperatures moderate but minimizes sunshine.

Topographically, the highest point in Estonia is the 318-meter (1,043 ft) Munamägi (Figure 6.1). The area surrounding Munamägi consists of rolling hills interspersed with farms and forest stands, not unlike Wisconsin or Minnesota. Having been glaciated approximately 10,000 years ago, the northern and western portions of the country are relatively flat. Numerous drumlins, eskers, and moraines and 1,440 lakes dot the landscape. Thirty-three percent of the landscape is covered by agricultural activity, forty percent by forests, and twenty-one percent by marshes and bogs.

Although at 45,100 square kilometers Estonia is only one third the size of Illinois, it possesses a variety of mineral and natural resources. The most prominent are the world's largest exploited deposits of shale oil, as well as phosphorite, peat, limestone and dolomite. It also has extensive forests and fertile soils, providing the nation with a solid economic base.

The most distinctive resource is the oil shale in Virumaa (the northeastern part of the republic), which is used to generate electricity and to produce household gas, commercial fertilizers and assorted chemicals. The extensive reserves (Table 6.1) would provide about a two-hundred-year supply at the current rate of extraction. Oil shale extraction dates from 1916, when production levels were relatively small. Much of the industry was lost during World War II, when all but 142 specialists with scientific degrees fled the country (Martinson, 1991, p. 235). After the war, production rebounded, peaked in 1981 at 31 million tons, was stable for many years, and then began to decline.

Approximately half of the almost 20 million tons extracted in 1991 were removed by conventional shaft mining and the other half by strip mining, introduced in the 1960s to increase production. Unfortunately, both mining methods yield large residue mounds. These have seriously polluted the groundwater supplies of the region, affecting both human habitation and agricultural activity. The underground mining has caused subsidence in many areas; as a result, former agricultural areas have flooded, creating bogs and

Table 6.1   Mineral Resources in Estonia

Resource	Explored Reserves	Mined Units in 1991
Oil shale	3,800 million metric tons	19.6 m.m.t.
Phosphorite	750 million metric tons	0.4 m.m.t. (1990)
Limestone, dolomite	250 million cubic meters	3.1 m.cu.m.
Sand, gravel	150 million cubic meters	6.9 m.cu.m.
Peat	2,400 million metric tons	1.8 m.m.t.

Source: National Report of Estonia to U.N. Conference on Environment and Development 1992, Tallinn: Ministry of Environment, 1992.

causing coniferous trees to prematurely lose their needles and die. The surface mining has totally altered the landscape, and although much land is reclaimed, in northern climates it takes many years to restore original soil and vegetation. Still, over 80% of the 10,000 hectares affected by mining have been recultivated and reforested.

The oil shale region also includes Europe's largest deposits of phosphorite (see Figure 6.1). Although the phosphorite has been mined in the Maardu area (20 km east of Tallinn) since the 1920s, major new reserves were discovered east of Rakvere, at a site 40 kilometers west of Kohtla-Järve. Due to public protests all phosphorite production ceased in 1991 after 391,000 tons were mined in 1990. It appeared to the local population that the extracted minerals would be largely shipped to the Soviet Union, and since many of the employees were non-Estonians, the Estonians would suffer from the environmental degradation but not receive any of the industry's benefits. The phosphorite mining has produced both radioactive and self-igniting waste materials (Taagepera, 1989).

A second important fuel is peat. There are approximately half a million hectares of peat bogs and fens scattered over 1,600 sites, with at least 10 hectares each. They are easily accessible from all parts of Estonia, and at the current rate of extraction, there are ample supplies for centuries. Peat is used locally and is also exported to northern European countries for a variety of agricultural purposes.

Industrial Development

Estonia's main industrial products are agricultural commodities, forest products, and mineral resource extraction and processing. Fishing is also an important industry.

Despite a northern location, Estonia's farms are major producers of dairy products. Supply and market disruptions that have accompanied both the establishment of a free market economy and the separation of Estonia's economy from the rest of the former Soviet Union have caused recent declines in butter and cheese production.

In the long run, agricultural production, including grains and meat as well as dairy products, should rise with the conversion to a free market system, where owners have the incentive to produce with efficiency and in quantity. By the beginning of 1991, there were 2,339 privatized farms. Another 2,000 are in process. Agricultural products are also the basis for the wine and spirits industry.

Forty percent of Estonia is forested; its forest stands of 1.16 hectares per capita ranks behind Finland (4.1), Sweden (2.7), and Norway (1.7) but ahead of Latvia (1.0) and Lithuania (0.5). Other countries in central Europe, such as Denmark, Germany and Poland, have less than a quarter of a hectare per person. There are a total of 264 million cubic meters of timber, or 144 cubic meters per hectare. The increase in timber production from 2.887 million cubic meters in 1990 to 3.010 in 1991 (each year accounts for a little over 1% of the existing forest) indicates a basic reality in the current economics of industrial production: it is more lucrative to export raw materials than to sell them to domestic industries. As the economy matures, Estonia will need to sell more value-added products.

The forests consist principally of pines (41%), birch (28%), spruce (23%) and a variety of alder, aspen, oak, ash, linden and elm. These forest resources have been long appreciated; the forests of the major islands have been under some form of protection since 1254. The first written regulations regarding forest management were introduced in 1782. Much of the current timber production emphasizes short-term gain, and even with reforestation programs, growth in this northern climate is slow. Environmental damage from acid rain, polluted groundwater and inadequate conservation techniques during harvesting has affected much of the existing forest. Many trees are also afflicted with root diseases, in part caused by high water tables. Mistakes in drainage channeling and road building have raised water levels, now a problem in about 40% of Estonia's forests (*Environment '90*, 1991, p. 18).

In terms of processing primary materials, northeastern Estonia has been as important to Estonia as the Ruhr region has been to Germany. It has met some of the energy needs of the country while providing a manufacturing base for export items such as chemicals, fertilizers and electricity. A large chemical facility is located at the Kohtla-Järve mines; two electric power plants are 40–50 kilometers to the east. The major products are sulfuric acid (450,000 tons annually), urea (200,000 tons annually for agricultural uses), and ammonia (as a raw material for fertilizer).

Regarding energy production, the emphasis has shifted over time from low quality household gas production to electricity, with power produced at two large facilities, the Estonia and Baltic Power Plants. The Baltic has a 1,435 MW capacity and the Estonia 1,610 MW. Estonia's heating systems are run on petroleum products, which have to be imported; Estonia formerly sent electricity to Russia and received heating fuel in return. Supplies were assured during the Soviet period but are not guaranteed any longer. Inadequate heat and hot water were major problems during the last several winters.

The shortage of heating fuel has placed additional emphasis on the Virumaa shale oil production, but the transition to a free market and concerns over environmentally unsound production methods have led to production declines. Electric production has decreased 7% in eight years, shale oil mining has declined 25%, and mineral fertilizers are down 8%. The most serious decline occurred in the early 1990s. Electric production was down to 14,506 million kWhs in 1991 and was estimated at 12,000 million in 1992, as compared to 18,900 million kWhs in 1980 (when production peaked). Russia's inability to purchase energy for hard currency is a major factor. Russia purchased 3,607 million kilowatt hours of electricity from Estonia in 1990, 1,598 in 1991, and none in 1992. At the same time Estonia continues to buy natural gas from Russia, but also in declining amounts. In 1992 it was projected to be at 60% of the 1.5 million cubic meters purchased in 1991. In 1993, Russia briefly shut off all gas supplies into Estonia as part of a dispute over payments and the status of ethnic Russians in the republic. Latvia's electric imports from Estonia also dropped from 5,150 million kWh in 1990 to about 3,500 in 1991, but it, too, faces payment difficulties.

The economic problems of Estonia can be summarized in the words of Hendrik Meri, deputy chief of the Department of Planning, who in speaking of the Soviet era said, "All the Union Republics form part of one economy, one single complex. . . . Every republic is assigned specific tasks. . . . The attempt is to solve a problem not in the interest of a particular region but of the whole country" (Singh, 1979, pp. 50–51). There was a distinct effort to integrate the country economically and socially, and while the social integration did not succeed, the economy of Estonia is still deeply intertwined with the CIS. The abrupt discontinuation of raw materials and markets has been a severe shock to all. The Soviet command economy also left a system of "tremendous waste and corruption" (Martinson, 1991, p. 237).

The World Bank planned to make a $30 million loan to Estonia by the end of 1993 for the conversion of boiler houses so that they can use local fuel, for the reconstruction of existing central heating systems, and for the introduction of new technologies in the energy sector. Until these sorts of structural, long-term changes are implemented, energy supply shortages are likely to continue.

Major Environmental Problems

A major source of Estonia's environmental problems is the great emphasis placed by the Soviet regime on industrial growth. Industrial output, rather than agricultural production, was seen as the way to build a strong economic empire. In Estonia, stress was placed on oil shale mining, electricity generation and textile production. Oil shale production was used to generate electricity and to produce household gas, much of which was sent to St. Petersburg. The gas pipeline from Virumaa was first completed to St. Petersburg in 1948 and not extended to Tallinn until 1953, indicating that the USSR's needs overshadowed Estonia's needs. Additionally, little attention was given to the environmental consequences of meeting production goals.

Environmental issues have always been important to Estonians (Pryde, 1991, pp. 259–264). There is an emerging consensus that environmental concerns became the principal catalyst of the unrest that led to the ultimate independence of Estonia. An important early step occurred in 1977 when "18 Estonian environmentalists warned in an open letter against the on-going shameful exploitation and pollution of Baltic soil and sea" (Roos, 1985, p. 65). Almost a decade passed before internationally noteworthy actions were taken. "Major protests in Riga about the environment in November, 1986 had been followed by similar demonstrations in Tallinn in spring 1987. The latter successfully blocked the plans . . . to begin phosphate mining in north-eastern Estonia, already a major ecological disaster area" (Hiden and Salmon, 1991, p. 149).

In the 1980s Estonian environmentalists scored several successes: blocking plans to strip-mine phosphorite, build an oil terminal in Tallinn, and construct additional oil shale–burning power plants. In 1988 the Green Party was officially tolerated by the Soviet government as a political party. The same year the Congress of the Popular Front proclaimed its support for ecology over economics, and later that year an Estonian delegate to the USSR Supreme Soviet decried the pollution in northeastern Estonia and described the tumultuous demonstrations to close the facilities. The lack of resolve by the Soviet regime to address the root problems led the Estonian parliament to declare sovereignty by a vote of 58–1.

In the end, pollution "provided a crucial stimulus to the political reawakening of the Baltic republics" (Hiden and Salmon, 1991, p. 3). Soviet authorities simply did not appreciate the gravity of the Estonian concern for the environment, nor did the non-Estonians living in the republic at the time. In the 1987 Estonian Academy of Sciences survey appearing in the daily *Rahva Hääl*, 95% of Estonians responded affirmatively to the question "Do you consider an unpolluted environment important?" while only 25% of non-Estonians responded similarly (Ilves, 1991, p. 75).

Much of this concern stems from water pollution. Many of Estonia's lakes and rivers are seriously polluted. In 1989 there were no wastewater treatment facilities in Tartu, Kuresaare, or Tapa and only primary treatment facilities in Tallinn and Haapsalu. Rakvere and Pärnu were the only cities to have both primary and secondary (biological) facilities. In these latter cases the facilities are not always in operation, for want of spare parts.

Since the entire country is in the Baltic Sea drainage basin, much of this pollution is eventually discharged into the Baltic Sea. The Baltic is rather shallow, has little water exchange with the North Sea, and is vulnerable to pollution from its ten bordering countries, each of which has at least some heavy industry near the shoreline. Estonia became a member of the eighteen-year-old Baltic Sea Convention in 1992, as well as the new Helsinki Convention established in 1992. These call for reducing heavy metal and organic contaminants discharged into the sea. Because Estonia has few biochemical wastewater treatment facilities, 285 tons of oil products and several hundred tons of phenols annually reach the Baltic Sea (by contrast, the tanker *Kihnu* which ran aground in January 1993, spilled 40 tons of petroleum). While the levels of phosphorus in the sea continue to increase and will not likely stabilize in the next thirty years, the levels of PCB, DDT, and oil products in the sea are declining (*National Report*, 1992, p. 24).

In Estonia, most of the 175 million cubic meters of water consumed in 1991 came from groundwater sources. Only Tallinn and Narva use treated surface water. In almost half of the country, however, the upper aquifers have been contaminated by nitrates, largely from fertilizers. The most serious problems are in eastern Virumaa (Kohtla-Järve area), where sulfates and phenols are among the hazardous substances in the groundwater.

Estonia also has some alarmingly serious air pollution levels, mainly SO_2 (sulfur dioxide) and NO_x (oxides of nitrogen). Measured in per capita SO_2 emission, Estonia, with 140 kilograms, outranks the former East Germany (125 kg), the former Czechoslovakia (90), Hungary (58), Poland (56), and Lithuania (51). Countries such as Netherlands and Norway are under ten. The corresponding figure for Europe is about nine, while North America's is 19. Estonia may well lead the world in this dubious distinction (*National Report*, 1992, p. 26). The annual discharge of NO_x has been declining since 1986, as has SO_2, but it was still over 20,000 tons in 1990. In the mid-1980s, Estonia was identified as having the highest per capita air pollution among all fifteen of the Soviet republics (Pryde, 1991, p. 263).

Considering only stationary air pollution sources, Estonia produced 610,000 tons of pollutants in 1990. Of this, 302,000 tons were solid pollutants, and 208,000 were SO_2. "Approximately 75% of the main pollutants are emitted by the Baltic and Estonia Thermal Power Plants, which rank among the ten biggest sources of air pollution in Europe" (*National Report*, 1992, p. 26). The Baltic plant is only 5 km southwest of the city of Narva, and the Estonia plant, slightly smaller, is located 15 kilometers farther southwest. Both burn fossil fuels derived from shale oil. The most common wind direction is estimated from the southwest, so that Narva is frequently in the path of these pollutants (as is St. Petersburg). Because the plants' smokestacks are more than 150 meters high, airborne pollutants are cast over a large region. In addition to contributing to pollution in the St. Petersburg region, these plants deposit an estimated 19,000 tons of sulfur annually in Finland. Estonia is also a recipient of foreign pollution; acid rain is a problem in southwestern Estonia, where no significant local polluters are found.

Non-stationary sources account for another 130,000 tons of pollutants, mainly from cars, trucks and tractors. The 1990 level of 147 private vehicles per 1,000 inhabitants exceeded the figure of 128 in Lithuania and 99 in Latvia (Pihlak, 1991, p. 2). It is less than 50 in Uzbekistan, Kazakhstan, Azerbaijan, Moldova, Kyrgyzstan, and Tajikistan. The high level of motorization, the age of the equipment, and the type of motors (many run on 76 octane leaded fuel) contribute to airborne pollutants. All of Estonia's major cities, including Tallinn (484,000), Tartu, (115,000), Narva (82,000), and Kohtla-Järve (77,000), are adversely affected.

Nuclear fuel was produced for many years in Sillamäe, a coastal city northeast of the Kohtla-Järve. It is estimated that the presently closed Sillamäe military facility has left behind radioactive waste that includes 1,200 tons of uranium and 750 tons of thorium (*National Report*, 1992, p. 28). Without an extensive cleanup, it is likely that the radioactive waste will eventually contaminate the local groundwater and ultimately enter the Gulf of Finland. Assistance with this problem is coming from specialists in Finland and Sweden, where they have had many decades of experience in the handling and disposal of nuclear waste. Information on the impact of environmental contamination on public health has not been made publicly available, but cases of hair loss among children, improper bone development, anemia, and other medical abnormalities have been recorded in eastern Virumaa (Uibu, 1989).

The lack of concern about industrial waste and the blind drive to meet the goals of the Soviet five-year plans have given Estonia a legacy of large hazardous waste dumping sites and a continued pattern of waste production. For several types of waste products, the amounts deposited in waste storage sites is less than the annual accumulation. The most visually obvious accumulations of waste are near the Kohtla-Järve facility, where numerous high mounds of ash residue are located. Currently, 20 square kilometers are covered by 160 million tons of ash. Some are located close to densely inhabited settlements (see Figure 6.2), but the most extensive accumulations are near

Figure 6.2   Ash mounds, residue from oil shale mining, located near a high-rise residential complex near Kohtla-Järve.

the power stations. Since many of these mounds are over twenty years old, many now support a variety of vegetation, including stands of trees. Still, these mounds represent an environmental hazard. The ash contains both sulfuric acid and heavy metals; when it rains the acid dissolves the heavy metals, and the resulting toxic runoff contaminates rivers and groundwater supplies.

Due to a strategic location, Estonia was home in the early 1990s to twenty-one rocket bases, six military airfields, six abandoned bases, two military naval bases and an assortment of other training and manufacturing facilities. Of particular concern are the discarded hazardous by-products of this military activity. An hour's drive west of Tallinn is the Paldiski harbor, which houses two nuclear submarines. The Estonian government as of early 1993 had been unsuccessful in persuading the government in Moscow to remove these submarines.

Governmental Structure: The Environment

In November of 1988, Estonia declared its sovereignty from Moscow. Within a month the "parliament approved the Concept of Nature Protection and Rational Utilization of Natural Resources, which together with numerous other legislative acts has to guarantee the stable and environmentally secure development of Estonia" (*National Report*, 1992, p. 3). Currently the most comprehensive legislation is the February 23, 1990, Law on the Protection of Nature in Estonia. It is the third law since 1935 defining the rights, environmental responsibilities and liabilities of citizens and enterprises. Later that year regulations were passed that identified pollution taxes and compensation penalties for environmental damage.

In 1990 the Ministry of the Environment was reorganized. The Environmental Protection Fund, Forest Department, and Fisheries all report to the minister. The ministry also includes a special office for the chief inspector of nature protection and has over 20 units and departments, such as the Water Department, Nature Conservation Department, Sea Agency, Monitoring and Data Processing Center and Institute of Fish and Sea Research. These are supplemented by 19 local environmental protection departments. These units have established a comprehensive system of protected areas in Estonia, including the 644-square-kilometer Lahemaa National Park and five state nature reserves (Figure 6.1 and Table 6.2). In addition, in 1992 there were fourteen landscape preserves, six botanical-zoological preserves, 29 bog preserves, twenty ornithological preserves, and other assorted preserves, including fifty-three locally protected areas. A major issue in Estonia's environ-

Table 6.2   Preserved Areas in Estonia

Type of Preserve(a)	Number	Total area(b)	Average size(b)	% of Republic(d)
Nature Reserves (Zapovedniki)	5	625.13	125.03	1.39
Biosphere Reserves	0	0		0.00
National Parks	1	649.11	649.11	1.44
Natural Monuments (Zakazniki)(c)	57	2037.00	35.74	4.52
Total	63	3311.24	52.56	7.34

Nature Reserves (date created)	Hectares
Endlaskiy (1985)	8162
Matsalu (1957)	39697
Nigula (1957)	2771
Vil'sandskiy (1971; 1910)	10689
Viydumyae (1957)	1194
Total	62513

National Parks	Hectares
Lakemaa (1971)	64911

(a) For the definition of each type of preserve, see Appendix 1.2.
(b) In square kilometers.
(c) Data are from late 1980s USSR sources; at least 69 such areas existed in 1993.
(d) The area of Estonia is 45,100 sq. kilometers.

Source: Pryde (1991).

mental management has been the division of authority and responsibility between local and central government.

The Environmental Protection Fund was established in 1983 and continues to provide financial support for environmental protection and to generally reduce pollution. It receives much of its revenue from pollution taxes and penalties. In 1990, 4.8 million USSR rubles were expended on numerous programs. The "development of the material base of environment protection" and "execution of research and project activities" each received about 28% of the fund. Less than one percent was devoted to environmental education and 3.5% to protected areas.

An integral part of environmental management and planning has been the development of a computerized set of environmental maps at a scale of 1:500,000. The regions of Virumaa and Tartumaa are being implemented first. Virumaa is the center of the oil shale industry, and Tartumaa has suffered from the mismanagement of local Soviet air bases; groundwater supplies have been severely contaminated by gasoline and aviation fuels.

International Trade and Tourism

Given the limitations of the Port of St. Petersburg, Tallinn is the closest alternative. With its proximity to the deeper waters of the Baltic Sea, and its favorable natural harbor conditions, Tallinn is an excellent location for a port.

The Port of Tallinn consists of three major facilities: the City Port, Kopli (fishing and bulk goods harbor), and the new Muuga Harbor. The City Port has developed into a mixed use facility with passenger service and bulk cargo handling. With the completion of the Muuga Harbor in 1986, there was excess capacity, and the port authority is beginning to shift functions and will redesign the City Port for strictly passenger service in the future, as a scenic entry into the country. With a draft of 18 meters, the Muuga Harbor can handle any vessel entering the Baltic through the Straits of Denmark. A totally new facility, it has the most modern silo complex in Europe, with a storage capacity of 300,000 tons and refrigeration facilities capable of handling 5,000 tons (Laving, 1991, p. 10). The port was built in part to handle large grain imports into the Soviet Union, but such activity has begun to decline in recent years for both economic and political reasons. Coal shipping, however, has increased, as has the use of the harbor facilities by the Danes and Swedes for storage purposes.

The currently planned Via Baltica motorway will provide Estonia with a vital link to central Europe and beyond. Connecting Tallinn, Riga and Kaunas with Warsaw and Budapest, it will provide a variety of travel services, such as rest areas, motels, service stations and restaurants, on a facility designed for 100-120 kph travel. Another roadway, the Hansa Way, is being planned, connecting St. Petersburg through southern Estonia to Riga, Kaliningrad and points west.

For the last two decades international tourism to Tallinn—a quaint city of Gothic architecture and cobbled streets—was extensively promoted to attract

Western capital. The ferry crossing on the *Georg Ots*, from Helsinki to Tallinn, takes less than three hours, just enough time for tourists to frequent the many bars and duty-free shops, providing the Soviet Union with Western currency. In recent years slot machines and a casino were added to increase potential earnings. The service had the imagined advantage to the Soviets of allowing Estonian residents to see firsthand the behavior of foreign tourists, many of whom were rather intoxicated.

In recent years there has been an explosion of service to Tallinn. In addition to two more ferries, hydrocraft service is now available. In the summer of 1990 the firm Estline initiated service to Stockholm: the *Nord Estonia* currently departs Stockholm in the evening and arrives about twelve hours later in Tallinn. This increase in service has allowed the passenger total to rise from 960,000 in 1991 to projections of over one million in 1992. In 1985 there were only 132,000 tourists from capitalist countries (ENE, 1987, p. 343).

Air service to the West began in the late fall of 1989 when Aeroflot and SAS agreed to fly between Stockholm and Tallinn. It was the first post–World War II service by a Western carrier to the Baltic republics. Tallinn was chosen for a variety of business reasons, but perhaps above all it had a world class airport, totally rebuilt to handle the 1980 Olympic yachting traffic. There had been uncertainty about demand, but over 4,000 reservations were made in the first month after the service was announced. It was one of the most successful start-ups in the history of SAS.

International air service is now also provided to Helsinki by Finn Air. Lufthansa flies to Frankfurt from Tallinn, and Estonian Air flies to numerous destinations, including Frankfurt, Copenhagen and Amsterdam, and has replaced Aeroflot's service to Stockholm and Helsinki. In 1990, 20,319 passengers flew between Tallinn and Helsinki and 31,364 flew between Tallinn and Stockholm. Tallinn and Estonia in general are well connected with western Europe and will continue to promote tourism. It is one of the clear economic potentials of the country. The number of visitors from the former Eastern bloc countries has declined recently, but Western visitors have increased.

Conclusions

Due to political and economic changes, Estonia has lost Russia as its major export market, as well as its access to cheap petroleum products. Considerable pressure exists to provide much-needed hard currency by increasing electricity production and by mining phosphorite again, even though such moves would have negative ecological consequences. At the same time, Estonia has signed numerous international environmental agreements designed to preclude serious environmental damage from being a result of tempting short-term economic solutions.

While its future is unclear, Estonia's past is not. Five decades of mismanagement and disregard for the environmental consequences of large scale industrialization and military occupation have seriously damaged the quality of Estonia's air, land and water. It is to be hoped that the environmental movement that helped topple an empire will continue to play a key role as difficult economic choices are made by a newly capitalistic and independent Estonia.

Acknowledgments

The author would like the thank the following individuals for their assistance in various capacities in the preparation of this chapter: Igor Gräzin, Aleksander Kaldas, Ilmar Kaljurand, Juhan Lamp, Endel Lippmaa, Aadu Loog, Ingrid Niinemäe, Silvia Pülme, Jüri Sander, and Peet Sööt.

Bibliography

Clemens, Walter. 1991. *Baltic Independence and Russian Empire.* New York: St. Martin's Press.

Eesti Nôukogude Entsüklopeedia (ENE). 1987. Vol. 2, Tallinn: Valgus.

Environment '90, 1991. Tallinn, Ministry of the Environment.

Fenhann, Jorgen. 1991. *Energy and Environment in Estonia, Latvia and Lithuania.* Roskilde, Denmark: Riso National Laboratory, August.

Hiden, John, and Patrick Salmon. 1991. *The Baltic Nations and Europe: Estonia, Latvia, and Lithuania in the Twentieth Century.* London: Longman Press.

Ilves, Toomas. 1991. "Reaction: The Intermovement in Estonia." In Jan Trapans, ed., *Toward Independence: The Baltic Popular Movements.* Boulder: Westview Press, p. 75.

Laving, Jüri. 1991. *Estonian Transport.* Tallinn: Informare.

Martinson, Helle. 1991. "The Development of Chemical Science in Estonia from 1945 to the Present." *Journal of Baltic Studies,* 22, pp. 233–240.

National Report of Estonia to UNCED 1992. 1992. United Nations Conference on Environment and Development, Rio de Janeiro, 3–14 June 1992. Tallinn: Ministry of the Environment.

Parming, Tönu, and Elmar Järvesoo, eds. 1978. *A Case Study of a Soviet Republic: The Estonian SSR.* Boulder: Westview Press.

Pihlak, Ilmar. 1991. "The Problems of Traffic and Highway Capacity in Estonia." Tallinn: Tallinn Technical University. Mimeographed.

Pryde, P. R. 1991. *Environmental Management in the Soviet Union.* Cambridge: Cambridge University Press, especially pp. 259–264.

Raun, Toivo. 1987. *Estonia and the Estonians.* Stanford, CA: Hoover Institution Press.

Roos, Aarand. 1985. *Estonia: A Nation Unconquered.* Baltimore: Estonian World Council.

Singh, Darshan. 1979. *Soviet Family of Nations, A Profile of Estonia.* New Delhi: Sterling Publisher.

Statistika Aastaraamat. 1992. Tallinn: Eesti Raamat.

Taagepera, Mare. 1989. "The Ecological and Political Problems of Phosphorite Mining in Estonia." *Journal of Baltic Studies,* 20, pp. 165–174.

Taagepera, Rein. 1993. *Estonia: Return to Independence.* Boulder: Westview Press.

Uibu, J. 1989. "Appeal of the Estonian Republic Ministry of Public Health." *Sovetskaya Estonia,* May 16, p. 3.

World Conservation Union, East European Programme. 1993. *Environmental Status Reports, 1993: Estonia, Latvia, Lithuania.* Gland, Switzerland: IUCN.

7

Latvia

Juris Dreifelds

Latvia is located on the eastern shores of the Baltic Sea and enjoys over 500 km of coastline. Its neighbors include Estonia on the north (300 km of common border), Lithuania on the south (500 km), and Russia (300 km) and Belarus (200 km) on the east (Figure 7.1). While in popular perception Latvia appears tiny, its size of 64,589 square kilometers ranks it ahead of such countries as Belgium, Switzerland and Denmark. Its population of 2.6 million amounts to less than 1 percent of that of the former USSR. Latvia's latitude places it on the same level as Labrador; hence the daylight hours are significantly different from those in New York City (longer nights in winter and longer days in summer). Its landscape has been carved by the deposits of retreating glaciers and is heavily dotted with hills and three major areas of highlands. There are numerous lakes and rivers. This variety in landscapes has limited the size of farm fields, even though about 45% of Latvian territory is suitable for agriculture.

Latvia, Estonia, and Lithuania are collectively known as the Baltic republics. While there are many differences among them, such as language, religious background and political culture, in contrast to other Soviet republics they were all independent and internationally recognized states prior to their forcible incorporation into the USSR in the summer of 1940. This period of independence has played an important part in the maintenance of a strong national consciousness and a European orientation.

Latvia's geographical location on the Baltic Sea has provided it with a maritime direction and has made it an attractive center of trade. Its capital city of Riga is equidistant from Moscow and Berlin (850 km) and, because of its geopolitical and strategic advantages, has been a coveted object of both countries during their historical expansionist phases.

Latvia is unusual because of its mix of ethnic groups. Only 52% of the population was found to be Latvian in 1989. The decrease in the percentage of the

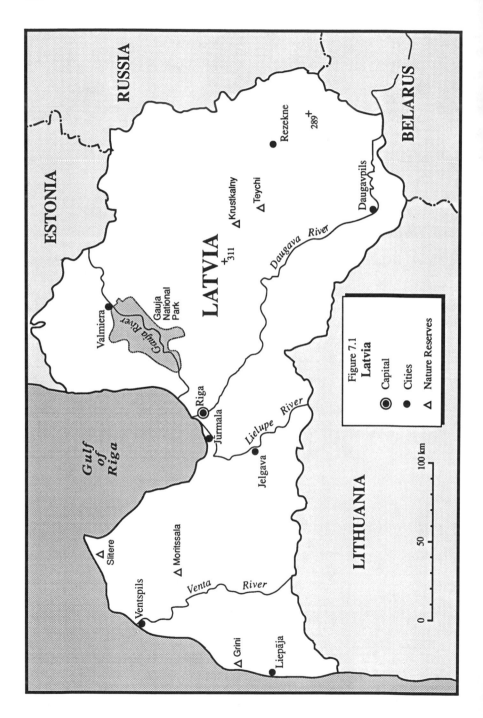

Figure 7.1
Latvia
◉ Capital
● Cities
△ Nature Reserves

Latvian population took place during the period of Soviet occupation from 1945 to 1991. Since 1991, however, there are signs indicating a slow Latvianization of the population.

History and Demography

Archaeological objects indicate the presence of human beings in Latvia as early as twelve thousand years ago. However, no one is certain about the ethnic composition of these people. The Latvians were one of the branches of five distinct Baltic peoples, only two of which have survived into the modern era (the other survivors are Lithuanians).

Beginning in the thirteenth century, the various Latvian tribes were conquered one at a time by Crusaders mobilized in Germany to Christianize the pagans. This conquest was completed by about A.D. 1300. Many of the victorious soldiers remained and formed the basis of the Baltic feudal baron class. This German-speaking ruling caste retained its power in spite of a succession of foreign regimes in all or part of the country during the next six hundred years (the Vatican, Denmark, Prussia, Poland-Lithuania, Sweden, Russia). The greatest impact on the history of Latvia besides the German barons has been that of its imperial neighbor, Russia. The process of attaching parts of Latvia to the Russian empire began in 1721 under Peter the Great.

Latvia was able to establish its independence in 1918 and was able to avoid the fate of so many other parts of the former Russian empire, which succumbed to Bolshevik domination. Latvia's period of independence lasted until June 1940, when Soviet troops occupied the country following the secret Molotov-Ribbentrop Pact of August 23, 1939. Many people perished as a result of this occupation by the Soviet army. The annexation of Latvia and the other two Baltic republics was never recognized by the United States. The oppression continued under the Nazis from 1941 to 1945 and once again under the post-war rule of the USSR. As in most other Communist countries, private property was confiscated, farmers were forced into collectives, and most freedoms were extinguished. Tens of thousands of people died as a result of deportations to Siberia, guerrilla warfare and political executions. The overt terror subsided after Stalin's death, but the long-range program of russification and Sovietization continued. As a consequence of post-war industrialization, hundreds of thousands of mostly Slavic workers settled in Latvia and formed a majority in all the largest urban areas (Table 7.1).

After Gorbachev introduced the policy of *glasnost*, Latvia became a leading center of liberalization. The first openly anti-regime demonstrations began on June 14, 1987, in Riga to commemorate the thousands who had been deported by the Soviets to Siberia. Many other demonstrations followed. During this period of awakening, most Latvians and, surprisingly, a majority of non-Latvians in the republic as well expressed their desire for independence (Dreifelds, 1989a). The first democratically elected government since the Soviet occupation declared on May 4, 1990, its intention to pursue independence. The goal came sooner than expected as a result of the failed coup of August 1991 and the subsequent recognition of independence by the USSR.

Table 7.1   Population of Latvia by Ethnic Origin, 1935-1989

Ethnic Origin	1935 1000s	1935 %	1989 1000s	1989 %	City of Riga %	City of Daugavpils %	City of Jelgava %	City of Rezekne %
Latvian	1467.0	77.0	1387.8	52.0	36.5	13.0	49.7	37.3
Russian	168.3	8.8	905.5	34.0	47.3	58.3	34.7	55.0
Belarusan	26.8	1.4	119.7	4.5	4.8	9.1	6.0	2.0
Polish	48.6	2.6	60.4	2.3	1.8	13.1	1.7	2.7
Ukrainian	1.8	0.1	92.1	3.4	4.8	3.1	3.9	1.6
Lithuanian	22.8	1.2	34.6	1.3	0.8	0.9	1.2	0.2
Jewish	93.4	4.9	22.9	0.9				
German	62.1	3.3	3.8	0.1				
Estonian	6.9	0.4	3.3	0.1				
Gypsy	3.8	0.2	7.0	0.3				
Other	3.9	0.2	29.5	1.1	4.0	2.5	2.8	1.2
Total	1905.4	100.0	2666.6	100.0	100	100	100	100

Sources: Latvija Sodien, p. 13; Cina, June 23, 1971; 1989 Gada Vissavienibas Tautas Skaitisanas Rezultati Latvijas PSR, p. 10.
Note: The 1935 data exclude the territory of Abrene, which was added to the RSFSR in 1944.

Soon thereafter, Latvia, as a sovereign country, received membership in the United Nations and other world bodies.

The Soviet period left Latvia with difficult demographic and linguistic dilemmas. As a result of the large migration of workers from other republics and differentiated birthrates, Latvians are almost a minority in their own country. They constituted about 83 percent of the population in 1945, but only 52 percent in 1989. In addition, by 1989 Latvians had become a minority in the seven largest cities of the republic. In the capital city of Riga the Latvians had been reduced to only 36.5 percent of the total population of 915,000. A similar situation applied in the next largest cities: Daugavpils (127,000) and Liepāja (114,000).

This condition has had an enormously negative impact; Riga accounts for 34 percent of the national population of Latvia and the bulk of publishing, higher education and culture. Since most non-Latvians have a minimal knowledge of Latvian, ethnic Latvians have difficulty conversing in their native language in their own capital city, and their daily life unfolds within a sea of Russian-speaking individuals. According to the 1989 census, 65.7 percent of ethnic Latvians knew Russian (the highest rate of any former republic), but only 21.1 percent of Russians living in Latvia knew Latvian. Thus, following independence, the government made Latvian the official state language and required a knowledge of Latvian in all jobs involving public contact (doctors, government clerks, etc.). This demand has created predictable strains within the non-Latvian population.

Another source of conflict has turned out to be the question of citizenship. As an occupied country, Latvia had no control over its borders or its immigration and thus received hundreds of thousands of foreign settlers. Today most of these people strongly favor "instant citizenship" for all those who desire it, without any pre-conditions such as language requirements or length of residence. Most ethnic Latvians, however, are opposed to such a blanket policy. The Latvian parliament (Supreme Council) in 1994 was considering a law requiring 10 years of residency, a knowledge of the state language (Latvian) and an oath of loyalty. The draft law also contains a quota limiting the number of new citizenships that can be granted annually.

Another lingering issue in early 1994 was that of the remaining Soviet military troops in the republic. Russia, now in charge of them, ties their removal to the status of the ethnic Russian residents in Latvia. A serious incident involving these troops and local Latvian officials occurred in January 1994, and all sides would like to avoid the possibility of such incidents escalating into armed conflict. This led to an agreement for the removal of the remaining troops by August 31, 1994, which was accomplished.

The upheavals of the last few years have wrought changes in the demographic patterns of Latvia. Beginning in 1990, more people left the republic than came to live in it. The net out-migration during 1992 was over 30,000. There has also been a shift in self-identification among a certain percentage of those from mixed marriage families involving a Latvian parent or from those of Latvian origin who had earlier assimilated to the predominant (Russian) power group. Now many of these have chosen to be identified as Latvians. The rates of natural increase have also changed. The birthrate of all groups has decreased, but that of the Russians has been particularly drastic. They now have a negative natural rate of change in population as a result of lower births and higher deaths.

Natural Assets and Resources

Latvia is not a highly mineralized region and contains relatively few metal and hydrocarbon resources. On the other hand, it is rich in biotic resources.

While Latvia is one of the oldest populated countries of northern Europe, it still contains significantly large and pristine wilderness areas. Over 42 percent of its territory is wooded. Scotch pine and Norway spruce form about two thirds of forest stands. A very high proportion of the timber crop is immature because of previous overcutting and the devastation wrought by several hurricane force storms in the recent past. Hence much of the local wood supply comes from thinning and improvement cuts. A very high percentage of harvested wood is utilized for combustion, and with increased prices of oil and other fuels, the popularity of wood furnaces and stoves has increased dramatically, even in cities. Wood is also used by the republic's paper industry and by its specialized plywood and furniture manufacturers. The traditional designation of "green gold" given to Latvian forests has recently been discovered by a myriad of private companies and "privateers," who have found a lucrative market in the export of lumber to neighboring countries, often without proper licensing or payment of taxes.

Ironically, while the Soviets overcut the allowable annual yield of wood, the area of bushland has increased since 1940. The abandonment and eventual overgrowth of many isolated, formerly private farms by low value scrub may not have added much in terms of timber value, but it did create ideal conditions for wildlife. The World Wildlife Fund in its 1992 Latvian project acknowledged the existence of many unique ecological sites and animal species rarely found in other parts of Europe (i.e., black storks, small eagles, otters, wolves, beaver, lynx). An added feature of Latvia's environment is the large territory occupied by lakes and marshes (over 10 percent). The variegated and rapidly changing environments of glacial moraines and lowlands have allowed temperate southern flora (oaks) to grow within a few hundred meters of northern flora (bog cotton and cloud berries). Indeed, one of the most appealing aspects of the Latvian countryside is the interspersing of glacial highlands (25 percent of territory) with undulating or flat plains. The recent trend to privatization of abandoned farms and the reckless and often uncontrolled cutting of timber stands for fuel and for quick profits may jeopardize the existing ecological sanctuaries.

To protect this natural wealth, Latvia has created 5 state nature reserves, totaling about 40 thousand hectares, and almost 150 (as of 1987) smaller nature preserves (Table 7.2). One of the first national parks in the former Soviet Union was created in 1971 along the Gauja River. A problem exists, however, with former private landholders in the area of some of the reserves wishing to have these parcels deeded back to them.

Latvia's location on the westernmost borders of the USSR and on a sea that also washes the shores of NATO countries created an unexpected windfall for naturalists. The Latvian sea coast was inadvertently protected by the Soviet border guards. These troops, for security reasons, destroyed many of the existing houses along the seashore and prevented the construction of new homes in this area. As a result, there are over 300 kilometers of unsullied and "undeveloped" seashore washing on mostly sandy slopes and dunes, bordered by natural pine and spruce forests. While laws have been passed to prevent any construction within one kilometer of the sea, many legal loopholes as well as the general ignoring of such laws has opened the prospects for the destruction of a wild coast not found in any other part of Europe. As yet, local entrepreneurs have not realized the long range prospects of developing ecotourism.

The more populated seaside of Jūrmala, with its many sanitoriums and tourist accommodations, was a key rest zone for the Soviet state and the Riga population after independence. Much has changed, however. Jūrmala beaches have remained closed to swimming since 1988 due to bacteriological contamination, and few visitors find their way here from Russia and other former Soviet republics. This resort area, with its striking tall pines and antique architecture, has the potential for becoming a major attraction for western Europeans, as it did in the interwar years.

The Latvian climate is humid, with high rates of precipitation. One of the benefits of this condition has been the ready availability of water for recreation and for industries. Indeed, Latvia has much more water per capita than almost all other republics of the former USSR. While this has helped pro-

Table 7.2   **Preserved Areas in Latvia**

Type of Preserve(a)	Number	Total area(b)	Average size(b)	% of Re-public(c)
Nature Reserves (<u>zapovedniki</u>)	5	396.72	79.34	0.62
Biosphere Reserves	0	0.00		0.00
National Parks	1	837.50	837.50	1.31
Natural Preserves (<u>zakazniki</u>)	148	1040.00	7.03	1.63
Total	154	2274.22	14.77	3.57

Nature Reserves (date created)	Hectares
Grini (1957; 1936)	1477
Krustkalny (1977)	2902
Moritssala (1912)	818
Slitere (1957; 1921)	15428
Teichi (1982)	19047
Total	39672

National Parks	Hectares
Gauya (1973)	83750

(a) For the definition of each type of preserve, see Appendix 1.2.
(b) In square kilometers.
(c) Area of Latvia is 63,700 sq. kilometers.

Source: Pryde, 1991.

cesses of self-purification, it has also lessened pressure for the recirculation of wastewater. In addition, this abundance has attracted industries producing large volumes of effluent.

As a coastal republic, it is not surprising that much of the water carried by Latvia's rivers is collected outside the country's boundaries. Thus over 60 percent of the annual water volume of the six largest rivers comes from abroad, mainly from Belarus and Lithuania. The dangers inherent in a lack of pollution cooperation were brought home to Latvians in November 1990, when a polymer complex in Novopolotsk, Belarus, accidentally spilled 128 tons of cyanide derivatives into the Daugava River (Western Dvina) and did not warn downstream users in Latvia. Only the presence of numerous dead fish forewarned Latvian inhabitants about the danger.

Water has also been a source of valuable electricity. Latvia's largest river, the Daugava, carries a large volume of water over its 370 km flow through

Latvia and has stretches of significant descent. There are presently three hydroelectric dams supplying over a third of the republic's consumption of electricity. It is noteworthy that the construction of the number two dam at Plavinas involved a wide ranging and surprisingly agitated confrontation between naturalists and resource exploiters in 1958—a period of ideological thaw when more liberal and nationally minded Latvian Communists dominated the Party in the republic. After their purge and replacement by ideological conservatives in 1959, the dam project was signed for construction.

The projection of another dam on the Daugava, dam number four near Daugavpils, precipitated another nationwide debate and confrontation between environmentalists and engineers. This time the engineers lost; the project was terminated in November 1987. This victory was a critical factor in the reawakening of Latvian consciousness, leading eventually to the vigorous pursuit of autonomy and then independence. The initiative for this successful campaign, which began in October 1986, was taken by two journalists, one of whom, Dainis Ivans, later became the first leader of the Latvian People's Front. Many groups in Latvia and to a lesser extent in Belarus were mobilized. Meetings, demonstrations, articles in the press and media events characterized this rising of the people against a seemingly untouchable project of the then-current five-year plan. The truly effective coup de grâce to this project was masterminded by the scientific community, not merely of Latvia but also of Belarus and, more important, of the USSR Academy of Sciences, which provided the much-needed credibility and legitimacy to change the minds of decision-makers in Moscow (Dreifelds, 1989b).

The abundance of water has created economic problems as well. A large part of Latvia's useful agricultural land requires constant draining. This has necessitated extremely expensive water amelioration projects involving the laying of drainage pipes, the straightening of natural streams, the digging of drainage ditches, and the construction of polder dams. During the 1960s and 1970s, drainage work absorbed about a third of all agricultural investments in Latvia. Indeed, Latvia, with less than one percent of the former territory of the USSR, claimed over 11 percent of all Soviet drained land.

Another negative aspect of the climate pattern is that the heaviest precipitation usually occurs at harvest time, in August and September. This hinders mechanized grain harvesting, leads to grain drooping, and forces heavy investment outlays in grain-drying structures and ventilation systems. In 1992, ironically, the biggest problem was lack of rain. Such a degree of dryness had not been experienced in over a century.

In general the climate has determined that the mainstay of agriculture in Latvia is clearly animal husbandry and dairying, although much attention is also paid to cereal and root crops. Most of the field crops (barley, oats, potatoes) have traditionally been utilized for animal feed. One of the important features of Latvian agriculture for many decades, as planned by Moscow specialists, was to grow pigs and other animals in large complexes utilizing feedstock from other republics. With the dissolution of the former patterns of inter-republic trade, many Latvians have been forced to cut back on animal husbandry, slaughtering their cattle and pigs because of a lack of affordable feed.

In spite of many problems, agriculture still presents one of the key resources of the republic. The privatization process has allowed over 50,000 individual farmers, mostly Latvian, to begin farming. In view of the small size of these farms (an average of 17 hectares) and the lack of previous experience by many, a large number of the novices will be involved in little more than subsistence farming, and many of the younger enthusiasts may soon become discouraged or go bankrupt. On the other hand, the loosening of agricultural quotas and tariffs by the European Community, as now seems probable, could raise the survival potential and even prosperity of Latvian farmers.

While forestry and agriculture are among the most important resources, a signal advantage of Latvia is its seaside location and year-round ports. The port of Riga, with its container terminal and freight traffic from Japan via Siberia, has particularly great potential for growth. The port of Ventspils is the end terminal for a Volga-Urals crude oil pipeline built in 1968. The port has three berths capable of servicing large ocean tankers. The American Occidental Petroleum Company (Oxy) built a giant industrial chemical complex here, thereby increasing the economic importance of this all-season port but at the same time creating dangerous conditions of pollution and a threat of chemical explosions within the boundaries of the city. The port of Liepāja was for many decades under the supervision of the Soviet military and at times even harbored Soviet atomic submarines. Not until May 1992 was Liepāja relinquished by the Russian military. Much rebuilding is in store, but the port holds much promise for the future. The post-independence co-optation of the Soviet merchant ships that were based in Latvia has provided the republic with a strong source of foreign currency. Many of the 150 or so ships with the Latvian Shipping Company, however, are old and dilapidated.

Other significant natural resources exist, such as raw materials for cement, gypsum, high quality clay, peat and construction materials such as gravel, limestone and sand. Fish from the Baltic Sea are also in great demand. Amber, which is washed up on the beaches of the sea, is a much sought after material for jewelry and has had a symbolic impact on the country, which is often called "amberland." Some minor deposits of oil have been found, but greater hope is placed in locating oil in the Baltic Sea within Latvian territorial waters.

Latvian Industry

During the Soviet period, Latvian industry was developed according to the concepts of a Moscow-planned division of labor. Most of the industries that were located in Latvia had to import workers and raw materials and export finished products. Exports as a proportion of Latvia's GNP accounted for 50 percent in 1988, a level similar to that of ten other republics. Only Russia had a relatively low export dependency, at around 15 percent (Grahm and Konigson, 1991, p. 6).

During the late 1980s, 60 percent of all industrial personnel in Latvia were employed in the engineering industry (42.8%) and the textile industry (20.3%). The other important fields were food industry (6.7%), wood industry (9.8%), building materials industry (5.2%) and chemical industry (6.7%). Certain military industries may not have been included in this calculation. Soviet enterprises often provided in-house services for their own employees, such as housing construction, food catering and retail trade, consumer sales, health care and recreational facilities. Such a practice skewed final employment figures (Grahm and Konigson, 1991, pp. 25–27).

In view of Latvia's export dependency and raw material import dependency on the former USSR, the entire industrial sector is undergoing adverse changes as a result of the rupturing of old trade patterns, the general chaos in currencies and finances, price hikes to world levels, and endemic and widespread thievery by managers and other leading personnel. Production in Latvian industry declined 44.4 percent between October 1991 and October 1992 (Latvijas Valsts, 1992, p. 8). Especially hard hit has been the engineering industry, which has not been able to sell most of its production. Over half of this sector was dependent on military orders from the Soviet armed forces, a market that has all but disappeared.

There is no doubt that the state, with its limited budget, will not be able to maintain industries that cannot sell what they produce. Massive unemployment appears to be on the horizon. Most of these workers, moreover, are non-Latvian. Privatization, which has been touted as the only way out of the economic gridlock, has not proceeded very far. Less than 10 percent of production is outside direct state control (but not outside indirect control). Plants having some foreign capital accounted for only 1.1 percent of industrial production in 1992 (Latvijas Valsts, 1992, p. 15).

There are signs of change. In 1991 most (88.2 percent) of Latvian exports went to the CIS and 3.2 percent to Western countries. One year later over 20 percent of exports went to the West (Latvijas Valsts, 1992, p. 23). The International Monetary Fund also praised Latvia in 1992 for its determined actions in stabilizing the currency and limiting the printing of money. As a result of this policy, inflation in Latvia was below 4% a month from December 1992 to April 1993. A major change in attracting foreign investments will occur when the former Soviet armed forces, numbering about 30,000, leave Latvia.

One of the most critical variables in changing the costs of production has been energy, and in 1991 Latvia imported 91% of the energy it consumed. Latvia is dependent on Russian oil and gas and Estonian and Lithuanian electricity. Russia is now charging close to world prices for its supplies, while Latvia's Baltic neighbors are strongly pushing for more realistic electricity prices. These price changes have affected all levels of the population. Most people cannot afford the high price of energy, and the state cannot afford to continue subsidies. Switching to wood, to gas meters and to smaller apartments is a step forward, but obviously such measures are not enough.

Environment and Pollution

Latvia as an urbanized (71%) and industrial republic has had to wrestle with a variety of endemic problems of pollution. However, these have not been of the same severity as in other heavily industrialized parts of the USSR, or in the pollution triangle of Poland, the former East Germany, and the Czech Republic.

The assault on the environment has come from many directions. The most pressing concern is water quality. Air pollution is less of a problem because automobile transportation is less developed than in the West. Also, cleaner natural gas and electricity have replaced dirtier energy sources, such as coal. There is growing concern over toxic wastes and the haphazard, unmonitored burial of industrial and commercial garbage. Abandoned explosives and poison gas canisters from World War II, dumped off the Latvian coast near Liepāja, have become a major source of tension (*Diena*, February 25, 1992).

The Daugava, Lielupe and Venta Rivers carry the bulk of water pollutants. Riga in particular, a city of about 900,000 people that straddles the Daugava less than 10 km from its mouth at the Gulf of Riga, has been the major source of contaminants. It accounts for two thirds of industrial production in Latvia, and as yet only about 20 percent of the city's sewage is properly processed (Figure 7.2). The construction of a treatment plant for Riga sewage has gone on for over twenty years, and many feel that it will continue for another twenty years.

Farming has been responsible for a growing share of water pollutants. Erosion of hilly terrain and high levels of fertilizers and pesticides have created difficult problems of containment. Two of the key debilitating aspects of rural areas have been a careless attitude and an ignoring of environmental laws. Animal barns are constructed alongside water bodies, fertilizers and pesti-

Figure 7.2 The Daugava River near the center of Riga; the light portion of water on the left is a source of polluted water entering the river.

cides are stored in ramshackle buildings, pollution treatment equipment is sloppily maintained, and oil storage depots have insufficient environmental safeguards.

In 1989, only 110 million cubic meters, or 30 percent of total effluent in Latvia, were adequately treated before being dumped into local waterways, a rate of purification somewhat ahead of Russia (11%) and Lithuania (25%) but exceeded by all other former Soviet republics (Goskomstat SSSR, 1990, p. 248). The bulk, or 86 percent of all inadequately treated waste water originated from commercial-industrial sources.

The Sloka Pulp and Paper Complex right alongside the resort city of Jūrmala has been a perpetual pollution delinquent. The complex was built during the tsarist period in 1895. It has been the focus of pollution criticism and charges ever since the 1930's, but particularly during the Soviet period when its production of paper increased over fivefold and its installation of purification facilities lagged far behind. The first protests about Sloka in the post-war period surfaced in 1956, but the primary pollution treatment complex was put into operation only in 1975 and the secondary or biological treatment stage in 1978. A third, more sophisticated chemical cleansing complex was planned but never installed. According to several oral sources, even the first two stages came about as the result of the personal intervention by Premier Aleksei Kosygin, who regularly vacationed in Jūrmala.

The major confrontation between the republic and the All-Union pro-Sloka forces began in 1987, after the victory in stopping the Daugavpils dam. This time, rather than ask for more control equipment, environmental activists were determined to shut the mill entirely. In the end Moscow won by simply threatening to cut off the flow of paper to Latvia. The mill, however, did decrease the volume of production and for one month in May 1990 stopped production entirely to clean out its settling ponds and to refurbish other pollution cleaning equipment. Together with Riga sewage, Sloka's wastes have forced the closing of almost all seaside beaches extending over 10 km on each side of the Daugava. Due to both environmental concerns and economic necessities, the Sloka mill was shut down again in 1993 for an indefinite period.

Eutrophication (excessive nutrients that can lead to algae blooms) is a growing problem in inland waters, as well as in the Baltic Sea. In spite of the various problems, however, and using microbiological indicators but not toxic contaminants, Latvia's waterways on average can be classified as clean to moderately polluted. Individual rivers, lakes, and sections of the sea, however, do vary and are listed in official categories from very clean, clean, moderately polluted, polluted, dirty, very dirty to extremely dirty (Latvijas Vides, 1991).

The total discharge of air pollutants by weight in Latvia was significantly smaller than in the neighboring Baltic republics, reaching only one third of Estonia's and two fifths of Lithuania's levels (Latvijas Vides, 1991, p. 5). In 1989 the total discharge of air pollutants was 584,780 tons, or 9.0 tons per square kilometer. The major share by volume of this pollution (73 percent) was provided by motor vehicles. Among the stationary sources, thermal power plants were the most significant contributors, followed by agriculture and the food industry (sugar, milk canning), building materials (cement and lumber), and municipalities (heating facilities).

While factories have been able to control 93 percent of solid emissions, 97 percent of their polluting gases and evaporated liquids have not received treatment. In 1990, only 40 gas purification facilities were in operation. A major source of air pollution comes from Lithuania, where the ejections from the Mazeikiai petroleum refinery and thermoelectric plant and Naujoji Akmene cement plant are carried north. About 247,647 tons of hazardous wastes are produced every year, but these are discarded in regular dumps or other unsuitable areas (Nordic Project, 1991, pp. 44–49; *Diena*, May 29, 1991).

The environmental movement was one of the major catalysts of the Latvian awakening. Between 1986 and 1990 the topic was on the agenda of every politician, newspaper and social group. The undisputed leader in this area was the Vides Aizsardzibas Klubs (Environmental Protection Club), led by forester and poet Arvids Ulme. The Greens even elected 7 deputies to a parliament of 201, and during the election campaign of spring 1990 almost all deputies claimed to be environmentally conscious. Since 1990, and especially since 1992, when rapidly growing economic hardships created major strains, environmental issues have been receiving little publicity.

The official governmental body responsible for environmental issues is the Environmental Protection Committee (EPC). Rather than being attached to the cabinet, it is under the direct jurisdiction of parliament. Initially this allowed for greater freedom of action for the committee, but its chairman in May 1992 indicated in an interview that it might be more effective if it was part of the cabinet. In 1992 the EPC had about one hundred people in its administrative offices and about 670 inspectors, scientists and technical specialists. The EPC has the power to shut down any object temporarily or permanently, but this is rarely done. All new building or production projects require an environmental impact assessment, which has to be signed by the committee. The committee also establishes pollutant emission standards and helps in setting the resource based "pollution tax." It is also in charge of the Environmental Protection Fund, a financial repository for fines and losses created by polluters.

An unexpected by-product of the slowdown in the economy has been the lowering of pollutant volumes. This gain, however, has been undercut to some extent by the decreasing funds available for pollution control equipment and programs.

International Position and Future Prospects

During Latvia's independence period before the war, many resources were allotted to the building of communications and transportation infrastructures. After the war, Latvia's strategic location within the Soviet Union helped promote a dense development of transportation networks. The east-west routes are the best developed due to the flow of trade and major contacts to the east, particularly with Moscow. The all-season ports should help Latvia expand maritime contacts with the countries along the Baltic Sea. Indeed, a very close economic relationship appears to be developing with Sweden and Denmark. There is a great potential for growth with the Baltic ports of Germany such as Rostock, Lübeck and Kiel. Riga was for several hundred years an important trade link and center for the historical free trade of the old Hanseatic League. There are now serious attempts to reactivate this league. Another project that could help international access for Latvia is the planned highway link between Helsinki and Warsaw (ferry from Helsinki to Tallinn).

There is much international interest in ameliorating environmental problems in Latvia. In particular, the Scandinavian countries and Germany have realized that their own shores of the Baltic cannot be fully protected unless all the countries around this sea aim for the same levels of cleanliness. Indeed, they have concluded that every unit of currency spent in the former communist countries has a far greater impact in lowering overall pollution levels than if spent at home. Hence, their numerous technical and educational initiatives for the abatement of harmful pollutants on the other shore of the Baltic are in reality a wise investment in their own ecological welfare. One of the most active institutional frameworks in this direction has been the steering agency of the Helsinki Convention on the Protection of the Marine Environment of the Baltic Sea Area. This convention was signed in 1974 and entered into force in 1980. The steering agency, or Helsinki Commission (HELCOM), created a special task force in 1990 to coordinate and assist the elaboration of concrete programs from each of the Baltic littoral countries, including Latvia. Latvia became a full member of HELCOM in March 1992.

The head of the Riga Environmental Committee acknowledged in May 1992 that much foreign advice is being provided but that not enough concrete financial aid has been forthcoming. At a time when Latvia is experiencing wrenching economic pressures and has reached close to subsistence levels of survival, it does not have the capacity to invest in costly ecological projects. Latvia is today in a unique position to maintain and enhance its exceptional natural endowments, such as the unspoiled beaches, salmon streams, forest tracts, marshes and other water bodies, and rare animal and plant species. Well managed ecological tourism, especially in such a central part of Europe, could be an environmentally successful option for stimulating the economy. On the other hand, the enticement of immediate cash from unscrupulous developers could turn Latvia into a weak and tawdry copy of the commercial tourist centers of Europe. Unless more concrete initiatives are undertaken by Latvians themselves and by wealthier neighboring countries, there is a great likelihood that Latvia's rich natural endowments will succumb to the forces of least resistance, and another link in the chain of the world's natural heritage will be lost for use and enjoyment by future generations.

Bibliography

The Baltic States: A Reference Book. 1991. Tallinn: Estonian, Latvian, Lithuanian Encyclopaedia Publishers.

Diena. Republic of Latvia daily newspaper.

Dreifelds, Juris. 1989a. "Latvian National Rebirth." *Problems of Communism.* July–Aug.

———. 1989b. "Two Latvian Dams: Two Confrontations." *Baltic Forum.* Spring.

———. 1990–1991. "Immigration and Ethnicity in Latvia." *Journal of Soviet Nationalities.* Winter.

Environmental Protection Committee, Republic of Latvia. 1992. *National Report of Latvia to UNCED 1992.* Helsinki: Government Printing Center.

Fenhann, Jorgen, ed. 1991. *Energy and Environment in Estonia, Latvia and Lithuania.* Roskilde, Denmark: Riso National Laboratory.

Goskomstat SSSR. 1990. *Narodnoe khoziaistvo SSSR v 1989 g.* Moscow: Finansy i Statistika.

Grahn, Leif, and Konigson, Lennart. 1991. *Baltic Industry: A Survey of Potentials and Constraints.* Stockholm, Sweden: Swedish Development Consulting Partners AB.

International Monetary Fund. 1992. *Economic Review: Latvia.* Washington, D.C.: IMF.

Jūrmala. City of Jūrmala weekly newspaper.

Latvia: An Economic Profile. 1992. Washington, D.C.: National Technical Information Service.

Latvijas Valsts Statistikas Komiteja. 1992. *Zinojums Par Latvijas Republikas Tautas Saimniecibas Darba Rezultatiem.* Riga: Latvijas Valsts Statistikas Komiteja, Nov.

Latvijas Vides Aizsardzibas Komiteja. 1991. "Vides Aizsardziba Latvijas Republika 1990. gada Parskats." Riga: Latvian Environmental Protection Committee. Mimeographed.

Management of the Nordic Investment Bank. 1991. *A Survey of Investment Plans and Needs in the Three Baltic Countries.* Copenhagen: Nordic Council of Ministers.

Nordic Project Fund. 1991. *Environmental Situation and Project Identification in Latvia.* Helsinki:

Rutkis, J. 1967. *Latvia: Country and People.* Stockholm: Latvian National Foundation.

State Committee for Statistics of the Republic of Latvia. 1991. *National Economy of Latvia in 1990: Statistical Year-Book.* (Text in English). Riga.

Westing, Arthur, H. 1989. *Comprehensive Security for the Baltic:* An Environmental Approach. London: Sage Publications, PRIO and UNEP.

World Conservation Union, East European Programme. 1993. *Environmental Status Reports, 1993: Estonia, Latvia, Lithuania.* Gland, Switzerland: IUCN.

World Wildlife Fund Project 4568. 1992. *Conservation Plan for Latvia Final Report.* (Text in Latvian). Riga: Vide.

8

Lithuania

Randy Kritkausky

Lithuania is one of the oldest nation-states in the European portion of the former Soviet Union, tracing its state history back to the early 14th century. Over the past two hundred years, however, there have been only about 25 years of independence, from 1918 to 1940 and since 1991. Today, the new country (whose official name in the Lithuanian language is Lietuva) is home to just under four million people and embraces a territory of 65,200 square kilometers. It is the only one of the former Soviet republics where Roman Catholicism is the dominant religion.

Ethnography and History

Lithuania's ethnic diversity, history of Soviet occupation, culture, language and religion provide common links as well as discontinuities with its Baltic neighbors. Ethnically, Lithuania is the most homogeneous of the Baltic societies. In 1991, ethnic Lithuanians made up nearly eighty percent of the total population of 3,751,000; Russians represented only nine percent. Consequently, Lithuanians have expressed less concern over and reacted with less severity to Russification than Estonia and Latvia, which have proportionately larger Russian populations.

During and after World War II, however, Russians were settled in towns and newly created industrial centers, such as the one around the Ignalina nuclear power station, where more than ninety percent of the residents are Russian. As a result, Lithuanian pollution problems, economic reform efforts, and plans for environmental remediation all have the potential to become intertwined with ethnic tensions.

Lithuanians live with the distant memory of leading great empires and a more recent memory of being absorbed into the Soviet Union. In the fourteenth century, under Grand Duke Gediminas (1316–1341) and his heirs,

Lithuania expanded south as far as Kiev and east as far as Novgorod. Between 1569 and 1795 Lithuania and Poland were ruled as a Commonwealth. Then, during the last decade of the eighteenth century, Poland was partitioned by Russia, Prussia, and Austria, and most of Lithuania fell under Russian control. Occupied by Germany during World War I, Lithuania declared its independence in the chaos after that war. Between 1918 and 1940 Lithuania was an independent nation, though slightly smaller in size than today (Figure 8.1). This experience with democracy was ended by the secret Molotov-Ribbentrop Treaty between Hitler and Stalin in 1939. Like the other Baltic republics, Lithuania was occupied by Soviet troops in June of 1940, a period of Soviet control disrupted only by German occupation between 1941 and 1945.

Lithuanian independence began anew in 1988 when scientists publicly opposed the expansion of the Ignalina nuclear power plant and thousands of Lithuanians joined in protest. The result was formation of a Lithuanian green movement, which acted as an umbrella for a wide variety of groups seeking comprehensive governmental reforms. The Green Movement prepared the way for creation of the Lithuanian Reform Movement, known as Sajudis, in 1988. Under pressure from these popular forces, Lithuania's communist government asserted limited independence, and the Communist Party eventually split into factions on the eve of elections in January 1990. Sajudis triumphed in these democratic elections, and under the leadership of Vytautas Landsbergis, the new parliament declared the restoration of Lithuania's independence. An economic blockade by the Soviet Union in 1990 and a violent attack in January of 1991 on the Vilnius television tower, radio station and publishing houses failed to discourage the parliament or Lithuanian people, who voted overwhelmingly (90.5 percent in 1991) for independence.

In September of 1991, following the failed coup attempt, the Soviet Union formally recognized Lithuania's independence. In October of 1992, Algirdas Brazauskas, head of the Lithuanian Communist Party during the early stages of the independence struggle, was returned to power, and the Sajudis-Landsbergis faction was voted out of its parliamentary majority. The 1992 "October election surprise" was seen as a response to economic uncertainty and the strong nationalist rhetoric of the Sajudis faction.

Contemporary Lithuanian culture is a combination of deeply rooted traditional cultural elements and more recent Soviet values. Added to this historical mixture is the impact of the profound political, social and economic transformations of the past five years.

Nowhere is this more apparent than in an examination of the "Baltic personality": disciplined and reasoned, friendly but cool, quietly determined, and ethnically self-conscious. These traits played a critical role in forming the tone of the firm and defiant, yet patient and flexible negotiations between Baltic independence movements and the Soviet Union. For example, facing repeated violent provocations, such as the 1991 killing of thirteen civilians by Soviet troops in Vilnius, Lithuanians exhibited extraordinary self-control and determination. They resisted the temptation of violent retaliation, which would have precipitated a massive use of Soviet force, and instead set a mod-

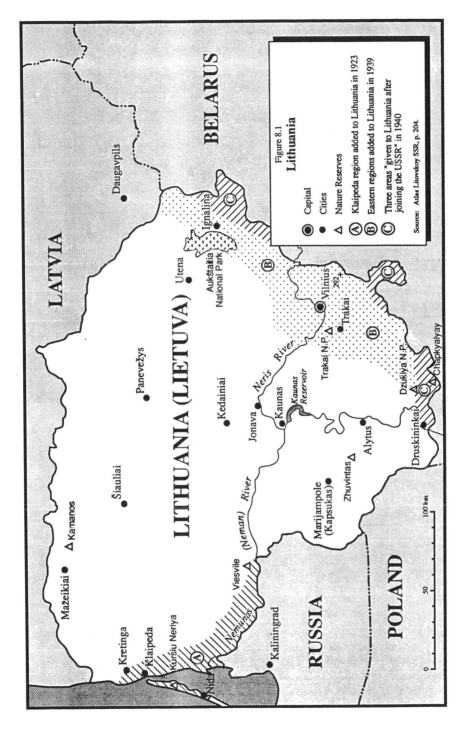

Figure 8.1
Lithuania

Capital ◉
Cities ●
Nature Reserves △

(A) Klaipeda region added to Lithuania in 1923
(B) Eastern regions added to Lithuania in 1939
(C) Three areas "given to Lithuania after joining the USSR" in 1940

Source: Atlas Litovskoy SSR, p. 204.

erate tone for Lithuania's precedent-setting independence effort. It probably helps explain why Lithuania was the first Baltic republic (in September 1993) to enjoy the removal of all Soviet military personnel from its soil.

Throughout the Lithuanian independence struggle, Lithuanians were surprised to find that the communist goal of a "new Soviet man" had not taken root as deeply as they had feared either on their own soil or in their own psyches. The "new Soviet man" was a Stalinist era concept of forging a universal socialist culture and language (Russian) and collectivist attitude. Today this concept remains a part of the Baltic cultural legacy but is most often used by individuals who self-deprecatingly refer to unwelcome characteristics in their own personalities.

Despite widespread negative characterizations of the Soviet legacy, Lithuanians remain quite fond of Russian literature, music and culture in general. But contemporary Lithuanian attitudes also reserve a special place for the more undesirable "Soviet" experiences, in particular for those responsible for forced migrations to Siberia, purges of intelligentsia, collectivization of small farms, environmental deterioration, and recent violence. It is necessary to keep in mind the extreme ambivalence that Balts have toward things Soviet and Russian if one is to understand Lithuanian society, its struggle for autonomy, and the struggle of individual Lithuanians seeking to break free from their past while maintaining some sense of continuity in their lives.

Natural Resources and Constraints to Development

Lithuania is situated on the eastern shore of the Baltic Sea and borders Latvia to the north, Belarus to the south and east, Poland to the southwest and the Kaliningrad region of Russia to the west (Figure 8.1). The 65,200 square kilometer surface area of Lithuania lies in the east European mixed forest belt but today is mostly gently elevated unforested plains. There are over 6,000 small lakes in Lithuania, half of them less than one half hectare in size and only twenty-five having a surface area of more than ten square kilometers.

Lithuania's Baltic coast is unusual and extraordinarily beautiful. Nearly half of the coastline is separated from the Baltic Sea by the Courland (Kurshskiy) Lagoon. The outer boundary of this lagoon is a long, narrow, sandy peninsula called the Courland Spit, half of which is on the territory of Kaliningrad. Its dunes and pine forests are a naturally protected region, with generally clean sandy beaches on the outer Baltic shore. These beaches are a major source of amber. During Soviet times, the nearly pristine ecology of this Baltic shore was severely threatened by intense military activity from nearby Kaliningrad, as munitions fragments sometimes mixed with amber on the beaches. In the summer of 1989, local environmental organizations collected and displayed the rubble, including bomb casings, at the resort town of Nida in order to publicize the problem (Figures 8.2 and 8.3).

Lithuania is crossed by a large number of small rivers and streams, of which the largest are the Nemunas (Neman) River, and its tributary, the Neris. Lithuania also has an abundance of clean subsurface groundwater, which provides most drinking supplies. Because Lithuania has been less in-

Figure 8.2   Recreational use of the beach along the Baltic coast of the Courland Peninsula at Nida, Lithuania. Photo courtesy of Randy Kritkausky.

Figure 8.3   Display by local Green group of beach debris, including bomb casings, collected along the coast near Nida. Photo courtesy of Randy Kritkausky.

dustrialized than many other former Soviet Republics, most of the ground-water is in relatively good condition. Agricultural runoff, not industrial chemicals, are the main contaminants of groundwater and surface water.

Twenty-eight percent of Lithuania is covered by woodlands, the majority of which are pine forests and softwoods. Bogs, once a significant part of the landscape, are now only six percent of the territory. Over the last few decades the intensification of large scale agriculture, cutting of forests, and draining of bogs has contributed to erosion and loss of soil productivity. Presently, fifteen percent of the nation's farmland is severely eroded.

Lithuania's potential energy resources are the focus of an emerging controversy. Fuel oil from Russia, natural gas from Ukraine, and electricity from the Ignalina nuclear power plant were once the energy lifelines of Lithuania. Growing concern over the safety of the Ignalina reactors and increased costs and uncertainties over the stability of oil supplies from Russia have forced Lithuania to look for alternative energy resources, preferably from internal sources. High quality oil reserves have recently been discovered off the Lithuanian Baltic coast. Although the ecological and tourist values of this coastal region present serious obstacles to petroleum development, Lithuania has decided to develop its oil reserves, to build an offshore oil terminal, and to modernize its refinery at Mažeikiai (Izvestiya, November 17, 1993).

Lithuania's other natural resources are fairly limited. Those that do exist pose certain dilemmas. Raw materials for the cement industry (limestone) and fertilizer industry (anhydrite) are abundant. So, too, is extremely high quality iron ore in the southwest. The difficulty in exploiting these resources is that many of them lie under Lithuania's remaining forests and in regions where groundwater could be easily damaged.

Aside from the above, Lithuania has few natural constraints to development. Its proximity to the Baltic Sea gives it a much milder climate than other parts of the former Soviet Union lying at the same latitude. Severe storms are rare, though drought, such as devastated Lithuanian agriculture in 1992, can periodically occur. The relative shortage of industrial raw materials is a factor of continuing concern.

Environmental Problems

Lithuania is predominantly an urban nation, with 68% of its population living in cities in 1989. Although the country has had a modest 0.8% average annual growth rate over the past twenty years, its largest cities have grown at two to three times that rate (Table 8.1).

Problems related to energy production are perhaps of greatest environmental concern. At present, Lithuanians obtain their petroleum from a refinery at Mažeikiai. It is Lithuania's largest industrial installation and a major source of sulfur dioxide and lead pollution (Banks, 1991). The refinery's supply of petroleum is from Russian wells. Only Mažeikiai's "strategic value" as a source of fuel for the Kaliningrad military installations has kept the petroleum flowing, and then only irregularly, since Lithuania regained its independence.

Table 8.1   Lithuania's largest cities

City	Population (1000s) 1970	1989	Ave. annual growth rate (%)
Vilnius	372	582	1.9
Kaunas	305	423	1.3
Klaipeda	140	204	1.5
Siauliai	93	145	2.1
Panevezys	73	126	2.1
Lithuania (total)	3128	3690	0.8

Source: 1989 Census of the USSR

Over 40% of Lithuania's electrical power is produced at the Ignalina nuclear power plant in the northeastern corner of Lithuania (Figure 8.1). Because the two reactors at this site are quite large, Lithuania produces more electrical power than it consumes, and nearly one quarter of Ignalina's output is marketed in Belarus and Latvia. Ignalina is thus a major source of hard currency.

The reactors are also a major source of domestic and international concern. Ignalina station has the largest RBMK, or Chernobyl-type, reactors in the world (1,500 MW each). Unlike other RBMKs, they have not been fully upgraded since the 1986 Chernobyl accident. The fact that Ignalina is constructed on an earthquake fault line made the attempted completion of a third reactor in 1988 an environmental and political turning point in Lithuania's history. Over 20,000 people formed a human chain around the reactor in September of 1988 in a successful demonstration preventing further expansion.

Ignalina's thermal pollution of Lake Druksiai, the largest in Lithuania, is a source of concern. The possibility of a nuclear accident is an even greater concern as the lake empties into a major Lithuanian river system. Tritium leaking from the site has added to the alarm. A history of small fires in the reactor facility has attracted international attention and some funding for safety programs from Scandinavian countries. A lack of proper on-site nuclear waste storage facilities and virtual elimination of the possibility of utilizing Russian waste disposal facilities will soon precipitate a crisis at the reactor. There will be no more space for spent fuel rods within two years.

Untreated industrial wastewater and sewage present a surface and underground water contamination potential throughout Lithuania. The Baltic port city of Klaipeda is a focus of this concern. Much of Lithuania's surface water enters the Baltic via the Nemunas River a short way south of here. Klaipeda's industry and sea traffic offer abundant opportunities for spills. Unfortunately, such accidents are common and included the breaking apart of a British tanker near Klaipeda in 1981. Klaipeda's sewage processing plant is only now being completed.

Klaipeda's water pollution problems are magnified by the fact that its pollution can be trapped in the inland waterway created by the Courland Peninsula. The threat to the Courland lagoon is enhanced by untreated industrial wastes dumped into the lagoon from the Russian controlled Kaliningrad Oblast region to the south. The lagoon has the potential to breed the same kinds of biological and health problems that have been associated with St. Petersburg's dike, which encloses that city's harbor (see Chapter 3). Unfortunately, both situations raise the same difficult questions. Unless local emissions are controlled, dangerous pollutants will become trapped behind barriers that impede normal water circulation, thereby endangering coastal populations. Until the sources of pollution are eliminated, it is likely that the flow of pollution into the already devastated Baltic Sea will increase.

The cumulative impact of industrial and sewage waste upon the Baltic Sea is magnified by the unusual nature of the Baltic. It is extremely shallow, and its waters are slow to flow into the Atlantic because of the narrow passage connecting it to the North Sea. Freshwater tends to "float" on the surface of the heavier salt water below. Consequently, pollution tends to stay concentrated at the surface. Seal kills and deadly algae formations in the Baltic have made international news in recent years. More recently, opening of Soviet-era archives has documented the dumping of chemical weapons into the Baltic at the end of World War II. Cylinders containing these wastes are now rusting through and releasing their contents.

While the inland waterways and groundwaters of Lithuania have been contaminated by untreated sewage, leakage from landfills, and agricultural runoff, these problems are easier and less costly to remedy than the persistent chemical and heavy metal contamination in the groundwater of some heavily industrialized regions such as northeastern Estonia. Much of the water pollution in Lithuania could be quickly halted by treatment facilities, landfill management, and new agricultural methods.

Another source of concern about industrial pollution in Lithuania is two chemical fertilizer factories north of Kaunas. Situated in Jonava and Kedainiai, these two giant installations produce phosphates and ammonium based fertilizers. Two problems result from the production. First, uncontrolled or improperly controlled emissions of chlorine, sulfur anhydride, fluorine, and heavy metal compounds cause chronic health problems. Nearly one quarter of the population living within 6 km of the Kedainiai facility suffers from conjunctivitis. The Kedainiai region also has Lithuania's highest rate of malignant tumors.

The second environmental problem associated with the fertilizer plants is a history of accidents. Leaking chemical storage tanks placed too closely together are a chemical time bomb. The most notable accident at these sites occurred in March of 1989 when a liquid ammonium tank broke open and exploded. A chain of fires was ignited, and the blaze was not extinguished for two days. Seven people were killed in this incident. Severe health problems were detected among local residents months after the accident.

Two environmental problems having significant human impact upon the general population are urban air pollution and food contamination. Urban air pollution in Lithuania can be threatening to human health. As in other former Soviet republics, automobiles are generally not equipped with air pollution control equipment, and trucks and buses normally pollute visibly. Official statistics indicate that about 60% of Lithuania's air pollution is caused by motorized transport. Recently, a growing market for imported used cars from Europe has introduced a large number of worn out, poorly tuned and ill-equipped vehicles. Combined with the fact that leaded gasoline is still commonly used, there is reason to be concerned about urban air pollution and particularly about lead poisoning in children. Ironically, the Soviet economic boycott in 1990 and recent interruptions of petroleum deliveries produced a temporary improvement in urban air quality. This respite alerted the public to the problems of urban air quality and mobilized some support for measures restricting traffic in the core of urban centers.

Contaminated food is a growing problem with environmental roots. The collapse of the old Soviet Sanitary Inspection Service, which was responsible for food inspection, has left a somewhat chaotic and poorly financed food inspection service in the republic to fill an enormous gap in public health protection. In this vacuum, there have appeared large amounts of unregulated food from Lithuania and neighboring countries. There is concern that some of the food brought in from Belarus may be from Chernobyl contaminated zones and represents products that could not be marketed at home. Without proper supervision and inspection, the food chain remains a potential pathway for environmental contaminants.

A balanced picture of Lithuania's environmental situation should also note some significant gains. After decades of secrecy, glasnost unleashed a flood of revelations about previously unknown ecological problems. This, however, may give the appearance of a rapidly deteriorating environmental situation in Lithuania when in fact conditions are probably beginning to stabilize or improve in many sectors.

Many of the improvements in Lithuania's environmental conditions, however, can be traced merely to the large decrease in national productivity characteristic of so many former Soviet economies. A positive result of this otherwise negative development is a dramatic reduction in the absolute volume of wastes produced in the manufacturing sector. Inefficient, noncompetitive and often wasteful production processes have been shut down. When brought back on line, they will hopefully have been modernized to operate in a more efficient, less wasteful mode. Some older factories may be the target of international buyouts and conversions, but others may be re-opened simply out of economic urgency. In any case, Lithuania's present economic conversion process may present opportunities for environmental improvement, though only time will tell to what extent this will be realized.

In certain areas, tangible environmental improvements are being made. Foreign investment banks are providing funding for such projects as wastewater treatment facilities and energy conservation programs. Comprehensive planning has begun for modern municipal and industrial waste minimization and disposal programs at the regional and national level.

Perhaps most encouraging are the multitude of microdecisions that businesses, consumers, and non-governmental organizations are making in an effort to improve the quality of the local environment. Locally initiated and funded, these programs involve environmental education, stream and landscape protection programs, and technology development. One of the most impressive examples of such activity is the upgrading of the Lapiu landfill in Kaunas. For the two decades prior to the election of "greens" to the city council in 1989, the Lapiu landfill outside Kaunas accepted a mixture of unsorted industrial and household wastes. Without a liner or leachate collection system, contaminated water ran into a local stream and the nearby Neris River. When several Greens from the Atgaya Club of Kaunas, an environmental NGO, were elected to office, they set their sights on improving operations at the landfill, hired a staff of twenty workers and stopped surface leachate runoff by using local clay. They then drilled wells on the perimeter of the site so that contamination could be monitored. Wastes were then separated so that liquids were not poured into the garbage. Recyclable materials were removed and sold. These steps, while preliminary, have reduced the damage caused by the disposal facility. The decision-making process at Kaunas reflects a productive pattern of cooperation between environmental NGOs and local officials. The improvements at the Lapiu landfill are all the more remarkable as they began during the hardships created by the Soviet economic blockade of Lithuania. They demonstrate the potential to solve environmental problems at the local level with local resources.

Environmental Management in
Independent Lithuania

During the Soviet period, Lithuania's environmental protection was in the hands of the State Committee for Nature Protection, which was responsible to the USSR Council of Ministers. In the Soviet command economy, the committee was overshadowed by the powerful economic ministries, and the goal of producing goods outweighed environmental concerns. In 1990, when the Lithuanian Environmental Protection Department replaced the Soviet Committee for Nature Protection, this new department was placed under control of the new Lithuanian parliament. It was hoped that this elevated legal status and independence would avoid many of the regulatory problems of the past.

The Lithuanian Environmental Protection Department is responsible for developing environmental policy, for enforcing laws and regulations, and for controlling the exploitation of natural resources. Lithuania has five national parks, four nature reserves, and 234 preserves, all of which are administered by the Environmental Protection Department (Table 8.2). A problem common to several of these preserved areas is that individuals whose families owned land in the area prior to 1940 are seeking to regain title.

There are eight regional agencies operating under the Environmental Pro-

Table 8.2   Preserved Areas in Lithuania

Type of Preserve(a)	Number	Total area(b)	Average size(b)	% of Republic(d)
Nature reserves	4	235.32	58.83	0.36
National parks	5	1409.00	281.80	2.16
Natural preserves (c)	174	1850.00	10.63	2.84
Total	183	3494.32	19.09	5.36

Nature Reserves (date created)	Hectares
Chapkyalyay (Čepkeliai) (1975)	10590
Kamanos (1979)	4300
Viesvile (1991)	3200
Zhuvintas (1946)	5442
Total	23532

National parks	Hectares
Aukstaitiya (1974)	30300
Dzukiya (1991)	55800
Kursiu Neriya (1991) (e)	26400
Trakai (1991)	8300
Zemaitiya (1991)	20100
Total	140900

(a) For the definition of each type of preserve, see Appendix 1.2.

(b) In square kilometers.

(c) 1985 data; the number in 1992 was about 240, covering ca. 2,500 sq. km.

(d) The area of Lithuania is 65,200 sq. kilometers.

(e) Of the total area of 26,400 ha., 16,700 is water (ocean) surface.

Source: Pryde (1991).

tection Department in Alytus, Kaunas, Klaipeda, Marijampole, Panevežys, Šiauliai, Utena, and Vilnius. In each of these regions there are district inspectorates. Larger municipalities also have inspectorates. In 1990, 371 air and water pollution cases were prosecuted or arbitrated, and 4,300,000 rubles in fines were collected. A separate environmental department exists within the government for coordinating the environmentally related functions of ministries.

Nature protection and environmental management in Lithuania are funded by fees or taxes imposed upon natural-resource-using industries engaged in activities that pollute the environment. Fees or taxes are to be increased by multiples when pollution exceeds allowable effluent levels; these were taxed at the 1992 rate of 464 rubles per ton for water pollution and five rubles per ton for air pollution. The result of this system is that Lithuania spent 0.6% of its national income on environmental protection in 1991.

One of the difficulties facing government authorities, businesses, and environmental organizations is a general lack of experience with making and enforcing environmental laws. There are few, if any, environmental lawyers in Lithuania. Environmental enforcement and management are in the early stages of developing, even as the entire governmental and civil structures of Lithuania simultaneously evolve.

During the late 1980s, environmental NGOs played an active role in formulating and influencing the enforcement of environmental laws and regulations. The Lithuanian Green Movement included top scientists and intellectuals who were able to influence action through public demonstrations, such as the 20,000 protesters who circled Ignalina in September 1988 and the milk boycott a year later. They were also adept at working behind the scenes using their expertise to influence environmental decisions. Authorities were aware that should scientific reasoning fail, a public demonstration could follow. In the late 1980s, Lithuania's officials were still unfamiliar with public protests and were still deeply concerned about how their superiors in Moscow would view the embarrassment. This pre-independence period was the high point of environmental NGO influence.

Ironically, Lithuania's environmental NGOs succeeded too well. In the elections of January 1990, many of the national environmental leaders were elected to the national parliament. These leaders soon became overwhelmed with the task of achieving national independence. Locally, in municipal and regional elections, Green leaders were elected to city councils or were appointed to administrative positions in environmental bureaucracies. The Lithuanian Green Movement's leadership was removed in a wave of democratic success. But the loss was no less devastating. Of the dozens of local Green clubs that constituted the Lithuanian Green Movement in 1989, only a handful remained in 1992.

At the same time, public concern with explicitly environmental issues, which formerly provided safe cover for more political concerns as well, went into a decline. First, independence commanded center stage. Then simple economic survival in a transition economy became nearly everyone's daily focus. While Greens in office began to implement many of their policies, such as the Kaunas landfill project discussed above, they, too, began to confront the grim realities of severely limited economic resources. In a highly competitive budgetary environment, funding for environmental programs began to decline. By 1991 and 1992, in a more democratic and independent Lithuania, Greens no longer had the organizational ability to mobilize the political support they so desperately needed.

Recognizing this need, in March of 1993 the Lithuanian Green Movement held its first congress in two years. Original Green Movement members shared the podium with new and younger aspirants. Discussions reflected a new, almost painfully deliberate dedication to democratic procedures. One young, newly elected member of the directing council offered to step aside so that a woman who had been nominated could serve. Congress participants examined the need to set a movement agenda that accommodated economic development needs along with environmental concerns. The Green Movement, which helped to nurture Lithuania's independence struggle, was rebuilding itself.

Lithuania's Green Movement shares with many government leaders a recognition that sound environmental management and enforcement practices will be possible only after a civil society has been established. Newly empowered and broad based environmental NGOs working in partnership with local and national authorities will be able to make progress on Lithuania's ecological problems as they did a few short years, but a political generation, earlier. Independence has not stopped environmental progress in Lithuania; it has simply stalled such progress in some areas.

Perhaps the final roadblock to environmental reform in Lithuania is slowed economic reform. Privatization through 1993 was slow in Lithuania and has slowed further since the election of Brazauskas. While somewhat favorable foreign investment laws are in effect, and banking policies allow for the repatriation of profits, it remains difficult, if not impossible, for foreign companies to gain title to property. Until full and free foreign investment is guaranteed, most of Lithuania's industries will not have access to the efficient processes and anti-pollution technologies that they need.

Agriculture is an area where environmental improvements can be and are being implemented with success and at a relatively low cost. Agriculture is a large part of Lithuania's economy. In 1990, it constituted twenty-five percent of the GNP (versus fifty-four for industry) but thirty-three percent of the national income, about the same as for industry. Breaking up large Soviet collective farms and redistributing the land to individual farmers are ending the era of monoculture and its reliance upon massive applications of chemical fertilizers and pesticides.

Making Lithuania's new agricultural sector economically stable is an issue mitigating against environmental reforms. In many cases, private farms have been made almost unmanageably and unproductively small. Equipment for small farms is in short supply. Russia, which in the past supplied livestock feed grains to Lithuania's animal husbandry industry, has reduced its shipments. Productivity in this sector, which represents sixty-nine percent of Lithuania's agricultural productivity, has dropped in the past two years. And in the absence of good sanitary inspection and monitoring of food supplies, market incentives for providing commodities that are not tainted with nitrates and pesticides remains small.

Balancing Economic Development and Environmental Preservation

Lithuania's future economic development focuses upon balancing a number of difficult energy production and environmental risk considerations. Continued operation of the Ignalina nuclear power plant and development of off-shore oil reserves could provide Lithuania with an energy supply capable of supporting industrialization. However, the environmental risks associated with this strategy, as outlined above, are enormous. In the case of the Ignalina reactor, the danger is potentially catastrophic, as a Chernobyl-scale accident could devastate a small country. As an alternative, turning away from further energy development and instead promoting energy conservation techniques could provide Lithuania with sufficient power for a modern agriculture-based economy.

Agricultural development is inviting to many Lithuanians as it ties into traditional Lithuanian values. As Lithuania is relatively unindustrialized, this development path would not be a radical departure. In fact, several of Lithuania's main industries, such as fertilizer production, are agriculturally related. As Lithuania's land is largely unpolluted, the opportunities to capitalize upon this resource and preserve it are inviting. Agriculture is a sector where Lithuania could practice sustainable development. Making Lithuania's agricultural products succeed in a highly competitive world market will be part of the formula for successful sustainable development in Lithuania.

Tourism presents a rich opportunity for Lithuania, both economically and environmentally. Germans have just rediscovered Lithuania's exceptional Baltic coast, and their hard currency is a major contribution to the republic's national economy. Lithuania's lake regions, such as around Aukštaitia National Park, could provide a similar resource with relatively few environmentally damaging trade-offs.

Lithuanians also discuss the possibility of utilizing their highly trained, and comparatively inexpensive, labor force to attract high technology industries and convert the existing industrial infrastructure. Such a strategy might complement an agricultural and tourism based economy and still preserve Lithuania's environment.

All of Lithuania's critical development decisions, and therefore its environmental future, depend upon when and how the country is integrated into the regional and global economy. Some of the decisions are already being made for Lithuania by external factors. Multinational banks have imposed budgetary and currency restrictions. These same institutions have imposed energy pricing demands upon Russia, which has used the opportunity to apply economic pressure on the rebellious Baltic republics.

Because of historical ties with the Soviet Union, Lithuania's trade situation and economic future are largely tied to that of Russia and other former Soviet republics, at least in the short term. But Lithuania is currently looking west-ward to Europe and especially north to the Scandinavian countries. The Danes, who are beginning to position themselves as the bridge between the West and the Baltic states, are becoming much more actively involved in the Baltics, forming joint ventures, acquiring property, and establishing cultural links. There is discussion among the three Baltic countries of forming a Baltic common market. But recent discussions concerning cooperative energy projects between Lithuania and Latvia, whereby Latvia would provide a petroleum depot at Ventspils and Lithuania would refine the oil at Mažeikiai, suggest an atmosphere of suspicion as much as a common Baltic interest.

Events over the past five years in Lithuania suggest that it is impossible to imagine where this republic will go. The world, excluding former Soviet leaders, has still not fully grasped and appreciated the role that Lithuania played in breaking open the Soviet empire. But it is clear to all that Lithuanians have a remarkable ability and a ferocious determination when it comes to reclaiming control of their own destiny. Exhausted after five years of living on the brink of a revolutionary abyss, Lithuanians are turning inward temporarily. Private homes, many of them in a grand style and scale that will undoubtedly be known someday as "post-independence celebration architecture," are springing up across the countryside and at the perimeters of cities. Even before they are completed, these homes begin to show signs of gardens being planned and planted as Lithuanians reconnect to household and nature. Lithuanians are affirming their cultural idea of a self-sustaining homestead.

Greeks used the word *oikos* to refer to this notion of a self-sufficient home. In English, we have derived the terms *ecology* and *economics* from the Greek word. In recent times, these two abstractions have been presented as polar opposites in many Western development debates. But Lithuanians, and other peoples of Eurasia, have talked of remarrying these two ideas and finding a new economic development path, "a third way," that avoids the environmental devastation of both capitalist and socialist societies. Lithuania is fertile ground for such a new experiment.

Bibliography

Aplinkos bukle, kitimo tendencijos, aplinkos apsaugos valdymas. Vilnius: Environment Protection Agency of Lithuania, 1992.

Atlas Litovskoy SSR. Moscow: GUGK, 1981.

Banks, A. *Lithuania's Environmental Problems.* Sandy Bay, Tasmania: Lithuanian Studies Society, 1991.

Bronius, K. *Musu Lietuva.* (Vol. 1). Vilnius: Lietuvos Enciklopedijos Leidykla, 1964.

Fenhann, J. *Energy and Environment in Estonia, Latvia and Lithuania.* Roskilde, Denmark: Riso National Laboratory, 1991.

Feshbach, M., and A. Friendly Jr. *Ecocide in the USSR.* New York: Basic Books, 1992.

Lietuva: Trumpas zinynas. Vilnius: Lithuanian Information Institute, 1992.

Lithuania—Information sheets. Vilnius: State Encyclopedia Publishers, 1992.

Mnatsakanian, R. A. *Environmental Legacy of the Former Soviet Republics.* Edinburgh: Centre for Human Ecology, 1992.

Natsional'nyy doklad, SSSR k konferentsii OON 1992 goda o okruzhayushchey sredi i pazvitiyu. Moscow: Goskompriroda, 1991, pp. 278–285.

Peterson, D. J. *Troubled Lands: The Legacy of Soviet Environmental Destruction.* Boulder: Westview Press, 1993, pp. 244–247.

Pryde, P. R. *Environmental Management in the Soviet Union.* Cambridge: Cambridge Univ. Press, 1991.

Sapoka, A., ed. *Lietuvas istorija.* Vilnius: Mokslas Publ., 1990.

Vardys, V. S. *Lithuania: A Rebel Nation.* Boulder: Westview Press, 1994.

World Conservation Union, East European Programme. *Environmental Status Reports, 1993: Estonia, Latvia, Lithuania.* Gland, Switzerland: IUCN, 1993.

9

Ukraine

Ihor Stebelsky

Among the republics of the former Soviet Union, Ukraine had the second largest population and economic importance; and, in reflection of this, it is discussed in two chapters. Chapter 9 will discuss the physical and historical background of the country and outline its main environmental problems. Chapter 10 will examine the various laws and institutions that have been developed to address these environmental concerns, as well as some of their shortcomings.

Located north of the Black Sea, Ukraine is the second largest country in area in Europe and, after Russia and Kazakhstan, the third largest in the former Soviet Union. In population, it is the second largest republic in the former USSR, but in Europe it ranks sixth after Russia, Germany, Italy, the United Kingdom, and France. It shares a boundary with Russia to the east and northeast and with Belarus to the north, and in the west, from north to south, lie Poland, Slovakia, Hungary, Romania and Moldova. As a former Soviet republic, Ukraine is a member of the Commonwealth of Independent States and has been a member of the United Nations since 1945. Since the demise of the USSR, Ukraine has transformed its role in the United Nations and other international bodies from reflecting Soviet policies to promoting an independent position. Its government is seeking peaceful resolutions to regional tensions at home and abroad. Pressured by the reformist opposition, the presidency is pursuing economic reforms, but the process is hampered by a majority of the legislators and most of the administrators, carryovers from the old regime who are reluctant to relinquish their former Communist bureaucratic power.

Ethnicity and History

Ukraine is inhabited mostly by ethnic Ukrainians. According to the January 12, 1989, Soviet census, of the 51.7 million inhabitants of Ukraine, 37.4 million (72.3 percent) were ethnically Ukrainian; the others comprised a large variety of minorities. Russians (11.4 million, or 22.1 percent) were by far the largest minority group. Jews and Poles, formerly much more numerous than at present, numbered about 0.5 and 0.2 million (0.9 and 0.4 percent), respectively. Conversely, 6.8 million Ukrainians lived in the rest of the former Soviet Union, mostly in Russia (4.4 million), Kazakhstan (0.9 million), Moldova (0.6 million), Belarus (0.3 million), and Central Asia (0.3 million).

Ukrainians are also found in large numbers in Poland (presently about 400,000), Slovakia (about 150,000) and Romania (over 250,000). There are also about 755,000 in Canada, probably 1 million or more in the United States, up to 400,000 in Brazil, up to 250,000 in Argentina, and smaller numbers in western Europe and Australia.

Minorities settled in Ukraine mostly as a result of a long history of various empires implementing policies of colonization. The Polish-Lithuanian state (16th–17th centuries) encouraged the acquisition of lands by Polish nobility and small gentry and the employment of skilled Jews (who had come from Germany in the 13–14th centuries). The Turkic-speaking Muslim Crimean Tatars originated from the Mongol-Tatar invasion (13th century), as did the Turks who accepted Orthodox Christianity and became known as the Gagauz. Gypsies have long wandered through Ukraine. Thousands of Hungarians and Romanians are located along Ukraine's border with these two countries.

Under the Russian Empire (18th–19th centuries), the southern steppes of Ukraine were colonized in part by Russian peasantry and military, as well as by invited German (mostly Mennonite) colonists and Bulgarian, Moldavian and Greek immigrants. Many of the Germans had immigrated to the west by the late 1920s or were removed in 1941 to Kazakhstan and Siberia. During the Soviet period, Ukraine received a large influx of Russian specialists and managers while losing its own to Russia and other republics. Along with the Russians also came Russian-speaking Belorussians, Volga Tatars, Azeris and others to fill managerial or worker positions in the industrial cities of Ukraine. Western Ukraine, when part of inter-war Poland, had acquired a large influx of Polish colonists, most of whom were "patriated" after World War II to Poland.

The history of Ukraine extends back well over a millennium. By the 8th century, the city of Kiev had grown in economic and political importance to become the center of a new political power: Rus. The establishment of the Rus principality in Kiev in the 9th century began the process of replacing tribal loyalties with the broader Rus identity. This process was strengthened by Prince Vladimir's adoption (988) of Byzantine Christianity as a state religion and its propagation, in the Old Church Slavonic, among the Slavic tribes of the Dnipro (Dnepr) River basin.

The subsequent Mongol-Tatar invasion (1237–1241) devastated the southeastern principalities and brought about a political realignment. In the ensuing centuries, Muscovy arose as a protectorate of the Mongol-Tatars, while Lithuania, Poland and Hungary annexed the western principalities of Rus. The old Rus elites were absorbed into these kingdoms' Roman Catholic landed gentry, while the masses were subjected to serfdom.

Ukraine's struggle for independence gained momentum with the emergence of a new identity among Cossacks in the steppe frontier. Protective of their freedom and proud of their Orthodox Christianity, the Cossacks gathered beyond the Dnepr rapids, where they organized a democratic-military order that fought both the marauding Tatars and Turks and the haughty Roman Catholic Polish gentry. Their elected leader, Bohdan Khmelnytsky (1595–1657), led a military campaign against Poland that ended in the establishment of a short-lived Cossack state. The territory of this state became known as Ukraine (literally, "the borderland"). This Cossack state was partitioned and its hetmanates (territories governed by their own elected hetmans) eventually became restless protectorates of Poland and Muscovy. By 1795 most of Ukraine had been absorbed into the Russian Empire, although the southwestern portion became part of the Austro-Hungarian Empire.

The identity of the people as Ukrainians emerged in conjunction with the name of their land, Ukraine, and became consolidated with their opposition to Muscovite expansionism. When Muscovy, transformed into the Russian Empire, subordinated the Hetmanate (late 18th century) into a province called Little Russia and bound the Cossacks in serfdom, the desire for freedom increased. In the 19th century, growing interest in folk culture, the development of a vernacular Ukrainian literature, and especially the poetry of Ukrainian bard Taras Shevchenko gave rise to modern Ukrainian national consciousness. By the end of the 19th century, most of the so-called Little Russians of the Russian Empire and even the Ruthenians of Galicia in the Austro-Hungarian Empire considered themselves Ukrainian.

Following World War I, with the collapse of both the Russian autocracy and the Austro-Hungarian Empire, Ukraine engaged in a brief struggle for independence (1917–20), losing to the Red Army of Russia, which incorporated the larger part of Ukraine as the Ukrainian Soviet Socialist Republic within the USSR (1923). The western territories of Ukraine were absorbed by Poland, Czechoslovakia, and Romania. As a result of the Hitler-Stalin pact and the events of World War II, the Soviet Union extended its territory westward, annexing most of the earlier Ukrainian territories into the USSR, nearly all of which became part of the Soviet Ukrainian SSR, and now Ukraine. In 1954, Khrushchev transferred the Crimean Peninsula from the Russian Republic back to Ukraine.

Physical Environment and Natural Constraints

Occupying the southern portion of the Eastern European Plain, Ukraine consists mostly of lowlands and gently rolling uplands that seldom rise above 500 meters. Except for the coast of the Black Sea and the Sea of Azov, Ukraine does not have any obvious physical boundaries. There are two mountain systems, consisting of the Carpathian range (rising to 1,700–2,000 m) in the west and the Crimean range (1,000–1,500 m) in the south (Figure 9.1).

The climate of Ukraine is temperate, cool and semi-continental. Temperatures increase from north to south, with mean annual temperatures of about 6°C at the Russia-Ukraine border, about 10°C in Odessa, and about 12°C in Yalta. Continentality increases eastward with distance from the Atlantic

144

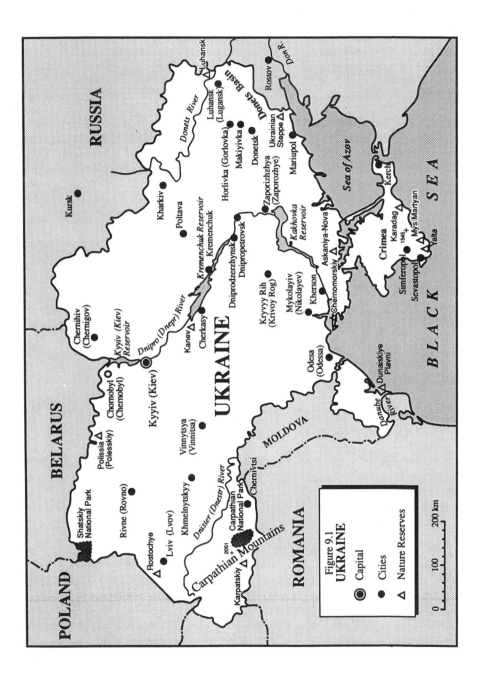

Figure 9.1
UKRAINE
◎ Capital
● Cities
△ Nature Reserves

Ocean, manifesting itself in colder winters, warmer summers, and increased annual ranges in temperature. There is an increase in aridity from north to south, which presents the potential for dust storms. The mean January temperatures are nearly everywhere below freezing (−1 to −8°C). Only the southern coast of Crimea, sheltered by its mountains from the cold air masses in the north, remains free of frost. The mean July temperatures range from 24°C in the south to 19°C in the northwest and to 16°C in the higher Carpathian Mountains.

Precipitation in Ukraine decreases from about 800 mm in the west to about 450 mm in the east and 300 mm or less along the coast of the Black Sea lowland but can be as high as 1,200 mm in the Carpathian Mountains. The monthly maximums occur either in June or July. Whereas in western Ukraine winter precipitation is substantial, in eastern Ukraine frequent high pressure blocks the eastward flow of maritime air masses and results in meager snow cover, especially in the south. In the spring and summer, the occasional invasion of continental tropical air from Central Asia may be accompanied by a hot, drying wind, known as the *sukhovii*, which can wilt crops in a matter of hours and in severe cases lead to dust storms.

Variations in climate and topography have resulted in a natural zonation of soils and vegetation. In the north, the glaciated and poorly drained lowland, known as Polissia, comprises a mosaic of forested or swampy ecosystems best left in a natural state.

South of Polissia is the forest-steppe zone, which is characterized by thick, rich soils. In the cooler, more humid areas, gray forest soils support deciduous forests. Further south are found the fertile chernozem soils, which originally supported a brightly flowering meadow steppe and forested steppe. Much of the forest and nearly all of the steppe have been transformed into cultivated land, which has produced much food but also resulted in biotic depletions, erosion, and water pollution.

South of the forest-steppe is the steppe. This broad grassland zone, which extends south to the Black Sea, may be subdivided into several subzones of increasing aridity. The northern subzone is characterized by rich, prairie chernozems, which are now largely in agriculture. South of this is a drier belt of southern chernozems with increasing accumulations of salts; the natural vegetation here was narrow-leaved fescue and feather grass steppe. Along the Black and Azov Seas, and in the Crimean lowland, are chestnut soils with considerable salt accumulations, overlain by a dry grassy steppe.

In the mountain province there is altitudinal zonation of soils and vegetation. The Carpathian Mountains have deciduous and mixed forests typical of the central European forest belt. At higher elevations, the forests include more beech, silver fir and spruce; the highest elevations support Alpine meadows.

The Crimean Mountains are characterized by oak, beech, hornbeam, and various pines. The highest elevations support pastures of low, thick grass. The southern slopes, at lower elevations, support a Mediterranean type of vegetation, including oak, juniper, cypress, magnolia, stone pine, olive and myrtle trees. To preserve portions of these diverse natural communities, a network of mostly small nature preserves, plus three national parks, has been created. These are presented in Table 9.1. Additional information on them is presented in Chapter 10.

Ukraine has few physical constraints to development. Except for the mountainous zones in the Carpathians and Crimea, where seismic activity is common, the East European platform to the northeast is geologically stable. Areas that may hinder agricultural development, such as marshes or steep, mountainous slopes, are small. Somewhat larger areas of podzolic soils, though not inherently fertile, may be improved for agricultural production. Perhaps more limiting to agriculture are the areas of the southern steppe that contain saline chestnut soils.

The greatest natural limitation to agriculture in Ukraine is the dry climate of the steppe. Here, in this warmest part of Ukraine, drought may occur as a prolonged period without rain and can result from the *sukhovii* (a hot, desiccating wind that occurs on the average 24–30 days/year). The more intense ones can cause damage to crops within hours. Strong easterly winds may cause dust storms (3–8 days/year), removing the fine particles of dry topsoil and transporting it great distances or building up dunes of coarse materials that cover up and suffocate young crops (see Figure 16.2).

Other weather hazards common to agriculture include early and late frosts, winter kills of winter wheat, and, in the summer, thunderstorms with torrential downpours and damaging hail. Thunderstorms are common in the steppe and forest-steppe (25–30 days/year) and in the Carpathians (up to 40 days/year), where they can produce damaging floods.

The greatest emerging physical constraint for agriculture, industry and municipal needs is the growing shortage of water. Both surface waters and groundwater depend on precipitation, most of which evaporates or infiltrates into the ground. Surface runoff in Ukraine is scanty. Only the Dnipro (Dnepr) River, with an average annual discharge of 40 km³/yr, is suitable for multipurpose river basin development. The Dnister (Dnestr) River, by contrast, discharges only 7–8 km³/yr, and the fluctuating flow is unreliable for navigation or power. Even less useful is the Donets (a tributary of the Don River), which releases a mere 4–5 km³/yr.

Natural Resources

Ukraine has a wealth of natural resources. Runova (1986) estimated that Ukraine, with an area only 2.7 percent of the former USSR, accounted for 13.1 percent of its combined mineral, hydroelectric, forest and agricultural land resources, including 18.2 percent of the agricultural land and 8.6 percent of the mineral resources. If the quality of Ukraine's resources is taken into account, then their true value becomes even greater. Thus Ukraine produced in the 1980s over 22 percent of the value of agricultural production and generated over 17 percent of the electrical power in the USSR.

Ukraine's fossil fuel resources have been significantly depleted. Only the coal deposits, especially the coking coals of the Donets basin, are still rated exceptionally significant, accounting for more than 25 percent of the former

Table 9.1   Preserved Areas in Ukraine

Type of Preserve(a)	Number	Total area(b)	Average size(b)	% of Re-public(d)
Zapovidnyky (Nature Reserves)(c)	1 2	1441.31	120.11	0.24
Above, that are Biosphere Reserve:	2	1206.55	603.28	0.20
National Parks(c)	3	1235.03	664.02	0.20
Zakazniki(c)	1103	4249.00	3.85	0.70
Total(c)	1118	6925.34	6.19	1.15

Zapovidnyky (date created)	Hectares
Askaniya-Nova (1921; 1874)	11054
Chernomorskiy (1927)	57048
Dunaiskiye Plavni (1981; 1973)	14851
Kanev (1968; 1931)	1035
Karadag (1979)	1370
Karpatskiy (1968)	18544
Lugansk (1968)	1580
Mys Mart'yan (1973)	240
Polesskiy (1968)	20104
Rastoch'ye (1984)	2080
Ukrainskiy Stepnoy (1961; 1926)	1634
Yaltinskiy (1973)	14591
Total	144131

National Parks	Hectares
Karpatskiy (1980)	50303
Shatskiy (1983)	32800
Sinevir (1989)	40400
Total	123503

(a) For the definition of each type of preserve, see Appendix 1.2.

(b) In square kilometers.

(c) Data are for 1990; new nature reserves and national parks have been created since 1991.

(d) Area of Ukraine is 603,700 sq. kilometers.

Sources: Pryde (1991);   Okhrana (1991).

USSR total. Even so, the most easily minable seams have been exhausted. The production of natural gas in Ukraine accounted for about 33 percent of the Soviet output in 1964 but dropped to 4 percent by 1989, while petroleum declined from 2.6 to 0.9 percent. There are abundant quantities of low pressure natural gas in Ukraine, but technologies are not yet available to harness it. For the nuclear power industry, Ukraine possesses very large graphite deposits (about 50 percent of the former Soviet total) and substantial uranium deposits. As graphite-moderated reactors are now considered unsafe, the future of this industry is questionable.

Ukraine has some of the richest deposits of iron ore (31 percent of the former Soviet total) and even larger deposits of the alloying metal manganese (70 percent). It also has rich deposits of mercury, as well as some titanium, bauxite, alunite, chromite, nickel, lead, zinc, copper, and gold. For the chemical industry, Ukraine possesses about 10 percent of the former USSR's common salts, 5.3 percent of the potash, and large deposits of magnesium salts and phosphorites. Ukraine is especially well endowed with kaolin clay, refractory clays, and limestones and has quartzite sands for glassmaking, quality granites, and a variety of precious stones. Mineral waters are found in the Carpathians and also in Crimea, where they combine with a coastal setting and a mild climate for outstanding resort and recreational opportunities.

Most of Ukraine has been cleared of its natural vegetation for agriculture, but forests still occupy 8.6 million ha (over 14 percent of the area), largely due to an active reforestation program. Ukrainian forests are particularly valuable because of their relatively fast growth, and because of the presence of hardwoods (15 percent of the oak, 20 percent of the beech and 10 percent of the ash stands in the former USSR). Conifers (pine, fir, and spruce), however, represent 54 percent of Ukraine's forest fund. Almost 40 percent of Ukraine's forest fund is in deciduous hardwoods (oak, beech, and hornbeam). Only 7 percent is occupied by softwood deciduous species, such as birch, aspen, alder, linden and poplar.

Agricultural land occupies over 41.8 million ha, or about 70 percent of the total land area of Ukraine. Of the land used for agricultural purposes, 81.7 percent is plowed and 15.8 percent is in hayfields and pasture.

The quality of Ukraine's agricultural resources may be appreciated in terms of the republic's contribution to the former USSR's total: 7.5 percent of the agricultural land but 15.0 percent of the land in crops, 22.6 percent of the total value of agricultural production, 25.9 percent of all vegetables, 26.0 percent of all grains, 26.7 percent of potatoes, 32.2 percent of flax fiber, 40.8 percent of sunflower seeds, and 53.3 percent of sugar beets. The feed base supports a large share of the former USSR's farm animals, such as cattle (21.3 percent), pigs (25.3 percent), and fowl (21.0 percent). As a result, Ukraine contributed about 22.0 percent of the USSR's meat, 22.5 percent of the milk, and 20.5 percent of the eggs.

Industrial Development

Modern industrial development began in Ukraine during the 19th century and was based almost entirely on raw material extraction and primary processing. Capital raised by the local gentry was used to construct grist milling, sugar refining, and some food processing industries. French, British and Belgian capital was invested to mine the Donets basin (Donbas) coking coal and Kryvyy Rih (Krivoy Rog) iron ore, smelt the iron ore, and build some heavy machinery in the southeastern part of Ukraine.[1] The Russian government funded the building of the railways. Ukraine's raw material resources and primary products were encouraged to move to manufacturing centers in central Russia (mainly Moscow and St. Petersburg), thus retarding the development of manufacturing industries other than steel in Ukraine. Even less industrialization occurred in western Ukraine under the Austro-Hungarian Empire. Here, the main industrial development involved lumbering and woodworking and petroleum extraction in the Carpathian foothills funded by British capital.

After World War I, in Soviet Ukraine a concerted effort was made to expand heavy industry. The fastest growth occurred in the development of steel production and heavy machine-building and metalworking. Despite Ukraine's more productive industries, a policy of developing new resources in the eastern regions of the USSR was initiated in the 1930s and acquired urgent strategic considerations just before and during World War II. As a result, the national share of Ukraine's industrial output began to decline in comparison to that of Russia. The industrial base, of course, was largely destroyed during the war.

Following World War II, Ukrainian industrial capacities were quickly rebuilt. The industries that developed rapidly during this period included basic chemicals (chemical fertilizers, sulfuric acid, cellulose), tractors and automobiles, aircraft and electronic instrument making. The steel industry, destroyed during the war, was rebuilt and expanded. The post-war industrial expansion caused many cities to increase rapidly in size (see Appendix 9.1). In the 1980s a policy emerged to develop energy- and water-saving industries and processes, reflecting resource scarcities that are impacting certain industries, cities, or entire regions of Ukraine.

The generation of electricity is indicative of the emerging constraints in energy resources. Electric power generation has increased forty times since World War II to meet the growing industrial needs of Ukraine as well as some energy export.

At first, electricity was generated from coal-fired power stations. On the eve of World War II, the Dnipro (Dnepr) Hydro-Electric Power Station (Dniprohes), located near Zaporizhzhya, entered production, and from the 1950s to the 1970s additional dams were built on the Dnipro. However, the share of their contribution to Ukrainian electrical production declined (from 17 percent in 1950 to 4 percent in 1989), as most of the growth in electricity generation came from giant regional coal-fired stations, atomic power stations, and urban heat and power plants.

By the 1970s, the Soviet nuclear power–generating program required the construction of several nuclear power plants in Ukraine, including the Chornobyl (Chernobyl), Rivne (Rovno), South Ukrainian, Zaporizhzhya (Zaporozhe), Khmelnytskyy, and Crimea stations. In 1992, the potential generating capacity of the nuclear power stations in Ukraine stood at 14,880 megawatts, with sixteen reactors available for service (Table 9.2). However, several of

Table 9.2   Nuclear Power Stations Operating in Ukraine
            (as of July 1992)

Station	Reactor Type	Location	Number of Reactors	Capacity (megawatts)
Chornobyl	RBMK-1000	Prypyat	3	3,000
Rivne (Rovno)	VVER-440/1000	Kuznetsov	3*	1,880
South Ukraine	VVER-1000	Prybuzhzhya	3	3,000
Zaporizhzhya	VVER-1000	Energodar	5*	5,000
Khmelnytskyy	VVER-1000	Netyshyn	2*	2,000
TOTAL				**14,880**

* The Rivne, South Ukraine, and Khmelnytskyy complexes each has an additional 1,000 MW reactor that has been completed but cannot be started up because of a moratorium on bringing new units online.

Sources: Marples, 1992; Pryde, 1991, pp. 36 - 40; and Post-Soviet Geography, vol. 32, no. 4 (April 1991), pp. 285 - 289.

them, including all the units at Chornobyl, were either temporarily or permanently shut down as of 1992.

There are a number of environmental implications from such a rapid buildup of electrical generating capacity. First, there is the problem of air pollution from coal-fired generating plants: the need for efficient scrubbers, the use of low-sulfur coal, or the replacement of coal with cleaner natural gas. Second, there is the problem of the exhaustion of cooling water resources in Ukraine. Third, in the aftermath of Chornobyl, there is the public fear that, because of shoddy workmanship in the original construction and inadequately trained personnel, another nuclear power plant accident is likely to happen (Marples, 1986).

Environmental Problems

The intensive utilization of land for agriculture and the heavy industrialization of Ukraine have brought about losses of plants and animals, degradation of the soil, and the pollution of air, water and land. Soviet government priorities of rapid development at minimum expenditure have tended to exacerbate pollution and industrial hazards.

For over a century, erosion has been one of Ukraine's most serious environmental problems. The expansion of cultivation on sloping lands has accelerated water erosion, gullying, the disappearance of small streams, and the loss of the rich loess-based chernozems. The clearing of the steep slopes of the Carpathian and Crimean foothills has resulted in severe erosion and flooding. Continuous cultivation of the dry steppes has resulted in wind erosion, and neither the planting of windbreaks nor improved tilling methods have eliminated this problem. The ill-advised drainage of the sandy soils of Polissia (in northern Ukraine) has brought about desiccation and wind erosion.

Irrigation in the dry steppe, by contrast, has resulted in waterlogging, soil salination, and degradation of the fertile chernozems. Agricultural chemicals have contaminated soils with pesticide residues and polluted both surface water and groundwater with nitrates and other chemicals. This condition is particularly acute in the southern steppes, where the heavy use of chemicals resulted in the 1980s in some of the highest rates of morbidity and mortality in Ukraine (Dorohuntsov, 1991). Chemical pollution has been intensified by the limited assortment of herbicides and pesticides available, their improper application, inadequate use of biological methods of pest control, and imbalanced application of mineral fertilizers.

Mining and primary processing have had a severe impact on land, water and air quality. In the Donets-Dnipro industrial region, some 250,000 ha of land have been disturbed by the mining of coal, iron ore, manganese and other minerals. Another 5,000 ha of land are lost annually to industrial waste storage and the disposal of slag (Zastavnyi, 1990, p. 212). Mercury is one of the most highly toxic of all minerals, and the Soviet Union's second largest mercury mines were located at Nikitovka, north of Horlivka. This is in one of the most highly polluted regions of Ukraine.

Smelting, thermal-electric power generation and chemical production have led to severe air pollution, including high emissions of oxides of nitrogen and sulfur, which have resulted in acid precipitation. Smelting, in particular, has contributed to heavy metal contamination of the areas surrounding several metallurgical cities. Automobiles, fueled by leaded gasoline and devoid of pollution control equipment, are major sources of air pollution in otherwise less industrialized cities, such as Kyyiv (Kiev), Lviv (Lvov), Vinnytsya (Vinnitsa), or Yalta. Such cities as Dniprodzerzhynsk, Donetsk, Mariupol, Zaporizhzhya (Zaporozhe), Dnipropetrovsk, Kryvyy Rih (Krivoy Rog), Kyyiv, Odesa (Odessa), Alchevsk (formerly Kommunarsk), Makiyivka, and others were listed in environmental documents in 1989 as particularly polluted (Pryde, 1991, Chap. 2; *Okhrana*, 1991, pp. 43–45). The cities with the most serious problems are shown in Table 9.3.

To reduce emissions from coal-burning power plants, the United States is currently assisting Ukraine with a process called reburning. This technology, initially applied at the Ladyzhin power plant, is designed to reduce the output of oxides of nitrogen.

Water pollution is equally a serious problem. Many large industrial enterprises and some municipalities have failed to treat some of their effluent, leading to the pollution of surface water with oxygen-depleting organic matter, phosphates, nitrates, cyanides, ammonia, phenols, PCBs and heavy metals. This has impacted not only potable water supplies but also river and coastal fisheries and the safety of water for swimming. Rivers flowing

Table 9.3   Most Polluted Ukrainian Cities

City (Russian spelling/name)	Air pollutants (1000 tons) (a)		
	1985	1987	1990
1. Kryvyy Rih (Krivoy Rog)	1314.2	1290.0	1041.7
2. Mariupol' (Zhdanov)	814.3	785.8	610.2
3. Makiyivka (Makeyevka)	375.0	318.8	305.2
4. Dniprodzerzhynsk (Dneprodzerzhinsk)	370.4	337.0	268.2
5. Dnipropetrovsk (Dnepropetrovsk)	354.3	321.2	254.1
6. Zaporizhzhya (Zaporozhe)	302.1	286.9	246.4
7. Alchevs'k (Kommunarsk)	369.1	251.4	187.8
8. Donetsk	208.1	192.8	171.0
9. Kremenchuk (Kremenchug)	174.9	194.2	151.4
10. Lysychansk (Lisichansk)	120.5	132.2	129.1
11. Yenakiyeve (Yenakievo)	136.5	120.8	125.4
12. Odesa (Odessa)	124.5	105.6	80.6
13. Kyyiv (Kiev)	99.2	93.7	54.7
14. Cherkasy (Cherkassy)	64.4	62.4	31.5

(a) From stationary sources only

Source: Okhrana okruzhayushchey ... (1991), pp. 43-45.

Note: Some major cities and important industrial centers, such as Kharkiv, Lviv, Luhansk, Kramatorsk, and Stakhanov, were not included in the list.

through heavily industrialized areas, such as the Donets, have become open sewers. Pollution of the Donets River contaminated the drinking water of Kharkiv (Kharkov) for years. Coastal resorts, concentrated in Crimea and along the Black Sea and Azov Sea littoral, have been affected by beach closures. Even groundwater, the main source of drinking water in southern Ukraine, is being threatened by critical levels of fertilizer, herbicide and pesticide pollution. Kyyiv's water supply may have been contaminated by fallout from Chornobyl. Cholera and cancer rates were unusually high in the Odesa region in the 1970s and 1980s (Feshbach and Friendly, 1992, pp. 124–125).

Pollution of the Black and Azov Seas is another growing problem. The Black Sea is polluted from chemicals flowing down the rivers that feed into it, from cities along its coast, and from boats that traverse it. As a result, toxic hydrogen sulfide levels are building up in the sea, and beaches near Mariupol, Odesa, and elsewhere have to be periodically closed. Oxygen supplies, necessary for fish life and confined to the upper 100 meters of the sea, are being depleted.

The shallow Sea of Azov is in even worse condition and is often described as dying. Its once abundant fishery is almost gone. It suffers from pesticides and nutrients from farming operations and from exceptionally high readings of such serious pollutants as mercury, ammonia, phenols, surfactants, and sulfur compounds. An introduced parasite has reportedly killed up to 80 percent of the plankton in the sea (Mnatsakanian, 1992, p. 53).

Perhaps the greatest environmental problem in Ukraine presently is the aftermath of the Chornobyl (Chernobyl) accident, the long-term exposure to radiation, and the hazard of a similar accident in the future. Although the official death toll from acute radiation exposure at the time of the accident stood at 31, the unofficial count of deaths (attributed mostly to work on radioactive cleanup) has ranged from 4,000 to 10,000 (Feshbach and Friendly, 1992, p. 146). Since the prevailing winds at the time of the reactor fire were from the southeast, the city of Kyyiv (2.5 million people) was spared, and the heaviest radioactive fallout became concentrated mainly in areas north of the reactor. Within Ukraine, rain deposited hot spots of radioactivity to the west in Polissia, to the Belarus border to the north, and to scattered locations of central Ukraine to the south of Kyyiv. Surveys indicate that the heaviest contamination with radioactive cesium occupies about 10,000 km^2, of which 7,000 km^2 is in Ukraine and the rest in Belarus. This zone contained 640 settlements with a population of about 250,000 (Zastavnyi, 1990, p. 225). To date, over 100,000 persons have had to be relocated out of the most highly contaminated regions of Ukraine. In the late 1980s, the undamaged reactors were put back into service, but in 1992 following independence, all units at the Chornobyl plant were shut down. However, the critical need for electrical energy caused the Ukrainian parliament in 1993 to order all available units back on line for the foreseeable future. Further, work on additional units at other nuclear power plant sites was reauthorized, after having been stopped for several years.

At the time of the accident, the Soviet authorities treated the event with secrecy and callous indifference to public welfare. When the accident became known internationally, an administrative approach was taken to evacuate a 30 km radius zone. There was great reluctance to evacuate all areas severely affected by radiation, and even by 1990 a number of such areas outside the 30 km zone had not yet been evacuated, and their records of morbidity had been suppressed. Food was not carefully screened for radioactivity, and farming in contaminated areas was encouraged to continue. Radioactivity in the Prypiat (Pripyat) River, the Kyyiv Reservoir on the Dnipro River (a source of drinking water for millions), and in the Dnipro River itself as it flows toward Kyyiv has been officially termed as being at "acceptable levels," but many

informed people question this (Figure 9.2; see also Figure 10.1). The Prypiat
River is so close to the reactor that contamination had to have occurred, and
the bottom sediments in the Kyyiv Reservoir are known to have elevated radiation levels.

Moreover, the natural areas of elevated background radiation in Ukraine,
particularly in the Ukrainian crystalline shield, make even a small increase
from radioactive fallout dangerous. Therefore, it is not surprising that the
population mistrusts the official statements regarding the safety of nuclear
reactors or the denials of health officials that increasing sicknesses are related
to radiation. It didn't help that a fire forced a second unit to be closed at
Chornobyl in 1991. In addition, in 1992 there were operating problems,
which required unit closures, at the Khmelnytskyy, South Ukraine, and
Zaporizhzhya (Zaporozhe) power plants.

A map, prepared by the Geographical Branch of the Academy of Sciences
of the Ukrainian SSR, identifies the main areas of ecological disruption
(Rudenko et al., 1990, p. 18). This map is reproduced as Figure 9.3. Ecological
disasters ("catastrophes") are identified in the area of Chornobyl and in the
irrigated zone of the southern steppe. Very severe ecological disruptions are
evident beyond the immediate disaster zones in these two regions and also in
the Donets and Dnipro industrial areas and in the hot spots of radioactive
fallout. Other highly degraded areas are scattered regions of soil erosion

Figure 9.2   The Dnipro (Dnepr) River at Kyyiv (Kiev), looking north. Just beyond the horizon
is the Kyyiv Reservoir, which may have received contaminated water from Chornobyl
(Chernobyl), 100 km farther north.

and chemical contamination south of Kyyiv and Vinnytsya and near Chernivtsi (Chernovtsy). Urban centers stand out as focal points for air and water pollution.

Figure 9.3 clearly depicts an unfortunate state of the natural environment of Ukraine. The implications are that vast sums will need to be spent to improve environmental living conditions, that a significant restructuring of both industrial and agricultural activities will be required, and that effective governmental agencies will need to be in place to supervise Ukraine's environmental improvement. The next chapter will examine these themes in more detail.

Ukraine's Future Prospects

Although Chapter 10 will discuss further aspects of Ukraine's administrative structure, it might be useful to conclude this chapter with a brief summary of the main advantages and uncertainties facing Ukraine's immediate future. Both are impressive.

Its advantages are readily evident. It enjoys an excellent natural resource base (except for oil) and exceptionally productive agricultural land. Its central location, with good land and water access to Europe, is a significant advantage. Its people are, in general, both well educated and industrious.

Unfortunately, its uncertainties are equally portentous. The environmental aftermath of Chernobyl is the most widely known and relates to a broader, very difficult energy supply problem that has to balance radiation, fossil fuel pollution, and balance-of-payments worries with Russia. In the early 1990s, Ukraine's economy was unacceptably weak, it owed Russia a large debt, and its inflation was perhaps the worst in the world. Such situations always lead to political unrest, authoritarianism, or both. The military relationship with Russia and the rest of the world, involving nuclear missiles, Soviet troops, and the Black Sea fleet, had been only partially resolved by the end of 1994. Ukraine had inadequate fuel supplies for the 1993–94 winter, and Russia linked further imports to a favorable resolution of the status of the Black Sea fleet. Finally, the future of the Crimean Peninsula, given to Ukraine by Khrushchev in 1954, is a very uneasy topic. Russian nationalists want it (and especially the military port city of Sevastopol) back; Ukraine, of course, does not consider this a negotiable issue. Yet it is one that will not easily go away, as evidenced by a 73% vote for Russian separatists in the Crimean election of January, 1994. A pro-Russia candidate was victorious (defeated) in the June 1994 presidential election.

In theory, the future of Ukraine should be one of the brightest of all the former Soviet republics. Ultimately, it may be, but such an optimistic scenario will depend on satisfactorily resolving the internal economic problems, and the Ukrainian-Russian political issues, that now cloud the contemporary existence of this ancient nation-state.

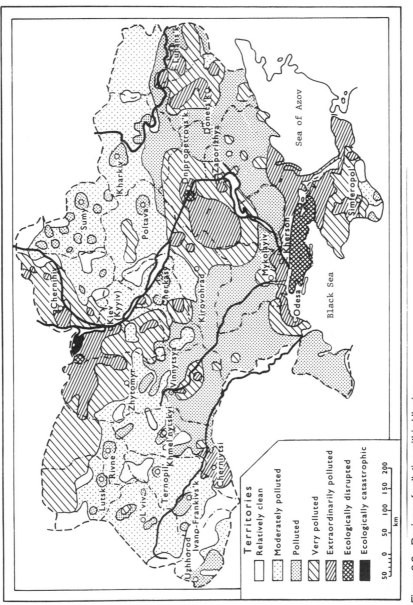

Figure 9.3   Regions of pollution within Ukraine
Source: Geographical Branch of the Ukrainian SSR Academy of Sciences, 1990

Appendix 9.1 Ukraine's Largest Cities

City (Former Name)	Major Function(s)[1]	Population (1000s) 1970	Population (1000s) 1989	% Increase 1970 - 1989
Kyyiv (Kiev)	C, P, Ch	1632	2587	58
Kharkiv(Khar'kov)	C, Ch	1223	1611	32
Dnipropetrovsk	C, F, Ch	904	1179	30
Odesa (Odessa)	C, P, Ch	892	1115	25
Donetsk	C, F, Ch	879	1110	26
Zaporizhzhya (Zaporozh'ye)	C, F, Ch	658	884	34
L'viv (L'vov)	C, Ch	553	790	43
Kryvyy Rih (Krivoy Rog)	F	573	713	24
Mariupol' (Zhdanov)	F, P	417	517	24
Mykolayiv (Nikolayev)	C, P	362	503	39
Luhansk (Voroshilovgrad)	C	383	497	30
Makiyivka (Makeyevka)	F	429	430	1
Vinnytsya (Vinnitsa)	C, Ch	212	374	76
Sevastopol'	P	229	356	55
Kherson	C, P	261	355	36
Simferopol'	C	249	344	38
Horlivka (Gorlovka)	Ch	335	337	1
Poltava	C	220	315	43
Chernihiv (Chernigov)	C, Ch	159	296	86
Zhytomyr (Zhitomir)	C, Ch	161	292	81
Sumy	C, Ch	159	291	83
Cherkasy	C, Ch	158	290	84
Dniprodzerzhynsk	F, Ch	227	282	24
Kirovohrad (Kirovograd)	C	189	269	42
Chernivtsi (Chernovtsy)	C	187	257	37
Khmel'nytskyy	C	113	237	110
Kremenchuk (Kremenchug)	Ch	166	236	42
Rivne (Rovno)	C, Ch	116	228	96
Ivano-Frankovsk	C	105	214	104
Ternopil'	C	85	205	141

[1] C = Oblast Capital; F = Ferrous Metallurgy; P = Port; Ch = Chemical Industries.

Source: 1989 USSR Census

Notes

1. Throughout this chapter, the former English transliterations (from Russian) of Ukrainian place-names are given in parentheses when they differ significantly from contemporary Ukrainian spellings. Some recent works persist in using the traditional Kiev rather than the Ukrainian spelling Kyyiv.

Bibliography

Dienes, L., and Shabad, T. 1979. *The Soviet Energy System: Resource Use and Policies.* Washington, D.C.: V. H. Winston.

Dorohuntsov, S. 1991. "Environment, Resources and Regional Development in Ukraine." A presentation by the director of the Council for the Study of the Productive Forces of Ukraine, the Academy of Sciences of Ukraine, at the University of Windsor, Windsor, Ontario, Canada, March 11.

Feshbach, M., and Friendly, A. Jr. 1992. *Ecocide in the USSR: Health and Nature Under Siege.* New York: Basic Books.

Kubijovyc, V. (ed.) 1963. *Ukraine: A Concise Encyclopaedia.* Vol. 1. Toronto: University of Toronto Press.

Marples, D. R. 1986. *Chernobyl and Nuclear Power in the USSR.* Edmonton: Canadian Institute of Ukrainian Studies, University of Alberta.

————. 1991. *Ukrainians Under Perestroika: Ecology, Economics and the Worker's Revolt.* New York: St. Martin's Press.

————. 1992. "Chernobyl and Nuclear Energy in Post-Soviet Ukraine," *RFE/RL Research Report,* vol. 1, no. 35 (Sept.), pp. 54–58.

Mnatsakanian, R. A. 1992. *Environmental Legacy of the Former Soviet Republics.* Edinburgh: Centre for Human Ecology.

Narodne hospodarstvo Ukrains'koi RSR u 1988 rotsi: Statystychnyi shchorichnyk. 1989. Kiev: Tekhnika.

Narodnoe khoziaistvo SSSR v 1989: Statisticheskii ezhegodnik. 1990. Moscow: Finansy i Statistika.

Natsional'nyi sostav naseleniia SSSR po dannym vsesiouznoi perepisi naseleniia 1989 g. 1991. Moscow: Finansy i Statistika,

Okhrana okruzhayushchey sredy i ratsional'noye ispol'zovaniye prirodnykh resursov. 1991. Moscow: Informtsentr Goskomstat SSSR.

Peterson, D. J. 1993. *Troubled Lands: The Legacy of Soviet Environmental Destruction.* Boulder: Westview Press.

Pryde, P. R. 1991. *Environmental Management in the Soviet Union.* Cambridge: Cambridge University Press.

Rudenko, L. H., Horlenko, I.O., Shevchenko, L.M., and Baranovs'kyi, V. A. 1990. *Ekolohoheohrafichni doslidzhennia terytorii Ukainy.* Kiev: Naukova Dumka.

Runova, T. 1986. "Prirodno—resursnyi potentsial osnovnykh ekonomicheskikh raionov SSSR." In Gerasimov, I., and Preobrazhenskii, V. (eds.), *Osnovy konstruktivnoi geografii.* Moscow: Prosveshchenie.

Shabad, T. 1969. *Basic Industrial Resources of the USSR.* New York: Columbia Univ. Press.

Simons, M. 1991. "For Black Sea, Slow Choking by Pollutants," *New York Times,* Nov. 24, pp. 1, 18.

Ukrainian Ministry of Environmental Protection. 1992. *Ukraine National Report for UN Conference on Environment and Development* (Brazil-92). Kiev: Chas.

Zastavnyi, F. D. 1990. *Heohrafiia Ukrainy.* Lviv: Svit.

10

Environmental Management in Ukraine

William E. Freeman

The major and most revealing features of environmental life in Ukraine in 1992 and 1993, as described in the preceding chapter, can be summarized in a few descriptive phrases. A line item in the Ukrainian state budget for 1993 provided for spending 0.25 percent of gross domestic product on the environment. This is less than the 1.2 percent the USSR claimed it spent annually in the 1980s on the environment and much less than the developed countries spend on their environment. As in many other former republics, measured pollution in Ukraine has decreased since 1990, but this has been primarily because of large declines in industrial production. Pollution will very likely increase proportionately when the economy recovers.

According to public opinion polls, at least until 1992, the environment remains one of the top issues of public concern in Ukraine, ranking higher than housing and energy. However, neither old-line party bosses nor the new free-marketeers pay much attention, even rhetorically, to the environment, and governmental economic reform programs rarely mention environmental issues.

Finally, Zeleny Svit (Green World) is the largest environmental organization in Ukraine, but almost half its local chapters are inactive. The Ukrainian Greens Party is among the two or three most popular parties in Ukraine, according to public opinion polls. However, as it was formed after the elections of 1991, it has no representatives in the Ukrainian Supreme Council (parliament); and since the public does not perceive it as a true political party, it is not likely to be a major electoral force in the near future.

The common thread that connects these vignettes is obvious: the "spontaneous" and paradoxical nature of environmental developments in Ukraine. On the one hand, the list indicates that there is a strong environmental awareness in Ukraine and, as newspaper reports have made clear, strong societal support for effective environmental action. On the other hand, it demonstrates that important developments affecting the environment are taking place without the influence or intervention of the institutions of society and government. Thus, it can be argued that environmental institutions in Ukraine must be strengthened before major and lasting environmental gains can be made.

The Soviet Environmental Legacy

As the preceding chapter showed, Ukraine suffers from severe environmental problems. Soviet economic development left Ukraine heavily reliant on nuclear power (30 percent), beset with industrial pollution (one of the highest per capita rates in Europe), short on water (second to last per capita among the former Soviet republics), and faced with the cleanup of the worst nuclear accident in history (see Figure 10.1).

This chapter examines in some detail the other part of the Soviet environmental legacy: the system of environmental management in Ukraine. This system has changed substantially since the attainment of independence. Since 1991, there has been a strong emphasis on the environment as a factor in Ukraine's national security, the country's environmental priorities have been revised, and Ukrainian environmental institutions have been reoriented

Figure 10.1   Aerial view of the Chornobyl (Chernobyl) nuclear reactor complex, showing the exploded Unit 4 in the center, and the cooling pond, which is adjacent to the Prypiat (Pripyat) River, in the background to the left. Photo courtesy of SovFoto.

toward Ukrainian interests. However, it has proven difficult to overcome the fundamental weaknesses of the old Soviet system: fragmentation of environmental authority among government agencies, a government structure in which the environment is often ignored, and a reluctance to break from former practices.

Fragmentation of Authority

In 1988, the USSR undertook a major environmental reform. This involved creating environment agencies within the government, including the USSR State Committee for Nature Protection (Goskompriroda), and analogous state committees for nature protection at the republic level. The purpose behind this reform was to unite the government's environmental functions in one agency and end fragmentation of environmental authority among more than a dozen different agencies.

In practice, however, the other ministries successfully resisted this attempt: the state committees for hydrometeorology retained their environmental monitoring functions, the state forestry committees kept their oversight over forests, and so on. By 1990 it was clear that this attempt at unification had failed. Environmental ministries had come into being, but in each Soviet republic they were only one of several agencies responsible for natural resource management or environmental protection.

Government Structures

After independence in 1991, environmental ministries and state committees in the former USSR republics tried several different ways to overcome fragmentation. In Latvia, Lithuania, and Moldova, the environmental ministries were subordinated to the parliament, at least temporarily, to give them increased attention. In Russia, there have been two attempts to raise environmental management to the deputy prime minister level, that is, the environment minister has been put in charge of all ministries and agencies in the "environment-resource bloc" and named deputy prime minister. In both instances, however, this attempt was overturned.

In Ukraine, as in most other former Soviet Union (FSU) republics, the environmental ministry has had to share environmental responsibilities with several others. In these cases, the deputy prime minister charged with oversight over environmental questions has no ex officio interest in the environment. Thus this topic has never found strong support within these new nations' governments. In some cases, presidential advisers on the environment have provided an additional source of influence on decision-making; in others, such advisers have ended up in bitter rivalries with the environmental ministries.

Post-Soviet Similarities

Most of the newly independent states have sought recourse in the passage of a comprehensive environmental law intended as a policy guide for subsequent, more detailed laws on specific environmental issues. Ukraine, together with Russia and almost all the other former republics, has passed such an environmental law (*Zakon*, 1991), although many of the ancillary bills have stalled in parliament owing to the press of other business. As a result, the legal authority of the new environmental ministries remains ambiguous. At the same time, the structure and functions of these new ministries remain largely unchanged.

When the Ukrainian Goskompriroda was formed along with those in other republics in 1988, there was a great deal of talk that these committees embodied a more progressive "functional" form of organization than did Western environmental ministries. Most of the successor ministries, including Ukraine's, have retained this basic Goskompriroda structure and made only superficial changes.

Ministry for Environmental Protection

The principal environmental institution in the Ukrainian government is the Ministry for Environmental Protection (MEP). According to the Ukrainian environmental law (*Zakon*, 1991), MEP has broad responsibilities, including "overall management in the field of the protection of the natural environment" and exercise of "state control over the utilization and protection of land, mineral resources, surface and underground water, atmospheric air, forests, other vegetation, the animal world, the marine environment, and natural resources of territorial waters, of the continental shelf, and of the exclusive (maritime) economic zone of the republic, as well as over the observance of ecological safety norms" (Article 20). However, it has proved difficult for MEP to exercise these responsibilities fully.

Leadership

Since Ukrainian independence in 1991 and the establishment of an independent Ukrainian environmental ministry, there have been two environment ministers, each with differing priorities. Yurii Shcherbak, who held the position from July 1991 to September 1992, is a writer, a physician, and a very popular politician in Ukraine. Elected to the USSR Supreme Soviet in 1989, he served on its Ecology Committee. He was a founder of Zeleny Svit, was head of the Greens Party, and at MEP was an active proponent of cooperation with citizen environmental groups. He was able to assert a Ukrainian national environmental agenda and keep the environment a national priority. Upon coming into conflict with the president, however, he left MEP to become Ukraine's ambassador to Israel.

Yuriy Kostenko, the minister since September 1992, is an engineer by training, a mountain climber by avocation, and, like Shcherbak, an elected politician (the only representative of Rukh in the current government). His primary interest is the environment as a part of national security. In particular, he has shown a continuing interest in the question of nuclear power development in Ukraine and, as a member of the Supreme Council, the question of Ukraine's accession to the START I treaty.

Two environment ministers in two years does little to establish continuity in environmental policy or to build the institutional capacity of MEP. It would be unfair to expect much more than what has already been accomplished. Time must pass and great efforts will have to be made in order to refashion MEP for Ukrainian conditions and make its authority equal to the problems it must solve.

Staffing

Staffing has been a major problem for MEP, and currently MEP does not have enough staff. At present, the central headquarters staff in Kyyiv (Kiev) now has only about 120 employees, down from 175 in July 1992. For a country of 52 million people and severe environmental problems, this number is clearly insufficient for a central environmental ministry. The quality of MEP staff is also a question. In 1988–89, new MEP staff was being taken in from other ministries and agencies; these staff members had no particular interest or expertise in environmental matters. In 1992, one Western source estimated that 30–50 percent of the central staff in Kyyiv were "ballast" (Simm and Rosen, 1992). Shcherbak selectively replaced many of the senior management inherited from his predecessor. Kostenko intensified this process, requiring that MEP staff, at least at management levels, be "recertified" through a series of examinations and interviews. As a result, more than 60 percent of senior (nonpolitical) management were replaced at MEP.

MEP staff members are heavily oriented toward science and engineering. Many were educated as scientists, and the current MEP training program emphasizes technical instruction. Moreover, the MEP's scientific and research institutions appear to dwarf the MEP central staff in Kyyiv. For example, the Ukrainian Scientific Center for Marine Ecology, in Odesa, has almost 900 staff members. By contrast, MEP tends to lack economists, policy analysts, and experienced environmental managers.

Budget

Funding for MEP is not commensurate with its responsibilities. The 1992 MEP budget was about 500 million karbovantsi; in 1993 it was about 3.1 billion (equal to about U.S.$3 million). However, with inflation taken into account, it appears that the 1993 budget was slightly lower than that of 1992. MEP accounts for about 10 percent of all government spending on environmental issues, which was 33 billion karbovantsi in 1993. MEP's budget is only about 3 percent of that of the Chernobyl ministry, which was about 600 billion karbovantsi in 1993.

Although MEP budgets are low, it appears that support for MEP is large enough to cover some programmatic expenses, not just basic salary, expenses, and maintenance. MEP expenditures in 1992 provide an indication of the MEP budget breakdown (Ministry, 1992). These figures are not broken down by pollution type; as is the case in most FSU republics where the water lobby is very strong, MEP probably spent more money on water than on air or soil pollution.

In 1992, twelve percent of the budget went to other ministries and oblast governments for measures such as the construction of wastewater treatment facilities, the construction of plants for reprocessing toxic waste, the liquidation of slag heaps, the demineralization of saline mine water, scientific research, and design work for wastewater treatment on small streams and rivers.

Fifty-five percent went to equipment and other material for MEP, primarily for monitoring and inspection, especially in badly polluted areas; for laboratory buildings in Donetsk, Khmelnytskyy, Chernihiv, Severodonetsk, and Dnipropetrovsk; and for the purchase of vehicles, computers, communications equipment, and copy machines. The final thirty-three percent went for environmental review, information and education, and nature reserves.

One bright spot for 1993 was that for the first time, MEP's budget appeared as a line item in the state budget. This introduced an added element of predictability into MEP's programmatic operations; it is probable that in 1992, given inflation and the Ukrainian government's fiscal difficulties, MEP regularly had to solicit the Ministry of Finance for additional allocations, which no doubt by the end of the year accounted for a sizable portion of MEP's budget.

As of May 1993, when the 1993 state budget was passed, 3.1 billion karbovantsi were worth about $3 million. It is likely that for the next few years, until MEP funding is increased, foreign assistance for the environment in Ukraine will constitute a relatively large sum, possibly equaling the annual budget of MEP and accounting for perhaps as much as 5 percent of total environmental spending in Ukraine.

Organization

Within MEP, the minister has two first deputy ministers and several other deputy ministers, who oversee the work of about fifteen main departments. These departments, which typically have staffs of five to ten workers, are the principal operating units of MEP.

These departments appear to fall into three primary groups. The first group, which includes the departments for personnel, finances, and administration, provide the main support for MEP operations. Although these departments include a mix of new and pre-independence staff, they are nevertheless embedded in a broader government system that is inflexible, inefficient, and antiquated, in which many of the habits of the Soviet bureaucracy still prevail. The internal MEP budget process, for example, remains largely unknown to most MEP staff. Further, it appears that department heads do not have a firm budget allocation for their department at the start of each fiscal year and must later apply for additional allocations (Simm and Rosen, 1992).

The second group comprises what might be called traditional departments, such as protected natural territories, science and technology, monitoring, international relations, and information and public relations. All their functions are fairly obvious and largely similar to departments found in other FSU environmental ministries. That is not to say that these functions are not extremely important within MEP. It is simply that the nature of the problems these departments face is relatively clear; that the solutions, though in many cases very difficult, are straightforward; and that the functions themselves generally fit into well-defined niches in the environmental management system inherited from Moscow.

The Zapovidnyky and Other Protected Natural Territories Department serves as an example of this group of departments. It is an extension of the analogous department under the former USSR Goskompriroda and has inherited the problems that its Soviet predecessor never fully resolved. This MEP department has to worry principally about finding the money to pay field personnel in the nature reserves (*zapovidnyky*) and national parks. With the severe reductions in allocations from the central state budget, the maintenance of the *zapovidnyky* has been a source of great concern in Ukraine, as in Russia and other republics. Local governments may have had to take upon themselves some of the funding needed to preserve and maintain protected natural areas. A second problem is that MEP has had to struggle with other government agencies that are resisting the transfer of protected areas. The 1992 Ukrainian environmental law calls for the transfer of the *zapovidnyky* and national parks to MEP. As of 1993, despite pressure from the Greens, this transfer had not taken place. As in the USSR, the national parks remain de facto under the jurisdiction of the forestry ministry. The *zapovidnyky* are still split among the education ministry, the Academy of Sciences, the Academy of Agricultural Sciences, and the forestry ministry. The question of jurisdiction is now before the Ukrainian Supreme Council.

The Zapovidnyky Department, though, has had some notable successes. It added two new *zapovidnyky* (Medobor and Dnipro-Orilsk) to the existing system, enlarged others, and transformed some hunting preserves once used by the privileged elite into *zapovidnyky* and national parks (Stetsenko, 1992). Nevertheless, with only about 2 percent (1.2 million hectares) of total land area under protection, Ukraine should make the addition of *zapovidnyky* and national parks a continuing priority. This effort will be crucial to threatened species, such as great bustard, demoiselle crane, and steppe eagle, which will very likely not be able to survive outside protected areas. In addition, the *zapovidnyky* have attracted environmental funding from abroad, to protect, for example, the Danube Estuary Zapovidnyk and the Carpathian Zapovidnyk and National Park, both as part of efforts to create protected areas that cross international boundaries.

MEP's Monitoring and Science and Technology Departments also have meager resources and difficult institutional problems inherited from the past. The Monitoring Department has the responsibility of creating a standardized environmental monitoring system for Ukraine. Presently, as in Russia, environmental monitoring in Ukraine is carried out by a dozen or more government agencies and Academy of Sciences institutes. MEP, among the poorest of these agencies and institutes, must find a way to lead and coordinate the others. Similarly, the Science and Technology Department must assert leadership in a national effort to develop a unified policy for environmental science and research. Otherwise, MEP will remain relatively powerless vis-à-vis the Academy of Sciences and its institutes. The legacy of Soviet science includes grand and costly proposals for sophisticated monitoring networks, a tendency to gather data for the sake of data, and environmental programs that rarely translate into practical action plans. MEP must offer better alternatives in science and monitoring so as to assert leadership and attract funding.

The third group of four or five departments, whose functions are not entirely self-evident, represents the first step in breaking away from the management system inherited from Moscow. The Optimal Nature Exploitation Department, for example, is in charge of the pollution fee system, the national environmental fund, and, evidently, the new system of payments for resource use. Though these systems originated primarily in Moscow (with the participation of Ukrainian environmental economists), their application to Ukrainian conditions will likely require additional adaptations over the next few years. Consistent with his interests in nuclear safety, Kostenko has added a department for nuclear and radioactive security, which has been active in the public debate in Ukraine about closing Chernobyl and nuclear power in general. This new department is probably the first serious attempt by MEP to regulate the activities of other government ministries. These departments represent the core of MEP's effort to reform itself into a modern environmental ministry.

The expectation that MEP's departments can be arrayed in a pyramidal hierarchy on an organizational chart is probably unrealistic at this point. There seem to be no clear lines of authority between departments. Moreover, the influence of personalities, never a factor to be underrated in any bureaucracy, is likely to be especially critical in MEP, whose authority is not now strictly derived from legislation. The decision-making style in MEP is highly personal, the organizational scheme is mostly horizontal, and both are likely to remain so until MEP gains in size, numbers, and funding.

An assessment of MEP's capabilities must also note what structures it does not have. For example, it lacks a policy department and therefore tends to contract out much of the policy work to Academy of Sciences institutes. This situation, much like that in Russia, makes it more difficult for MEP to be heard within the government. MEP has an interest in taking part in the national debate on economic reform and privatization, but until it has a strong policy office, it will have difficulty doing so.

Neither does MEP have clearly identified responsibilities for air, water, and waste; these functions seem to be fragmented throughout MEP. To complicate matters, two new institutions, not within MEP's structure, have recently been formed. First, MEP's department for State Ecological Inspection was made into a separate, independent inspectorate that reports to the environment minister. This department was the largest in MEP, and the reasons for its separation are unclear. The second is the Dnipro Commission, first formed in 1992. Chaired by Kostenko, it is the principal institutional framework for resolving environmental questions in the Dnipro River basin and apparently has major funding. With a 1993 budget of 7.9 billion karbovantsi (more than double the size of the MEP budget), it plans, funds and evaluates the programs it finances. The role of these two new institutions will probably become clearer, but for the moment it remains difficult to sort out responsibilities within MEP and associated government structures.

Regional Offices

MEP has offices in each of Ukraine's twenty-five oblasts and in the cities of Kyyiv and Sevastopol. A typical oblast office has 50 to 70 employees, working in an organizational structure that tends to reflect that of the central ministry in Kyyiv. In Donetsk Oblast, one of most important, the local MEP office has about 200 employees, who work in five departments. The funding for the oblast offices comes from the central budget, sometimes augmented by money either from local governments or from the environmental funds. In Russia, by contrast, the environment ministry has for the past two years been unable to fund its oblast and lower-level offices, so oblast and city governments have had to step in and provide financing. The regional offices perform the bulk of MEP's work.

Policy Instruments

The policy instruments available to Ukraine to achieve national environmental goals have for the most part been little altered since independence in 1991. It is beyond the scope of this chapter to analyze all of these instruments, but it is useful to look at three key elements of Ukrainian environmental policy, namely, (1) environmental norms, permitting, and compliance; (2) pollution fees and environmental funds; and (3) environmental review.

All three of these policy instruments have their origins in Soviet environmental policy of the late 1980s. In the USSR such policy was very new and largely experimental; nevertheless, Ukraine and many other successor states have adopted similar practices. All three policy instruments were provided for in general USSR environmental law, but none was the object of specific Soviet legislation; they were implemented on the basis of instructions or directives, which lack the full force of law. Ukraine has thus far preserved this characteristic as well.

Environmental Norms, Permitting, and Compliance

Permitting is the key regulatory tool available to MEP. MEP issues each factory or production facility a permit, which defines the kind and amount of pollutants it may release, a timetable by which it must comply with MEP requirements, and background materials. Once issued, the permit is usually good for five years.

Like similar permitting systems elsewhere, the Ukrainian permitting system is technically and administratively complex. The key concepts in the permitting process are the maximum permissible concentration, the sanitary-protection zone (SPZ), and the limit established for each enterprise's release of pollutant.

The maximum permissible concentration is the ambient norm set for a given pollutant. Each MPC is set by the health ministry at a level that, at least in theory, poses zero risk to human health. If there is no MPC for a substance, then a temporary MPC is set, pending further research, which is usually funded by the polluting enterprises. MPCs, once established, are rarely revised. (By contrast, U.S. standards are generally revised every three to five years.)

The sanitary-protection zone is the area around the pollution source, usually no more than one kilometer beyond its boundary, in which no people can live, so as to protect the health of the population. If it is expected that the MPC will be exceeded at the perimeter of the SPZ, in theory the pollution source cannot be built, and an exception must be sought. If the MPC will not be exceeded, the size of the SPZ may be reduced, with the agreement of MEP and the health ministry.

MEP (primarily at its local offices) sets limits for the emission source for each pollutant released into the environment. For air, these limits are called maximum permissible emissions (MPEs), and for water, maximum permissible discharges (MPDs). The limit represents the level of release at which the MPC will be attained at the perimeter of the sanitary zone. MEP establishes limits for one year and must communicate the limits to the source by January 1 of each year. MEP can also set temporary limits that apply until the source of the emissions attains MPE or MPD limitations.

Any pollution in excess of the MPC at the perimeter of the sanitary-protection zone triggers any one of a variety of enforcement procedures. The MPE/MPD limit is also a key element in the pollution fee system. Limits, it should be emphasized, are often established, not by actual measurements of pollution effects, but by simple back-calculation from the MPC. It is assumed that the pollution is predictable according to mathematical formulas.

The norms and permitting system have not been very effective in Ukraine, for several reasons. First, Ukraine tries to regulate a very large number of MPCs, far more than most other countries do. There are more than 1,000 MPCs for air quality: more than 500 MPCs and another 500 involving temporary MPCs. There are equivalent numbers of MPCs for surface water. The demands on MEP staff are quite high, and staff review of permits and limits is reportedly often perfunctory.

Second, based as MPCs are on the assumption of a near-zero risk to human health, in Ukraine they are often very stringent, making compliance very difficult. Because pollution concentrations in some cities consistently exceeds MPCs, the MPC has come to be perceived principally as a unit of measurement. Local newspapers often report, for example, that the level of sulfur dioxide is today at six MPCs.

Third, MEP lacks the equipment and instruments to carry out effective measurement and monitoring of pollution releases. Most enterprises report their own pollution, which is not unusual, and MEP lacks the means to check the figures they report.

Finally, enforcement is weak. The penalties for violations are often so low as to be meaningless, and the court system is so poorly developed that little judicial recourse is available.

Pollution Fees and Environmental Funds

At present, the system of pollution fees and environmental funds is probably the most effective environmental policy instrument in Ukraine, although exactly how effective it is in practice is open to some debate. Ukrainians speak of this system as a "market-based" instrument, as opposed to a "command-and-control" approach, because it is supposed to provide a financial incentive for polluters to reduce pollution. In the absence of a true market and a mature regulatory system in Ukraine, however, the distinction tends to be lost, and there is not much evidence that polluters regard pollution fees as anything but another tax or fine they must pay.

Pollution fees have been introduced in Ukraine in stages over the last four to five years. In 1989–1990 they were introduced on an experimental basis in six different regions; similar experiments were going on in many other parts of the USSR at the same time. In 1991, Article 44 of the Ukrainian environmental law mandated the use of pollution charges throughout all of Ukraine, and a later decree established the procedures for levying and collecting the fees. In practice, the full system has been in place in Ukraine less than two years.

In this system, polluters (including mobile and nonpoint sources) must pay for their pollution of the air, land and water (surface, marine, or ground), usually in karbovantsi per ton of pollutant released. Payments are made quarterly in advance, and adjustments for actual pollution are made at year's end, based on the enterprises' annual reports of pollution releases. Companies dealing in hard currency must make pollution payments in hard currency. Pollution payments do not exempt polluters from reimbursing actual damages caused to the environment.

For any pollution source, oblast governments establish the amount of the fee based on four main factors. First are the limits the MEP sets for each pollutant in the permit. Up to the limit, the normative payment applies and is treated as a production cost. Beyond the limit, payments are increased by a factor of up to five and taken out of profits. Second, the more toxic the pollutant, the higher the fee. A substance such as mercury, for example, is likely to be 100 times more expensive than a relatively benign substance. Third, the more polluted the region where the polluter is located, the higher the fee. The charge may be raised by a factor of as much as 1.75 for a badly polluted region. Fourth, if a source does not have duly confirmed limits, it is assessed above-limit payments.

The current Ukrainian pollution fee system is comparatively lenient toward polluters. For example, local governments may partially or fully exempt failing and bankrupt enterprises from payment of the pollution fee. In addition, as a temporary measure prompted by the economic crisis, all polluters are exempt from fees until January 1, 1996, for pollution within the limits of their MPEs and MPDs.

Recent changes have removed some of the weaknesses in the pollution fee system. In 1993, for example, MEP increased the fee schedule by up to 39 times and indexed the payments for inflation. Also, it is encouraging that local soviets have exempted only 1.3 percent of enterprises from paying the fees, and almost all of these are publicly owned, such as wastewater treatment plants. Judging from anecdotal evidence from Ukraine and Russia, however, there remains ample scope for abuse on the part of recalcitrant enterprises. It should be noted that Ukraine is introducing a companion system of payments for natural resource use. The features of this system are unknown, but it is likely that much of the money collected will go into general budgets at the local level, not into earmarked environmental funds.

The money collected through the pollution fee system is deposited in a system of environmental funds specially earmarked for environment purposes. Article 46 of the 1991 environmental law provides that 70 percent of the money goes into local environmental funds, 20 percent into oblast environmental funds, and 10 percent into the Ukrainian national environmental fund. The cities of Kyyiv and Sevastopol, which enjoy special status, retain 90 percent of the money collected. These funds do not constitute part of the regular governmental budgets at any level.

At the national level, MEP is in charge of the national environmental fund, with its spending decisions subject to confirmation by the Cabinet of Ministers. In 1992 the total amount of payments and fines into the national environmental fund was 90 million karbovantsi, and in 1993, it is expected to be 700 million karbovantsi. This is not a lot of money in any case, and it appears that when inflation is taken into account, less usable money will be collected in 1993 than in 1992.

It should be emphasized that the national fund is quite new, having been set up only in 1992. Inflation is a major problem for the fund, and fund managers must seek ways to protect the value of its deposits. The expenditures from the national fund are unclear, and it remains to be seen whether fund managers will avoid the pressure to fund established interests, such as environmental science, as opposed to actual pollution cleanup.

Environmental Review

Environmental review in Ukraine, as in Russia and most other republics of the former USSR, is a two-step process that is mandatory for all projects and activities that can have an adverse impact on human health and the environment. The first step in this process is an environmental impact statement (EIS), which the project proponent prepares. The second step is an official state environmental review of the EIS, usually carried out by a panel of experts either from MEP or designated by MEP and working under MEP supervision.

In theory, no work on any project can begin until the state environmental expert review approves the EIS. In the USSR, this prohibition proved ineffective, so in 1990 a provision was added that financing for the project could not proceed without a positive conclusion. Ukraine has preserved this provision in Article 29 of the 1991 environmental law.

More than 90 percent of the state environmental expert reviews are done at the oblast and local levels. In 1992 the central ministry staff in Kyyiv carried out approximately 100 state environmental expert reviews, only for the largest and most important projects. MEP staff in each oblast carried out, on average, 50 to 100 expert reviews. In all, about 1,500 to 1,700 such reviews were carried out in Ukraine, a figure that has remained stable over the past few years ("Derzhavna," 1992).

More often than not, state environmental expert reviews in Ukraine return a negative conclusion (about 70 percent in 1992). In Kyyiv Oblast in 1992, 87 out of 197 conclusions were negative. When the conclusions of the state expert review are negative, the project should be scrapped or modified, at least in theory. It is unclear, however, to what extent this prohibition has been enforceable.

Environmental review in Ukraine preserves a number of progressive features inherited from the old USSR practice. First, it is comprehensive. It covers both government and private activities and not only new construction projects but also planning documents, new standards and technologies, and changes to existing facilities, including those in the defense sector. Second, the EIS must include an analysis of the alternatives that were considered for the project and an explanation of why they were not chosen. The expert review, in turn, is supposed to analyze these alternatives and confirm the choice made in the EIS. Third, the EIS must contain a section that presents or summarizes the views of the public made known during the EIS preparation.

Nevertheless, environmental review in Ukraine has not been as effective as it should be. First, MEP does not have the capacity to manage the environmental review process adequately. The number of central ministry staff devoted to environmental review is now fewer than ten, and the number of oblast-level staff devoted to the process is proportionately not much larger. The draft environmental review law recognizes this problem and provides MEP with the capacity to bring in outside experts to sit on environmental review panels. The draft law also stipulates that the project proponent has to pay for the expert review process in an amount up to 5 percent of the total worth of the project. Until the draft law is adopted, though, MEP appears not to have full control over the environmental review process either at the central or local level.

Second, the environmental review system in Ukraine appears to lack the ability to negotiate changes in a project design before it is too late to alter the project without great expense. There appears to be no formal scoping procedure, and the expert review begins at a point when the project preparation work has been completed, often at great cost but perhaps in an environmentally unacceptable manner. At that point the choice between economic development and environmental protection is very difficult. An emphasis on EIS preparation and negotiations earlier in the process could alleviate problems encountered when the project progresses without MEP consultations.

Conclusion

In conclusion, three overriding points are worth emphasizing. First, MEP is at this point more a technical support ministry than a strong regulatory ministry. Its principal roles at the moment include promoting responsible use of nuclear power, providing technical expertise to other ministries and enterprises, and providing advanced methodologies to oblast and local offices. Potentially, it has a strong role to play with regard to foreign assistance and investment in the environmental sector in Ukraine. However, MEP's capacity to manage regulatory programs is still insufficient. It will take time for MEP to strengthen the policy instruments it has at its disposal and use them effectively to attack specific problems. Given this situation, it would be a mistake to assume that the best way to improve the environment in Ukraine in the short run is to pass strong laws and regulations and strictly enforce them; as of now, MEP is unable to do the latter.

The second point is that there has been a significant devolution of environmental authority to the oblast and local levels in Ukraine. Permitting is done almost entirely at these levels, ninety percent of the pollution fees are collected and spent at these levels, and almost all of the environmental reviews are done here as well. Such decentralization of environmental functions is desirable in most circumstances, although it must be noted that in Ukraine, as opposed to many other countries, it is a relatively weak central ministry that is devolving its authorities to the local level.

Third, the principal opportunity for MEP at present, and its greatest challenge, is to contribute to economic recovery and development in Ukraine. The strong environmental consciousness among the people of Ukraine and the strong Green movement make it likely that the environment will not be forgotten as a national priority, and it is also likely that many Ukrainian political leaders are not anti-environment but simply do not know how to harmonize economic development and environmental protection. Some of the impetus for this effort will come from abroad, since most Western companies will not invest heavily in Ukraine (or other former USSR republics) without a clear understanding of their environmental liability and obligations. If MEP can help provide solutions, it will stand a better chance of evolving into the sort of environmental ministry more familiar in the West.

Bibliography

"Derzhavna ekologichna ekspertiza." 1992. *Ridna Pryroda,* nos. 2–3, pp. 10–11.

"E taki partii." 1992. *Visty z Ukrainy,* July 9–15.

Hoffer, Ron. 1992. "Regulatory Aspects of Water Quality Programs in Ukraine: Summary Observations and Recommendations." September. Unpublished ms.

"Kontseptyya Derzhavnoi programy okhorony navkolishn'ogo pryrodnogo seredovyshcha i ratsional'nogo vykorystanyya pryrodnykh resursiv Ukrainy." 1992. *Uriadovyy kur'er,* April 22.

Kostenko, Yuriy. 1992. "Ekologiya—nayefektyvnisha ekonomika." *Kyyvs'ka pravda,* November 11.

Marlar, John, 1993. "Water Quality Management in Belarus." January 2. Unpublished ms.

Ministry for Environmental Protection. 1991. "Ministerstvo Okhorony Navkolyshn'ogo Pryrodnogo Seredovyshcha Ukrainy." Kiev: August 30. Press release.

———. 1992. "Pro plan pershochergovykh zakhodiv po okhoroni navkolyshn'ogo pryrodnogo seredovyshcha na 1992 rik, jaki finansuyut'sya za rakhunok derzhavnogo byudzhety (500 mln. krb.)." Kiev: July.

Pace, Thompson G., and Joseph W. Paisie. 1992. "Trip Report: Belarus and Ukraine." August. Unpublished ms.

"Polozhennya pro Ministerstvo okhorony navkolyshn'ogo pryronogo seredovyshcha Ukrainy." 1991. August 14.

"Poryadok vyznachennya platy i styagnennya platezhiv za zabrudnennya navkolishn'ogo pryrodnogo seredovyshcha." 1992. January 13.

Simm, Ian, and Seth B. Rosen. 1992. "Ministry of Environmental Protection of Ukraine: Institutional Issues and Recommendations for Development." Report to the World Bank. Cambridge, MA: Harvard University, Program on Economic Reform in Ukraine, July.

Stetsenko, M. 1992. "Models of Nature: What We Must Do to Protect Them." *Holos Ukrayny*, January 28, as translated in Joint Publications Research Service. *Central Eurasia*, May 22.

Ukrainian Television. 1993. "Zayava partii zelenykh ukrainy." January 23.

U.N. Conference on Environment and Development. 1992. *Ukraine National Report*, Kiev: Chas. (In Ukrainian and English).

U.S. Information Agency. 1992a. "Ukrainians Say Economy Bad Now, Divided on Economic Future." Washington, DC: Office of Research, Opinion Research Memorandum, April 1.

———. 1992b."Ukrainians Less Wary of Political Changes Than of Political Leaders." Washington, DC: Office of Research, Research Memorandum, April 20.

Vyshnyak, Oleksandr, and Volodymyr Oliynyk. 1992. "Seven Percent for . . . Communism." *Molod Ukrayiny*, April 2. In Foreign Broadcast Information Service. *Daily Report: USSR*, April 25.

Zakon Ukrains'koi Radyans'koi Sotsialistichnoi Respubliki pro Okhoronu Navkolyshn'ogo Pryrodnogo Seredovyshcha. 1991. Kiev: Vydavnystvo Ukraina.

Zapovedniki SSSR: Zapovedniki Ukrainy i Moldavii. 1987. Moscow: Mysl'.

11

Belarus

Oleg Cherp and Nadezhda Kovaleva

Belarus (previously Byelorussia or White Russia) is situated near the western border of the former Soviet Union, with a population of 10.3 million people (1990) and territory of 207.6 thousand km². Two recent events have made the world more aware of this little-known country. The first was the Chernobyl disaster, which severely affected the Belarusian population and territory. The second was the meeting of the heads of Russia, Ukraine and Belarus in December of 1991, which took place in an ancient Belarusian forest, Belovezhskaya Pushcha, and declared the end of the USSR and the establishment of the Commonwealth of Independent States. The central agencies of the new confederation were placed in the Belarusian capital of Minsk. As a result of independence, the spelling of the names of most Belarusian cities has been changed from the old Russian (Cyrillic) form to a preferred Belarusian form; in this chapter, the latter will be given first with the Russian version in parentheses.

Ethnicity and History

The Belarusians, who represent one of the three East Slavonic nations, constituted in the 1989 census about 78% of the population of the former Belorussian Republic. The remainder includes Russians (13%), Poles (4%), Ukrainians (3%), and Jews (1%). The Belarusian language is close to both Russian and Ukrainian but is also influenced by the Polish and Baltic languages. Approximately three quarters of churchgoing Belarusians belong to the Russian Orthodox church; most of the rest are Roman Catholics.

In 1926, before the onset of industrialization, only 10% of the Belarusian population lived in towns. Vast areas of forests and swamps used to hinder the development of Belarusian villages. These features, as well as the unique location of the country as a frequent battlefield between East and West and the variety of religions and languages of the people settling in Belarus, have formed the Belarusian character. The Belarusian self-image emphasizes secretiveness and reluctance to accept foreign ideas but at the same time also embraces religious and national tolerance, cheerfulness and rich imagination. Perhaps these features help explain why Belarus remains virtually the only country of the former Soviet Union not affected by severe nationalistic tensions or political extremism.

About 15 centuries ago, the Slavs began to arrive at the territory of modern Belarus, which was populated by Baltic tribes. In the 8–10th centuries A.D., in the upper basins of the Dnepr and Western Dvina Rivers, the synthesis of Baltic and Slavonic populations resulted in the formation of the ethnic communities of the Belarusians' ancestors. In the 9th to 13th centuries, the territory of Belarus belonged to the early feudal state of Kievan Rus, a political and military union of Eastern Slavonic principalities.

In the 13th century, Kievan Rus was defeated by the Tatar-Mongols. The people of the western part of the country, however, managed to defend their independence. This fact accounts for one of the poetic legends of the name of the country, Belarus, which was first used in a Polish chronicle in the early 14th century. White Russia might mean the part of Russia that was "free" or "independent" (of Tatars).

The need to resist the pressure of Tatars and German crusaders forced the people of Belarus to consolidate around the rapidly expanding principality, with the capital of Navahrudak (Novogrudok) ruled by a Lithuanian prince Mindaugas. By the middle of the 14th century, all the territory of modern Belarus was attached to the Great Principality of Lithuania, Russia and Zhamoytiya (GPL). By the 15th century, the territory of the GPL had expanded from Brest to Smolensk and from the Baltic to the Black Sea. The origin of the Belarusian language, the Belarusian culture and the Belarusian nation itself should be looked for in the GPL, where 90% of the population was Slavonic and the state language was old Belarusian. The current borders of Belarus in the east, the south and the west almost coincide with that of the GPL in 16th century. The modern emblem of both Belarus and Lithuania is "Pagonya"—the GPL's coat of arms. The first Belarusian book (it was also the first book in an Eastern Slavonic language) was printed in 1522, in GPL's capital Vilniya (Vilnius), by Francis Scaryna, a Renaissance Belarusian enlightener.

In the 16th century, in the face of the threat from the east, the GPL united with the Polish Kingdom (1569) to form Rzecs Pospolita. This state started a series of exhausting wars with the Russian tsars that once resulted in occupying Moscow (1610–1612). However, Rzecz Pospolita was not able to withstand Russia in the long term. At the end of 18th century, this state ceased to exist. In 1772, the eastern part of Belarus was attached to Russia, in 1793 the central portion, and in 1795 the western one. Ironically, the unification with Russia, a country close to Belarus in language and religion, led to the deterioration of the Belarusian culture. This was partly because Russians always considered the Belarusians "spoiled" by Polish-Lithuanian rule, and much effort was exerted by the tsarist government to correct this "discrepancy."

After the Revolution of 1917 Belarus was one of the major battlefields of the civil war. According to the Riga Treaty (1921), the western part of Belarus went to Poland. The eastern part formed the Byelorussian Soviet Socialist Republic—one of the four founding republics of the USSR in 1922. In 1939, the two parts of Belarus were united as a result of the USSR's actions against Poland at the beginning of World War II. This war was most disastrous for Belarusians, as one in four died in the battles or during the three years of German occupation. The population returned to its pre-war level only in 1972.

The post-war policy of the USSR government was to convert Belarus into a country of modern labor-intensive industry. This industrialization was accompanied by rapid urbanization. This process was disastrous for the national language since the main practitioners of the language were rural dwellers. By the 1970s, the Belarusian language had been practically withdrawn from life in the larger cities. For example, there were no Belarusian schools in Minsk. Now, some efforts are being exerted to revive what the 19th century poet A. Mickewicz called "the most perfect and best preserved of the Slavonic languages."

Physical Environment

Belarus is situated on the western part of the Russian plain. It stretches for more than 500 km from north to south and for 600 km from west to east and shares borders with Lithuania, Latvia, Poland, Ukraine and Russia (Figure 11.1).

Belarus is mostly a plain with an average altitude of 160 m, crossed by the Belarusian Ridge from east to west, with heights not exceeding 346 m (Dzerzhinsky Peak, near the capital). This chain of uplands serves as a watershed divide between the Baltic Sea basin and that of the Black Sea. Southward from the Belarusian Ridge elevations decrease gradually. Pleistocene glaciation of Scandinavian origin was the major factor responsible for the present topography. The country can be divided into three main physical-geographic provinces.

Poozerye, the lake province, is located in the north in Vitsyebsk (Vitebsk) Oblast, in the terminal zone of the Valdai glacial deposits (comparable with the Wisconsin glaciation in North America), and has the freshest and most unchanged glacial relief. The widespread terminal moraines and numerous lakes of glacial origin are characteristic of this type of landscape and give the province its name. Similar landscapes continue northward into the taiga zone and westward past the border of Belarus, forming a vast lake belt.

The Predpolesye is in the central part of Belarus and is confined to the area around the Belarusian Ridge and its southern foothills, which are also of glacial moraine origin from the Moscow glaciation (comparable with the Illinoisan in North America). There are almost no lakes in this area.

The Polesye province in the south, in the Pripyat River watershed, is a flat-bottomed basin formed by tectonic troughs. Its high water table causes large portions of it to be marshy and of diminished fertility.

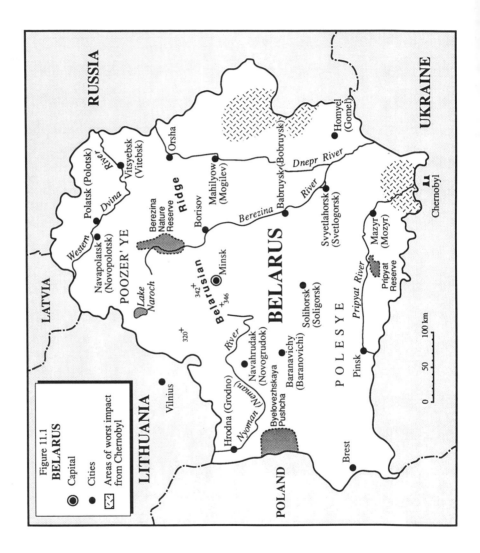

Figure 11.1
BELARUS

⊚ Capital
● Cities
▨ Areas of worst impact
from Chernobyl

The climate of the country is moderately continental and relatively cool, with distinct seasons and western winds prevailing in winter and summer. The precipitation slightly exceeds evaporation. Belarus lies in the area of maximum precipitation on the Russian Plain (500–700 mm a year), with twice as much precipitation occurring in summer as in winter. Snow cover thickness is 10–30 cm on average. The average temperature in January varies from −4°C (in the southwest) to −8°C (in the northeast). In July it varies from +17°C in the north to +19°C in the south. Belarus's topography provides conditions for more than 10,000 lakes and about 21,000 rivers, the latter having a total length of 91,000 km. Most of the Belarusian rivers are fed by snow and groundwater and are frozen for 2–3 months. Some of the rivers are suitable for navigation; the largest of these are the Dnepr, Pripyat, Berezina, Western Dvina and Nyoman (Neman).

The surplus of precipitation, together with certain geomorphological features such as low soil permeability and the vast lowland in the south, results in a major characteristic of the Belarusian landscape: the abundance of wetlands. These are especially widespread in the Polesye region.

The central part of Belarus is situated in the mixed forest zone; Polesye is in the broadleaf forest zone, while the northern forests are of the southern taiga type. Pine forests are more common for Poozerye and for the sandy soils of Polesye. Oak forests are typical for the southwest. The mosaic of relief types and the large number of lakes, bogs and forests result in the striking variety of soil cover, plant and animal species; 1,050 higher plant species, 280 species of birds and 73 species of mammals inhabit Belarusian forests, which occupy more than one-third of the territory.

Major soil types are forest podzols (11% of the total), peat bog (50%), and floodplain (37%). Most of the soils are acidic, low in both humus content and mineral salts.

Belarus has certain physical constraints on its industrial development and agriculture. Domestic energy resources (including wind energy and hydro energy) are too small to satisfy the country's demand. Belarus also lacks some other important natural resources, such as metallic ores and direct access to a sea. Although the Belarusian climate is generally quite suitable for agriculture, its low winter temperatures impose constraints. Moraine topography in Poozerye causes interruptions in the region's arable lands; combined with the stoniness of soils due to glacial deposits, it also prevents the efficient use of agricultural machines. However, the main difficulties for agriculture are created by boggy landscapes.

The natural soil fertility in Belarus is not sufficient for intensive agriculture. Mineral soils (mostly podzolized) are low in humus content and basic nutrients; their structure is weak. Organic peaty soils are also low in nutrients and undergo wind erosion, as do some of the upland soils. On these types of soils nutrients must be added.

Favorable natural features of Belarus include its advantageous geographical position, diverse natural resources, availability of water, predominantly flat landscape, relatively mild and moist climate, and absence of natural hazards such as earthquakes, droughts and dry winds.

Natural Resources and Industry

More than 4,000 mineral deposits involving 30 types of raw materials have been explored in Belarus, most of them in the Pripyat depression (Matesovich, 1990). Only a few of the deposits are of industrial significance, with potash salts among the most important. There are also numerous deposits of peat (about 800 extraction sites in all), rock salts, oil (small deposits in the southeast), and building materials. Among the resources of lesser importance are brown coal, dolomite, and mineral waters. Oil shale, phosphorites, and metals (mostly iron) have been found but are not extracted currently.

An important feature of Belarusian water resources is the availability of large volumes of near-surface groundwater (normally, 0 to 10 meters). In 1990, about 40% of the country's water needs were satisfied by groundwater ("Ekologicheskiye," 1991, p. 44). Until recently, only groundwater was used for domestic purposes in the capital.

Belarus accounted for 1.7% of the territory of the USSR and 3.6% of its population in 1990. At the same time, it produced 4.2% of the GNP. Among the major Belarusian industrial developments are the following:

- Extraction of potash salts (in the Solihorsk industrial region) and production of mineral fertilizers (53% of the USSR total)
- Oil refinery and petrochemical industry in Navapolatsk (Novopolotsk)
- Synthetic fibers production (34% of the USSR total) in Mahilyow (Mogilev) and Svyetlahorsk (Svetlogorsk)
- Manufacture of harvesters (54%) in Homyel (Gomel), tractors (14%) and heavy trucks in Minsk

Raw materials for these industries are mainly brought in from other countries, while the final products are largely exported (93 to 96% of trucks and tractors, 87% of potash fertilizers, 70 to 74% of synthetic fiber).

Agriculture produces about a fifth of the gross national product of the country. The main branches of agriculture are farming livestock and growing flax, potatoes, and buckwheat.

Peat was the main source of energy for a long time. Because of the new oil developments in the southeast of the country and the construction of a gas pipeline from Russia, a policy was adopted to switch the largest power plants to fuel oil and gas. However, because of the large concentration of energy-intensive industry in the country, domestic resources can provide for less than a tenth of the energy demand. Currently gas is supplied from the Urals, oil from the Volga region, and coal from Ukraine. This dependency in energy sources may lead to a political dependency on Russia or Ukraine. Thus, certain groups in the government feel there is a necessity to develop Belarusian domestic sources of energy. These might be either new oil or brown coal developments or nuclear energy. Such decisions could sharply increase the environmental problems of the country.

Major Environmental Problems

Unfavorable environmental situations exist in Belarus in the area affected by Chernobyl, in the largest industrial cities (Minsk, Navapolatsk, Vitsyebsk, Mahilyow, Hrodna, Mazyr, Homyel, Svyetlahorsk, Babruysk), in the Solihorsk industrial region, in the regions of Polesye negatively affected by land reclamation, and in areas where large livestock and poultry farms are located.

Chernobyl

Due to climatic conditions, about two-thirds of the radioactive fallout from Chernobyl fell on Belarus. In May 1986, the radioactivity of ground-level air in Belarusian cities increased by anywhere from a few dozen to a hundred thousand times. The number of Belarusians who suffered from the disaster is estimated to be between 2.5 million and 4.8 million (or 25% to 45% of the total population). Twenty percent of the country's agricultural land and 15% of the forests have been lost. Over a hundred thousand people have been relocated. There are about two thousand suffering from thyroid cancer (one in five is a child), and the occurrence of this illness has increased dramatically since 1986 (see Table 11.1).

Although there is a little visible evidence of the effect of Chernobyl on the natural environment, this disaster strongly affected the economic situation of the country by, among other things, necessitating the diversion of sizable funds from environmental protection programs. For example, the withdrawing of agricultural land increased the pressure to intensify land reclamation,

Table 11.1   Incidence of Thyroid Cancer in Children in Belarus

Region of Belarus	1986	1987	1988	1989	1990	1991	1992*	Total
Brest	0	0	1	1	6	5	5	18
Homyel	1	2	1	2	14	38	13	71
Hrodna	1	1	1	2	0	2	6	13
Mahilyow	0	0	0	0	2	1	1	4
Minsk	0	1	1	1	1	4	4	12
Minsk City	0	0	1	0	5	2	1	9
Vitsyebsk	0	0	0	0	1	3	0	4
Total	2	4	5	6	29	55	30	131**

* First six months of 1992.

** The World Health Organization reported that by April 1993 the total had increased to 168 children, and by December 1993 to 196.

the dangerous environmental consequences of which are discussed later in this chapter. The economic impact of Chernobyl becomes more onerous because of the collapse of the USSR and cancellation of strategic assistance programs funded from former all-Union sources.

In October 1989, the USSR government asked the International Agency on Nuclear Energy for an assessment of the safety of people living in areas contaminated by Chernobyl. In 1991 the international committee formed by the agency issued a report with its conclusions (The International Chernobyl Project, 1991). The principal disputable statement of the committee was what it felt was an absence of evidence of the harmful consequences of radiation on people's health. The changes in the population's health were attributed to "radiophobia" and the deterioration of social-economic conditions.

The scientists criticizing these conclusions indicate some inconsistencies in committee's methods. The committee had examined only 1,356 people, the vast number of whom had been relocated from the 30-km zone, whereas the people who took part in the cleanup at the site (some 600,000 to 800,000) were not considered. The committee also employed a static, rather than a dynamic, approach, not taking into account possible long-term effects associated with migration and transformation of radionuclides.

In contrast with the committee's conclusions, the *Nabat* independent newspaper reported 1,638 people (including 55 children) suffering from thyroid cancer by January 1991. By the end of 1993, the number of children so afflicted had reached almost 200 (Table 11.1). For the twenty pre-Chernobyl years only 5 cases were registered in Belarus (all adults). The level of cancer diseases increased by 23% (*Nabat*, 1991, no. 55). According to an article published in *Nature*, there were 80 cases of thyroid cancer per one million children in the Homyel (Gomel) region, while normally there is only one (Kazakov et al., 1992).

Air and Water Pollution

In general, the larger Belarusian cities (listed in Table 11.2) are relatively free of air and water pollution. Only one of them, Mahilyow (Mogilev), was placed on the list of the most polluted cities of the USSR in 1989. The main polluter in Mahilyow is the Khimvolokno industrial association, which produces synthetic fibers and has been identified as one of the most dangerous plants of the USSR (Yakubovich, 1989, p. 4). Specific pollutants in Mahilyow are sulfur compounds and methanol.

Oil refineries and petrochemical plants have resulted in serious environmental deterioration in Navapolatsk, where the air is polluted by hydrogen sulphide, benzene and ammonia and where bronchial sickness increased 1.5 times between 1985 and 1990 ("Ekologicheskiye," 1991, p. 4). The Navapolatsk industrial complex also pollutes air in Polatsk, one of the oldest of the Slavonic towns.

In terms of pollution subject to international treaties, Belarus emitted 281,000 tons of sulfur dioxide, and the same amount of nitrogen oxides, in 1990. From 1980 to 1990, sulfur dioxide emissions decreased by 24%, and there were plans to decrease them by another 30% by 1993. The main means

Table 11.2   Largest cities in Belarus

City (alternate spelling)	Population (1000s) 1970	1989	% increase
Minsk	907	1589	75
Homyel (Gomel)	272	500	84
Mahilyow (Mogilev)	202	356	76
Vitsyebsk (Vitebsk)	231	350	52
Hrodna (Grodno)	132	270	105
Brest	122	258	112
Babruysk (Bobruysk)	138	223	62
Baranavichy (Baranovichi)	101	159	57
Borisov	84	144	71
Orsha	101	123	22
Pinsk	62	119	92
Mazyr (Mozyr)	49	101	106
Belarus (total)	9002	10200	13.3

Source: 1989 USSR census

of combatting sulfur dioxide emissions is the gasification of power plants, but this may be difficult due to a sharp increase in gas prices after the collapse of the USSR. For example, Minsk Power Plant 4 has recently had to switch from gas to oil with a high sulfur content (*Ekologia Minska*, 1992, no. 10).

Belarusian rivers are referred to as moderately polluted (the third of seven categories in the water quality classification), the main pollutants being oil products, nitrates and ammonia ("Ekologicheskiye," 1991, p. 5). Approximately 93% of the discharges that require mandatory purification are treated (in 1988, this figure was only about 30% for the USSR as a whole). However, the inefficiency of the treatment plants is a serious problem, as is pollution from non-point sources. There is no provision for the treatment of urban and industrial runoff. Another major water pollution problem is associated with large livestock farms. For example, the Byelovezhski pig farm (108,000 head) in Kamenets has a serious negative impact on the environment close to the Belovezhskaya Pushcha nature reserve (Matesovich, 1990, p. 112). Agricultural pollution of groundwater is a serious problem in rural areas, where one-fifth of the wells have become unsuitable for drinking because of contamination (Yakubovich, 1989, p. 11).

Another water pollution problem is the eutrophication of small lakes. Half of all Belarusian lakes are being excessively silted (Yakubovich, 1989, p. 12). The problem of eutrophication is affecting the biggest and the most beautiful of Belarusian lakes, Lake Naroch, which has important recreational and tourist value. The concentration of blue-green algae has increased 80 times in Lake Naroch over the past 35 years. In part, it is due to accidental discharges from sewage pipelines that are too close to the shoreline.

The Problems of the Capital

Overall, Minsk is a well-planned modern city, rebuilt after the Second World War (when 96% of its buildings were destroyed). In 1989 it had 1.6 million inhabitants. Minsk has a unique landscape in the form of its green belt. The afforestation of the Minsk district is 27%, extremely large for a big city. There are even plans to establish the Belaya Rus National Park in the Minskaya upland north of Minsk. The green areas and artificial water bodies in the city, together with industry having been shifted away from the center, make Minsk much more attractive than most large industrial centers of the former Soviet Union. Perhaps this attractiveness has been among the reasons that Minsk is one of the fastest-growing cities in the former USSR. Its environmental problems, typical for such cities, are mainly associated with the failures of the USSR's planned economy.

Minsk was always famous for its high quality drinking water supplied from underground aquifers, which underwent a minimal chlorine treatment. The problems with the water supply began in the 1970s and were caused not only by groundwater pollution but also by the uncontrolled consumption and wasting of water. Minsk dwellers consumed up to 330 liters per capita per day, more than people in western Europe and North America do. The ability to provide so much water was considered to be a great achievement of the socialist economy. In the late 1970s, the city government was forced to put into operation a surface water supply system in order to satisfy the growing demand in new residential areas. This resulted in a rapid increase in the sickness rate in those areas as it proved to be difficult to provide clean water from surface sources.

There is only one sewage treatment plant in Minsk. Its capacity is not sufficient to cope with the peak flows, and therefore it permanently pollutes the Svisloch River. For 100 km downstream of Minsk, the river is "absolutely dead," and for 150 km it does not meet water quality standards (Yakubovich, 1989, p. 7). Additionally, a single treatment plant serving a large city represents a high risk: the environmental consequences of any emergency situation at the plant may be disastrous.

Although the air in Minsk is relatively clean, some of the local levels of pollution are much higher than the standards. Most of all, this applies to the residential areas around the tractor plant. The plant was constructed in the post-war period in a southeast suburb, taking into account the prevailing westerly winds. However, some decades later, a new housing development took place around it, including portions that were inside the exclusion zone (Figure 11.2). In this area, the average annual concentrations of sulfur dioxide are 6 to 8 times the maximum permissible concentrations, NO_x reaches 7.5 to 8 MPCs, and benzene reaches 2–7 MPCs (Yakubovich, 1989, p. 7). Vehicular air pollution is checked, but fines for violations are very small.

Figure 11.2   Industrial air pollutants being released adjacent to a residential area in Minsk. Photo by Boris Akhremichev.

Similar mistakes were often committed in designing new road developments, which resulted in disturbing the residents by noise and air pollution. One remedy envisaged by the city government is to require environmental impact assessment on all new developments (including housing and road construction) in the city (Fridlyand, 1992).

The Negative Impacts of Mineral Extraction and Reclamation

According to Bulygina (1992), mineral extraction in the Solihorsk industrial region has the largest negative industrial influence on the Belarusian environment, and its consequences will be second only to the Chernobyl disaster if the proper measures are not taken immediately. Continuing to use the ore processing technologies of the 1960s means generating 1 to 1.3 m³ of solid waste and 0.75 m³ of liquid waste during the production of each ton of potash salt. Vast volumes of wastes (30 million tons of salts and brine annually) are dumped onto the land, causing the loss of large areas of fertile land (at the current rate of 100 ha/year; five thousand ha of land have been withdrawn to date [Bulygina, 1992, p. 3]).

The moist climate of Belarus results in brine infiltrating from the waste storage sites into water-bearing strata. The effect of groundwater salinization (about 300 g/l in aquifers covering more than 10,300 ha means not only the loss of more agricultural land but also an enormous threat to the whole hydrological system of Polesye, because the leading edge of the salinization moves toward the wetlands of Polesye at the speed of 60 m/year [Yakubovich, 1989, p. 15]).

The most realistic alternative to the storage of wastes in landfills seems to be to dump them into abandoned mines. This would also help prevent the problem of the "sinking" of the surface in mined areas, which now covers 120–130 km² (Bulygina, 1992, p. 11). Such a procedure, however, needs much more research to ensure the absence of leakages. Among other alternatives, lining and covering the landfills and recycling the wastes are possibilities.

The total area of marshy land that needs some regulation of its water regime to be usable for crops is 48% of the total agricultural land in the country (6.1 million ha). As a result, a period of intensive land reclamation in Belarus began in the late 1960s. There has always been strong economic pressure to reclaim more land as its productivity increases by 5–6 times after such melioration (Skoropanov et al., 1982). Currently, the reclaimed areas yield 30% of Belarusian crop production. By 1 January 1990, about 3.19 million ha (36.1% of the agricultural land) had been meliorated (mainly drained), about half of this in the Polesye region. In some districts of Polesye, up to 65% of the agricultural land has been meliorated (Lishtvan and Yaroshevich, 1991, p. 15).

Drainage of wetlands has led to severe environmental problems in the Polesye region, most of which are associated with developments in the 1960s that employed many archaic technologies. First, the water regime was altered and streams disappeared. From 1945 to 1973, the level of water in Polesye rivers decreased by 7 to 51 cm, and by 20 cm in the major river Pripyat, even though the climate remained the same (Lishtvan and Yaroshevich, 1991, p. 21).

Second, drainage leads to the deterioration of the soil moisture regime in adjacent territories. The peat formation is replaced by the destruction and mineralization of the soil's organic content. This also increases the problem of soil erosion, which is already quite severe in Belarus, where 30% of soils are inclined to water erosion and about 8% to wind erosion. Because of erosion, the area of agricultural land decreased by 173.1 thousand ha for 1976–1985 and by 123.8 thousand ha for 1986–87. One million tons of soil are blown away by wind from reclaimed peat bogs each year.

Third, agriculture on reclaimed lands leads to increased water contamination by erosion products and fertilizers. Fourth, soil drainage adversely affects water and marsh birds and reptiles. The majority of birds in the Belorusian list of endangered species (the Red Book) inhabit wetlands.

Last but not least, the loss of wetlands means great aesthetic damage. Wetland landscapes have played an important role in the formation of the Belarusian culture. It is sufficient to note that there are almost two dozen words in the Belarusian language to refer to marshy land.

Forestry, Nature Conservation and Tourism

Forests occupy 34.7% of the territory of the country. This fraction has not decreased since 1973, but the quality of the forests has deteriorated. Mature forests account for only 2.4% of total forested land. Forestry mismanagement and the increased risk of fires on meliorated peat areas pose threats for Belarusian forests, including the most valuable and endangered oak woods. To help protect these forests, numerous protected natural areas have been created. By 1993 there were 76 protected areas, including the Berezina and Pripyat Nature Reserves, one planned national park, the Belovezhskaya Pushcha Hunting Preserve, and 73 nature preserves (*zakazniki*) of state importance in Belarus (see Appendix 11.1). Additionally there are 186 areas designated as local nature monuments. The total area of protected territories is 4.4% of the country (0.67% in nature reserves); there are plans to increase this up to 10% (Matesovich, 1990, p. 5).

Fluvioglacial and alluvial plains are represented in the Berezina Biosphere Reserve (established in 1925, 76,201 ha), and Belovezhskaya Pushcha (established in 1939, 87,600 ha). Belovezhskaya Pushcha (the Forest of White Tower), which is one of the oldest reserves on the territory of the former Soviet Union (and extends westward into Poland), has a special status of "preserved hunting area." In the 1930s, the population of European bisons (*zubr*) was protected and recovered there. Now, the *zubr* is often used as a symbol of Belarus since more than two hundred of them live in the country. Recently, the World Bank has allocated a million dollar grant for the Belarusian and Polish governments to preserve the Pushcha.

The complex landscapes of Polesye, including peat bogs, are preserved in the Pripyat Reserve (established in 1969, 62,213 ha), which is situated in the broadleaf forest zone. A characteristic feature of this region is its high degree of afforestation (about 55%). All species of trees grown in Belarus are represented there. The landscape of the Pripyat Reserve symbolizes Polesye: vast picturesque oak forests on floodplains with stork nests in the oaks.

The Polesye Radiation-Ecology Reserve was established in 1988 in eastern Polesye to analyze the impacts of higher background radiation on the ecosystems in the Pripyat basin where the Chernobyl disaster took place. There is a plan to establish Naliboksky Reserve in the central part of Belarus in Minsk and Hrodna (Grodno) Oblasts in the oak-dark conifer forest subzone. The most valuable area here is a large forested area where 23 rivers form the upper portion of the Nyoman (Neman) River watershed.

There are numerous problems to be solved with regard to nature reserves. First, the existing preserves do not fully reflect the variety of Belarusian landscapes. The following landscapes are completely absent in the existing nature reserves: (1) glacial lake plains (in Poozerye), (2) loess plateau (in central and eastern Belarus on the Belarusian Ridge), and (3) high hill plains (outside the Valdai glaciation area, on the Belarusian Ridge). Second, the preservation of natural water bodies has hitherto been outside the scope of plans for new reserves. Third, it would be desirable to preserve high (oligotrophic) moors in the upper reaches of rivers, which help maintain the ecological equilibrium in a region.

The Belarusian landscape also provides favorable conditions for the creation of national parks, which require the development of tourist zones. In national parks, not only natural but also some cultural and historical sites might be preserved (cultural buildings, architectural ensembles, etc.). One national park, Braslavskye Ozyora, is currently being planned.

Solving these nature protection problems will require considerable effort not only because the withdrawal of lands is difficult in this relatively densely populated region, but also because there is little experience in combining several uses in a single area (e.g., tourism and recreation) while at the same time preserving land use patterns and other cultural traditions.

For many reasons Belarus seems to be a good place for international tourism. Among these are the easy access from all parts of western Europe, the Baltic region and Russia. The road system is relatively good by Soviet standards. The moderate climate of the country is another advantage. Last but not least, Belarus provides a level of political stability, which cannot be seen in any other republic of the former Soviet Union.

Some disadvantages must also be noted. The first of them is the effect of the Chernobyl disaster, which forces even local Belarusian residents to leave the country for the sake of their health (see Figure 11.1 for the main areas impacted). The infrastructure for tourism in Belarus is much less developed than, for example, in the Baltic countries (on the other hand, it offers less expensive service).

Among the assets to tourism in Belarus are the picturesque hills and lakes of Poozerye, which is an ideal place for boating, windsurfing, fishing and camping; nature reserves (Berezina and Belovezhskaya Pushcha already have some tourist facilities); the Belovezhskaya Pushcha, which can provide hunters with an opportunity hunt in a virgin European forest; and the old castles of Hrodna, Navahrudak, Mir and other cities (many of which need to be restored).

Visiting Belarus, tourists can enjoy vast woodlands and complex marshlands, wild heath moors and small forest lakes. They can also see the original way of life of Eastern Slavs, which is still preserved in some of the Polesye villages. There is a opportunity for a visitor to learn much about the intriguing and little-known pages of European history—dramatic battles between the Roman-Catholic West and the Orthodox East that took place on Belarusian territory.

Governmental Structure and Legislation

The State Committee on Nature Protection of the former Byelorussian SSR was formed in the 1960s. At that time, its main function was the protection of natural water bodies and wildlife. Occupational hazards, drinking water quality, and residential environment were under the authority of the Ministry for Health Protection, and air and surface water monitoring was the responsibility of Goskomgidromet (the State Committee on Hydrometeorology). In 1989, all environmental protection became the responsibility of Goskompriroda, which in 1991 in Belarus was renamed Dzyarzhkamecalogia (the State Committee on the Environment). However, it currently lacks the necessary equipment and personnel to perform its responsibilities in full. Thus, for the time being the Goskomgidromet and the Ministry of Health Protection continue their monitoring. Nature reserves are under the authority of a special agency within the Council of Ministers rather than the Dzyarzhkamecalogia. All of the environmental protection activity within individual ministries is supervised by the Committee of the Council of Ministers on Emergency Situations, the Consequences of the Chernobyl Disaster, and the Environment. A special parliamentary commission and governmental committee deal with the problems associated with the Chernobyl disaster, according to S. Rudneva, the chief environmental specialist of the Belarusian Council of Ministers.

In terms of legislation, the first Belarusian environmental law was adopted in the fall of 1992 (the State Law on Environmental Protection). The Law on Environmental Safety and the Law on State Environmental Assessments were being discussed in the media in 1993.

Among the Belarusian non-governmental environmental organizations, the Belarusian Ecological Union (BEU) and the Belarusian branch of the Social-Ecological Union should be mentioned. The Minsk branch of BEU succeeded in stopping a proposed industrial development in the city center in 1992. It also publishes the *Ekologiya Minska* weekly, the only city environmental newspaper in the former Soviet Union that in 1993 was being delivered to the U.S. Library of Congress.

There are also more than two dozen citizen groups and foundations dealing with the consequences of Chernobyl. The largest of them is the Belarusian Social-Ecological Union Chernobyl, affiliated with SEU, which for more than two years has published the *Nabat* newspaper distributed in Russia, Ukraine, and some other countries.

Belarusian human and natural resources provide excellent potential for resolving environmental problems and mitigating the devastating impacts of the Chernobyl disaster. The necessary preconditions for doing this are political factors such as peace, good relations with neighboring countries, and internal stability. To this end, Belarus took the significant step in 1994 of closely integrating its economy with that of the Russian Federation, including adoption of the Russian ruble and credit control by the Russian Central Bank. In return, Belarus receives oil and natural gas from Russia on more favorable terms. A pro-Russia president of Belarus, Alexander Lukashenko, was elected in summer 1994.

The Belarusians demonstrated that maintaining peaceful conditions remains the highest national priority when on February 4, 1993, the Belarusian parliament voted to adhere to the Nuclear Non-proliferation Treaty and to ratify the 1991 Strategic Arms Reduction Treaty. Thus, Belarus became the first state in history to give up its nuclear arms. This is a positive sign which allows considerable hope for a better future for this new country.

Appendix 11.1   Preserved Areas in Belarus

Type of Preserve(a)	Number	Total area(b)	Average size(b)	% of Republic(c)
Nature Reserves (<u>zapovedniki</u>)	2	1384.14	692.07	0.67
Biosphere Reserves	1	762.01	762.01	0.37
National Parks	0	0.00	0.00	0.00
Natural Preserves (<u>zakazniki</u>)	50	6067.00	121.34	2.92
Hunting Preserves	2	985.47	492.74	0.47
Total	54	8436.61	156.23	4.06

Nature Reserves (date created)	Hectares
Berezina (1925)	76201
Pripyat (1969)	62213
Total	138414

Hunting Preserves	Hectares
Belovezhskaya pushcha (1940)	87600
Telekhanskoye (1977)	10947
Total	98547

(a) For the definition of each type of preserve, see Appendix 1.2.
(b) In square kilometers.
(c) Area of Belarus equals 207,600 sq. kilometers

Source: Pryde, 1991.

Bibliography

Bulygina, T.G. 1992. "Ecologicheskiye problemy rayonov deyatel'nosti kaliynykh predpriyatiy." An analytical report prepared for the government. Minsk. Unpublished ms.

"Ekologicheskiye aspekty social'no-economicheskogo razvitiya Belorussii i ispol'zovaniya prirodnykh resursov." 1991. (The Report of the State Committee on the Environment to the Council of Ministers). Minsk. Unpublished ms.

Ekologiya Minska. (The Minsk city weekly environmental newspaper). Various issues.

Fridlyand, M. 1992. Head of the Minsk City Council Environmental Committee. Personal communication.

Goyev, V.Ya., and Kochanovskiy, S.B. 1990. *Obzornaya informatsiya, 1989: Novoye v reshenii problemy okhrany okruzhaiushey sredy v Belorusii.* Minsk: BelNIITI.

The International Chernobyl Project. 1991. An Overview. Report by the I.A.N.E. International Advisory Committee.

Kazakov, V.S., Demidchik, E.P., and Astakhova L.N. 1992. "Thyroid Cancer after Chernobyl." *Nature* 359, pp. 21–22.

Kratkaya Belorusskaya Sovetskaya Entsiklopediya (KBSE). 1977–1978. Vols. 1–5. Minsk: Goskomizdat.

Lishtvan, I.I., and Yaroshevich L.M. 1991. "Problema melioratsii i okhrana prirody." In *Ekologicheskiye aspekty melioratsii: Sbornik nauchnykh trudov.* Minsk: BelNIIMiVKh.

Marples, D.R. 1992. "Post-Soviet Belarus and the Impact of Chernobyl." *Post-Soviet Geography,* vol. 33, no. 7, pp. 419–431.

Matesovich A.A. 1990. *Aktual'nyie problemy sostoyaniya i okhrany prirodnoyi sredy v Belorusii.* Minsk: Obshestvo Znaniye.

Mil'kov, F.N. 1961. *Srednyaya polosa Evropeyskoy chasti SSSR.* Moscow: State Geographic Literature Publishing.

Rudneva, S. 1992. Chief Environmental Specialist of the Belorusian Council of Ministers. Personal communication.

Skoropanov, S.G., Karlovskyi, V.P., and Brezgunov, V.S. 1982. *Melioratsiya zemel' i okhrana okruzhayushchey sredy.* Minsk: Uradzhayi.

Yakubovich, L.S. 1989. *Okhrana okruzhayushchey sredy v BSSR.* An analytical report prepared for the government. Minsk. Unpublished ms.

Zapovedniki Pribaltiki i Belorussii. 1989. Moscow: Mysl'.

Zaprudnik, Jan. 1993. *Belarus: At a Crossroads in History.* Boulder: Westview Press.

12

Moldova

Adriana Dinu and Matthew Rowntree

The independent Republic of Moldova presently consists for the most part of the old Moldovan Republic of Bessarabia, which was created by Romanians in 1359, together with a narrow strip of former Ukrainian territory east of the Dnestr River (locally called the Nistru River), which was annexed in 1940 (see Figure 12.1). Moldova has an area of 33,700 km^2 and a 1992 population of 4,359,100, of which 3,900 km^2 and a population of 600,000 lie in the trans-Dnestr region. It is the second smallest of the former Soviet states. Moldova is situated between Romania to the west and Ukraine to the north, east and south. Chisinau (Kishinev) is the capital, Romanian the national language, and Eastern Orthodoxy the dominant religion. It became a member of the Council on Security and Cooperation in Europe on 30 January 1992 and of the United Nations on 2 March 1992.

History and Demographic Characteristics

Being strategically positioned, Moldova was fought over and fragmented by the great imperial powers of Austria, Russia and Turkey for much of its history. In 1484, the southern region of Bessarabia was given to the Turks. In 1600, Milhai Viteazu combined the countries of Valachia, Transylvania and Moldova to form a united Romania. After the Russo-Turkish War (1806–1812), Russia annexed 44,500 km^2 of Romania east of the Prut River. Following the Paris treaty of 1859, Moldova regained Bessarabia. But that territory was lost again to Russia in 1912. In January 1918, following the collapse of tsarist Russia, Bessarabia declared its independence from Russia when it was named the Democratic Republic of Moldova and was united with Romania in March of that year (Nistor, 1991).

The Soviet republic of Moldova was created by Stalin in 1939 under the Molotov-Ribbentrop Pact. It includes the former Romanian provinces of

Figure 12.1
MOLDOVA
◎ Capital
● Cities
▨ Trans-Nistru (Trans-Dnestr) Region

Bessarabia and Bukovina and former Ukrainian territories to the east of the Dnestr River, which were exchanged for Moldovan territories to the south of the republic. By creating a new republic and concentrating the industrial centres in the Russian-speaking, former Ukrainian territory of (trans-)Dnestr, Stalin was able to gain greater control over the Moldovans by reducing their population majority, increasing their dependence on the Ukrainian dominated areas for power and industrial produce, and undermining future territorial claims by Romania (Fleck, 1991). Stalin further strengthened his hold on Moldova by making Russian the official language, thereby favoring ethnic Russians for government positions. Stalin is also blamed for allowing a series of famines, with the result that close to one million Romanians were displaced between 1940 and 1964. Many of these people were replaced with immigrants from Ukraine and Kazakhstan (Nistor, 1991).

The glasnost period leading up to the collapse of the USSR in December 1991 generated new feelings of ethnic identity among the Moldovan people.

In August 1989, the Moldovan government adopted a law reinstating Romanian as the official language and in August 1991 declared its independence from the Soviet Union.

The population of Moldova reflects its turbulent past, with its mixed ethnic composition of nearly 4.4 million. Included in this number are about 3 million Romanian-Moldovans (64%), over 1 million Russians (13%) and Ukrainians (13.8%), over 150,000 Gagauz (3.5%; these are Turkish Christians), with the remainder being Jews, Bulgarians, and others (see Table 12.1). The country experienced a 10% population growth rate between 1979 and 1989 with Chisinau, the capital, accounting for 655,000 people (15.4% of the total population) at the beginning of 1989. According to the 1989 census, there were 2.06 million males and 2.27 million females; of the total population, 46.5% were classified as urban. Moldova is divided into 40 administrative districts and four major urban centers: Chisinau, Tiraspol (182,000 population in 1989), Balti (Beltsy, 159,000), and Tighina (Bendery, 130,000).

Ethnic tensions have increased since 1990. Among Romanian-Moldovans, the Russian and Ukrainian populations have become increasingly unpopular as a result of past privileges. These groups are now considered foreigners. Further antagonism has developed as the Russian and Ukrainian majority in the Province of Dnestr in eastern Moldova seeks independence as the Soviet Socialist Moldovan Republic of Transdnestria (or the Dnestr Republic). This is partly in response to having failed to gain support from Russia or Ukraine to form an autonomous state within either of them (Fleck, 1991). The nationalism expressed by some of the majority of the Ukrainian and Russian residents of Transdnestria is becoming increasingly significant in the region's future; they have already used their industrial and transport advantages to blockade the rest of Moldova. Civil disputes and unrest in the region's capital, Tiraspol, as well as in Dubasari (Dubossary) and Tighina, resulted in a

Table 12.1   Characteristics of Moldovan Population, 1989

Nationality Background	1000 People	% of Country	Urban % of Ethnic Group
Romanians	2794.7	64.5	33.5
Ukrainians	600.4	13.8	63.1
Russians	562.1	13.0	86.1
Gagauz	153.3	3.5	41.2
Bulgarians	88.4	2.0	45.5
Jews	65.8	1.5	99.2
Others	70.8	1.7	68.0
Total	4335.4	100.0	

Source: Data adapted from Soviet Geography, April 1991, p. 228.

state of emergency being set up in the summer of 1990 and 20 deaths in Tiraspol in March 1992. Ethnic Romanians are also being encouraged to leave some towns, particulary Tighina, 20 km to the west of Tiraspol on the Dnestr River. The Gagauz population is also becoming unpopular as it, too, seeks an independent state in the south of Moldova.

Physical and Biotic Environment

Moldova is a relatively flat country, with one third covered by plains (the North Moldova Plain, or Baltului Steppe, and the South Moldova Plain, or Buceagului Steppe) and fluvial terraces. It has a mean height of 147 m above sea level and a maximum height of 429 m in the central part of the country. The territory has been classified into nine geomorphological regions from north to south and three natural zones: forest, forest-steppe and steppe. The steppe region is in places broken by rugged rock outcrops (Figure 12.2).

The region's climate is semi-arid and continental with little snow and a mean winter temperature of −3°C in the south and −5°C in the north during the coldest month (January) and a summer mean of 22°C in the south and 19.5°C in the north during the hottest month (July). The mean annual rainfall is 400–500 mm, with most precipitation falling between April and October. Rainfall does, however, tend to be sporadic, and droughts occur three years in ten.

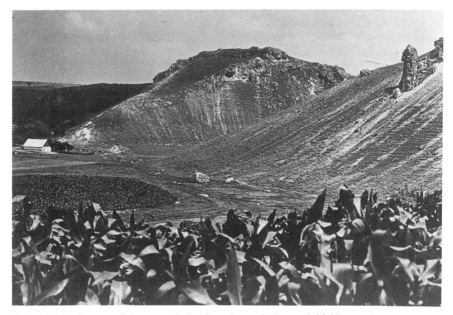

Figure 12.2   An area of steep, eroded rocky outcrops in the north Moldovan steppe region near the city of Edinetz. Photo courtesy of P. Cocirta.

Moldova was originally covered by steppe vegetation in the south and broadleaf forest in the north and sustained fauna representative of eastern Europe, the Balkan Peninsula and the Black Sea's north shores. However, economic development and exploitation have led to a widespread reduction in the country's biodiversity, particularly with reference to steppe and wetland habitats. Furthermore, in 1989, the USSR State Committee on Nature Protection reported that there was no natural landscape remaining in Moldova (Mnatsakanian, 1992), presumedly meaning landscapes unmodified by human activity. Forests, however, do cover 243,100 ha, or 7.2 percent of the country, although there is a high incidence of tree damage (IUCN-EEP, 1991; Pryde, 1991, p. 114).

The country, moreover, still retains 260 bird, 80 fish, 400 other vertebrate species and 4,500 invertebrate species, although these numbers continue to decrease. Between 1900 and 1950, eight bird species were recorded as no longer occurring in Moldova, including the Dalmatian pelican (*Pelecanus crispus*), the black vulture (*Aegypius monachus*) and the steppe eagle (*Aquila rapax*) (Tarabukin, 1978). In 1990, there were 8 mammal, 17 bird and 4 reptile species listed as protected; this number is expected to increase, especially for fish species, as overfishing and hydrotechnical works at Stînca Costesti have prevented fish from entering the Danube-Prut system.

Two state nature preserves were designated during the 1970s, the Kodry State Zapovedniki (5,177 ha) and the Redenskiy Les Hunting Preserve (5,664 ha). Together, they cover 0.32% of the country and contain samples of middle European forest, dominated by species of oak and acacia. These reserves are primarily preserved as scientific institutions for the study of their natural complexes and are established on land excluded from economic utilisation. In 1988, the smaller Yagorlyk Zapovednik was created. By 1989, 11 nature sanctuaries or partial reserves called *zakazniki* (two zoological and 9 botanical) had been designated, which cover 3,200 ha, in addition to the two *zapovedniki* and one hunting preserve just noted. These are statistically summarized in Table 12.2.

Being relatively flat and well drained, Moldova has no topographical constraints to development. The climate permits 2 to 3 agricultural crops per year, but the country is relatively poor in metallic and petrochemical deposits. Although Moldova is currently self-sufficient in steel, it lacks many other essential metals for development. Unless further reserves of coal and oil can be found, Moldova will continue to have an energy deficit (Turnock, 1980).

Moldova receives a total of 13.6 billion m^3 of water annually, with 657 km of the Dnestr River providing 56% of the country's needs and 695 km of the Prut River providing 16%. But despite 3,200 water courses, there are occasional water shortages due to low precipitation and high evaporation rates. These shortages lead to occasional crop failure and rivers drying up (the 1992 drought caused an estimated 40 billion rubles' worth of losses). When flash flooding does occur, it results in erosion of agricultural areas, with landslides and the formation of gullies.

Table 12.2   Preserved Areas in Moldova

Type of Preserve(a)	Number	Total area(b)	Average size(b)	% of Re- public(c)
Zapovedniki	2	60.77	30.39	0.18
National Parks	0	0.00		0.00
Zakazniki	11	32.00	2.91	0.09
Hunting Preserves	1	56.64	56.64	0.17
Total	14	149.41	10.67	0.44

Zapovedniki (date created)	Hectares
Kodry (1971)	5177
Yagorlyk (1988)	900
Total	6077

(a)   For the definition of each type of preserve, see Appendix 1.2.
(b)   In square kilometers.
(c)   Area of Moldova is 33,700 sq. kilometers.

Source: Pryde (1991).

Agriculture and Industry

Moldova's natural productivity is due largely to its rich agricultural soils, with chernozems covering 69% of the country. Agriculture accounts for 24% of Moldova's gross national product and 34% of the work force. Ninety-five percent of the country is under active economic development, with 2.5 million ha, or 74% of the country, dedicated to agriculture (Mnatsakanian, 1992). Of this, 1.8 million ha are under arable production, 408,600 ha are under plantations, and 350,000 ha are under pasture and hay fields. Crops produced include wheat, tomatoes, potatoes, tobacco, cucumbers and grapes, with the latter forming half of the 200 food processing enterprises in the country. In addition to wine grapes, Moldova is also noted for its extensive orchards, which are located mainly on the fertile fluvial terraces. Moldovan wine is considered to be quite good.

In the past, much of Moldova's agricultural produce was exported to other regions of the former USSR at very low prices, and the land was overworked. As a result, there has been extensive soil degradation resulting from careless cultivation and contamination with agricultural chemicals (IUCN-EEP, 1991). Only 20–25% of the total arable land now has a humus content greater than 3%, and large areas of the country are becoming increasingly susceptible to erosion. The dependence on agricultural chemicals has decreased since the late 1980s, though this might partially be caused by shortages of supplies or money. Agriculturalists and distributors still have to reduce the post-harvest loss, which is estimated at 60%, in order to make their operations more efficient (Berry, 1992). In the future, there is potential for Moldova to combine with Romania to form an "agricultural super-power," providing food for European as well as former Soviet countries.

Moldova is further favored with extensive deposits of high quality construction rocks, clay, gravel, limestone, and sands, as well as small deposits of brown coal, oil, and iron ore that were discovered after 1948 (Turnock, 1980). Over 35 million tons of minerals are extracted annually, with operations based on 98 open cast mines and 16 underground mines. However, increasingly large areas of arable land are being destroyed as a result of these extraction processes, and it is likely that conflicts between the needs of agriculture and mineral companies will become more significant in the near future.

A large proportion of Moldova's industry, was created during the 1950s and now accounts for over half of the gross national product. Over one third of the total industrial production is based on the food industry, and over half of these companies are associated with viniculture.

One third of industrial production and 80% of Moldova's energy capacity, however, are made in or controlled from the Dnestr region (*Eastern European Newsletter*, 1992a), including metal and cement works in Ribnita (Rybnitsa) and hydroelectric plants in Dubasari. If the Transdnestr region was declared independent, the opportunities for Moldova's future growth would be severely constrained and dependent upon retaining economic links with the Dnestr region or establishing and developing trade and energy agreements with neighboring states, particularly Romania.

Moldova also contains over 260 large and 400 small intensive livestock farming enterprises. However, their current operation is making a significant contribution to the environmental degradation experienced in Moldova, as over 40 million m^3 of wastes are produced each year (Asevskii and Cocirta, 1989), polluting both water and air with nitrates and ammonia.

Major Environmental Problems

Like many of the former Soviet republics, Moldova has experienced wide-scale, intensive, rapid and unsustainable development. Air, soil, and water pollution is common and is the attributed cause of Moldova's high incidence of abnormal births, infant mortalities, and lowered mental abilities (*Observer*, 15 Jan. 1989; Ziegler, 1992, p. 27; Feshbach and Friendly, 1992, p. 67).

Air pollution is particularly common in large towns and cities such as Balti (Beltsy), Ribnita (Rybnitsa), Chisinau (Kishinev) and Tiraspol. Most of this pollution is caused by vehicles, with 76.2% of the 132,000 tons of pollution emitted in Chisinau during 1988 coming from vehicles (Mnatsakanian, 1992, p. 37). Over half of the pollution from stationary sources comes from energy generating complexes. The giant regional coal-burning power plant near Dnestrovsk accounts for 53% of all pollution from stationary sources, in part because it increased output following the Chernobyl disaster of 1986. Most of this pollution is in the form of SO_2 and particulates (dust) (see Table 12.3). In addition, further pollution has resulted from accidents, such as at the weapons manufacturing complex at Tighina (Bendery), when explosions at a biochemical plant released ammonia and chlorine gases. National air pollution levels are monitored by fourteen stationary and five mobile stations.

After the Second World War, the Soviet leadership encouraged the exploitation of agriculturally rich republics, such as Moldova, to feed other areas. Small farms were converted into state and collective farms and saturated with agricultural chemicals to increase production and reduce pest damage. Between 1965 and 1989, the average mineral fertilizer use increased from 28 kg/ha to 196 kg/ha. From 1967 through 1986, the average application of pesticides in Moldova was over 17 kg/ha, more than ten times the average in western countries. Pesticide use in Moldova was thirteen times higher than even the USSR average (Feshbach and Friendly, 1992, p. 67). Although Moldova's dependence on chemicals has been reduced and experiments with biological pest control have proved successful, food and soil contamination is still extensive, with 25% of the food produced in 1990 found to be polluted with nitrates. Furthermore, DDT is still found in soils in concentrations up to 9.2 mg/kg (Mnatsakanian, 1992, p. 41), even though it was officially banned in the USSR in 1970. High concentrations of the herbicides Simazine and Atrazine are still found in soils, although their concentrations are decreasing (IUCN-EEP, 1991).

Further soil degradation has occurred due to a decline in the country's soil-humus content, causing the soil structure to weaken. One quarter of the arable land in Moldova suffers from water erosion, and 28% of the arable land is subject to deflation (wind erosion). It is estimated that 18 million tons of topsoil erode annually from Moldova's arable land, equating to a loss of 1 ton/ha per year (Mnatsakanian, 1992, p. 41).

Another major environmental problem is based on Moldava's difficulty in securing perennial supplies of potable water and reducing the pollution lev-

Table 12.3   Atmospheric Emissions in Moldova, 1989 (1000 tons)

Pollutant	Total Emissions	%	Emissions from Stationary Sources	%
Carbon Monoxide	544.6	51.4	48.6	11.5
Sulfur Dioxide	237.8	22.4	237.8	56.1
Hydrocarbons	112.2	10.5	9.5	2.2
Nitrogen Oxides	82.8	7.8	45.8	10.8
Dust	79.5	7.5	79.5	18.8

Source: State Committee on Nature Protection, 1990.

els in existing supplies. Only 8% of Moldova's water comes from aquifers, and only 50% of this can meet Soviet drinking standards. Many of the wells near major cities are drying up, and many of the rural wells are contaminated with high mineral concentrations and bacterial counts.

Moldova's water pollution stems from both point and non-point sources, with the dominant point sources being industrial, municipal and sanitary waste sites and livestock farms; with agricultural chemicals, wastes, and soil erosion constituting the major non-point sources. During 1986, 13 million m^3 of untreated water were discharged into the Dnestr basin, and in 1989 this rose to 21 million m^3 (including 610 tons of petroleum products and 19,000 tons of organic compounds). In addition, over 8 million m^3 of water are used annually in the management of wastes from livestock farms, much of which seeps back into water systems, contaminating supplies with nitrates, parasite eggs and pathogens.

Much of the water pollution caused by agriculture is derived from nitrates and soils that are washed directly into adjacent rivers. The Prut and Dnestr River valleys are under extensive agricultural production and have little or no vegetation to intercept chemical-rich water and soil once the harvest has taken place. The Reut River, in an area dominated by agriculture in the north and center of Moldova, had pesticides in 95% of its water when sampled in 1990 and also contained high concentrations of ammonia and nitrogen (IUCN-EEP, 1991). Further contamination results from the direct runoff of used irrigation water, which contains both agricultural chemicals and salts. Serious water pollution has occurred on the Dnestr River as a result of damage to a dam and the non-operation of the sewage works at Dubasari following civil disturbances.

Government Structure and Citizen Activism

Moldova's environmental policies remain a legacy of the former Soviet government, although the new State Department for Environment and Natural Resource Protection (formed in July 1990) is in the process of drafting new laws and has had exclusive control over natural resource administration and nature preservation since October 1990. The new laws will be divided into three components: (1) the use and protection of the environment, (2) the Republic of Moldova State Department for Environment and Natural Resource Protection, and (3) the Ecological Fund of Moldova. They must be approved by the Ecological Commission of the parliament of Moldova. The State Department for Environment and Natural Resource Protection has 2,921 employees, including 1,720 members of the Forest Directorate, 521 members of the Ecological Inspectorate, 405 members in the hydrometeorology division, 185 members of the National Ecological Institute and 90 employees at the department's central office.

As with many other former Soviet republics, non-governmental organizations and citizen activist movements were banned in Moldova by the ruling Communist Party and had no influence in government programs until the end of the 1980s. However, in November 1988, the Moldavian Green Movement was set up by Chisinau intellectuals. Although originally opposed by the government, it was able to draw attention to some of the environmental problems caused by agriculture, power generation, and the pollution of the Prut River. A second NGO, the Ecological Movement, became affiliated with the Moldavian Popular Front, which subsequently gained control of the Supreme Soviet, an action that led to the declaration of independence from Moscow (Ziegler, 1992, p. 28).

Non-governmental organizations are developing in Moldova, although many currently lack basic communication and management skills. The Ecological Movement and the Green Party have, however, developed public awareness and education programs in the mass media; published their own journal, *Ave natura*; organized lessons in schools; and arranged scientific expeditions. They have also developed links with Romania and Ukraine for international research projects in the Dnestr and Prut River basins.

External Ties and Economic Potential

Moldova is still dependent on the former states of the USSR as markets for its goods, although there is considerable potential to develop links with Romania and, through better management programs, become a major European source of agricultural produce. Commodities such as Moldovan wine could potentially become major export items. Furthermore, Romania may be able to provide Moldova with the energy and raw material supplies that are required for future growth, and this in turn could be a step in the direction of a potential reunification.

However, at present Moldova is still highly dependent on Dnestr Province, and authorities in Tiraspol have in the recent past used sanctions on the rest of Moldova to protest the arrest of the Dnestr Republic's president, Igor Smirnov (Fleck, 1991). Dnestr holds considerable advantages when negotiating terms and conditions for future trade and transport agreements with the rest of Moldova as it controls most of Moldova's power and transport capacity. Perhaps in reflection of this, former Communist officials did well in the February 1994 national elections; candidates favoring re-unification with Romania did not. As has been mentioned, Moldova's industrial development will also be limited by the availability of energy resources even if Dnestr officials do not impose sanctions, as their current energy budget runs at a deficit (Turnock, 1980). Energy production will be further restricted if international environmental legislation imposes penalties on severely polluting countries, like Moldova, that still rely on inefficient factories and power generating plants.

Opportunities for the development of Moldova's tourism potential may be restricted due to its relative lack of beaches and outstanding scenery. However, its pleasant climate, historic thirteenth and fourteenth century towns, and abundance of vineyards could be the basis for establishing and developing a potentially thriving tourist industry, assuming a peaceful resolution to current ethnic disagreements.

Acknowledgments

The assistance of the East European Programme of the World Conservation Union (IUCN), and of its personnel in Cambridge, UK; Gland, Switzerland; and Bucharest, Romania, is gratefully acknowledged.

Bibliography

Anon. 1991. *Sostoianie prirodnoi sredî v SSR Moldova v 1989 godu.* Kishinev: Universal.

Asevskii, V., and Cocirta, P. 1989. *Ispalozovanie vodî v jiuvotnovodstive.* Kishinev: Cartea Moldoveneascǎ.

Berry, R. 1992. "Proposed Village Study in the Republic of Moldova." Copy of letter received at the East European Programme, Cambridge, England.

Cocirta, P. 1989. *Vodnîi resursî Moldavii: ispolizovanie i ohrana.* Kishinev: Znanie.

Eastern European Newsletter. 1992a. "Moldova Fused," vol 6. no. 6 (March 16).

——. 1992b. "Moldova/Romania: Anatomy of the Local War," vol. 6, no. 8 (April 13).

——. 1992c. "Romania," vol. 6 no. 25 (December 14).

ECE and UN. 1992. *The Environment in Europe and North America—Annotated Statistics, 1992.* New York: United Nations.

Feshbach, M., and Friendly, A. 1992. *Ecocide in the USSR.* New York: Basic Books.

Fleck, F. 1991. "Russians Resist Slide Towards Romanians." *The Guardian,* September 5.

IUCN-EEP. 1990. *Protected Areas in Eastern and Central Europe and the USSR* (An Interim Review). Cambridge: IUCN Publications.

——. 1991. *Environmental Status Reports: 1990.* Vol 3, *The USSR.* Cambridge: IUCN Publications.

Mnatsakanian, R. 1992. *Environmental Legacy of the Former Soviet Republics.* Edinburgh: University of Edinburgh, Chap. 6.

Moldova State Department for Environmental and Natural Protection. 1991. *Status Report for Moldova in 1990.* Kishinev.

Moldova State Department for Environmental and Natural Resources Protection and National Institute of Ecology. 1992. *Report for the World Bank Regarding the Environmental Status of Moldova.* Kishinev.

Nistor, I. 1991. *Istoria Basarabiei.* Bucharest: Ed. Huminitas.

Pryde, P. 1991. *Environmental Management in the Soviet Union.* Cambridge: Cambridge University Press.

State Committee on Statistics. 1989. *Okhrana okruzhayushchey sredy i ratsional'noye ispol'zovaniye prirodnykh resursov v SSSR: Statisticheskiy sbornik.* Moscow: Goskomstat.

Tarabukin, B. (ed). 1978. *The Red Data Book of the Moldavian SSR* (In Russian), Kishinev; cited in Wilson, M., and Boswall, J. 1987. *Birds in the Soviet Red Data Books,* for ICBP, European Continental Section Conference, Hungary.

Turnock, D. 1980. *Eastern Europe (Studies in Urban Geography).* London: Dawson.

Yablokov, A. 1988. "Pesticide Ecology and Agriculture." *Kommunist,* no. 15, pp. 34–42.

Ziegler, C. 1992. "Political Participation, Nationalism and Environmental Politics in the USSR." in Massey Stewart, J. (ed.), *The Soviet Environment—Problems, Policies and Politics.* Cambridge: Cambridge University Press.

13

Georgia

Lynn Richards

Georgia (which refers to itself as the Sakartvelos Respublika) is the western-most of the three Transcaucasian republics of the former Soviet Union and the only one of the three fronting on the Black Sea. It includes, under Soviet classification, two autonomous republics, Abkhazia and Ajaria, and one autonomous region, South Ossetia (Figure 13.1).

Georgia is home to an ancient civilization, and its Black Sea coast was well known in Roman times. A Georgian state dates from the fourth century B.C., and Christianity was introduced in the fourth century A.D. For the next millennium and a half, Georgia was occupied alternately by Persians, Turks, and Mongols, with only brief periods of independence. In 1801, the core of the country came under the control of tsarist Russia. Georgia was briefly independent from 1917 to 1921 but was forcibly joined to the USSR in 1922.

Unfortunately, considerable ethnic unrest and armed conflict exist in two of Georgia's three autonomous regions as this chapter is being prepared (in 1994); only Ajaria remains peaceful. Because of this internal instability, Georgia has not yet been able to stabilize its economy. The environmental situation in Georgia stands out as one of the silent victims of the social and political strife in that country. Since 1991, some forms of pollution have temporarily decreased because of fuel shortages, ethnic conflicts, and consequent economic downturns. However, with few exceptions, rather little attention has been given to the environmental consequences of the collapse of the nation's political, economic and social infrastructures.

Contemporary Ethnic Conflicts

Georgia is characterized by tremendous ethnic diversity. Of Georgia's 5.4 million people, 70.1% are Georgians (who traditionally refer to themselves as Kartveli); 8.1%, Armenians; 6.3%, Russian; 5.7%, Azeris; 3.0%, Ossetians;

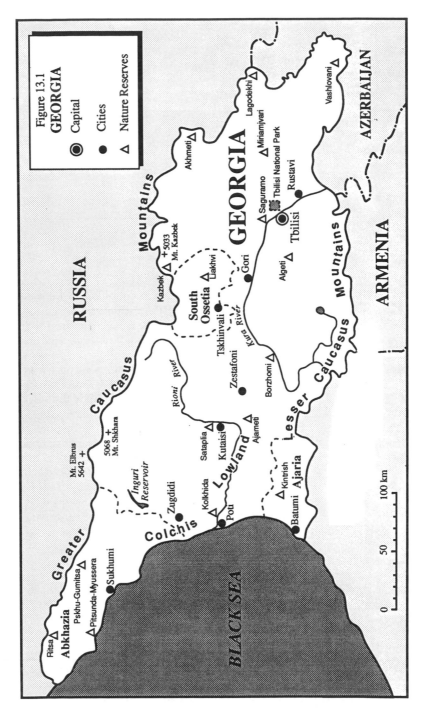

Figure 13.1
GEORGIA

◎ Capital
● Cities
△ Nature Reserves

1.8%, Abkhaz; and less than one percent, Ajars. The 1989 census counted 14 officially recognized national minorities in Georgia, nine of which represented more than 30,000 people (see Table 13.1).

Ethnic conflicts have long plagued Georgia. Presently, the Abkhazians and Ossetians present the most organized independence movements. Over the past seventy years, Georgia's minorities have lacked equal access to political and economic power and faced social and educational disadvantages, despite stated Soviet ethnic equalization policies. The results of these policies are being felt today as Georgia undergoes ethnic and nationality crises.

Problems in Ossetia intensified in December of 1990 when regional elections were organized to form a new South Ossetian parliament. That same month, the late Zviad Gamsakhurdia, then president of Georgia, abolished the South Ossetian Autonomous Region, arrested South Ossetian leaders, and declared a state of emergency. Since then, a civil war, exacerbated by the introduction of Russian Interior Ministry troops, has produced close to 100,000 refugees, who have fled South Ossetia to North Ossetia or other parts of Russia (Jones, 1992, p. 31). As of 1994, the situation remains tense and unsettled.

However, the conflict in Abkhazia has taken precedence over problems in South Ossetia and saps most of Georgia's political and social energy. While the Abkhazians represent only about 18% of the total population in the autonomous republic, they hold the majority of the seats in the local government through the old electoral laws established during the Stalin era.

Table 13.1   Major Ethnic Groups in Georgia

Ethnic group	Dominant religion	1989 pop'n in Georgia (1000s)	Percent of total Georgian pop'n (1989)
Georgians	Georgian Christian	3787	70.1
Armenians	Armenian Apostolic	437	8.1
Russians	Eastern Orthodox	341	6.3
Azerbaijani	Shiite Moslem	308	5.7
Ossetians	Eastern Orthodox; Islam	164	3.0
Greeks	Greek Orthodox	100	1.9
Abkhaz	Islam; Eastern Orthodox	96	1.8
Ukrainians	Eastern Orthodox	52	1.0
Ajars	Sunni Moslem	30-50	<1.0
(Others)		50-100	1+
Georgia, total	Georgian Christian	5449	100

Sources: Wixman, 1984; Schwartz, 1991.

Vladislav Ardzinba (Rdinba), elected to the Supreme Soviet of the USSR in 1989, began to govern in Abkhazia without the consent of parliament in 1991 (Chagelishvili, 1993). In protest, the Georgian representatives stopped attending the sessions and tensions escalated.

From December 1991 to January 1992, during the Georgian civil war, President Gamsakhurdia was removed from power, and massive numbers of weapons and ammunition were spread throughout western Georgia, effectively arming gangs. After Gamsakhurdia's deportation, his supporters gathered in western Georgia and blockaded railroads and robbed and pillaged trains and villages in protest. To protect the railroad lines, the Georgian government, then headed by Eduard Shevardnadze, sent troops to the area. Ardzinba, with the armed support of Gamsakhurdia's supporters and Abkhazia nationalists, responded by illegally creating a homoethnic national guard. Georgian troops and the National Guard lined themselves on either side of the mountains near Zugdidi. At this time, Shevardnadze warned Ardzinba that his guard had to step down and allow Georgian and Russian troops to protect the railroads from the bandits. In August 1992, 13 people, ministers and other high ranking officials, were kidnapped and taken to the Gali region, just inside the Abkhazia border. Georgian troops then made the decision to cross into Abkhazia. The Abkhazian National Guard met them with gunfire. Seven Georgian soldiers were killed and the war began (Chagelishvili, 1993). Throughout 1993, the Abkhazian separatists had the upper hand in the fighting, but with the support of Russian troops, Shevardnadze was able to regain control in late 1993. In 1994, 3,000 Russian troops were deployed as a peacekeeping force along the Abkhazia border.

While armed conflicts continue in Abkhazia and South Ossetia, it is impossible to assess the almost certain environmental damage. Almost all factories have ceased normal operations, and while these closures help abate some of the environmental problems, this remains an unsatisfactory and temporary solution.

Physical Characteristics

The nation covers a land area of 69,700 square kilometers and supports a high degree of biodiversity, with over 100 different types of landscapes and 23 physical geographic regions. Because of this level of diversity, Georgia has a high potential for natural resource development and exploitation.

Northern Georgia is entirely bounded by the Greater Caucasus Mountains; to the south lie the Lesser Caucasus Mountains. The highest peaks in the Greater Caucasus rise to over 5,000 meters and include dormant volcanoes. The Black Sea shoreline extends over 320 kilometers and supports wetlands and other types of coastal ecosystems. Between Zestafoni and the Kura River lies the relatively low watershed divide (a little over 1,000 meters) that separates the humid Colchis lowland in the west from the drier eastern half of the country. The Rioni and Kura Rivers drain these two regions, respectively.

Rainfall is plentiful in the western and alpine portions of Georgia and results in a humid subtropical climate in these areas. The coastal region has one of the mildest climates in the former Soviet Union, and as winter frosts here are usually mild, some citrus fruits (oranges, lemons, etc.) can be commercially grown in Ajaria. Eastern Georgia receives less moisture, and consequently more arid landscapes are encountered. As one travels eastward, the Caucasus Mountains become similarly more arid, with fewer forests and more meadows, pastures and savannas. The Lesser Caucasus Mountains are likewise wet in the west, drier in the east. Indeed, Batumi is the rainiest city in the former Soviet Union, receiving an average of 2,500 millimeters (100 inches) of precipitation a year.

Zapovedniki, or nature reserves, cover 2.4% of Georgian territory; over half of the reserves were founded before 1950 (Table 13.2). Currently, Georgia has only one national park, not far from Tbilisi, with a total area of 20,053 ha. This park does not extend into the high mountains, and is more in the nature of an urban greenbelt forest.

For the past three years, the World Wildlife Fund (WWF) has been working to create seven new national parks, covering 30% of Georgian land territory, which will greatly increase the amount of protected land in Georgia. The parks will follow international standards and have the full support of the Georgian government. Currently, the natural resources and potential of these areas are being assessed and analyzed, while plans are being made to create the first park in the Borgeomi (Borzhomi) region. Five of the proposed parks are located in forested and mountainous areas, one in a savanna area in central Georgia, and one in a wetlands area on the Black Sea coast (Shanshiashvili, 1993). As of February 1993, management plans were being developed to create a series of management zones for each park. The first zone will be a strictly protected area. The second zone will be a historical-cultural area intended for limited use. The third zone, a buffer area, will be a managed nature zone.

Georgia's natural constraints to development are compounded by anthropogenic environmental problems, such as erosion and deforestation. Problems such as landslides and avalanches are often a direct consequence of deforestation and severe wind erosion. In addition, Georgia is subject to serious floods, especially in spring. Snowmelt collects in mountain rivers and streams, causing significant amounts of soil to be lost during these spring floods. For example, in 1987 and 1989, eighty-three thousand ha of arable land were inundated as the result of two unusually heavy floods (Mnatsakanian, 1992, p. 65). As mentioned earlier, no part of the country is entirely free from frost.

Earthquakes are common and frequently disrupt both local landscapes and Georgian life. Most of the quakes are centered in the mountain regions, but some nevertheless affect populated areas. Earthquakes in the summer of 1991 leveled several villages about 100 km north of Tbilisi, and the 1988 Armenia earthquake was felt strongly in southern Georgia.

Georgia's relative lack of fossil fuels is another constraint to economic development. However, the country's location on the Black Sea gives it an economic advantage not enjoyed by either of the other two Transcausasus republics.

Table 13.2   Preserved Areas in Georgia

Type of Preserve(a)	Number	Total area(b)	Average size(b)	% of Re-public(c)
Zapovedniki	16	1686.46	105.40	2.42
Zapovedniki that are Biosphere Reserves	0	0.00		0.00
National Parks	1	200.53	200.53	0.29
Zakazniki	1	100.00	100.00	0.14
Total	18	1986.99	110.39	2.85

Zapovedniki (Date created)	Hectares
Ajameti (1957; 1946)	4848
Akhmeti (1980)	16297
Algeti (1965)	6822
Borzhomi (1959; 1935)	17948
Kazbek (1976)	8707
Kintrish (1959)	13893
Kolkhida (1959; 1935)	500
Lagodekhi (1912)	17818
Liakhvi (1977)	6385
Miriamjvari (1959; 1935)	1040
Pitsunda-Myussera (1966; 1926)	3645
Pskhu-Gumista (1978; 1946)	40819
Ritsa (1957; 1946)	16289
Saguramo (1957; 1946)	5247
Sataplia (1957; 1935)	354
Vashlovani (1957; 1935)	8034
Total	168646

National Parks	Hectares
Tbilisi (1973)	20053

(a) For the definition of each type of preserve, see Appendix 1.2.
(b) In square kilometers.
(c) Area of Georgia is 69,700 sq. kilometers.

Source: Pryde (1991).

Natural Resources and Industrial Development

Georgia is rich in natural resources, but the industries that have been built around them take a toll on the environment. Some of the world's largest manganese deposits are located in Georgia at Chiatura, which in 1990 supplied about 12% of the USSR's needs. There are also small coal and iron ore reserves, plus some copper, lead and zinc and the former Soviet Union's main deposits of barite (used in the production of computer chips). There are also abundant construction materials and good agricultural land. In normal times, the country's main exports include tea, grain crops, fruits and wine.

Georgia also has access to geothermal resources, "earth heat," which represent an attractive non-conventional energy source. The most practical development of geothermal energy in the former Soviet Union has focused on space heating, water heating, and agricultural applications. In Tbilisi, 25,000 people benefit from geothermal heat, and a few smaller towns have been entirely or mostly supplied from this source since the 1970s (Pryde, 1991, p. 69). Two associated phenomena are numerous hot mineral springs, widely developed for health spas, and cold mineral springs that provide a variety of mineral waters.

Chemical, energy, and metallurgical plants and mining operations play a major role in polluting the natural environment. A manganese metallurgical plant is located in Zestafoni. Rustavi hosts two major industries: an iron and steel complex (built at Stalin's insistence) and a large chemical complex. Tbilisi and Kutaisi also contain chemical plants. In addition, there are a petroleum refinery at Batumi, a ship building factory in Poti and a military production plant in Tbilisi. These factories consumed 25% of all energy used in Georgia, and often the cities in which they are located are at the top of lists for environmental problems, including air and water pollution.

Georgia, with 70% of its landmass originally covered by forests, is confronted with a problem of extreme deforestation. This, in turn, compounds other environmental problems and deteriorates the economic and social state of the country. It is estimated, though unconfirmed, that 40–50% of Georgia's forests have been cut (Crkonia, 1993). Rangers who are supposed to be protecting the forests are underpaid and therefore must take other employment and in some cases are apt to participate in the cutting of forests. In addition, the rangers work for the Forestry Ministry, and this ministry still views forests as a source of income.

While any kind of private cutting is illegal, individual citizens are chopping down trees for fuel due to a severe energy shortage or for profit due to economic difficulties. A truckload of trees can sell for the equivalent of $5,000. Custom officials between Georgia and Turkey are quite lax, and consequently much lumber crosses the border. Officially, it is illegal to export any wood from Georgia, but that law is rarely enforced. The Eco-Police (a new project under the Environmental Ministry, which employs 300 people nationally to protect nature from armed bandits and thieves) is taking some steps toward enforcement. For example, in Batumi, the Eco-Police arrested the crews of four boats filled with lumber headed for Turkey (Nogaideli,

1993). Timber is one of Georgia's greatest resources as well as part of the culture for many in the region. The effects of deforestation include increased soil erosion, landslides, a decrease in potential tourism, and an increase in the decimation of rare and endangered animals.

In western Georgia, a broad, flat area known as the Colchis lowland is drained by the Rioni River. Its natural flatness caused it to have drainage problems, and consequently a massive "reclamation" project was undertaken here to lower the water table and place the land into crops. Because the soil here is only moderately fertile, large applications of fertilizers are necessary to maintain its important agricultural output.

Pollution Problems

While Georgia's soil and forestry problems can act as an indicator of ecological deterioration, the problem of household and industrial wastes points to another serious shortcoming: due to current civil, economic and political strife, many systems for collecting and handling wastes have ceased to operate. For example, in 1993 regular garbage pickup in Tbilisi no longer occurred. Recycling is at a standstill. In 1989, paper wastes were being recycled by three factories, which turned them into writing paper, toilet paper, cardboard, cartons and shingles (Zhvania, 1993). The largest was the Zugdidi pulp and paper plant; however, it no longer runs due to political unrest and an inability to obtain fuel. In 1993, the recycling factories were collectively handling only 3,000–5,000 tons of waste paper.

Sewage poses another major environmental and health threat. In Batumi, only 60% of the sewage system is effective, causing 110 tons per year of organic contaminants to flow directly into the Black Sea and 1,220 tons of suspended solids. In Sukhumi, 50% of the city's sewage system does not work, and the other half has little effect because of malfunctioning equipment. The result is a flow of dirty, untreated water near beach and recreation areas; 846 tons of flowing organic contaminants and 660 tons of suspended objects are deposited yearly. In Poti, only 20% of the equipment for the wastewater treatment system is working, which results in 300 tons per year of organic substances and 220 tons per year of suspended solids flowing directly into the Black Sea (Georgian, 1992, p. 1).

Outdated and unmaintained equipment also results in contamination of the Black Sea. In Poti, a fish processing plant with primitive refining equipment accounts for 200 tons per year of organic substances and 30 tons of suspended solids being dumped directly into the sea (Ministry, 1992, p. 10). The collective result is a contaminated water system and the destruction of surrounding ecosystems.

Severe energy problems also plague Georgia. Energy resources include hydroelectric power, poor quality coal, and very limited gas and crude oil reserves. The largest hydroelectricity producer is the Inguri dam, which has 1,600 installed megawatts. Natural gas is imported from Turkmenistan, Russia and Iran (Vakhrang, 1993). However, 35–40% of all energy produced is lost because of technical problems, inefficient use, and inadequate transportation lines. No specific legislation exists regarding energy production or usage. It is estimated that the Georgian people need only one third of what is currently used and that individual factories are using up to eight times more energy than similar factories in the West (Nogaideli, 1993). Poorly designed international agreements aggravate this problem. The Inguri region imports electricity from Turkey in the winter and exports similar amounts in the summer. The energy Turkey exports, however, is four times more expensive than the energy Georgia exports.

Georgia's own natural resources could help alleviate its energy problems only at a high price. For example, the country has many fast, small mountain streams that could provide additional hydro power in the spring and summer to many of the small villages, but this would entail environmental losses. Georgia's only major fossil fuel is coal, and while it could be used to help alleviate some energy problems, it is of poor quality and produces high levels of atmospheric emissions when burned.

Although currently air pollution has decreased as a direct result of fuel shortages, fewer cars on the roads, and many factories unable to operate, it still remains a problem and is expected to increase because of outdated and ill-maintained equipment once factories resume operation (Figure 13.2). In 1989, air pollution levels were 100–120 percent of the national average of the former Soviet Union (Zhvania, 1993). There are four large industrial centers in Georgia (Zestafoni, Rustavi, Kutaisi, and Tbilisi), and all were included among the 85 most polluted cities in the Soviet Union in 1989 (Table 13.3).

The city of Rustavi is heavily polluted with dust, ammonia, phenols and benz(a)piren. In 1989, Tbilisi also had high pollution levels due to a combination of auto emissions and the city's location in a valley, which caused pollutants frequently to become trapped under inversions. The main pollutants are nitrogen oxides, carbon monoxide, formaldehyde, lead, phenols, and particulates. Thirty-seven percent of Tbilisi's air pollution treatment equipment worked inadequately in 1988 (Mnatsakanian, 1992, p. 60). In Zestafoni the main pollutant is manganese as well as benz(a)piren and particulates; and in Kutasisi, the main problems are particulates, phenols, and benz(a)piren. In 1989, the total volume of air pollutants released into the Georgian atmosphere was 1.37 million metric tons, of which about 70% originated from motor vehicles (State Committee, 1990).

While there has been an improvement in recent years in air quality, it results mainly from economic problems. It is generally accepted that once the fuel crisis is resolved, the air pollution figures will again climb, since there has been no improvement in the equipment used to control pollution levels.

The exploitation and deterioration of soils are a direct result of agricultural methods practiced under the communist regime. The introduction of monocultures into Georgia eliminated crop diversity and traditional farming methods. Monocultures were developed during the Stalin regime, when it was decided that western Georgia should produce mainly tea and eastern Georgia, mainly grain products (Zhvania, 1993). Five hundred years ago, Georgian peasants knew how and where to plant a variety of crops using terraces, which take into account and help conserve Georgia's fragile soil. Dif-

Figure 13.2   Dense hydrocarbon pollution being given off at a small industrial enterprise at Ambrolauri, on the upper Rioni River in the Caucasus foothills. Photo courtesy of the Georgian Greens.

ferent soil types were used for different crops. The implementation of mono-cultures eliminated this diversity and introduced the use of heavy machinery from Russia which further compounded the soil erosion problem. As a result of these practices, in 1989, of Georgia's 2,990,000 ha of agricultural land, 205,000 ha were salinated (6.9%), 855,000 ha were eroded (28.6%), 419,000 ha needed irrigation (14.0%), and 44,000 ha were waterlogged (1.5%) (Mnatsaka-nian, 1992, p. 65).

In addition, since World War II, about 700,000 ha of cultivated land have been lost to cities, roads, and industry. While the use of pesticides has dimin-ished somewhat in recent years due to public pressure, nearly 64% of the soil samples examined in 1989 contained pesticides (Mnatsakanian, 1992). Agri-cultural chemicals, fertilizers and pesticides are used three times more in

Table 13.3   **Major Urban/Industrial Centers in Georgia**

City	Population (1000s) 1970	1989	% increase	On 1989 "most polluted" list?
Tbilisi	889	1260	42	Yes
Kutaisi	161	235	46	Yes
Rustavi	98	159	62	Yes
Batumi	101	136	35	No
Sukhumi	102	121	19	No
Zestafoni	n.a.	23	n.a.	Yes
Georgia, total	4686	5449	16	

Sources: Soviet Geography, May 1989;   Mnatsakanian, 1992.

Georgia than in the West. In addition, sheep migrations in eastern Georgia compound the erosion problem. Over 100,000 sheep cross the mountains yearly, eating grasses and bushes, which act as natural barriers to erosion, and damage the soil with their hooves. The result of this migration is substantial soil erosion during rainstorms (Zhvania, 1993).

Georgia's abundant freshwater resources are threatened by current and past practices, which include poor regulation of factory effluents and a policy of heavy pesticide and fertilizer use. Rivers in Georgia are extremely polluted with pesticides used on tea and citrus plantations, which result in severe groundwater pollution (Zhvania, 1993). Near Batumi, the small rivers of Bartskana and Kubitsilakhi are extremely polluted with phenols, organic matter, ammonia, and nitrates all at four to twenty times the maximum permitted concentration (Mnatsakanian, 1992, p. 62). The Vere River is polluted from sewage water from Tbilisi and the Mashavera River, from the Madneuli ore enrichment plant (Ministry, 1992, p. 15). Both rivers flow into the Kura. Finally, industrial plants along the Kutai River dump wastes directly into the river, causing extreme environmental degradation in a fertile area.

For a little over a decade, problems of the Black Sea have dominated environmental discussions in Georgia. The Georgian Black Sea coast has a local population of 1.5 million in the regions around the three major port cities of Batumi, Poti and Sukhumi. Many resorts lining the Georgian shore lack sewage treatment or have inadequate systems that contaminate the beaches with bacteria (Georgian, 1992, p. 1).

The Black Sea used to have a vital fishing industry. In 1989, 900,000 tons of fish were caught from 23 different species, but in 1992 only about 120,000 tons were caught from 5 species (Zhvania, 1993). The decline, which intensifies economic problems, is blamed on the increased pollution in the Black Sea. For further comments on the Black Sea problem, see Chapter 9.

In addition, an oil pipeline between Baku and Batumi conveys crude oil for export. The purpose of this line was to produce hard currency for the Soviet Union, but now the profits go to Azerbaijan, and Georgia is left with the environmental damage. The Batumi plant that refines the oil spills 59 tons per year of oil into the water and 10 to 15 tons per year into the ground, as well as emitting 17,600 tons per year of harmful substances into the air (Georgian, 1992, p. 1). As a result, the sea waters in Batumi Bay are constantly polluted with oil from the refinery and oil tanks. Poti's harbor is also polluted with oil, up to four times the maximum permissible concentrations, as well as with phenols (four times the MPC) and surfactants (Georgian, 1992, p. 1). Poti's other major polluters are communal sewage and the shipyard.

In addition to these types of pollution, the Black Sea shoreline loses 15 ha of land yearly to erosion, primarily in the area around Batumi (Zhvania, 1993). The sea coast destruction is caused by wave action along the shore, which acts to erode away beaches and bluffs, especially under storm conditions. However, this land is not being adequately replaced because the dams on the rivers emptying into the Black Sea are preventing new sediments from reaching the shore.

Environmental Management Infrastructure

The environmental protection structure within the Georgian government is still developing. Georgia created the State Committee for the Protection of Natural Resources in 1974. Under this system each municipality throughout the republic had its own environmental management structure, which was primarily responsible for monitoring the environment. This network remains intact. In 1991, the State Committee was abolished, and the Ministry of Ecology and Use of Natural Resources (the Ministry of Environment) was formed. The Ministry's mandate consists of protecting the environment, controlling the use of natural resources, and implementing state policy concerning environmental protection. On November 25, 1992, Shoto Adamia was confirmed by parliament as the new head of the Ministry of Environment.

The ministry lacks direct authority over the polluting industries. This authority falls under the purview of the Ministry of Industry, which must report to the Ministry of Environment. Unfortunately, this places the latter Ministry one step removed from the source of the problems. Adamia is endeavoring to draft legislation that would have the factories report directly to the Ministry of Environment. Meanwhile, he is trying to restructure the ministry into a well-functioning operation. In the long run, he hopes to implement a plan whereby economic sanctions would be used to deter pollution. To that end, on January 1, 1993, a law was passed that will require polluting factories to pay a fine in direct relation to their pollution levels. This law became effective April 1, 1993. The regional offices within the ministry, with assistance from non-governmental organizations, will monitor and prepare reports on the amount of pollution from each factory (Adamia, 1993). This law is expected to more strictly control those that pollute.

The parliament's Ecological Committee, which works independently of the Ministry of Environment, was founded after the October 1992 elections and is responsible for drafting and passing environmental legislation. Although it has no formal ties with the ministry, the two organizations work in close cooperation.

While the environmental protection structures are still being formed, legislators have been working to create and implement new environmental laws. In September 1992, the Georgians passed a law prohibiting the import and export of all industrial, household and toxic waste. The catalyst for this was a Belgium firm attempting to export its wastes, and those from other European firms, to Georgia for processing and storage. In April of 1992, the Black Sea Convention was signed and adopted by countries bordering the Black Sea and called for protection in three areas: protection of the sea from polluted rivers, protection of the sea from industrial dumping and spills, and regulation of the use of biological resources (Adamia, 1993). Georgia also maintains several bilateral agreements with Germany concerning the Black Sea, cooperation on solving the soil erosion problem, and cooperation on the development of seven national parks (Zhvania, 1993). The environmental minister is looking for opportunities to sign other international environmental agreements.

On October 12, 1992, Georgians elected Eduard Shevardnadze president of Georgia and also voted on 150 seats in the parliament. The Green Party, the political arm of a non-governmental organization called the Georgia Greens, won 12 seats, making it the second largest faction behind the Liberal Democratic Party (Chagelishvili, 1993). These elections helped stabilize the Georgian government as a political institution. The structures for environmental protection, however, still need reform. Obstacles facing the development of a coherent environmental protection mechanism include a struggling economy, inadequate legal enforcement and implementation, organizational fragmentation for nature protection, and corruption within the government (Gzivishvili, 1992, pp. 65–66). While the government structures are changing, it is reasonable to assume that the obstacles blocking a solid environmental protection plan are still in place.

The non-governmental environmental movement in Georgia has been strong since the late 1980s. Since the October 1992 elections, however, the Greens have taken on new responsibilities and new importance. Founded in 1988, the Georgia Greens are made up of the Green Movement and the Green Party. The total membership is 6,000 people and is made up of smaller Green organizations in 42 different regions of Georgia.

Zurab Zhvania, founder and co-chair of the Georgia Greens, is now speaker of the Georgian parliament and one of five secretaries of the European Green Party. He has played an instrumental role in shaping environmental activism in Georgia for the past several years. In addition, the Greens have been successful in putting environmental concerns on almost every political platform. In fact, environmental minister Adamia was nominated by the Greens and is a member of the Green Party. In addition to political involvement, the Greens have several major projects that they develop and maintain. These include organic farming, waste recycling, environmental education, purification of sewage systems, development of alternative energy programs, soil re-cultivation, prevention of deforestation, work on Black Sea pollution problems, and development of ecotourism.

The Georgia Greens, both the movement and the party, have been successful in raising public awareness about serious environmental problems and then building local and federal coalitions to address those problems. In 1990, the Greens sponsored an Earth Day event to replant a forest that had been decimated. They received a donation of 25,000 seedlings, and the local community gathered to plant trees. This has become a yearly event and has grown in popularity each year.

In 1991, the Greens sponsored the first international conference on the problems facing the Black Sea. That conference laid the groundwork for the Black Sea Convention adopted the following year. From 1988 to 1990, the Greens created and hosted the Caucasian Common House for members of environmental groups in Georgia, Armenia and Azerbaijan. This was a forum for these people to gather and discuss common environmental concerns and develop common platforms for action. Within environmental circles, this program went far to help ease ethnic tensions. However, in early 1991 Gamsakhurdia forbade this group to meet. More recently, the Greens sponsored the campaign against the Belgium firm trying to export its wastes to Georgia. They successfully raised public awareness and drafted legislation that was later passed. The Eco-Police concept was originally the Greens' idea, and the Ministry of Environment was able to implement it. Finally, the Greens and the Ecological Committee organized a special commission to investigate Bastomi Lake, a unique ecosystem that was being contaminated by oil spills; their recommendations were implemented.

Economic reform has been stalled, with little progress toward privatization and a market economy due to the ongoing social and political strife. Even so, Georgia is now a member of the International Monetary Fund, the World Bank, and the United Nations and is exploring trade options with Turkey, Iran and Germany. In 1993, it became the last non-Baltic former USSR republic to join the Commonwealth of Independent States. Environmental problems are currently taking a backseat to more pressing economic, political and social problems, but clearly progress is being made to reverse the adverse environmental effects of earlier communist rule.

A great deal of optimism and energy currently reside within the new parliament members. They feel they have been successful in beginning to restructure the Ministry of Environment as well as drafting and implementing new legislation of the type just described. In addition, the ministry has taken active steps to determine the state of the environment in Georgia and was preparing a report in the summer of 1993 containing current environmental information gathered from independent sources.

However, reforms remain hampered by the other ministries whose activities directly affect the environment, such as forestry, energy, and industry. Communist bureaucrats still control these and other ministries that impact the natural environment. Until these ministries can be restructured and the communist bureaucrats removed from their positions, reform in environmental protection policies will be hampered. Without question, Georgia's independence from the Soviet Union has had a positive effect on environmental protection structures, legislation that includes implementation and enforcement, and citizen activism. While Georgia continues to struggle with the effects of the Soviet legacy on its political, social and economic mechanisms, the environment remains a clear victim both of past administrative policies and contemporary ethnic unrest. The political realities of Georgia's ties with the old USSR, however, allowed Russia to sign a treaty with Georgia in 1994 permitting continued presence of Russian military forces in Georgia to help end the fighting there.

Prior to the present period of internal conflict, Georgia was a land of great physical beauty and a diverse and productive economy. It has adequate natural resources, especially for agriculture, and a well-educated and talented population. Given a stable internal environment, Georgia would have exceptional tourist potential, focused equally on its scenic mountains, balneological spas, and attractive coastal facilities. Until such time as a peaceful and permanent solution can be found to present ethnic difficulties, however, this potential for international tourism will remain unfulfilled.

Bibliography

Adamia, Shoto. 1993. Minister of Environment, Georgia; interview with author, February 7, Tbilisi, Georgia.

Chagelishvili, Rezo. 1993. Deputy Minister, Ministry of Environmental Protection; interview with author, February 4, Tbilisi, Georgia.

Crkonia, Goga. 1993. Coordinator, Georgia Greens Forestry Program; interview with author, February 6, Tbilisi, Georgia.

Georgian Ministry of Environmental Protection. 1992. "The Incentives for Urgent Investments from Pollution in the Republic of Georgia." September.

Giragosian, Richard and Aram Hamparian, eds. 1992. *Transcaucasus: A Chronology.* Armenian National Committee of America, Vol. 10, October.

Gzivishvili, Tengiz. 1992. Interview with Guliko Marozashvili. "We Need an Ecological Fund," October 25, 1991; published in JPRS 92-002, Environmental Issues, January.

Jones, Stephen. 1992. "Indigenes and Settlers." *Cultural Survival Quarterly,* Winter.

Kiknadze, A. G. 1981. "The Contemporary Condition and Problems of a Man-Made Defense of the Black Sea Coast Within the Borders of the Georgian SSR." *Nature Protection in Georgia.* Georgian Academy of Sciences.

Ministry of Environmental Protection of Georgia. 1992. "Report on the Black Sea." August.

Mnatsakanian, Ruben. 1992. *Environmental Legacy of the Former Soviet Republics.* Edinburgh: Centre for Human Ecology.

Nogaideli, Zurab. 1993. Chairman, Commission of Environmental Protection and Natural Resources, Georgia Parliament; interview with author, February 4 and 8, Tbilisi, Georgia.

Pryde, Philip. 1991. *Environmental Management in the Soviet Union.* Cambridge: Cambridge University Press.

Schwartz, Lee. 1991. "USSR Nationality Redistribution by Republic, 1979–1989." *Soviet Geography,* vol. 32, no. 4, pp. 209–248.

Shabad, Theodore. 1969. *Basic Industrial Resources of the USSR.* New York: Columbia Univ. Press, pp. 157–164.

Shanshiashvili, Paata. 1993. World Wildlife Federation National Park and Program Co-
    ordinator; interview with author, February 7, Tbilisi, Georgia.
State Committee of the USSR for the Protection of Nature (Goskompriroda). 1990. *Re-
    port on the State of the Environment in 1989.* Moscow: Goskompriroda.
Vakhrang, Zaprya. 1993. Coordinator, Georgia Greens Energy Program; interview with
    author, February 7, Tbilisi, Georgia.
Wixman, Ronald. 1984. *The Peoples of the USSR: An Ethnographic Handbook.* Armonk,
    NY: M.E. Sharpe.
Zhvania, Zurab. 1993. Founder, Georgia Greens; interview with author, February 6, 7, 8,
    Tbilisi, Georgia.

14

Armenia

Armen L. Valesyan

The Republic of Armenia covers 29,740 km² in the northeastern section of a wide mountainous area known as the Armenian plateau. Located at approximately the same latitude as northern Colorado, Armenia stretches 360 kilometers from northwest to southeast and at its widest is 200 kilometers from west to east. It is bordered by Azerbaijan, Turkey, Georgia, and Iran (Figure 14.1). Declared an independent republic on September 21, 1991, there are 37 administrative regions and 21 cities in the republic, including the capital, Yerevan.

An Overview of Armenia

The Armenian plateau is one of the ancient hearths of human civilization. The original culture of the Armenian people developed on this territory over the course of several hundred years. It has been suggested that the Armenians' name for themselves, *Khai*, comes from Khaiasa, a country mentioned in the Khettskoi stone tablets from 1000 B.C. The Kingdom of Ararat (Urartu, 9th–6th centuries B.C.) developed the traditions of an advanced civilization; the Armenian kingdom led into the golden age of Great Armenia (around 100 B.C.). However, the Armenians' subsequent history took a tragic shift as Armenia lost its political independence for many centuries.

Armenia was the first state in the ancient world to adopt Christianity as its official religion. But throughout the 7th–15th centuries, it was the target of repeated foreign invasions of Arabs, Byzantines, Seljuk Turks, Mongol Tatars, and Timur (Tamerlane). From the 16th–18th centuries, Armenia was divided between Persia and Ottoman Turkey, and from the beginning of the 19th century it was under Russian control. An independent republic of Ar-

Translation by Holly Strand.

menia was proclaimed on May 28, 1918, but it lasted only two and a half years before the region was incorporated into the USSR.

The population of Armenia is 3,648,900 (1992), of which about 93% are Armenian. About 3% are Azeri, and less than 2% each are Kurdish and Russian. This is the smallest Russian population in any former republic. There are no ethnic sub-units; Nakhichevan, which is almost entirely surrounded by Armenia and Iran, is ethnically and politically part of Azerbaijan. Armenians, like Georgians, belong to the Indo-European ethnic family. Armenian is one of the oldest written languages; Mesrop Mashtots created the alphabet at the beginning of the 9th century.

Armenia's pattern of settlement is quite irregular. Although the average density is 123 persons per square kilometer, this figure rises to 389 persons on the Ararat Plain. For the country as a whole, 68.9% of the population is urban. The largest cities are Yerevan, with 1,199,000 people in 1989; Gyumri (Leninakan), with 120,000; and Vanadzor (Kirovakan), with about 100,000.

Machine building, chemical, non-ferrous metallurgy, light goods and food production are major branches of industry in Armenia. Viticulture and orchards dominate agricultural production. Milk cows, meat cattle and sheep are the main animal stock. There are 820 kilometers of railroad tracks and 7,700 kilometers of public roads.

Since 1988 the republic has been in conflict with neighboring Azerbaijan for control of Nagorno-Karabakh, an Armenian enclave within the territory of Azerbaijan (see Figure 14.1). By 1994, armed conflict had resulted in Armenian forces temporarily occupying several portions of western Azerbaijan. A cease-fire was agreed to by Armenia and Azerbaijan in early 1994; peace talks will hopefully follow.

Physical and Biotic Characteristics

More than 90% of the republic's territory is over 1,000 meters above sea level (see Table 14.1). The highest point is the summit of Mount Aragats, a very broad-based shield volcano rising to 4,090 meters. The lowest points, located in the extreme north in a canyon formed by the Debed River and in the south on the Araks River, are close to 400 meters above sea level. The complex structure of the relief, which is characteristic of the entire Armenian territory, gives the landscape a certain scenic appeal. Mountain ranges of over 3,000 meters border the territory. An orographic map of the republic would distinguish three major forms of relief: intermontane basins, volcanic plateaus, and folded mountains.

The folded block ranges (Somkhet, Bazym, Pambak) of the central Lesser Caucasus stretch across the northeast of the republic, between which lie deep tectonically formed valleys. The Aiotsdzor, Bargushat, Eranos, Zangezur and

Table 14.1   Elevational Characteristics of Armenia

Elevation Above Sea Level, Meters	Square Kilometers	Percent of Republic
380 - 500	20	0.07
500 - 800	530	1.78
800-1000	2370	7.97
1000-1500	5430	18.26
1500-2000	9300	31.27
2000-2500	7290	24.51
2500-3000	3800	12.78
3000-3500	970	3.26
above 3500	30	0.10
Total	29740	100

Source: Calculated by author.

other ranges form the Armenian plateau in the south and southeast. Mountain ranges occupy over half of the entire area of Armenia.

Young volcanic surface rock is widespread over the central part of the republic in the form of volcanic plateaus and shield ranges. In contrast to folded block ranges, the volcanic uplands and plateaus are less extensive and less distinguishable on the surface. The Ararat plain is located at an elevation of 800–1,200 meters in the southwest.

Practically the entire territory of the republic is seismically active; strong earthquakes are common (e.g., Gyumri in 1926, Spitak in 1988), as well as slumping, landslides and mudflows. The 1988 earthquake was especially devastating, killing an estimated 25,000 persons in the Gyumri, Spitak, and Vanadzor regions.

Armenia is located at the same latitude as Spain, Italy and Greece. Latitude, together with topography, determines the more important climatic characteristics. In the summer, continental air masses invade from the Iranian plateau to the south. In the winter the air on the Armenian plateau cools dramatically, and a zone of high atmospheric pressure is established. This results in many clear, cold days in the winter. An abundance of solar energy and high meteorological variability are characteristic of the climate, and vertical climatic/vegetation belts are well expressed on the mountain slopes. The climate is dry and almost subtropical on the Ararat Plain, in Megrinskoye canyon, and in the extreme northeast; but with increasing altitude it becomes progressively cooler.

A large amount of solar radiation is typical for the republic, about 2,700 hours per year on the average. On the Ararat plain and in the low mountains, the average July temperature is 25° to 27° Centigrade. The average January temperature is around −5°C, the normal absolute minimum is around −30°C. In the medium elevation mountains, temperatures in the summer average 18° to 20°C and in the winter, −8° to −12°C. A historic absolute minimum of −43°C was registered on the shore of Lake Arpi.

The average annual precipitation in the republic is 550 mm; the maximum falls in the spring and the beginning of summer, the minimum in the second half of summer and winter. The Ararat Plain experiences the least amount of precipitation at around 200 to 250 mm. Heavy downpours and hail are common. Snow cover in the low mountains is variable, but in the middle and high mountains snow remains late into the spring, with depths up to 100 cm.

The river system is distributed very unevenly over the territory. Seventy percent of the annual flow occurs during the spring, when the snowmelts and maximum precipitation levels are reached. Most (76.5%) of the territory is part of the Araks River basin, which begins in Turkey and flows along part of the Armenian-Turkish border. The main tributaries are the Akhuryan, Kasakh (and the Metsamor), Razdan, Azat, Vedi, and Arpa. A cascade of hydroelectric stations totaling 556,000 kilowatts has been built on the Razdan, and there are reservoirs on many rivers to regulate the flow. The Debed River, which flows into the Kura in Georgia, has the largest volume of water in Armenia after the Araks.

There are very few lakes in Armenia, and most of them are very shallow. The jewel of them all is Lake Sevan, at 1,900 meters above sea level and occupying an area of over 1,200 km. Twenty-six rivers and streams flow into the Sevan, but only one, the Razdan, flows out.

Soil cover of the republic is extremely varied. Semi-desert brown and gray soils are found at lower elevations—on the Ararat Plain and in the extreme north and south. They are used for vineyards, orchards, and melon crops. Brown-chestnut and chestnut soils are common at elevations of 1,300 to 1,700 meters on dry steppes. These soils are suitable for cultivation of fruits and tobacco; grapes can be found in the lower regions. Mountain chernozems can be found in mid-altitude mountains from 1,600 to over 2,000 meters. They are planted to grains, sugar beets, potatoes and other vegetables. Only about 12% of the republic's territory is forested, mostly in the mountainous regions; alpine meadows are found above 2,000–2,400 m.

The plant and animal kingdoms of Armenia are rich and diverse. About 3,200 different species of plants grow here, including 180 endemics. There are 450 species of vertebrates and more than 10,000 non-vertebrates. In the extreme northwest and south, semi-arid landscapes occur, dominated by sagebrush, but with almond trees, wild pear, buckthorn and cushion plants being very common. Rodents include field vole, suslik, and sanderling, while Caucasus agama, Greek turtle, viper and Armenian viper are among the reptiles present.

The steppe is the most common form of landscape in Armenia. Needle grass, broom sedge, and various other grasses and forbs are characteristic forms of vegetation. Steppe fauna is similar to that of the semi-desert and is mainly represented by hares and rodents, together with their predators, such as foxes, badgers, raptors and wolves.

Deciduous species predominate in the forest, including beech, oak, elm, maple, and hornbeam; wild apple, pear, sweet cherry, prunes, dogwood shrubs, and wild rose are also present. The forest provides a habitat for roe deer, wild boars, bears, squirrels, and many other species.

Subalpine meadows stretch from 2,200–2,400 to 2,800–2,900 meters above sea level and are dominated by forbs and mixed grasses. Alpine meadows occupy the summits of the mountain zone. The fauna of the alpine meadow is quite diverse: foxes, wolves, mountain goat, mouflon (wild sheep), quail and others.

Armenia has a rich variety of useful minerals. They include copper deposits near Alaverdi and Kafan, nephelite syenites (a source of alumina) in the Pambaks, iron veins near Razdan and in the Bargushats, molybdenum near Kadzharan, and gold near Zod. There are also polymetallic veins, signs of platinum, and concentrations of antimony, mercury and arsenic. Volcanic and sedimentary rocks provide excellent building materials. Volcanic tuff, in colors of orange, yellow, lavender, rose and black, is the best. There are rich deposits of marble, travertine and limestones and a major salt deposit near Yerevan. The copper, molybdenum, and gold deposits are the most extensive and valuable (Shabad, 1969).

Armenia has almost no fossil fuel resources. The armed conflict of the early 1990's caused all fuel pipelines into the republic to be severed. However, in 1993, Turkmenistan agreed to sell natural gas to Armenia, although the method by which it would be delivered was not specified.

Numerous mineral springs arise from artesian wells and fissure-veins. The most famous are Dzhermuk, Dilizhan, Vzhni, Ankavan, and Sevan. Armenia is also rich in semi-precious and decorative gemstones, such as agate, jasper, amethyst, heliotrope, obsidian, turquoise, and onyx.

Natural Resources and Environmental Problems

The following factors are characteristic of natural resource problems in Armenia: (1) intense geological and geomorphological activity and changes due to relatively youthful landforms and relief, seismicity, continental climatic conditions, active slope processes and a number of related phenomena; (2) a relatively long and continuous history of human influence on the natural environment; (3) a high density of population and production; (4) a rapid rate of industrialization and urbanization; (5) an increased proportion of economic activity directly based on exploitation of natural resources; and (6) a predominance of extensive (and therefore often wasteful) methods of land use.

A wide variety of ecological problems have developed in the republic, with negative repercussions on public health, as well as on future economic development. The areas whose environments have been most adversely affected include:

1. The Yerevan metropolitan area, where more than a third of Armenia's population lives and where more than 60% of the industrial potential (including chemical processing, thermal energy, nonferrous metallurgy, and raw materials for construction) are concentrated (Figure 14.2).
2. Other industrial cities: Vanadzor (formerly Kirovakan) has chemical and thermal energy production industries, Razdan specializes in construction materials and thermal energy, and Ararat produces asbestos. All three cities have high population densities and industrial concentrations, resulting in a degraded environment accompanied by a serious decline in public health.
3. Regions where mining and enrichment facilities for non-ferrous metallurgy exist (Kadzharan, Kafan, Agarak, Akhtala, Zod), as well as areas of extensive extraction of non-metallic minerals (Artik and elsewhere), which have resulted in decreased fertility or loss of arable land, severe soil erosion and destruction of forests.
4. Lake Sevan, which suffers from eutrophication, degradation of water quality, loss of 40% of its water volume, and the disappearance of unique, endemic species of trout.
5. Resort and health spa zones with mineral springs (Arzni, Dzhermuk, Dilizhan), where degradation is being caused by anthropogenic impacts.
6. Those regions of northern Armenia that suffered the most as a result of the severe 1988 Spitak earthquake (Figure 14.3).
7. Regions suffering from military actions arising from the Armenia-Azerbaijan conflict.

Figure 14.2   View south over the city of Yerevan, with smoke from the heavily polluted industrial district in the background. The haze and pollution prevent Mount Ararat, 70 km away in Turkey, from being visible.

Figure 14.3   A rural region near the earthquake-destroyed city of Spitak, Armenia, showing typical buildings vulnerable to seismic damage as they stood prior to the 1988 earthquake.

The following paragraphs look at the state of the environment in more detail.

Land Resources

The generally steep relief, abrupt changes in elevation, active seismic processes, landslides, erosion, and avalanches serve to greatly limit land use suitability. Without counting damage from the Spitak earthquake, these processes have rendered 130,000 hectares of formerly productive land unusable in the past few years. Intensification of erosion and mudflows is caused by improper methods of plowing, watering, grazing, irrigation and road construction. Each year losses of the fertile soil layer approach 8 million tons, and about 1,000 hectares of earth are lost due to gullying (Figure 14.3). Secondary salinization of the soil is another critical problem. Other problems associated with conserving the land resources in the republic, such as the isolation and insignificant size of some land plots, not only complicate remedial measures but make soil conservation measures more expensive. Unfortunately, the existing procedures to protect land resources in Armenia still do not produce the needed effect.

Forest Resources

The republic's forests are not in satisfactory condition. This is partly due to the natural processes just described, as well as to anthropogenic pressures, such as solid waste disposal, logging, roads, livestock farms, and recreational activities. In the 25 year period ending in 1991, the forest cover of the territory grew by only 2%. According to the Ministry of Forestry, illegal forest logging has increased 8 to 10 times as a result of the energy crisis of the past few years. Twenty-five thousand separate cases were registered in 1992 alone, and the city of Yerevan was extensively deforested during the winter of 1992–93. Cutting the forests leads to a change in the species composition: for example, oak forests change to hornbeam forests. The small amount of forest cover in Armenia is one of the reasons erosion and mudflows are such a problem, which in turn decreases the productivity of arable land.

Water Resources

When the natural flow from Lake Sevan and half of the border rivers Araks and Akhuryan is taken into account, the average surface water flow of the republic is 6.54 billion cubic meters. There is 8 times less water per person than in the rest of the former USSR. In these arid conditions, without large rivers and with unequal distribution of flow and extremely intense demand, water problems are of great significance.

The chief polluters of surface waters are collective farms (81.8%), the chemical industry (11.2%), and the agro-industrial complex (3.3%). According to the Ministry of Environment, among the polluting substances thrown into water bodies in 1988 were 2,413,000 tons of sulfate salts, 2,302,000 tons of chloride salts, 454 tons of nitrogen, 250 tons of oil by-products, 235 tons of nitrates, 132 tons of phosphorous, 22 tons of iron, and 3 tons of copper. The Pambak-Debed, Razdan, Akhuryan, Agstev, and Vokhchi are the most polluted rivers of the republic.

Lake Sevan's situation deserves special attention. The problem began in the 1930s, when water reserves that had taken millennia to form were used up for irrigation and the production of hydroelectricity over a 50 year period, thus drying up much of Lake Sevan. It was proposed to leave a small lake with an area of 239 square kilometers in the middle, to be called Little Sevan. By the time it was publicly acknowledged that Sevan's water should be preserved for future generations as well, the lake level was already down 18.5 meters, its area reduced by 13%, and the volume of water reduced by 42%. Both the oxygen regime and the lake's chemical composition had been altered, the water became three times less transparent, and eutrophication had begun. Many species of endemic fish had disappeared for good. Newly exposed areas became subject to wind erosion.

Additional inflow of water was necessary to raise the falling lake level without completely ignoring the demand for irrigation and hydroelectric energy. Therefore, water from the Arpa and Eksegis Rivers was fed to Sevan through a 48.4 km tunnel. Sevan received about 250 million cubic meters of water through this tunnel every year, which was enough to support the present level of water when outflow and evaporation were taken into account. According to specialists, several centuries are needed to return the lake to its original biosystem and then only after the minimum level has been raised by six meters and toxic substances are no longer thrown into the waters that feed into the lake. It has been proposed to construct another 21 kilometer tunnel to divert water from the Vorotan River.

By declaring Lake Sevan and the surrounding area a 150,000 hectare national park, some amount of anthropocentric stress on the region has subsided. However, other legislative actions aimed at establishing a protective regime for using the natural resources of the lake and its basin exist only on paper.

Air Pollution

In 1988, stationary sources emitted approximately 250,000 tons of polluting substances into the air basin, including sulfuric anhydride, nitric oxides, hydrocarbons, chloroprene, and others. This total dropped to 150,000 tons in 1989 as a consequence of the damage caused by the 1988 earthquake. The majority of emissions were caused by the following industries: energy production (35% of the total volume of industrial emissions), non-ferrous metallurgy (19%), construction materials for industry (10%), and chemicals (9%). Automotive emissions accounted for about 490,000 tons, or over 60% of the total volume of atmospheric pollutants.

Those enterprises contributing the most to air pollution are the Yerevan factories Nairit, Polivinilatsetat, and Kanaz, as well as the Vanadzor chemical plant, Ararat cement-slate factory, and Razdan cement producers. The Nairit plant has been particularly controversial (Peterson, 1993, pp. 244–247). The republic's most polluted cities, Yerevan, Vanadzor (Kirovakan), Razdan, and Ararat, are located in intermontane basins where, because of the extremely high potential for atmospheric pollution (aggravated by frequent calms and temperature inversions), the atmosphere's ability to purify itself is impeded.

The yearly average concentration for many substances is significantly higher than standard norms: particulates at 7 times the maximum permitted concentration in Razdan and Ararat, sulfur gas at 8 MPC in Vanadzor and Razdan, nitrogen dioxide at 7 MPC in Yerevan and Vanadzor, ammonia at 10 MPC in Vanadzor, ozone at 1.1 MPC, and choloroprene in Yerevan. It is not uncommon that for discrete periods, the concentration level of polluting substances may surpass the MPC by a factor of 10 or even occasionally by 100. As of the year 1988, Armenia was cited as having the lowest percentage in the USSR of air pollution sources equipped with emission control devices, only 24.3% (Mnatsakanian, 1992, p. 66).

It might be noted that one option for reducing Armenia's air pollution, the Armenian nuclear power station near Oktemberyan, has been shut down for several years due to both internal and earthquake-related safety concerns. However, economic necessity, aggrevated by fossil fuel shortages, forced the announcement in 1992 that its two 440 MW reactors would be started up again. If this did not happen, other types of power plants would have to be built, but as noted earlier, Armenia has very few fossil fuels. Restarting the nuclear reactors will be very controversial.

Mineral Resources

In general, the exploitation of mineral resources in Armenia is complicated and inefficient. In spite of enormous volumes of waste produced by mineral extraction and processing, an overall average of only 0.014% of the disturbed subsurface material is actually used. A number of valuable substances are thrown away, especially those associated with the extraction and processing of the copper and copper-molybdenum deposits. In all over 400 million cubic meters of tailings and waste products are produced by non-ferrous metallurgy, storage occupies 300 hectares of land, and 2,300 hectares have been degraded by mining. Likewise, the non-metallic mineral industry produces 45 million cubic meters of waste products and occupies 1,500 hectares.

Plants and Animals

There are 400 species included in the list of rare and threatened plants in the republic's Red Book of endangered vegetation. Furthermore, almost twenty species are already extinct, including ezhovnik, Tetradiclis, halophilous gladiola, yellow water lily, and others. Several species of bog vegetation also face threat of extinction. The republic's fauna has suffered in the face of anthropogenic pressure as well. The leopard, snow leopard, porcupine, hyena, manul, and both steppe and forest wildcat have almost totally disappeared. Indeed, southern Armenia has the highest density of endangered species of any region within the former Soviet Union (Pryde, 1987, p. 27).

In response to these biotic problems, a number of protected territories have been created in the republic. Aside from the aforementioned Sevan National Park, they include four *zapovedniki* and 16 *zakazniki* (Table 14.2).

Khosrov Zapovednik is the largest in the republic and is located in the upper basin of the Khosrov and Azat Rivers, tributaries of the Araks River. It represents a unique combination of the flora and fauna of the arid sparse forest. There are more than 80 endemic species of plants; rare animal species

Table 14.2   Preserved Areas in Armenia

Type of Preserve(a)	Number	Total area(b)	Average size(b)	% of Re-public(c)
Nature Reserves (<u>zapovedniki</u>)	4	720.12	180.03	2.42
National Parks	1	1500.00	1500.00	5.03
Preserves (<u>zakazniki</u>)	16	851.00	53.19	2.86
Total	21	3071.12	146.24	10.31

Nature Reserve (date created)	Hectares
Dilizhan (1958)	24232
Erebun (1981)	100
Khosrov (1958)	29680
Shikahogh (1975)	18000
Total	72012

National Parks	Hectares
Sevan (1978)	150000

(a) For the definition of each type of preserve, see Appendix 1.2.
(b) In square kilometers.
(c) The area of Armenia is 29,800 sq. kilometers.

Source: Pryde (1991).

include Armenian mouflon, wild goat, leopard and the Mediterranean turtle. The avian population is extremely rich: golden eagle, bearded vulture, peregrine falcon, Caspian snowcock, and stone partridge are among the more noteworthy species.

Over 80% of Dilizhan Zapovednik is located in the upper and middle reaches of the Agstev River. Mostly composed of beech and oak-hornbeam forests, the relict yew groves found within them are of special interest. Among other fauna, the noble deer, European roe deer, wild boar, and southern golden eagle are found here.

Forests also dominate in the Shikahogh Zapovednik, located in the upper basins of the Tsav and Shikahogh Rivers. There is a relict plane tree grove here, as well as mountain goat, wolf, marten, partridge, hawks, and Caspian snowcock. In the smaller Erebun Zapovednik, situated just west of the capital, rare species of wild wheat are preserved.

Since *zapovedniki* are not a united or continuous territory, it is difficult for them to maintain their protected populations. There are various parcels of settlements and farms wedged in among them. Conflicts constantly arise over hay mowing, which destroys nests, burrows, lairs and wild plants; hay fields and cattle pastures represent human subsidized competition with wild animals.

The border area between Armenia and Azerbaijan illustrates an especially serious ecological situation, because of the armed conflict there in the early 1990s. Forest fires are a frequent by-product of the systematic shelling; they kill wild birds and animals or force them out of their habitats. A relict plane tree grove, located 6 km from the Azerbaijani border, has been destroyed. The risk of epidemics in this zone has already increased dramatically as it is impossible to properly maintain purification facilities, water supply and sewage systems.

Governmental Actions and Future Prospects

The following are among the more significant environmental improvement measures taken in Armenia within the past few years: (1) the new Yerevan wastewater treatment plan is a bio-purification facility with a capacity of 220 million cubic meters per year; (2) the Armenian nuclear energy plant at Oktemberyan has closed down; (3) a production line of primary aluminum refining at the Kanaz factory in Yerevan was shut down, eliminating fluoride wastes and resinous compounds; (4) production of cyanamide, melamines, nitric acids and ammonia compounds was stopped at the Vanadzor chemical factory; (5) production was cut at the Kauchuk-I and Nairit plants in Yerevan; and (6) the Alaverdi mining and metallurgical combine has been restructured by eliminating sulfuric acid and certain operations, including ore firings and fusion.

The Ministry for the Conservation of Nature and the Environment provides general guidelines and coordinates the republic's conservation and rehabilitation measures. There are executive departments for land use strategy and international cooperation, as well as the following subdivisions: atmospheric protection, protection and conservation of water resources, protection of plant and animal life and their habitats, protection of soil and subsurface features, and state environmental impact assessments. The ministry also operates interregional territorial inspection stations. The Ecological Commission is a standing committee of the republic's Supreme Soviet. The Armenia Green Party and the Society for the Conservation of Nature in Armenia are the largest public organizations with an ecological agenda.

Obviously, Armenia's future environmental and social well-being will depend heavily on the course of events in the political and economic arenas. The cessation of the military conflict with Azerbaijan is paramount; as noted earlier, some hopeful signs appeared in early 1994. Also needed are mutually profitable cooperation with neighbors, the creation of reliable and diversified ties with the global community, internal political stability, and the development of democratic institutions. Without these, one cannot expect any improvements in the quality of the republic's environment.

Many of the stumbling blocks in the economic arena fall into the category of building a foundation for a market economy. Above all, it is necessary to reform the various types of land use so that they can help improve socio-economic conditions through the widespread adoption of non-intensive resource technologies, the development of alternative forms of energy, tourism and recreation, and other innovative projects. And, of course, the organization of environmental education for a population whose environmental consciousness is extremely low is especially important, as is the establishment of an open and effective monitoring system for environmental quality.

Much will depend on the extent to which Armenia is drawn into the international environmental arena. In particular, President Levon TerPetrosian's idea of turning Armenia into a research region for ecological-human environment experiments merits attention. The concept, which was suggested at the 1992 Rio conference for conservation and development, is to develop an effective environmental program that could then be applied to other small countries as well. This idea is, of course, dependent on peace being achieved; still, in ways such as these, this small republic with serious environmental problems is nevertheless looking to the future with hope.

Bibliography

Abovian, Iu. 1989. "The Ecological Situation of the Armenian SSR and the Concept of Nature Preservation." *Asparez*, vol. 80, no. 8579, Aug. 5.

Abovian, Iu., I.E.G. Bunatian, and L.V. Davtian. 1982. *Okhrana prirodnykh resursov Armianskoy SSR*. Yerevan: Aiastan.

Airapetian, E.M., and L.V. Arutiunian. 1983. *Osnovy okhrany prirody*. Yerevan: Luys. (In Armenian).

Bardacarian, A.B., ed. 1966. *Sovietskii Soyuz: Geograficheskoye opisanie*. vol. 22, T. Armenia. Moscow: Mysl'.

Barsegian, A. M. 1985. "Sovremennoe sostoianie flory i rastitel'nosti Armenii i zadachi ikh okhrany." In *Geographical Aspects of Rational Exploitation of Nature in Armenian SSR*. Yerevan: AN Armenian SSR, pp. 6–11. (In Armenian).

Belyi, V.N., and I.V. Belaya-Barsegian. 1990. *Armenia. Encyclopedia for Travelers*. Yerevan: Central Publishing House of Armenian Soviet Encyclopedia.

Feshbach, M., and A. Friendly Jr. 1992. *Ecocide in the USSR*. New York: Basic Books.

Kelegian, P. 1993. "Paradise Suspended: The Challenge to Armenia's Nature Preserves." *Surviving Together*, vol. 11, no. 2 (Summer 1993), pp. 12–13.

Khalatov, V. Yu., and R. Kh. Gaginyan. 1991. "Geoekologicheskaya klassifikatsia landshaftov Respubliki Armenia." In *Ratsional'noe priridopol'zovanie gornykh stran*. Bishkek: pp. 23–24.

Mnatsakanian, R. 1992. *Environmental Legacy of the Former Soviet Republics*. Edinburgh: Centre for Human Ecology.

Mulkidzhanian, Ya. I. 1975. *Zapovedniki i zakazniki Armianskoi SSR*. Yerevan: Aiastan. (In Armenian).

Okhrana okruzhayushchei sredy i ratsional'noe ispol'zovanie priodnykh resurov v Respublike Armenia. 1990. Yerevan: Statisticheskii Sbornik.

Peterson, D.J. 1993. *Troubled Lands: The Legacy of Soviet Environmental Destruction*. Boulder: Westview Press, pp. 244–247.

Pryde, P.R. 1987. "The Distribution of Endangered Fauna in the USSR." *Biological Conservation*, vol. 42, no. 1, pp. 19–37.

———. *Environmental Management in the Soviet Union.* Cambridge: Cambridge University Press.

Shabad, T. 1969. *Basic Industrial Resources of the USSR.* New York: Columbia University Press.

Suny, R.G. 1993. *Looking Towards Ararat: Armenia in Modern History.* Bloomington: Indiana University Press.

Valesyan, A. L. 1984. "Geograficheskie problemy prirodopol'zovaniya i okhrany prirodnoi sredy v Armianskoi SSR." In *Sovietakaya Geografia.* Leningrad: Nauka, pp. 218–230.

———. 1990. "Environmental Problems in the Yerevan Region." *Soviet Geography.* vol. 31, no. 8, pp. 573–586.

———. 1991. "Ekologicheskii labirint: Est' li vykhod?" *Zvartnots,* no. 3, pp. 25–28.

Zhdanko, T.A. et al. 1984. *Strany i narody: Nauchnoe-popularnoe geograficheskoye etnographicheskoe izdatel'stvo v 20 t.* (Sovietskii Soyuz: Respubliki Zakavkaz'ia, Respubliki Srednei Azii, Kazakhstan). Moscow: Mysl', pp. 101–104.

15

Azerbaijan

Ze'ev Wolfson and Zia Daniell

Azerbaijan is perhaps the most strategically situated of the three Transcaucasus republics, fronting on the Caspian Sea and connecting Russia with Iran. Like the rest of the Transcaucasus region, it was well known even in Roman times. It is well endowed with natural resources, although its major one, petroleum, is now becoming depleted, at least on land. The development of this and other branches of the Azerbaijan economy in the Soviet period has resulted in high levels of pollution and biosphere deterioration, problems that have been well known for some time (Komarov, 1980). As an independent nation, Azerbaijan will need to move swiftly to address these problems, but unfortunately in 1993 armed conflict with Armenia was placing a heavy drain on available resources.[1]

Population and History

Azerbaijan, the only independent Muslim republic in the Transcaucasus, comprises a total of 86,600 square kilometers, an area roughly the size of Austria. With a population in 1989 of over 7 million, Azerbaijan also ranks as the most populous in the region. Both the republic's history and topography vary tremendously: for thousands of years, numerous groups have overrun the rocky mountains and fertile lowlands of Azerbaijan. Even today the bloody conflict with Armenia threatens to shatter the nation. A look at the history of Azerbaijan indicates this current struggle is far from unique; it is only the most recent in a long list of battles fought over Azerbaijan.

In the 9th century B.C., the territory of today's Azerbaijan was occupied by slave owners. The state of Urtatu, spanning much of the Caucasus region, reached its peak during the late 9th and early 8th centuries B.C. By the turn of the 4th century B.C., tribes in the region known as Albanians had banded together into alliances in northern parts of contemporary Azerbaijan. These tribal units lasted until the invasion of the Romans in the last century B.C. By the time of Christ, Rome had annexed all of the Transcaucasus to the Roman Empire. In the 7th century A.D., the area came under Arab, and eventually, Islamic influence.

In the 13th century the region was conquered by the Mongols, but soon the waning Mongol influence led to the division of the territory of Azerbaijan. In the 15th century, the territory broke into units loyal to different nomadic tribes. By the turn of the 16th century, however, the region was facing two new repressive forces: the Turks and the Persians, with the latter dominating. Russia's victory over the Mongols gave the Russians access to the Volga River, thereby securing a direct transportation link between Russia and Transcaucasia. Communities in Transcaucasia once again flourished as the Volga-Caspian became a major silk trading route. Russia took a particular interest in the region, establishing a number of new Russian communities in the area.

By the beginning of the 17th century, however, Persian feudal lords had seized power from the Azerbaijani aristocracy. A peace treaty between Turkey and Persia in 1639 ceded the eastern Transcaucasus region to Persia, and for years the Azerbaijan economy suffered under Persian domination. The 1813 Peace of Gulistan returned northern Azerbaijan to Russian hands, but Russia's attempts to pull Azerbaijan toward capitalism met with widespread resistance. As a result, Azerbaijan was not fully integrated into Russian culture but became an important supplier of agricultural goods and raw materials for its parent state. The discovery of oil in Azerbaijan in the 1890s enhanced its value to the Russian regime.

The consolidation of Soviet power that followed the 1917 October Revolution encountered severe problems in the Transcaucasus region, due largely to strong nationalist tendencies and the less developed social and economic conditions in the region at that time. Resistance penetrated from the outside as well. In 1918, foreign troops entered Azerbaijan and briefly overwhelmed the ruling Soviet regime, but the anti-communists fell to Soviet forces just two years later. On April 28, 1920, the Azerbaijan Soviet Socialist Republic was formed.

Seventy-one years later, on August 30, 1991, Azerbaijan rejected its status as a republic of the Soviet Union and declared itself an independent state. By the end of the year, the independent Republic of Azerbaijan was enjoying worldwide recognition.

Today ethnic Azerbaijanis make up over 80% of the population of Azerbaijan. Russians and Armenians constitute much of the remainder, with Lezgians, Jews, Talysh, Kurds and Tats present in small numbers (Table 15.1). Much of the internal strife in Azerbaijan has centered around the enclave of Nagorno-Karabakh, an area predominantly populated by ethnic Armenians. Bitter fighting over the area has ravaged the two nations for years, while numerous foreign efforts have had little success in resolving the conflict. With a tenuous cease-fire holding in 1994 and no effective peace treaty in sight, the Republic of Azerbaijan may witness continued instability in the years to come.

Table 15.1   Ethnic Groups in Azerbaijan

Group	Population (1000s) 1959	1989	% change, 1959-89	% of 1989 total
Azerbaijanis	2494	5805	132.8	82.7
Armenians	442	391	-11.5	5.6
Russians	501	392	-21.8	5.6
Lezghians	98	171	74.5	2.4
Avars	17	44	158.8	0.6
Jews	40	25	-37.5	0.3
Others	106	193	82.1	2.8
Total	3698	7021	89.9	100.0

Source: Soviet Geography, April 1991, p. 237.

Physical Geography

Although Azerbaijan ranks only 8th in size among the former republics of the USSR, the nation's territory encompasses a wide range of landscapes. Mountains rim the northern, western and southern borders, while the Kura and Araks Rivers meander through a fertile lowland in the central and eastern parts of the republic. To the east lies Azerbaijan's Caspian Sea coastline.

Three separate mountain ranges surround the republic of Azerbaijan. The Greater Caucasus forms part of the northern border and contains the nation's highest peaks, including Bazar-Dyuzi (4,466 m), Shakh-Dag (4,243 m) and Tufan (4,205 m) (Figure 15.1). Limestone formations and hot springs dot the snow-capped landscape. This northern portion of Azerbaijan is subject to moderately strong earthquakes.

To the west of Azerbaijan lie the Lesser Caucasus Mountains. Although lower and less steep than their northern counterparts, the Lesser Caucasus still boasts peaks of up to 3,900 m. The range much of the border with Armenia, creating a physical barrier between the two warring republics. Directly to the east of the Lesser Caucasus foothills lies the disputed Nagorno-Karabakh enclave.

The final mountain range within Azerbaijan lies tucked away in the far southeastern corner of the nation. The Talysh Mountains, stretching 100 km southeast toward the Caspian Sea, constitute a small portion of the Azeri-Iranian border. Peaks reach heights only half those of the Greater Caucasus.

Yet despite the mountainous borders, much of the interior of Azerbaijan is typified by agricultural lowland. The Kura River spills into the Mingäçevir (Mingechaur) Reservoir in northwestern Azerbaijan, then wanders through an extensive plain before emptying into the Caspian Sea south of Baki (Baku).

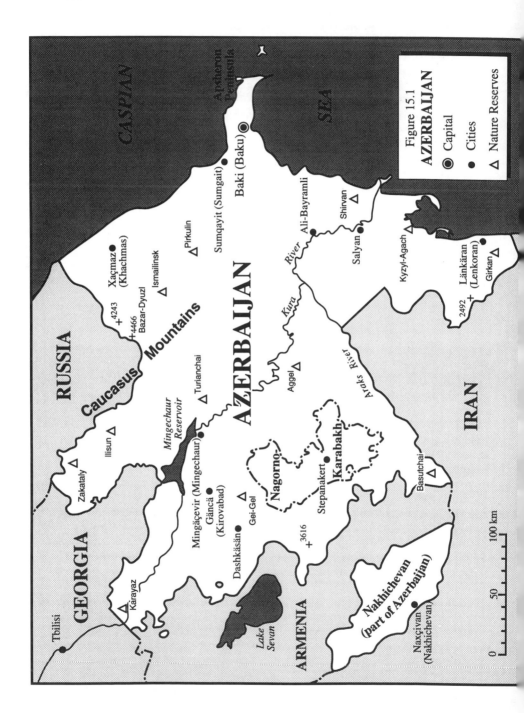

Figure 15.1
AZERBAIJAN

◉ Capital
● Cities
△ Nature Reserves

Numerous other rivers such as the Araks and the Karkarchay also flow through this fertile plain, connected by a series of canals for irrigation.

Irrigation plays an important role in the lower Kura region, where precipitation reaches only 8 inches per year. Virtually the entire region relies on irrigation to produce crops; the sole exception lies near the city of Länkäran (Lenkoran) on the Caspian, where precipitation greatly exceeds evaporation.

The Caspian Sea has a moderating effect on temperatures in Azerbaijan, where average winter temperatures in the lowlands remain above freezing, though nighttime frosts occur. Inland regions tend to be warmer and drier, while the climate to the southeast is slightly more subtropical. According to Soviet data, 36% of agricultural land in Azerbaijan is considered plowable, 52.3% is devoted to pastures, and 7.2% goes toward orchards and vineyards. The climate over much of the Apsheron Peninsula, combined with locally saline soils, greatly inhibits natural vegetation there.

The State of Biotic Resources

Azerbaijan is characterized by varied ecological conditions and a wealth of fauna, including 97 species of mammals, 357 species and subspecies of birds, 50 species of reptiles, 11 species of amphibians and 95 species of fish. With the goal of preserving the full spectrum of a diverse animal kingdom, the republic has a network of protected areas including *zapovedniki* (totaling 186,800 ha in 1992) and *zakazniki* (278,500 ha). The twelve *zapovedniki* of Azerbaijan occupy about 2% of the republic's territory (Table 15.2).

The implementation of land development projects and massive amounts of agricultural pesticides and weed killers have limited natural habitats and reduced the number of wild animals in Azerbaijan. Many other valuable habitats have been deteriorated or destroyed by oil development, air and water pollution, and urban-industrial activities.

Other factors have had equally damaging effects. Oil drilling and sewage from industry, agriculture and other sources have polluted the Caspian Sea and the republic's reservoirs, reducing the areas used as spawning grounds and causing a drop in the quantity of rare fish. The building of dams on the Kura and Araks Rivers and the increase in water used in manufacturing and irrigation have also contributed to the decline in the number of fish. Due to severe pollution in portions of the Caspian coast in Azerbaijan (Baki [Baku] Bay, the Sumqayit (Sumgait) seacoast, and the Neftianie Kamni Islands), "dead zones" have been created where fish and other sea life have disappeared.

Until the mid-1950s, 80% of the fish catch in the Caspian Sea consisted of valuable species (herring, sturgeon and salmon varieties). By the mid-1980s, the proportions were reversed: only 20% of the catch was rare fish, while 80% included common varieties (sprats, etc.). At present, sprats make up almost 100% of the catch.

According to statements from different sources, fish caught in the Caspian often contain toxic substances, such as phenols, and are inedible. The sturgeons, which yield black caviar, are in a particularly critical situation. Most

Table 15.2   Preserved Areas in Azerbaijan

Type of Preserve(a)	Number	Total area(b)	Average size(b)	% of Re-public(c)
Nature Reserves (<u>zapovedniki</u>)	12	1779.22	148.27	2.05
Zapovedniki that are Biosphere Reserves	0	0	0.00	0.00
National Parks	0	0	0.00	0.00
Natural Preserves (<u>zakazniki</u>)	16	2628	164.25	3.03
Total	28	4407.22	157.40	5.09

Nature Reserves (date created)	Hectares
Aggel [Ak-Gel] (1978)	4400
Basutchai (1974)	107
Gei-Gel' (1965; 1926)	7131
Girkan (1969)	2904
Ilisun (1987)	9345
Ismailinsk (1981)	5778
Karayaz (1978)	4155
Kyzyl-Agach (1929)	88360
Pirkulin (1968)	1520
Shirvan (1964)	17745
Turianchai (1958)	12634
Zakataly (1929)	23843
Total	177922

(a) For the definition of each type of preserve, see Appendix 1.2.
(b) In square kilometers.
(c) Area of Azerbaijan is 86,600 sq. kilometers.

of the schools of sturgeon that live in the Caspian and the Volga have developed fatal diseases caused by severe chemical poisoning and are near total extinction; the use of these sturgeon and their caviar for food poses a serious health risk. Although studies are incomplete, Soviet experts believe the degree of pollution of the caviar and the sturgeon schools inhabiting the coasts of Azerbaijan and Turkmenia (and Iran as well) are slightly lower than those in the Volga, but some types of disease are more widespread there.

In 1989 the Azerbaijan Red Book was created, into which 14 species of mammals (about 15% of all mammals), 36 species of birds (about 10% of birds) and 5 species of fish (about 5% of fish) were entered. By the beginning of the 1980s, measures were being developed to preserve and restore the plants and animals listed in the Red Book. These measures prevented the total extinction of such animals as the *dzheiran* (antelope). According to aerial data compiled in October 1989, the *dzheiran* population in Azerbaijan had reached 12,800 as compared with 400 in 1968 ("Environmental Situation," 1992, p. 257).

Land Deterioration and Waste Disposal

Approximately 100 years ago, Azerbaijan began to suffer its first real environmental degradation as oil extraction commenced near the capital of Baki (Baku) (Figure 15.2). The twentieth century witnessed even further deterioration as the republic began to develop heavy industry and pursue more intensive agriculture. The compounded effects of such detrimental practices have proven lethal for the environment in Azerbaijan, and today policy-makers struggle to determine how to begin dealing with the myriad of problems that have emerged over the past century.

Azerbaijan's territory currently contains more than 70 oil and other fuel deposits, over 340 various mineral deposits, and around 200 mineral and thermal complexes. Today, leading industries include oil, chemical, petrochemical, engineering, light and food industries, as well as ferrous and nonferrous metallurgy. Most are situated in the industrial centers of Baki-Sumqayit, Gäncä-Dashkäsan, Mingäçevir-Evlakh, and Mugano-Salyany ("Environmental Situation," 1992, p. 248). Despite this industrial emphasis, the major indicators of economic development in the republic stagnated dur-

Figure 15.2   Offshore oil extraction facilities, such as these at Baki (Baku), have locally polluted the Caspian Sea coast of Azerbaijan.

ing the 1985–1988 period, with GNP increasing by only 1%, industrial output increasing by 5% and agriculture declining by 5%.

Azerbaijan's land reserves consist of over 8.6 million hectares, of which agriculture occupies over 4.2 million ha, or 49%. Population increases and poor land husbandry have caused a persistent decrease in the area of arable land per capita, from .38 ha in 1958, to .26 ha in 1978, to only .21 ha in 1992. Significant losses of fertile land in the republic are a result of the laying of large pipelines (on average, 4 ha per kilometer) and the creation of industrial landfills. Every year recultivation projects are planned; however, they are not fully implemented.

In Azerbaijan, 1.37 million hectares, or 32.2%, of the area of agricultural land are exposed to erosion. Over 200,000 ha are subject to wind erosion. Plans for anti-erosion measures (creation of protective forest strips, terracing of steep slopes) are poorly implemented.

The salination of irrigated soil in the Republic of Azerbaijan has had the most detrimental effects on agricultural production. The total area of salinated soil adds up to 1.2 million ha, and over 500,000 additional ha of irrigated land are exposed to salination. Only 4.1% of operating canals in the republic are lined, and for this reason state irrigation systems alone lose up to 3 billion cubic meters of water yearly. Reducing the water loss amount by half would permit increasing the irrigated area of the republic by 150–200,000 ha. Seepage from the canals results in a significant rise in the water table, in places causing waterlogging and secondary salination of the soil.

In recent years, the republic has suffered an intensification of soil pollution by pesticides and mineral fertilizers. Every year the agricultural-industrial complex uses over 300,000 tons of mineral fertilizers and around 40–60,000 tons of pesticides. In 1991, the amount of chloro-organic pesticides alone that were used was 5 kilograms per ha, compared to a USSR average of 1.5 ("Environmental Situation," 1992, p. 255).

Waste utilization problems remain acute. In areas surrounding factories and mines, dumping grounds contain deposits of 50 million tons of iron ore wastes, 9 million tons of alunite waste, 3.65 million tons of bauxite waste, 1.1 million tons of salt, 250,000 tons of lead ore and 10,000 tons of molybdenum ore.

Because of the lack of landfill facilities for industry, the city of Sumqayit (Sumgait) is presently forced to deposit toxic waste directly on site or to transport it to city dumps. As a result, 19 dumps, occupying 120 hectares, have sprung up in the city.

At Sumqayit's superphosphate plant, every year around 150 tons of chemical waste collect; only 1,700 tons of chemical waste from this plant have been transported to a dump. At the Amalgamated Productions Khimprom, 50,000 tons of mercury-containing materials (wastes of the highest danger) have collected in unenclosed areas. In Baku (Baki), one firm sent to the city dump 7 million defective mercury-containing luminescent lamps.

In 1988, two years later than planned, the republic activated a landfill facility for the burial of agricultural chemicals (DDT, etc.). The capacity of the landfill facility is 8,500 tons, of which 76% has already been filled. Unfortunately, during its construction, a number of errors were committed. Because the cells into which pesticides and weed killers are deposited are not impervious, dispersion and leakage of toxic substances into subsoil water occur.

In addition, the problem of avoiding radioactive pollution is not being resolved adequately. Over 100 radioactive anomalies have been revealed that significantly exceed the natural background level. This is most directly connected with areas where old oil fields are located. The total volume of polluted soil, given the average level of irradiation of 500 mkR/h, comes to 10,000 tons ("Environmental Situation," 1992, p. 256).

Air Pollution

In 1989, 912,500 tons of various pollutants were discharged into the Azerbaijan atmosphere. However, these data do not include automobile emissions, which are about 50% of the total of industrial emissions, that is, around 450,000 tons a year. The overwhelming part of the emissions were discharged from Baki (657,000 tons, or 72%), followed by Sumqayit (64,000 tons, or 7%), Ali-Bayramli (55,000 tons, or 6.1%), Mingäçevir (48,000 tons, or 5.2%) and Gäncä (33,500 tons, or 3.6%) ("Environmental Situation," 1992, p. 248).

In Baki, average yearly concentrations of particulates and nitrogen dioxide in 1989 exceeded maximum permissible levels by one and a half times, while concentrations of chlorine and formaldehyde were three times in excess. Baki has been consistently listed as one of the most heavily polluted cities in the former Soviet Union, ranking second in this dubious category in 1990 among all cities listed (*Okhrana*, 1991, p. 43).

In 1989 in Sumqayit, 64,800 tons of noxious substances were discharged by stationary sources. Average yearly concentrations of dust, chlorine, sulfur dioxide, and nitrogen dioxide exceeded the maximum permissible levels by 1.3 to 1.7 times, while fluorine hydride was two and a half times in excess. Under unfavorable weather conditions, the content of these substances exceeded sanitary norms by 10 to 15 times. In Mingäçevir, emissions totaled 48,000 tons, 89% of which was discharged from Azerbaijan's Electric Power Station.

By 1992, according to official Azerbaijan statistics, the air quality situation had deteriorated significantly. A total of 1,394,000 tons of pollutants were emitted that year into the atmosphere of Baki alone (Zeinalov, 1992). According to data from the Moscow Committee on Statistics, this figure is much higher than the quantity of pollutants discharged from major cities such as Moscow and St. Petersburg. In Sumqayit, the 1992 figure had risen to 96,400 tons; in Gäncä, to 55,000 tons; in Mingäçevir, to 42,900 tons; and in Ali-Bayramli, to 69,800 tons.

Water Quality Problems

Pollution and inefficient usage of water resources, both from freshwater sources and the Caspian Sea, are central to the environmental problems of Azerbaijan. The total quantity of clean water used in Azerbaijan is around 12 billion cubic meters. Of this amount, 3.19 billion cubic meters go toward industry; 8.39 billion cubic meters, toward agriculture; and .40 billion cubic meters, toward drinking and private consumption. In 1989, discharge pollutants reached 292 million cubic meters; 220 million cubic meters of this amount were dumped without any purification process. Water sources were polluted with 3,690 tons of petroleum products, 689 tons of surfactants, 27.9 tons of carbolic acid, 32,700 tons of substances in suspension, and 2,023,000 tons of sulfates ("Environmental Situation," 1992, p. 251).

In agriculture, out of just over 8 billion cubic meters of water used for irrigation, around 3 billion cubic meters are returned back to rivers, reservoirs or the Caspian Sea. This water contains significant concentrations of chemical substances (fertilizers and pesticides).

In addition to being subjected to massive pollution, fish and other aquatic fauna are adversely affected by the general reduction in river discharge. The Kura's water supply to the Caspian has been halved since the construction of the reservoirs and irrigation systems (Khlilov, 1991). Closed-circuit water systems are not yet widely used in Azerbaijan, averaging 32% of the total waste volume. This was below the USSR average and was much lower than in the neighboring republics of Georgia and Armenia, which stood at 48% and 78%, respectively (Golub, 1992).

The Soviet policy of building large numbers of reservoirs is evident in Azerbaijan. At present there are about 40 reservoirs in the republic; an additional 35 were planned. Their role in irrigation and power generation is important, but at the same time they have created problems that are typical of irrigation projects in the former Soviet Union. These problems include low efficiency of irrigation systems, up to 50% leakage due to primitive canal technology, flooding of excessive fertile lands by the reservoirs, large evaporative losses of water, damage to or complete destruction of fish stocks, and so on.

Reservoirs also have an adverse effect on water quality in rivers due to reductions in downstream flows. The issue is significant since the Kura is the main water source for Baki, a city of 1.5 million inhabitants. Since 1991, the problem has become more serious, as the overall economic disintegration becomes reflected in Azerbaijan's water systems. Neither water treatment tanks nor new chlorination units, which were planned many years ago, have been constructed. The old facilities, meanwhile, are operating below sanitary or technological standards.

The bacteriological pollution of reservoirs and public water supplies has increased and has caused sanitation authorities to demand that water treatment facilities be shut down. At the same time, Soviet sanitary norms for potable water issued in 1991 allowed much higher concentrations of pollutants than previously and even tolerated the presence of various dioxins in the water (Golub, 1992).

In 1992 a critical situation arose in Baki: the city was unable to provide its inhabitants with even the minimal quantity of water. Water leakage in the city's water-piping system was evaluated at 40 to 50% of the total quantity even before the crisis; at present, it appears that the figure exceeds 60%. Water is transported in cisterns to many surrounding areas of Baki and sold by the bucket. Clearly, in such a situation, controlling the water quality is difficult by any standard.

Having recognized the severity of the situation, the leadership in some areas is trying to implement drastic measures. For example, in 1992 in Sumqayit, a decree halted the activity of 30 plants and factories. The construction of water-cleaning systems was begun with the assistance of Chinese and Dutch firms ("Tak budet," 1992).

Public Health Considerations

Industry, agriculture, and urbanization contribute to a growing public health problem. According to the Health Ministry, pollution of the air, water, and foodstuffs appears to be the main cause of an increase in cancer cases, allergy problems and weakened immune systems among Azerbaijanis. Urban populations seem to be most at risk; in cities registered cancer cases exceed those of rural areas by 3 to 4 times (Zeinalov, 1992).

In Azerbaijan, the insecticide DDT was allowed to be used "as an exception" from 1970 to 1988. On farms where it was used, skin diseases in children and nutritional and metabolic ailments were 4 to 5 times greater than normal (Feshbach and Friendly, 1992, p. 67). Incorrect and unregulated usage of fertilizers and pesticides has resulted not only in the pollution of soil, but also in a high concentration of these substances in foodstuffs, especially fruits and vegetables. Beginning in the 1980's, experts noted dangerous concentrations of DDT and other chemicals in food samples. However, it was forbidden to publish these data, and the information had no influence on policy in the areas of agriculture and public health services.

In 1982, a comparative study of rural areas in Ukraine and Azerbaijan was carried out. Two zones were selected in each of the republics: an experimental area and a control area containing active and limited pesticide use, respectively. Healthy adolescents between the ages of 14 and 17 were studied for cellular genetic disorders. The frequency of cytological disorders in both the experimental and control areas of Azerbaijan was considerably above average. It was convincingly demonstrated that excessive pesticide use increased the risk of disease. The situation was particularly ominous in areas with widespread cotton cultivation (Zeinalov, 1989).

It was not until 1989, however, that a special research center was established in Baki, and a health program was started to reduce the impact of chemicals on human health and the environment. Despite the extremely difficult economic and political situation, the program has been partially implemented, although important indicators, such as the infant mortality rate (about 33–36 per thousand), still remain high.

Caspian Sea Problems

Unlike the Aral Sea, the Caspian Sea does not suffer from a lack of water. Currently, its water level is rising, rather than falling, and this rising sea level is an increasing cause of concern. Fifteen years ago, the situation was reversed: the water level was falling, and engineers were planning to transfer water from the Volga to save the sea from drying out. In the last 25 years the level of the Caspian has risen 175 to 182 centimeters and is forecasted to rise another 1.5 meters by the year 2010. Even today beaches, highways and bridges along the coast near Baki are flooded. The lowlands of Azerbaijan at the Iranian border are especially affected since many roads, houses and other structures lie within the coastal area. The rising water also hurt the unique Kizyl-Agach Nature Reserve, where millions of ducks, geese, herons, pelicans and other birds used to winter on the coastal shoals. Massive poaching and various business activities of the local farms have reduced the effectiveness of the reserve to a minimum (Komarov, 1980), while the rising water has destroyed the vegetation that provided shelter and food for the birds.

The sharp rise in the level of the Caspian along the coast of Turkmenistan has created an extremely dangerous situation. In some areas the sea now stretches two to three kilometers inland, threatening industrial and residential areas, wastewater treatment plants, oil pipelines and highways. The most dangerous situations are on the Chelikan Peninsula, where a number of chemical and oil-producing enterprises are located, and at oil storage facilities in the town of Ufa, where a rise in the water level could lead to a major oil slick (Golub, 1990).

There are similar problems along the Caspian coast in Russia and Kazakhstan, where oil and gas deposits are also situated within the low coastal plain. Here the land is very flat, and even a small rise in water level can result in the sea coming hundreds of meters closer to the drilling towers. The northern Caspian coast is locally characterized by unstable ground, and in places "black holes" have emerged, into which parts of highways, buildings, and livestock have fallen. The water in the new lakes that emerge is similar in composition to the Caspian Sea (Wolfson, 1990).

Periodic level fluctuations have occurred in the Caspian in the past, but never anything like the 10-centimeter annual rise occurring during the past several years. In the summer of 1991, Azerbaijan initiated the first regional conference on the Caspian Sea problems. During the conference in Baki, a number of papers were presented that contributed greatly to the understanding of the problems. Yet at the same time, the meeting demonstrated an increasing politicizing of the issue, one example being Azerbaijan's use of the word *Khazar* for the Caspian Sea, since for Russian-speakers, *khazars* has a negative connotation.

The next meeting of the five Caspian countries was held in Tehran in October of 1992. In 1991, Iran did not take part in the conference. This time, Turkey did not participate, and the meeting reflected the political aspirations of Iran, which is trying to create a collaborative organization of the Caspian countries within a framework wider than that of environmental collaboration. At this meeting, the word *Khazar* was avoided both in official and unofficial speeches. Iran both proposed the idea of the organization and offered to cover the organization's expenses for the first three years. The conference did not reach significant progress, but it reflected clearly enough the approaches of its participants. Azerbaijan and Turkmenistan sided with Iran's position on practically all the points; Russia and Kazakhstan objected to almost all the points ("V zentre," 1992). An apparent key issue involved Iran's assertion that Iranian ships have the right to pass through all parts of the Caspian and its tributaries. These demands were presented as a pre-condition for cooperation in the fight against pollution and for access to fishing resources, etc. Russia was apparently unhappy with the idea of allowing Iranian ships to transport cargo freely through the Volga and Don rivers and Black Sea.

Cooperative efforts by the Caspian countries regarding the protection of the sea's resources and the prevention of pollution are also complicated by disagreements and conflicts within each country. Thus, Russia is unable to provide unified norms (even on paper) for controlling pollution of those Caspian river basins that flow through Russia's territory. In Azerbaijan itself, the Planning and Economic Committee, despite objections from the Environmental Committee and the Foreign Ministry, signed an "agreement regarding the usage of biological resources" with Russia ("V zentre," 1992).

Azerbaijan, due to its geographic location and dependence on the Caspian Sea, is expressing the greatest concern about the sea's condition. However, due to political and economic constraints, it cannot become a real leader in unifying efforts to conserve resources and limit pollution. Apprehensive of Russia's dominant role, Azerbaijan is trying to gain support from its Muslim neighbors, Turkey, and, more recently, Iran.

Regardless of political orientations and aspirations, both the Baki (1991) and the Tehran (1992) conferences reflected the growing preoccupation of all the basin countries with the fate of the Caspian, but at the same time these conferences showed the dominance of purely political and economic interests in what is called environmental politics.

Environmental Management and Policy

Regulatory agencies dealing with the environment of Azerbaijan began to be created later than in other republics of the Soviet Union. Until the mid-1980s the agencies were dispersed and distributed among numerous governmental departments and organizations. The creation during the 1980s of the Republics' Committee for the Environment and Efficient Use of Natural Resources (Environmental Committee) barely altered the situation. Citizen pressure on legislative and executive organs appeared in Azerbaijan significantly later and in a weaker form than in the European part of the USSR.

Since 1991 the Environmental Committee has been trying to consolidate its control over most regulatory functions that involve the creation of protected reserves and inspection of development projects. One of the first steps in this direction was the committee's recommendation of a whole package of legislative proposals, which were expected to be adopted in 1993 by the *Mejlis* (parliament). The heart of these proposals is the Law Concerning Environmental Protection and Natural Resource Utilization in the Azerbaijan Republic. In contrast with previous laws of the Soviet Union, which, according to Azerbaijan ecologists, were of an abstract and declarative character, these proposals are based on the experience of Western nations and should promote accelerated improvement in environmental practices. It is too early to evaluate the effectiveness of the new laws.

Funding is a major problem. The current head of the Environment Committee, Arif Mansurov, speaks of a disastrous financial situation in the environmental protection system. As an illustration, he points to the unavailability of 15–20 million rubles (in summer 1992 prices, a modest sum by Western standards of around $100,000) for the creation of a national park in Karabakh ("Nastoyashchee," 1992).

The latest available data concerning environmental inspection of development projects (1990) show that 185 technical projects and 359 land-use projects were examined. Additional environmental protection requirements were introduced into 195 projects. One hundred thirty-seven projects were refused on environmental grounds; however, this does not mean that they were not carried out.

The Environmental Committee today is strongly committed to environmental education through schools and through informal organizations and to the elucidation of the situation through the media. The committee subsidizes two periodicals dealing with protection of the environment. Environmental education is one of the few spheres that have undoubtedly benefited from the political changes of the past few years. The reasons are that environmental education demands minimal expenses and does not require the creation of new structures. Also, regardless of political inclinations, the new leaders are seen as people compelled to save the country, to drag it out of the economic, political, and environmental abyss into which the Communist empire had pushed it.

Green organizations have recently appeared. With their help, the first nongovernmental environmental research, service and production companies have appeared. In the post-Soviet period, a green party has been organized, and it has become a noticeable force in the Mejlis. In the beginning of June 1992, before the convening of the world conference in Rio de Janeiro, the Greens made a statement directed at the conference participants in which they pointed to the critical situation existing in Azerbaijan and the Caspian Sea. According to their statement, 60% of the country's land territory, 90% of its water sources, and 40% of the surface area of the Caspian Sea should be considered zones of environmental disaster. In particular, they pointed out that 250 tons of waste collect daily from oil drilling. This entire amount is dumped into the sea, despite the fact that the waste contains about 40 highly toxic elements and its destructive impact on the maritime environment greatly exceeds that of oil. For many years, scientists have observed with alarm the spread of "dead zones" on the Caspian Sea, where no signs of life remain.

The Green Party actively supports the Environmental Committee and its legislative initiatives in the Mejlis. It similarly insists on even wider and more active international cooperation and on an orientation, first of all, toward neighboring states (Turkey and Iran) and toward Western states, as opposed to the states of CIS, even though many believe the latter remain natural partners in many spheres. Thus, the Greens (and the director of the Environmental Committee, Arif Mansurov) protested against the signing in Moscow of an agreement on a multi-state environmental council of CIS in February 1992, as they saw in this agreement the rebirth of imperial structures. Although Azerbaijan officially signed the Moscow CIS agreement, in practice the republic is doing very little to implement the accord. Yet Azerbaijan's behavior is little different than that of other CIS members.

The oil industry in Azerbaijan may well be revitalized as Western firms begin to provide assistance. This may become yet another serious threat to the environment. Kazakhstan, Russia, Azerbaijan and Turkmenistan have all signed large oil development contracts with at least one Western partner, without coordinating with the other republics. All of them hope that the participation of Western firms will guarantee a solution to environmental problems. Yet even those who give credit to Western experience and technology know that local environmental officials are often unprofessional, corrupted, or both. Further deterioration of the political and economic systems would impede local authorities from demanding environmental protection measures, even if they were willing to do so. It seems that in many cases, if the projects do continue, the Western firms will determine the environmental protection program to be followed and then regulate their own activities (Zeinalov, 1992).

The environmental consequences of the Armenian-Azerbaijani conflict have been great. Last year, the Azerbaijan Republic's State Committee on Environmental Protection published an official statement in which it noted that military actions had caused over 10,000 hectares of arable land and longtime plantations and 600 hectares of forests to be destroyed. The statement also suggested there was intentional pollution of inter-republic rivers, as well as considerable damage to several nature reserves. It is clear that a satisfactory resolution to this conflict is key to Azerbaijan's short term economic and environmental improvement.

Thus, the final picture does not engender hopes for quick improvements in the environmental situation in Azerbaijan and the Caspian basin or for rapidly halting the current destructive rates of pollution and deterioration of the environment. Internal stability must be achieved, together with administrative reforms, before long-term improvement in Azerbaijan's economic and environmental situation can be realized.

Acknowledgments

The authors are grateful to Professor N. Vorontzov, former head of the Committee for Environmental Protection of the USSR, for providing the unpublished copy of "Report of the Committee 1991" and to Dr. Roma Tzvang and Mr. Efraim Meidan at the Mayrock Center of the Hebrew University for their assistance in collecting recent periodical publications on Azerbaijan and the CIS, as well as to Julia Fayngold and Faith Segal for their kind help.

Notes

1. The Nagorno-Karabakh conflict with Armenia continues to dominate all aspects of life in Azerbaijan, including both the economy and the environment. It affects not only the physical environment, but also the availability of up-to-date information and accu-

rate analysis of the current situation in Azerbaijan. The deterioration of all civic systems influences much of the statistical data and scientific activity in Azerbaijan, thus sometimes forcing the use of fragmentary, although quite plentiful, publications whose data cannot be verified. Data for 1991 and 1992 proved to be particularly unreliable, and figures on population, GNP and several other indicators should be treated as estimates.

Bibliography

"Environmental Situation in the USSR." 1991. Report to the U.N. Conference on Global Environment, Rio de Janeiro, 1992, by the Committee for Environmental Protection and Rational Use of Nature Resources of the USSR. Moscow.

Feshbach, M., and A. Friendly. 1992. *Ecocide in the USSR*. New York, Basic Books.

Golub, R. 1992. "The Caspian/Khazar Sea." *Environmental Policy Review*, vol. 6, no. 1, pp. 1–10.

Khlilov, S. 1991. "Chto na dne vodokhranilishch?" *Bakinskii Rabochii*, January 16, p. 3.

Komarov, B. (Z. Wolfson). 1980. *The Destruction of Nature in the Soviet Union*. White Plains, NY: M.E. Sharpe.

Mnatsakanian, R. A. 1992. *Environmental Legacy of the Former Soviet Republics*. Edinburgh: Centre for Human Ecology.

"Nastoyaschee i buduschee." 1992. Interview with Arif Mansurov, Head of Environmental Protection Committee of Azerbaijan, *Bakinskii Rabochii*, June 17, p. 2.

Okhrana Okruzhayushchey Sredy i Ratsional'noye Ispol'zovaniye Prirodnykh Resursov. 1991. Moscow: Goskomstat.

"Tak budet li voda v Baku?" 1992. *Bakinskii Rabochii*, June 6, pp. 1–2.

"V zentre vnimania—problemy Kaspia." 1992. *Bakinskii Rabochii*, October 23, p. 2.

Wolfson, Z. 1990. "The Caspian Sea: Clear Signs of Disaster." *Environmental Policy Review*, vol. 4, no. 2, pp. 13–18; see also *Environmental Policy Review*, vol. 7, no. 1 (1993), pp. 14–21.

Zeinalov, O. 1992. "Ne razbazarivat' bogatstva." *Bakinskii Rabochii*, June 6, p. 3.

Zeinalov, T., 1989. Director of the Pesticides Toxicology Lab of the Azerbaijani Academy of Sciences, interviewed in *Bakinskii Rabochii*, April 20, pp. 2–3.

16

Kazakhstan

David R. Smith

Among the former Soviet republics, Kazakhstan, at almost three million square kilometers, is second only to the Russian Federation in territorial extent. Indeed, Kazakhstan is now the ninth largest nation on earth in land area. It is also one of the most sparsely populated (Appendix 16.1).

Kazakhstan is the largest of the group of so-called Muslim republics of Central Asia that have emerged as independent countries following the collapse of the former Soviet Union. Its location between Russia to the north and the other Muslim republics to the south explains a cultural and economic-geographic division between the northern part of the republic and its southern flank. One of the consequences of its size is a great diversity of not only cultural attributes, but also physical geographic characteristics and natural resources. A familiarity with the spatial characteristics of Kazakh ethnic populations, industry and agriculture may help in understanding some of the key environmental and developmental problems that Kazakhstan will face in years to come.

History and Ethnicity

Kazakhstan exists in its contemporary political form as a result of its territorial acquisition by tsarist Russia at the end of the nineteenth century. Its present borders, drawn to define the limits of "Kazakh" territory, were delineated under Soviet rule in 1924. An important characteristic that separated the Kazakhs as a people from the Russians to the north and the sedentary peoples to the south was their nomadic lifestyle. For centuries, the Kazakhs wandered the steppes across western China and southern Russia, owing allegiance to families and tribes, until the incorporation of their territory into the tsarist empire.

Little is known about the early history of the Kazakhs. Early travelers concentrated on trade with regional urban centers and had little contact with the nomadic Kazakhs (Olcott, 1987, p. 3). The breakup of the Golden Horde and the acquisition of the territory by the descendants of the Mongol/Turkic peoples who arrived in the thirteenth century suggest a plausible theory of the Kazakh people's origin. By the mid-16th century, they were calling themselves Kazakhs; political and tribal allegiances served to separate the Kazakhs from their Kyrgyz and Uzbek neighbors. Some suggest the only distinguishing characteristic separating the Kazakhs from the Kyrgyz and Uzbeks is the degree of Mongol ancestry. In any case, with the arrival of the Russians in the 17th and 18th centuries, the Kazakhs were to be confused by the Russians as Kyrgyz until the formation of the Kazakh Republic in the 1920s.

Under Soviet rule, periodic border unrest occurred as a result of the large population of Kazakhs in neighboring Sinkiang (Xinjiang) Province of China. Prior to communist rule in China, Soviet collectivization efforts provoked a large migration of Kazakhs into western China. When the new Chinese government began to exert influence over the nomadic Kazakhs in western China, a reverse movement of Kazakhs into Soviet Kazakhstan began.

The Kazakhs identify themselves with the Sunni branch of Islam, although the strength of their commitment has varied over time. Islam was expanding into the cities in southern Kazakhstan by the eighth century. Even though most Kazakhs had embraced Islam by the eleventh century, elements of their nomadic lifestyle, characterized by shamanism, were to remain until the creation of the Kazakh Republic (Olcott, 1987). Until the Soviet-era creation of political units and economic lifestyle changes, the nomadic Kazakhs had very little contact with their more urban neighbors to the south.

With the Bolshevik promise of national self-determination came gradual political recognition for nationality groups. The new "Stalin" Constitution of 1936 involved the creation of eleven ethnically based political units, one of which was the Kazakh Soviet Socialist Republic. However, until 1989, the Kazakhs were a minority in their own republic. Even today, the Kazakhs (at 40%) represent only a plurality, not a majority, of the total population (Appendix 16.2).

In 1991, Kazakhstan had a territorial extent of 2.7 million square kilometers, the largest of the ex-Soviet republics after Russia. It is divided into 19 oblasts (provinces), and in 1991, its population was almost 17 million. The majority of the people (58%) live in urban areas, unlike the other Central Asian republics, and reflect the dominant role of industry in the economy. Table 16.1 shows that between 1951 and 1991, the population grew by 147 percent. This population increase was a result of in-migration as industrial and agricultural expansion occurred, as well as a higher than average birthrate. The capital city, Alma-Ata (Almaty),[1] was one of the fastest growing cities in the former Soviet Union. Table 16.2 provides a list of the new names of major Kazakhstan cities and their growth rates.

Detailed census data for Kazakhstan have revealed concentrations of Kazakhs and Russians in particular regions of the country (Table 16.1). Russian majorities existed in the six northern and northeastern oblasts, whereas the Kazakhs dominated in the far south along the Syr Darya (river) in Kyzl-Orda Oblast and in Guryev (now Atyrau) Oblast along the north coast of the Caspian Sea.

Table 16.1   Regional Population Distribution and Ethnic Composition of Kazakhstan by Oblast

Region/ Oblast	Year[a] 1951	Year[a] 1991	Per- cent change	Pop- ulation density in 1991 (p/km^2)	Percent urban in 1991	Ethnic composition in 1979 (percent) Kazakh	Ethnic composition in 1979 (percent) Russian
West							
Ural'sk	298	648	117	5	43	52	37
Gur'yev	218	447	105	4	62	76	18
Mangyshlak	26	332	1180	2	89	44	40
Aktyubinsk	306	753	146	3	55	52	25
TOTAL	848	2180	157	3	58	47	25
North and Northeast							
Kustanay	383	1074	180	10	53	17	47
North Kazakhstan	353	610	73	14	48	17	63
Kokchetav	336	669	99	9	40	26	40
Tselinograd	381	794	108	7	57	21	47
Pavlodar	320	957	199	8	65	28	46
Karaganda	479	1340	180	16	85	15	55
TOTAL	2252	5444	142	10	62	18	46
Central and East							
Turgay	94	305	225	3	34	37	32
Dzhezkazgan	172	496	188	2	79	41	39
Semipalatinsk	401	842	110	5	52	48	39
East Kazakhstan	582	949	63	10	65	25	68
TOTAL	1249	2592	108	4	60	34	45
Southeast							
Kyzl-Orda	283	665	135	3	65	76	15
Chimkent	722	1879	160	17	41	51	19
Dzhambul	430	1056	146	8	48	44	30
Alma-Atinsk	348	993	185	10	22	38	34
Taldy-Kurgan	394	731	86	7	45	46	37
TOTAL	2177	5324	145	8	42	42	23
KAZAKHSTAN	6813	16793	147	7	58	36	41

[a]Figures in thousands.
Sources: Calculated from information in Goskomstat SSSR, 1988; Informatsentr Goskomstata SSSR, 1991; and from offical census results.

The Kazakhs' centuries-old nomadic lifestyle, their cultural diversity and religious affinity with neighboring territories, the ethnically bipolar nature of the population, and the relatively recent political creation of the country suggest possible long-term problems of political stability. In the early 1990s, though, the strong leadership of President Nazarbayev, and an absence of significant political opposition, made Kazakhstan one of the more stable and economically progressive of the Soviet successor states.

Table 16. 2   Largest Cities in Kazakhstan

City	New Name	Population (1000s) 1970	1989	Percent Increase
Alma-Ata	Almaty	733	1128	54
Karaganda	Qaraghandy	523	614	17
Chimkent	Shymkent	247	393	59
Semipalatinsk	Semey	236	334	42
Pavlodar	(same)	187	331	77
Ust-Kamenogorsk	Oskemen	230	324	41
Dzhambul	Zhambyl	187	307	64
Tselinograd	Aqmola	180	277	54
Aktyubinsk	Aqtobe	150	253	69
Petropavlovsk	Petropavl	173	241	39
Kustanay	Qostanay	123	224	82
Temirtau	(same)	166	212	28
Uralsk	Oral	134	200	49
Shevchenko	Aqtau	59	159	169
Kzyl-Orda	Qyzylorda	122	153	25
Guryev	Atyrau	114	149	31
Kokchetav	Kokshetau	81	137	69
Ekibastuz	(same)	44	135	207

Sources: Soviet Geography, May 1989; U.S. Board on Geographic Names.

The Physical Environment

Kazakhstan has a varied geographic character, as would be expected for such a large territory. Four distinct physical and economic zones can be distinguished: (1) the west, or north Caspian lowland (west of the Turgai Trough), where significant petroleum resources are located; (2) the north and northeast, which is an eastward extension of the steppe-chernozem zone found in European Russia and Ukraine, and, a place where wheat farming on the former "Virgin Lands" is the dominant economic activity; (3) the center and east, where vast mineral and fossil fuel resources are located; and (4) the south and southeast, where glacier-fed streams and the Syr Darya provide water for an irrigated agricultural economy that resembles that of other Central Asian republics (see Figure 16.1).

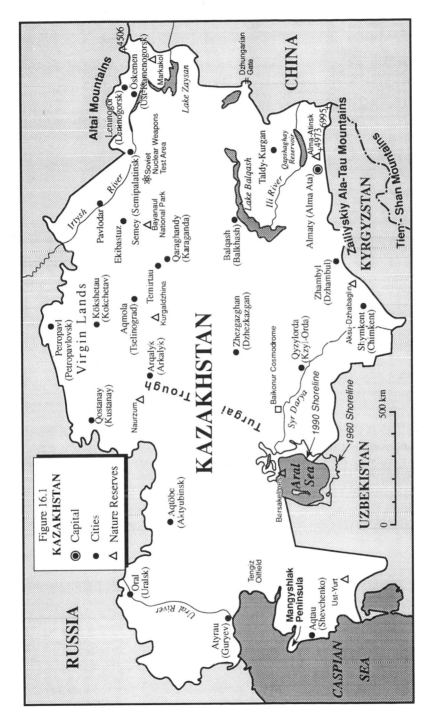

Figure 16.1
KAZAKHSTAN

◉ Capital
● Cities
△ Nature Reserves

The West

This area is bisected from north to south by the slow-moving Ural River, originating in the southern Ural Mountains of Russia and emptying into the Caspian at the city of Guryev. The portion of western Kazakhstan that borders on the Caspian Sea lies below sea level.

To the north, the terrain rises into the Mugodzhar uplands, the farthest southern extension of the Ural Mountains. This region is heavily mineralized with iron ore and chromium. To the south near the Caspian Sea is a major oil extracting region.

The northern half of the Aral Sea basin lies within Kazakh territory. The center of an interior drainage at the southern end of the Turgai Trough, the Aral Sea has been decreasing in area as upstream diversions have increased in the past twenty years along the two river systems that feed it.

The North and Northeast

Most of the territory between the cities of Kustanay (Qostanay) and Semipalatinsk (Semey), north to the Russian border, is known as the "Virgin," or "New," Lands. This extensive territory was sown to wheat in the 1950s under Khrushchev in order to improve the nation's food supply. There are numerous lakes in this region, some of them saline. The Turanian Depression, or Turgai Trough, separates the southern Urals in the west from the central Kazakh uplands to the east.

The Center and East

The dominant physical features of this region include the semi-desert central uplands and the foothills of the Altay Mountains in the east. The central uplands around Karaganda (Qaraghandy) (maximum elevation: 1,565 meters) slope down to the basin of the north-flowing Irtysh River in the east. The major cities of eastern and central Kazakhstan, such as Semipalatinsk, Ust-Kamenogorsk (Oskemen), Karaganda, and Dzezhkazgan (Zhezgazghan), are engaged mainly in industrial activities associated with mining a variety of minerals such as coal, iron ore, copper, lead and zinc. Lake Zaysan, a reservoir along the upper Irtysh River, and the Irtysh itself, provide water for industrial and municipal needs.

The South and Southeast

This region of Kazakhstan includes Kyzl-Orda (Qyzylorda), Chimkent (Shymkent), Dzhambul (Zhambyl), and Alma-Ata (Almaty) Oblasts, which border on Kyrgyzstan and Uzbekistan to the south. The border follows the Tien Shan Mountain range, with highest elevations rising to almost 7,000 meters, culminating at Khan Tengri Peak (6,995 meters). The Betpak Dala desert covers much of the territory. Glacier-fed streams flowing north out of the mountains, as well as the larger Syr Darya and Ili Rivers, provide water for extensive irrigated agriculture to take place. To the north lies Lake Balkhash, fed by the Ili River and other streams flowing westward out of China.

Physical Constraints to Development

Some of the more important physical deterrents to development in Kazakhstan include harsh climatic conditions, dust storms, soil salinity, seismicity and landslides, and the vast distances that have to be overcome to transport people, raw materials, and manufactured goods.

With high mountain barriers to the east and south, Russian Siberia to the north, and the vast Russian steppes to the west, Kazakhstan has a very continental climate. This means that without the moderating influences of large bodies of water, summers are usually hot and dry and winters are quite cold and relatively dry.

Temperatures and precipitation amounts vary across such a large land mass. Average July temperatures range from 24.6°C (76°F) at Kyzl-Orda in the south, to 20.4°C (69°F) at Kustanay in the north. January temperatures vary from −9.6°C (15°F) at Kyzl-Orda to −17.8°C (0°F) at Kustanay. Semipalatinsk has experienced a difference between historic maximum and minimum temperatures of 91°C, from a high of 42°C (108°F) to −49°C (−56°F).

Precipitation decreases from north to south; Kustanay averages 268 mm (10.5 in) per year, with a summer maximum, while Kyzl-Orda averages only 114 mm (4.5 in) per year, with a winter and spring maximum (Lydolph, 1977). Occasional dry winds, known as a *sukhovey*, can be significant in Kazakhstan. When they occur in the spring and early summer, they can destroy crops and lead to dust storms occurring over wide areas. These dust storms are a significant problem for agriculture in Kazakhstan (Figure 16.2).

Another problem for agriculture in northern Kazakhstan is soil salinization. It was noted that there are many saline lakes in the Kazakh steppe region, and the soils around them are often somewhat saline as well. Such lands cannot be used for agriculture. The desiccation of the Aral Sea to the south has also created a serious salt problem. Newly exposed lake-bottom lands contain a high salt content, and winds have periodically picked up these sediments and created "dust-salt storms," which can severely harm agricultural lands downwind.

A moderate seismic threat exists in the mountains along the southern and eastern margins of the republic. The hazard is greatest in the vicinity of the capital, Alma-Ata, which suffered a major earthquake in 1911. The entire central, northern, and western portions of the republic have little earthquake potential.

The steep mountain slopes near Alma-Ata, combined with the earthquake potential, create one other type of hazard for the southern border region: landslides. Landslides (the term is used here to include mudflows, avalanches, and debris flows as well) are a continuing threat in the Ala-Tau mountain ranges, and expensive dams and barriers have been built across the valleys leading out of the mountains to protect the city of Alma-Ata (Figure 16.3).

One final constraint to economic development is distance. Not only is the republic vast (3,000 km across), but it is also landlocked. With no easily accessible outlet to the world ocean, export goods must be transported enor-

258

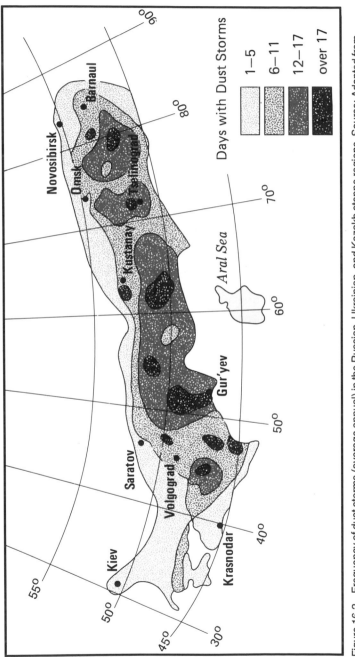

Figure 16.2 Frequency of dust storms (average annual) in the Russian, Ukrainian, and Kazakh steppe regions. Source: Adapted from Sazhin, 1988, p. 936. Reprinted with permission of V. H. Winston & Son, Inc.

Figure 16.3   The Olympic training facilities at Medea, as well as downstream areas near the Kazakh capital city of Almaty (Alma-Ata), are protected from landslides and mudflows by this large retention dam.

mous distances by rail, barge, or pipeline, generally through Russia. This will tend to make Kazakh commodities more expensive and the participation of foreign firms in Kazakh development more desirable.

Natural Resource Advantages and Existing Industry

Due to the abundance of mineral resources, Kazakhstan had the third most highly developed economy among the former Soviet republics. With about 7% of the USSR's population, it produced over 5% of the USSR's electricity, 4% of the oil, 19% of the coal, 10% of the iron ore, and 14% of the grain crops for the country as a whole (Goskomstat SSSR, 1988).

Electricity

Electricity is essential to economic development. Kazakhstan produced about 87 billion kilowatt hours of electricity in 1990, most of which was consumed by industry. Since the 1970s, the use of fuel oil and gas in thermal electric plants has risen as coal use declined. As the increasing value of oil for other uses is recognized, focus may shift to the more abundant and less expensive coal deposits in Kazakhstan to provide electricity. Conversion to coal would be expensive and entail an increase in air pollution. The republic's largest thermal electric station (4,000 megawatts), located in the city of

Ekibastuz, exploded in September of 1990, apparently caused by a hydrogen gas leak (Sagers, 1991).

Hydropower is an important electrical energy source along the Ili and Irtysh Rivers. Completed in 1979, the Kapchagay (Qapshaghay) hydroelectric station on the Ili River is the largest multi-purpose reservoir in Kazakhstan. Its construction has resulted in a reduction of discharge into Lake Balkhash and has produced the numerous detrimental socio-economic consequences that were predicted by conservationists before construction began (Bond et al., 1992).

The only nuclear reactor in Kazakhstan, a 350 megawatt fast breeder reactor at Shevchenko (Aqtau) on the Caspian seacoast, went off-line for repairs in early 1990 (Sagers, 1991). There has been some discussion of expanding this facility.

Fossil Fuels

Kazakhstan ranked third in the former USSR behind Russia and Ukraine in the production of fossil fuels. Two of the most important mineral resources to industrial development, oil and coal, are in relatively abundant supply, while natural gas is not.

The Emba oil fields near Guryev (Atyrau) have been in production since 1911. Regional oil production increased in the 1950s with the discovery of oil underneath the Mangyshlak Peninsula. A new major oil producing region takes in the Korolevskoye and Tengiz fields, both located in Guryev Oblast along the north Caspian coast. Production began in the Tengiz field in April of 1991 with the help of Chevron Corporation and is expected to top 3.5 million tons annually by the year 2000 (Sagers, 1992). The Tengiz field may have larger oil reserves than the north slope of Alaska. Other oil producing regions are in Kyzl-Orda Oblast and to the south of Dzhezkazgan. Long distance pipelines from the Tengiz fields for oil export and for oil transport to refineries in eastern Kazakhstan have been proposed, but if built, they will provide increased chances for accidents and leaks to occur.

Unlike the other Central Asian republics, Kazakhstan produces relatively small amounts of natural gas, mainly in conjunction with petroleum production near Shevchenko and Uralsk. The large-scale development of the Tengiz or other fields might change this (Sagers, 1993).

Kazakhstan is a major coal producer. The Karaganda underground mines and Ekibastuz open pit mines west of Pavlodar supply most of the republic's coal. Associated iron and steel plants have helped make the Karaganda region the most highly developed in Kazakhstan. The high ash content of both coals, however, has limited their attractiveness for industrial use.

Minerals and Metallurgical Production

Kazakhstan has large iron ore and manganese reserves, was the USSR's largest supplier of copper ore, and is the world's largest supplier of chromite ore. Iron ore deposits in Kustanay Oblast were the source of most of the 24 million tons produced in the republic in 1990, most of which was shipped to steel mills near Karaganda and Pavlodar. Southwest of Karaganda in Dzhezkazgan Oblast lies the former Soviet Union's largest copper ore deposit; other large deposits lie north of Lake Balkhash. Almost all of the 3.6 million tons of chromite ore produced in 1990 came from the region around Chromtau, east of Aktyubinsk (Aqtobe) in northwestern Kazakhstan. North of Lake Zaysan near the city of Ust-Kamenogorsk (Oskemen) lie major deposits of polymetallic ores, which include zinc, lead, and copper (Shabad, 1969).

Agriculture

Throughout the 1980s, the total sown area in Kazakhstan remained around 35 million ha, or about 13% of the territory of the republic. More than half of the total sown area is located in the Virgin Lands in the northern part of the republic. In the mid-1950s, a desire to increase animal fodder led to the replacement of wheat by corn in the Russian steppes and Ukraine. Between 1954 and 1960, over 43 million hectares of new (or virgin) lands from the Volga to the Altai Mountains were sown to wheat to replace land lost to corn. The two most important crops in Kazakhstan's Virgin Lands are wheat for food and barley for livestock fodder. By 1990, wheat and barley represented about 60% of the total crops sown in the republic. Spring planting is necessary because of harsh winter conditions in Kazakhstan's northern provinces, where most grain crops are grown. Rice, cotton, and a variety of vegetables and fruits are grown on irrigated areas in the southeast.

Pesticide and fertilizer use on fields in Kazakhstan began a sharp decline in the mid-1980s due to both economic and environmental concerns. By 1990, fertilizer and pesticide use had dropped by more than half as compared to two or three years earlier.

Major Environmental Problems

Air and water contamination from industrial sources and water and soil pollution from agricultural and urban areas continue to be the major environmental problems in Kazakhstan. Of particular importance are industrial emissions, areas of radioactive contamination, the desiccation and pollution of Lake Balkhash, water and soil pollution of Kazakhstan's northern portion of the Aral Sea basin, and the desiccation of the Aral Sea itself.

Air Pollution

As a consequence of the concentration of fuel and mineral resources in the northeast and central parts of the republic, together with associated industries such as ferrous and non-ferrous metallurgy, air pollution in these regions is among the highest in the former Soviet republics. The most serious air pollution occurs in regions where metallurgical, oil refining, and chemical industries are concentrated. Pavlodar, Karaganda, and Dzhezkazgan Oblasts are not only the focus of Kazakhstan's industrial production but of its air pollution as well. Almost 60% of total republic emissions, at an average of over one ton of pollutant per person, was emitted into the atmosphere in those three oblasts in 1988.

Lead and zinc production in East Kazakhstan Oblast and oil refineries along the north Caspian seacoast in Guryev Oblast were other major polluters in Kazakhstan. Sulfur dioxide emissions from Guryev Oblast were reportedly the second largest amount from any oblast of the USSR in 1989 ("Panel," 1990, p. 407). Karaganda Oblast produced the most air pollutants in 1988 among all of the republic's oblasts. About 1.5 out of 5.2 million tons of total emissions in Kazakhstan were from metallurgical plants in the oblast. Karaganda Oblast alone emitted more atmospheric pollutants than the entire Republic of Uzbekistan in 1988 (Goskomstat SSSR, 1989, p. 252).

Many other cities in Kazakhstan have serious pollution problems as well. In 1990, lead pollution emissions in excess of ten times the maximum permissible amounts occurred 31 times in Leninogorsk and 19 times in Chimkent (Popov and Erokhina, 1991). Temirtau had the third highest total amount of atmospheric emissions of all cities in the USSR in 1988. In addition, the second largest amount of nitrogen oxide emissions among all cities in the former USSR occurred at Leninogorsk in 1989 ("Panel," 1990, p. 407). Alma-Ata, Dzhambul, Zyryanovsk, Ust-Kamenogorsk and Temirtau were all considered cities with the highest level of unfavorable sanitary and hygienic conditions for 1989.

Ferrous and non-ferrous metallurgy, electricity generation and motor transport are the key polluters. Table 16.3 shows that transportation sources were the major causes of air pollution only in the capital city of Alma-Ata, while stationary sources (factories, etc.) were the major causes elsewhere. The main emissions in most cities in 1989 were composed of gases and liquids. Solid (particulate) emissions, which are very high in Temirtau and Ekibastuz, may damage the lungs. Overall, Pavlodar, Ekibastuz, and Temirtau may be the most unhealthy cities in Kazakhstan.

Dangerous emissions sometimes occur due to accidents. The most serious recent one involved a release of toxic beryllium oxide gas into the air from what once was a secret nuclear fuel producing metallurgical plant in Ust-Kamenogorsk in September of 1990. The accident led to increasing protests over radioactive waste sites in East Kazakhstan and Semipalatinsk Oblasts and their effect on cancer rates among the local populace (Feshbach and Friendly, 1992, p. 177).

Water Pollution

The large size and arid nature of Kazakhstan contribute to a very uneven water distribution regime. Polluted runoff from industry and pesticide and fertilizer contamination from agricultural fields are also typical. The type of water pollution depends on the dominant economic activities within a region.

There has recently been an apparent decline in the overall amount of polluted water in Kazakhstan. Water quality tests conducted in 1985 and in 1990 for chemical and bacteria content of water supplies throughout Kazakhstan revealed that the percentage of samples not satisfying public health norms

TABLE 16.3. Air Pollutant Emissions for Selected Cities in Kazakhstan in 1989 (thousand tons)

Region/City	Total emissions	Kilograms per person[a]	Total from non-stationary sources[b]	Total from stationary sources	Stationary sources		Gases and liquids, by ingredient[c]			
					Solids	Gases and Liquids	SOx	NOx	CO	VOC
West										
Gur'yev	61	389	23	38	3	35	10	3	3	19
North and Northeast										
Tselinograd	132	453	36	96	43	53	32	9	10	0.2
Pavlodar	329	917	72	257	102	155	100	22	14	19
Ekibastuz	737	4973	21	716	438	278	187	89	2	0.01
Karaganda	235	386	84	151	57	94	38	13	42	0.5
Temirtau	868	3823	19	849	231	618	99	34	482	3
Central and East										
Ust'-Kamenogorsk	167	505	40	127	22	105	62	14	29	0.2
Leninogorsk	44	555	9	35	7	28	21	3	4	0
Zyryanovsk	18	335	7	11	6	5	2	0.3	3	0.01
Southeast										
Dzhambul'	152	487	52	100	28	72	50	13	3	0.7
Alma-Ata	208	179	165	43	9	34	15	4	11	1.03

[a] Calculated using city population in 1991.

[b] 1987; mainly automobile emissions.

[c] Figures may not add exactly due to rounding. SOx: sulphur oxides, NOx: nitrogen oxides, CO: carbon monoxides, VOC: volatile organic compounds (hydrocarbons).

Sources: Feshbach and Friendly, 1992, pp. 289-296; Popov and Erokhina, 1991, pp. 89-93.

for chemical content declined from 16% to 14% and for bacteria content, from 11% to 7% (*Vestnik Statistiki*, 1991, p. 61). While the general level may have decreased, the same source notes that an increase of 65 million cubic meters of polluted waters accumulating behind reservoirs in Kazakhstan between 1985 and 1990 may pose a regional or local hazard.

Industrial discharges from ferrous metallurgy and petroleum refining have resulted in high levels of particularly dangerous chemical compounds in the Ural and Irtysh Rivers. The average levels of selected pollutants have come close to, and sometimes exceeded, the maximum permissible concentrations in those rivers for selected years between 1985 and 1990.

Draining into the Caspian Sea, the Ural River had average levels of oil and other refinery by-products exceed MPCs for each year recorded and came close to matching or exceeding MPCs for phenols. World-renowned caviar production from Caspian fish has been seriously affected by phenol contamination (Golub, 1992, p. 4). The declining amount of dissolved oxygen in the Ural River is also of growing concern.

The Irtysh River, which is located in the heart of Kazakhstan's industrial zone, is also highly polluted. Both average and maximum levels of oil and phenol pollutants measured well above permissible standards in recent years. In addition, the maximum observed biological oxygen demand of effluents discharged into the river was several times the MPC in each year.

Solid Waste Disposal

The amount of waste generated from municipal and industrial sources is increasing in Kazakhstan. The number of household and industrial waste disposal sites in urban areas declined from a total of 327 in 1985 to 277 in 1990 (*Vestnik Statistiki*, 1991, p. 60). During the same period, the percentage of urban area landfills that reportedly exceeded public health standards rose from 39% in 1985 to almost half of all dumpsites in 1990. Most toxic industrial waste is generated from industrial sources in Karaganda, East Kazakhstan, Semipalatinsk, and other industrialized oblasts. No quantitative data were available on hazardous wastes.

Radioactive Contamination

From 1949 to 1963, an area west of Semipalatinsk (located roughly halfway between Karaganda and Ust-Kamenogorsk) was the major nuclear testing site for the former USSR, including a large number of atmospheric tests. As a result, radioactive wastes are causing significant problems in the eastern portions of Kazakhstan. Tens of thousands of square kilometers are contaminated by dangerous levels of cesium-137 and other radioactive elements, and thousands of persons have been diagnosed as having received high radiation dosages (Bradley, 1992). Public protest, in combination with international treaties and moratoriums, has caused all testing to be terminated there and the site has been closed (Peterson, 1993, pp. 202 ff).

Lake Balkhash

The Ili River is fed by melting glaciers in western China and flows eastward into Kazakhstan, emptying into the southern part of Lake Balkhash (Balqash). The construction of the Kapchagay (Qapshaghay) Reservoir along the middle reaches of the river has led to declining lake levels and deterioration of Lake Balkhash's flora and fauna in a manner similar (though on a smaller scale) to the Aral Sea disaster to the west (see Bond et al., 1992).

Environmental concerns at Lake Balkhash center on water salinity and increasing pollution. As inflow has diminished, salinity has increased, especially in the shallower eastern half of the lake. After the filling of Kapchagay Reservoir, salinity levels in the eastern portion of the lake rose from 3.32 grams per liter in 1970 to 4.28 grams per liter in 1987 (Bond et al., 1992). Water pollution in the lake comes from three major sources: ore processing; past testing of rocket components, including fuel leakages; and power plant construction and operation.

The city of Balkhash (Balqash), on the northern shore, was one of the former Soviet Union's three largest copper ore producers. Waste from mining, smelting, and refining the ore has entered the air and waters around the lake. Smelters around the city of Balkhash emit around 80,000 tons per year of particulate matter, much of which may be settling on the lake surface. Mine drainage and acidic drainage from ore washing may be leaking into groundwater flowing into the lake.

Caspian Sea

The Caspian Sea, unlike the Aral, is not in danger of drying up; rather, its volume is increasing. While most of the flow into the Caspian is from the Volga River, the Ural River is a significant and growing pollution source. Industrial pollution of the sea comes mainly from petrochemical plants along its shores. (For a fuller discussion of the Caspian problem, see Chapter 15.)

Kazakhstan is the only republic that suffers from both the Caspian and Aral Sea problems. Careless water policies and an ongoing drive to develop natural resources are reasons cited by other republics to blame Kazakhstan for delays in finding solutions to the problems (Golub, 1992, p. 8), although these policies may have been more Soviet than Kazakh. Water resources management will become an increasingly important concern to all Central Asian republics as a result of their recent independence.

Nature Reserves and Preserves

State nature reserves (*zapovedniki*) have been established to protect particular types of ecosystems and to conduct environmental research. By 1991, there were 7 nature reserves established in Kazakhstan, two in the northern steppes, one set up in the foothills of the Altay Mountains in East Kazakhstan, two along the northern foothills of the Tien Shan Mountains near Alma-Ata and Chimkent, one near the Caspian Sea, and one on the island of Barsakelmes in the Aral Sea (Pryde, 1991).

Kazakhstan has 37 natural preserves (*zakazniki*), established for the specific purpose of protecting a particular landscape or habitat characteristic. The 15 zoological and 22 botanical preserves may face competition from future regional land use development plans. Kazakhstan also has one new national park, Bayanaulskiy, created in 1985. These preserved areas are summarized in Table 16.4.

The Aral Sea Dilemma

At one time the world's fourth largest lake, the Aral Sea has for many years been drying up, as water from its two major feeder rivers, the Amu Darya

Table 16.4   Preserved Areas in Kazakhstan

Type of Preserve(a)	Number	Total area(b)	Average size(b)	% of Re- public(c)
Zapovedniki (nature reserves)	7	8061.08	1151.58	0.30
Zapovedniki that are Biosphere Reserves	0	0.00		0.00
National Parks	1	505.82	505.82	0.02
Zakazniki	37	4081.00	110.30	0.15
Total	45	12647.90	281.06	0.47

Zapovedniki (date created)	Hectares
Aksu-Dzhabagly (1927)	75094
Alma-Ata (1961; 1931)	73342
Barsakel'mes (1939)	30000
Kurgal'dzhina (1968; 1959)	237138
Markakol (1976)	75040
Naurzum (1965; 1934)	87694
Ust-yurt (1984)	227800
Total	806108

National Parks	Hectares
Bayanaulskiy (1985)	50582

(a) For the definition of each type of preserve, see Appendix 1.2.

(b) In square kilometers.

(c) Area of Kazakhstan equals 2,717,300 sq. km.

Source: Pryde (1991).

and Syr Darya, had largely been diverted for upstream agricultural use. The northern half of the Aral Sea, including the lower portion of the Syr Darya, lies within Kyzl-Orda Oblast of Kazakhstan (Figure 16.1). Because of upstream irrigation water withdrawals, together with water losses that average 50% or more through evaporation and seepage from unlined canal systems, the flow of the Syr Darya from 1974 through 1986 did not reach the sea (Bortnik et al., 1992, p. 315). The same trend applied to the larger Amu Darya. As a result, regional environmental effects caused by the drying up of the sea include changes in climate and water quantity and quality, in addition to a variety of socioeconomic impacts along the lower courses of the Syr Darya and Amu Darya. In February of 1992, the Kazakh parliament declared the Aral Sea basin an ecological disaster zone.

As the sea has diminished in size and volume over the past several decades, its moderating influence on regional climate has declined. At the city of Aralsk, formerly located on the northern shores of the sea, the seasonal range of temperatures has widened by several degrees over the past 30 years. In the delta of the Syr Darya, the growing season has shortened; today, spring comes a week later and autumn, almost two weeks earlier. In some areas rice, an important local food crop, can no longer be grown.

The Aral Sea was radically transformed in early 1990 as it split into two pieces: the northern Maloye More (or Little Aral Sea), with its source the Syr Darya, and the Bol'shoye More (Large Sea) in the south, with its source the Amu Darya (Figure 16.4). In 1990, inflow into the upper Syr Darya delta was 3.4 km^3, of which about 2.0 km^3 reached the Maloye More (Shekhovtsov and Bortnik, 1991, p. 98).

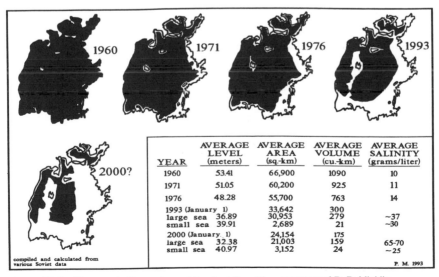

YEAR	AVERAGE LEVEL (meters)	AVERAGE AREA (sq.-km)	AVERAGE VOLUME (cu.-km)	AVERAGE SALINITY (grams/liter)
1960	53.41	66,900	1090	10
1971	51.05	60,200	925	11
1976	48.28	55,700	763	14
1993 (January 1)		33,642	300	
large sea 36.89		30,953	279	~37
small sea 39.91		2,689	21	~30
2000 (January 1)		24,154	175	
large sea 32.38		21,003	159	65-70
small sea 40.97		3,152	24	~25

compiled and calculated from various Soviet data

P. M. 1993

Figure 16.4   Changes in the surface of the Aral Sea. Map courtesy of P. P. Micklin.

Water pollution along the lower Syr Darya remains very high. River salinity reached over 1.5 milligrams per liter near Kazalinsk along the lower river course in 1990. Pesticide pollution from upstream agricultural use is also a serious problem. Although officially banned in 1970, DDT was used throughout the 1980s, and concentrations along the lower Syr Darya averaged 5 times above maximum permissible levels. Average concentrations of the insecticides Lindane and Hexachlorane were 5–7 times above MPC, reaching a maximum in 1990 of 91 and 74 times the MPC respectively (Shekhovtsov and Bortnik, 1991). In addition, increased concentrations of nitrites (1–3 times MPC) from fertilizer runoff were found in the waters of the Syr Darya below the city of Kyzl-Orda in 1990.

The simultaneous decline of water availability and increase in pesticide and fertilizer-laden upstream runoff have contributed to large increases in morbidity and mortality rates among the population along the lower Syr Darya. Groundwater supplies may not necessarily be an alternative. For example, the city of Kyzl-Orda has no waste purifying facilities. Local groundwater supplies have become contaminated, and the addition of large amounts of chlorine may have resulted in increased incidences of cancer among the population of the city (Wolfson, 1990, pp. 33–34). In addition, periodic outbreaks of bubonic plague have affected the population living along the shore of the northern Aral Sea (Micklin, 1991, p. 94).

As if all of this wasn't enough, Vozrozhdeniya Island in the Aral Sea has recently been identified as one of the Soviet Union's major chemical weapons testing areas.

The many proposed solutions to the Aral Sea problem emphasize one or all of the following: (1) prevent the disappearance of the sea, (2) provide water to adjacent land areas, and (3) address regional public health concerns (Bortnik et al., 1992, p. 318). Increased water availability as a result of drastic basinwide reductions in irrigated land (or more efficient use of water) would address all three aspects. It would also entail the cooperation of all the Central Asian countries that share the water resources of the basin and perhaps the Russian Federation as well.

Governmental Structure and Environmental Activism

The coordination and implementation of natural resource use and environmental protection measures in Kazakhstan were dominated by national policies and agencies until independence in 1991. While remaining politically conservative, Kazakhstan authorities have allowed the formation of several loosely organized private environmental organizations, whose main concern is specific ecological and environmental problems.

Environmental Protection Agencies

Before the demise of the Soviet Union in 1991, several public agencies were responsible for environmental and natural resource protection in Kazakhstan. They included the Kazakh State Ecological Commission, the Main

Administration for Game Management and Nature Reserves, the State Committee for Forestry, the State Committee on Environmental Protection (Goskompriroda), and the Department of Nature Conservation within the USSR State Planning Commission (Gosplan).

With independence and the disappearance of USSR environmental protection agencies, responsibility for environmental problems in Kazakhstan has fallen on several government agencies, including the newly created Ministry of the Environment, local and republic deputies sitting on parliamentary environmental committees, and the data-gathering State Committee for Hydrometeorology and Environmental Control. Many Kazakhstan offices of former USSR environmental agencies still exist in some form. A wide variety of scientific research institutions monitor and study specific regional environmental problems.

Private Agencies and Citizens Groups

Officially sanctioned private environmental agencies in Kazakhstan include the Ecological Foundation in Alma-Ata and the Green Movement of Kazakhstan, based in Dzhambul. One of the lesser known groups is called the Alma-Ata Ecological Fund. The fund, formed in the late 1980s and a member group of the Moscow "umbrella" organization called the Socio-Ecological Union, attempts to deal with the health effects of pollution. Its current activities include providing medicine to victims of air and water pollution around the Balkhash metallurgical center and working toward the establishment of a national park near Zyryanovsk, a heavily polluted region in the foothills of the Altai Mountains in eastern Kazakhstan (Rubin, 1992).

While not the case in many countries (including Russia and the United States), government officials in Kazakhstan work closely with environmental NGOs. However, the Kazakhstan government remains conservative and keeps a tight rein on the activities of private environmental groups, mainly through the dependence of such groups on government monetary support.

The two most important environmental issues in Kazakhstan, ecological deterioration around the Aral Sea and nuclear weapons testing and radioactive waste disposal near Semipalatinsk, have generated individual environmental initiatives among a growing number of scientists within research institutes.

The Nevada-Semipalatinsk Movement, established in 1989, is one of the most effective environmental groups in the former USSR (Figure 16.5). It was formed as a result of health concerns relating to the more than 400 nuclear tests conducted above ground (1949–1963) and below ground (1963–1990) in Semipalatinsk Oblast (see Pryde, 1991, pp. 256–257; Peterson, 1993, pp. 202–206; and Feshbach and Friendly, 1992, pp. 238–239). The recent creation of the Semipalatinsk Polygon program to document the health effects of regional nuclear weapons testing in eastern Kazakhstan and southwestern Siberia may lead to further environmental cooperation among the republics of the former USSR.

Figure 16.5   An American Indian and a Kazakh native are the
symbols on the banner of the Kazakhstan-based Nevada-
Semipalatinsk Movement, which opposes nuclear testing.

Communication, Trade, and Economic Potential

Kazakhstan occupies a territory approximately one-third the size of the
United States. Great distances separate population centers in Kazakhstan. In
addition, raw materials such as petroleum, coal, iron ore, lead, zinc, and
other valuable metals necessary for industrial and economic development
are abundant but widely scattered throughout the territory of the republic.
Large cities centered around natural resource exploitation, for example, are
located far from one another. While Kazakhstan may be considered the richest of the new Central Asian republics in terms of natural resources, it faces
some of the same developmental problems that Russia faces in attempting to
integrate Siberian resources into the rest of the Russian economy. Transportation costs remain high, especially for coal and iron ore. Investment in Kazakhstan in petroleum development and the building of pipelines and other
infrastructure may reflect a growing emphasis on industrial diversification
and on better integration of the economies and territories of the republic's
far-flung regions.

Internal trade and communication within Kazakhstan are difficult because of its large size and because its population is located mostly on the periphery and is ethnically polarized in territories separated by vast distances. Economic specialization and ethnic polarization tend to orient peripheral areas of the country more toward neighboring territories than inward toward a politically and economically unified Kazakhstan. On the other hand, more than half a million Kazakhs live in the southern Urals of Russia, and another million live in western China. They have been invited back to Kazakhstan, which is large enough to hold them, but they would probably return only after sustained economic progress (Henze, 1992, pp. 52–53, 58). There has been some talk about moving the capital from Alma-Ata to Aqmola (Tselinograd), which is closer to the major concentrations of population and industry.

Along with Ukraine, Kazakhstan was a principal supplier of grain to the other republics. With independence came lower trade volume in grain as food supplies became uncertain. Kazakhstan has also been a major supplier of fossil fuels and ores essential to industrial production, especially in the Urals region of Russia. Because of this economic interdependence, regional trade will most likely continue, but Kazakhstan may increasingly look to international help to exploit its natural resources potential. Kazakhstan also contains the large cosmonaut base at Baikonur; Russia apparently wishes to continue to make use of this facility.

In the early 1990s, much of the official communication and cooperation between Kazakhstan and countries other than the former Soviet republics was in the area of economic and natural resource development. Kazakhstan's economic development potential was given a boost with its acceptance into the International Monetary Fund on April 27, 1992. Numerous joint ventures have been carried out with foreign firms from a large number of countries. The U.S. petroleum corporation Chevron, mentioned earlier, has an agreement to carry out future Kazakh oil development around the northern Caspian. Other countries have taken considerable interest in the development of Kazakhstan, particularly Turkey. In early 1994, the United States pledged $400 million in aid to Kazakhstan in exchange for the latter's agreement to adhere to the Nuclear Non-proliferation Treaty.

With a small population and large territory, Kazakhstan has the greatest economic potential of all the Central Asian countries. Despite its remoteness, it has considerable tourist potential. For example, the region from the attractive city of Alma-Ata east to the Chinese border has spectacular mountain scenery, culminating in peaks almost 7,000 meters high. The southeastern portion of Alma-Ata Province could easily be a very popular new national park, specializing in managed ecotourism.

Kazakhstan also has perhaps the greatest environmental problems of all the Central Asian republics. Public opinion and pressures on the government to address environmental issues have had some success. Even so, the desire for economic progress by the government of Kazakhstan through gaining international help in exploiting the republic's abundant natural resources may involve at least short-term increases in environmental pollution. Political and social stability within Kazakhstan may depend on balancing the desire of its citizens for an increased standard of living and coping with the detrimental environmental effects that would result, as well as those that already exist.

Appendix 16.1   Ten Largest Nations of the World in Land Area

Country	Area (1000 sq. km.)	1989 Population (1000s)	Density (persons per sq. km.)
Russian Federation	17,075	147,386	8.63
Canada	9,977	25,334	2.54
China	9,576	1,069,628	111.70
United States	9,373	247,498	26.41
Brazil	8,511	153,992	18.09
Australia	7,682	16,090	2.09
India	3,280	833,422	254.09
Argentina	2,758	32,617	11.83
Kazakhstan	2,717	16,538	6.09
Sudan	2,505	25,008	9.98

Source: Compiled by author from information in World Almanac and Book of Facts.

Appendix 16.2   Major Ethnic Groups in Kazakhstan

Ethnic group	Population (1000s) 1959	1989	% increase, 1959-1989	% of 1989 total
Kazakhs	2,795	6,535	133.8	39.7
Russians	3,974	6,228	56.7	37.8
Ukrainians	762	896	17.6	5.4
Germans	660	958	45.2	5.8
Tatars	192	328	70.8	2.0
Uzbeks	137	332	142.3	2.0
Belarusians	107	183	71.0	1.1
Uighurs	60	185	208.3	1.1
Koreans	74	103	39.2	.6
Azerbaijanis	38	90	136.8	.5
Others	496	626	26.2	3.9
Total	9,295	16,464	77.1	100.0

Source: Data adapted from Schwartz, 1991, p. 238.

Notes

1. In this chapter, the traditional names of cities are given (or given first, with the new name in parentheses). Unlike many other republics that engaged in occasional renamings, Kazakhstan renamed, or put into Kazakh lettering, virtually every major city; in addition, most of the names are sufficiently different from the Soviet form that they would not be immediately identifiable. Thus, to avoid considerable confusion, the old name is given first in this chapter. A reference list of the larger renamed cities is presented in Table 16.2. There is an occasional tendency on recent Western and Russian maps to retain the old spelling of the capital, Alma-Ata.

Bibliography

Bond, Andrew, Philip P. Micklin, and Matthew J. Sagers. 1992. "Lake Balkhash Dwindling, Becoming Increasingly Saline." *Post-Soviet Geography*, vol. 32, no. 2, pp. 131–134.

Bortnik, V. N., V. I. Kuksa, and A. G. Tsytsarin. 1992. "Present Status and Possible Future of the Aral Sea." *Post-Soviet Geography*. vol. 33, no. 5, pp. 315–323.

Bradley, D.J. 1992. *Radioactive Waste Management in the Former USSR*. Vol. 3. Richland, WA: Pacific Northwest Laboratory, June.

Feshbach, Murray, and Alfred Friendly Jr. 1992. *Ecocide in the USSR*. New York: Basic Books,

Golub, Roman. 1992. "The Caspian/Khazar Sea—Polluted and Politicized." *Environmental Policy Review*, vol. 6, no. 1, pp. 1–10.

Goskomstat Kazakhskoy SSR. 1989. *Narodnoye Khozyaystvo Kazakhskoy SSR v 1989 g.* Alma-Ata: Kazakhstan,.

Goskomstat SSSR. 1988. *Naseleniye SSSR: Statisticheskiy Sbornik*. Moscow: Finansy i Statistika.

———. 1990. *Narodnoye Khozyaystvo SSSR v 1989 g.* Moscow: Finansy i Statistika.

Gosudarstvenniy Komitet Kazakhskoy SSR po Statistike i Analizu. 1991. *Statisticheskiy Yezhegodnik Kazakhstana*. Alma-Ata.

Henze, Paul B. 1992. "Turkestan Rising." *Wilson Quarterly*, Summer, pp. 48–58.

Informatsentr Goskomstata SSSR. 1991. *Okhrana Okruzhayushchey Sredi i Ratsional'noye Ispol'zovaniye Prirodnykh Resursov*. Moscow: Statisticheskiy Sbornik.

Lerager, J. 1992. "Second Sunset." *Sierra*, March-April, pp. 60–65.

Lydolph, Paul. 1977. *Climates of the Soviet Union*. Vol. 7. In *World Survey of Climatology*. New York: Elsevier.

Micklin, P.P. 1991. "Touring the Aral: Visit to an Ecological Disaster Zone." *Soviet Geography*, vol. 32, no. 2, pp. 90–105.

———. 1992. "The Aral Crisis: Introduction to the Special Issue." *Post-Soviet Geography*, vol. 33, no. 5, pp. 269–282.

Molosnova, T. I., O. I. Subbotina, and S. G. Chanysheva. 1987. *Klimaticheskiye Posledstviya Khozyaystvennoy Deyatel'nosti v Zone Aral'skogo Morya*. Moscow: Gidrometeoizdat.

Olcott, Martha Brill. 1987. *The Kazakhs*. Stanford, CA: Hoover Institution Press.

"Panel on the State of the Soviet Environment at the Start of the Nineties." 1991. *Soviet Geography*. vol. 31, no. 6, pp. 401–468.

Peterson, D.J. 1993. *Troubled Lands: The Legacy of Soviet Environmental Destruction*. Boulder: Westview Press.

Popov, M. N., and T. B. Erukhina. 1991. "State of Atmospheric Pollution over the USSR Territory in 1990 and the Tendency Towards its Changing During the Last 5-Year Period." *Soviet Meteorology and Hydrology*, no. 4, pp. 88–93.

Pryde, P.R. 1991. *Environmental Management in the Soviet Union.* Cambridge: Cambridge University Press.

Rubin, Ann. 1992. "Kazakh Environmentalists Battle More than the Aral Sea." *Surviving Together,* Fall/Winter, pp. 23–26.

Sagers, Matthew J. 1991, 1992, 1993. "News Notes," *Soviet Geography,* vol. 32, no. 4, pp. 251–290, *Post-Soviet Geography,* vol. 33, no. 4, pp. 237–268, and *Post-Soviet Geography,* vol. 34, no. 1, pp. 66–69.

Sazhin, A.N. 1988. "Regional Aspects of Dust Storms in Steppe Regions of the East European and West Siberian Plains." *Soviet Geography,* vol. 29, no. 10, pp. 935–945.

Schwartz, Lee. 1991. "USSR Nationality Redistribution by Republic, 1979–1989." *Soviet Geography,* vol. 32, no. 4, pp. 209–248.

Shabad, Theodore. 1969. *Basic Industrial Resources of the USSR.* New York: Columbia University Press.

Shekhovtsov, A. A., and V. N. Bortnik. 1991. "Present-Day Geoecological State of the Lower Syrdar'ya and Amudar'ya and the Aral Sea." *Soviet Meteorology and Hydrology,* no. 10, pp. 95–99.

Smith, D. R. 1994. "Change and Variability in Climate and Ecosystem Decline in the Aral Sea Basin Deltas." *Post-Soviet Geography,* vol., 35, no. 3, pp. 142–165.

Vestnik Statistiki. 1991. No. 12 (Russian monthly statistical journal).

Wolfson, Ze'ev. 1990. "Central Asian Environment: A Dead End." *Environmental Policy Review,* vol. 4, no. 1, pp. 29–46.

17

Turkmenistan

Philip Micklin

Turkmenistan is one of the five predominantly Muslim constituent republics of the former Soviet Union. The southernmost of the former Union republics, it shares a common border with Iran and Afghanistan as well as with the new states of Uzbekistan and Kazakhstan (Figure 17.1). At 35° north latitude, Kushka was the Soviet Union's southernmost city and an important entry point into Afghanistan. Turkmenistan's area is 488,100 km², and its population (on Jan. 1, 1991) was 3,714,000, placing it 4th and 13th, respectively, in these categories among the former republics of the USSR. The republic is predominantly rural (55% in 1990) and is the world's fourth largest producer of natural gas.

History and Ethnicity

Turkmenistan has a long history of human habitation. Nomads have roamed the area for millennia, and archaeologists have found evidence of cropping cultures in the south of the republic that date to 6000 B.C. Irrigated agriculture was in widespread use along the rivers (Amu Darya, Tedzhen, Murgab, Atrek) and at the margins of the southern mountains. During the first millennium B.C. states arose here (Margiana, Parthia, Medea) that were conquered, in turn, by the Persians and Alexander the Great. Turkic people had appeared in the area by the 10th century A.D. By this time, Islam had driven other, earlier religions from the region, and cities such as Merv (Mary) had become centers of Islamic culture and learning.

The Mongols (Tatars) under Genghiz Khan descended on present-day Turkmenia in the 13th century, and their domination lasted 150 years until broken by Tamerlane (Timur). Uzbek tribes began the dissolution of the Timurid Empire in the early 15th century with the capture of its capital of Samarkand. Several centuries later, what is now Turkmenistan was divided

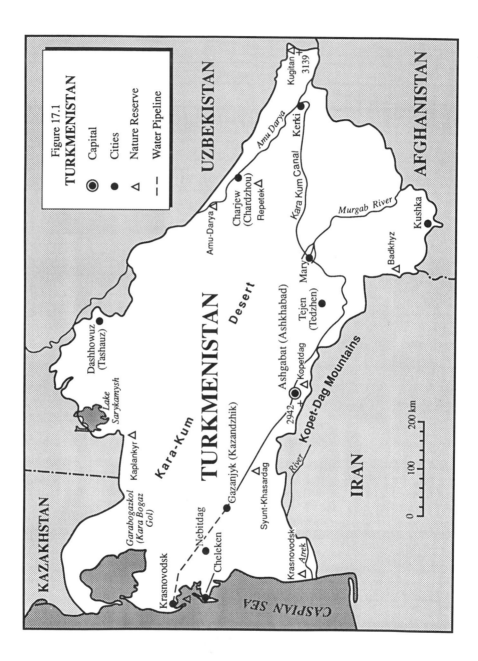

Figure 17.1
TURKMENISTAN

between the Khanates of Khiva and Bukhoro. During the last quarter of the 19th century, the Russian Empire incorporated, by conquest, all of Turkmenia. The whole of Central Asia under the Russians was called Turkestan, while present-day Turkmenistan was designated Transcaspia.

Turkestan was in political turmoil following the Bolshevik Revolution, with some groups (e.g., the Basmachi) showing organized and strong resistance to the imposition of Soviet rule. However, by 1924 most opposition had been crushed. In that year, Turkmenistan was created as a Union republic. Under Soviet rule, as in the rest of Central Asia, Islam was disparaged and pan-Turkism suppressed, collectivization of agriculture implemented, and industrialization and modernization begun. Turkmenia remained a bastion of Communist orthodoxy during the period of Gorbachev reforms, and the government leaders and party officials here (including current President Saparmurad Niyazov, a former first secretary of the Turkmen Communist Party) were not happy with the many aspects of perestroika, glasnost, and democratization that were being pushed from Moscow.

As with the other republics, statehood descended on Turkmenistan with the dissolution of the USSR at the end of 1991. After the failed August 1991 coup in Moscow, the Communist Party of Turkmenistan changed its name but continues its control of the government. The economy, as most aspects of life in Turkmenia, is still under tight control. Formal moves toward a market economy have made the least progress of any former Soviet republic, although private activities in the agricultural sector have been and continue to be significant. Political opposition is now "officially" legal but strongly discouraged.

Turkmenistan, like the other republics of the former USSR, is a multinational state, with more than 100 distinct ethnic groups recognized (Marchenkov, 1990). Turkmen constitute 72% of the population, according to the 1989 census, followed by Russians (9.5%), Uzbeks (9%), Kazakhs (2.5%), Tatars (1.1%) and Ukrainians (1%). It is curious, however, that persons of Persian descent were not isolated as a census category; it would seem likely there would be many such people in Turkmenistan.

The Turkmen are descendants of the Orguz Turks who migrated here at the end of the 10th century (Zickel, 1991, pp. 171–172). Traditionally a nomadic people (although forced by Soviet authorities during collectivization into more sedentary ways), the Turkmen still live predominantly in rural areas. The other nationalities, particularly Russians and Ukrainians, chiefly live in the larger cities, such as Ashgabat (Ashkhabad), with 398,000 residents; Dashhowuz (Tashauz), 112,000; Charjew (Chardzhou), 161,000; and Mary, 94,000. The 1989 census reported that 98% of those describing themselves as ethnically Turkmen considered the Turkmen language as their first language, with fluency in Russian listed by 25% of Turkmen respondents.

Physical Environment

The key physical feature of Turkmenistan is the vast Kara-Kum (in Turkic, Kara means "black" and Kum means "desert"), which covers some 80% of the republic. This mid-latitude desert has vast tracts of sand and sand dunes but also hard surfaced areas (rocky and clay-pan [in Russian, *takyr*]). Average annual precipitation here is the least of any place in the FSU, ranging from 70 to 200 millimeters. Summer air temperatures can rise to nearly 50° C and in winter fall to −35°C. The Kara-Kum has an extensive but sparse vegetation cover, with low bushes (e.g., camels thorn) and scattered small trees (e.g., black saksaul and acacia) common. Large areas of the Kara-Kum are used for pasturing of camels and sheep. The desert has a diversity of native mammals, reptiles, insects and birds, some of them endangered.

The Kopet-Dag Mountains stretch along the southern periphery of Turkmenistan and form the border with Iran and Afghanistan. Although rising to nearly 3,000 meters, they lack an alpine character and in many places are barren and dissected, reminding one of badlands (Alpat'yev et al., 1977, pp. 15–16). Nevertheless, many of the deep, steep, north-trending valleys on the Turkmen side are forested, contain streams, and are picturesque. A number of these have long been used for recreational and resort purposes. The highest point in the republic (3,139 m), however, is in the Kugitang-tau Mountains on the eastern border with Uzbekistan.

Although Turkmenistan is mainly desert, the country's physical environment is characterized by several important water resources. The Amu Darya, the heaviest flowing river in Central Asia, with an average annual discharge of 63 km^3, flows through and along the boundary of the extreme eastern part of the republic. Surface flow also arrives in streams from the foothills and mountains on the south and southeast of the republic (e.g., Tejen [Tedzhen] and Murgab Rivers). In all, the republic has access to aggregate surface flow resources of around 70 km^3/yr (Goskomstat SSSR, 1989, p. 64), although exploitable groundwater resources are estimated at only 2 km^3.

On the west, Turkmenistan borders on the Caspian Sea, the world's largest lake. In the northwest corner of Turkmenistan is a gulf on the Caspian Sea called the Garabogazkol (Kara-Bogaz-Gol), which is fed by overflow from the Caspian. It is very rich in mineral salts, such as sodium sulfate.

In the northern part of Turkmenistan, along its border with Karakalpakistan, lies Lake Sarykamysh. With an area of 3,000 km^2 and volume of over 30 km^3, this is among the larger lakes in the former USSR. It is unusual in that it grew from a much smaller, saline lake in the early 1960s owing to large inflows of used irrigation water (Micklin, 1991b, pp. 57–58). As a result, it is highly polluted with pesticide and fertilizer residues.

Physical Constraints to Development

The chief physical constraint to development for Turkmenistan is aridity. "Water is life" here; without a large and ensured supply of this resource, there can be no significant industrial development or large population centers, only extensive livestock raising based on desert and foothill pastures. Although Turkmenistan has access to significant water resources, there are problems. More than 90% of available river flow is in the Amu Darya, into which there is essentially no flow from Turkmen territory (it is generated almost totally upstream in Tajikistan). Further, the waters of the Amu Darya are under very heavy stress from huge withdrawals by Uzbekistan, both upstream and downstream from Turkmenistan. The much smaller groundwater supply is plagued by its dispersed nature, frequent high salinities, and natural losses via evapo-transpiration. Thus, water usage in the republic may already be above what is sustainable, providing a barrier to further water-intensive development.

There are two other constraints that deserve mention. Southern Turkmenistan, where most of the population lives, is a zone of maximum seismicity. Very powerful earthquakes occurred here in 1946 and 1948. The latter temblor destroyed Ashkhabad (Ashgabat) and killed a reported 110,000 persons (Marchenkov 1990).

The other problem relates to the Caspian Sea. Cyclical long-term fluctuations in the Caspian Sea level pose problems for development along that water body in western Turkmenistan. Port facilities in Krasnovodsk, as at other locations around the Caspian, have had to adjust to a 3 meter drop in surface elevation between 1930 and 1978, followed by a 1.5 meter rise since 1978. For additional discussions of the Caspian Sea, see sections on the Caspian in the chapters on Azerbaijan and Kazakhstan.

Natural Resource Advantages and Existing Industry

Turkmenistan has considerable resource potential. Most important are oil and natural gas deposits. Production of oil reached a peak of 15 million metric tons in 1975 and in 1990 was 5.7 million, fourth among the former republics of the USSR (Sagers, 1990). Natural gas production, which has climbed steadily, reached 88 billion cubic meters in 1990, or 11% of national production, putting Turkmenistan in second place among former Soviet republics after the RSFSR. Natural gas fuels electrical generating plants in all the major cities, and total reserves are estimated at 8 trillion cubic meters. Mineral resources of note are the brines of the Garabogazkol (Kara-Bogaz-Gol), the large gulf on the Caspian Sea in northwestern Turkmenistan, from which mirabilite (sodium sulfate decahydrate) and other commercially valuable salts are extracted. Other resources found in the republic include potash, iodine, bromine, and sulfur.

Although often overlooked, Turkmenistan's solar and wind resource potential is considerable. Solar radiation is the highest in the former USSR at 35 kilowatt-hours/km^2, while daytime wind speeds average 3–5 meters/second (Mints, 1969, pp. 279–280; Pryde, 1984). There has been some development of solar (water heating) and wind (farmstead electricity and mechanical pumping), but the potential has hardly been touched. The former USSR's Solar Energy Research Institute was located at the new suburb of Bikrova, outside Ashgabat. It is not known what Turkmenistan plans to do with this facility.

As is true of the rest of the Central Asian republics, Turkmenistan's industrial development is much below the average for the former USSR. The chief heavy industry is oil and gas extraction, with some local petrochemical production. Light industry is well developed here (at least as compared to heavy industry), with primary focus on processing of raw cotton and production of cotton textiles, wool processing and weaving, and silk production. Turkmen carpets are world famous, with a large share of the production sold internationally.

Irrigated agriculture plays a key role in the Turkmen economy. In 1990, the area with irrigation facilities reached 1.203 million hectares, accounting for about 6% of the USSR's irrigated zone (Goskomstat SSSR, 1991a, pp. 489–492). Cotton, grown on 52% of these lands, is the chief crop. Turkmenistan in 1990 produced 18% of Soviet raw cotton, second after Uzbekistan. Food crops (grains, vegetables, melons, and fruits) and fodder were raised on the remaining irrigated lands. The desert zone of Turkmenistan is important for the pasturing of sheep and goats, of which there were 5.5 million head in 1990. Camels are also an important part of both the Kara-Kum and the rural economy, serving as beasts of burden as well as sources of meat, milk, and hides (Figure 17.2).

Major Environmental Problems

Turkmenistan faces a variety of environmental/resource management problems. As is the case in the other republics of the former USSR, the largest Turkmen cities, such as Ashgabat (Ashkhabad), Charjew (Chardzhou), Dashhowuz (Tashauz), and Krasnovodsk, as well as smaller settlements where industry, mining, and thermal power plants are located, suffer from water quality deterioration and air pollution. Although there were thousands of point sources of air pollution in the republic in 1988, only 38 percent were equipped with pollution reduction equipment, and these often worked

Figure 17.2   Camels, some domesticated and some feral, are a familiar feature of the Kara-Kum Desert in Turkmenistan.

poorly (Mnatsakanian, 1992, pp. 108–112). Transportation is the chief contributor to air pollution in the larger cities. Charjew was the only Turkmen city listed among the 90 most polluted in the USSR in 1990.

Water pollution from industry and municipal sources was the lowest in the USSR in 1989 (irrigation return flows are not counted in these statistics). For Turkmenistan as a whole, water pollution and air pollution are less serious than in most former Soviet republics because of a low level of industrialization, small number of vehicles, and low population density. However, return irrigation flows containing pesticides, herbicides, mineral fertilizers, and defoliants, particularly from cotton fields, are a serious problem.

The chief environmental issues for Turkmenistan are to develop a rational management plan for its huge desert regions, to deal effectively with the problems of irrigated agriculture and water management, and to contend with rapid population growth and health problems. Covering 80% of the republic, the Kara-Kum Desert has constrained settlement and economic development of Turkmenistan to a narrow strip near the base of the moisture-capturing Kopet-Dag Mountains in the south, to oases along the Amu Darya on the east, and to several coastal settlements on the Caspian Sea in the west. The accepted wisdom under Soviet rule, which has not changed with independence, is that the desert must be used to further economic development. The problem, of course, is how to do this without severely degrading the resource while providing protection for critical desert ecosystems and species.

In 1962, the Desert Institute of the Turkmen Academy of Sciences was established in Ashkhabad to study the desert and develop plans for its utilization, protection, and improvement. Programs have been implemented to study desert soils and water resources in order to formulate a rational plan for their use, to find means of stabilizing sand dunes and protecting structures from them, to develop cropping systems suitable for use in the desert, to find means for improving the quality of desert pastures, and to aid in the study and preservation of critical ecosystems and biota. The institute operates a system of desert research stations and manages the Repetek International Biosphere Reserve. The Desert Institute has extensive international contacts and runs an international training course on desertification for UNEP (United Nations Environment Programme).

The work of the Desert Institute and other organizations has led to the development of ecologically sound methods for more intensive economic use of the Kara-Kum. However, such efforts are still mainly limited to the experimental stations and have not received broad dissemination. In spite of an ongoing program to combat desertification in the Kara-Kum (defined as the intensification or spreading of desert conditions in arid regions), this process continues (Figure 17.3). This is partially the result of natural occurrences (e.g., climate change), but most results from human influences. The most serious and widespread negative impacts result from overgrazing, which degrades and simplifies vegetation communities, exacerbates erosion, impoverishes the soil, and depletes groundwater (through withdrawals for livestock). Earlier this century, widespread cutting of brush and small trees for firewood caused serious damage. In more recent decades, industrial develop-

Figure 17.3   Dense, hardy vegetation has been planted in an effort to stabilize the shifting sands of the Kara-Kum and limit desertification. Photo by P. P. Micklin.

ment, particularly for oil and gas extraction, with its accompanying need for new roads and settlements, has caused serious harm.

Laudable efforts have been made in Turkmenistan to preserve critical desert ecosystems and their biota, including the creation of several nature reserves, as shown in Figure 17.1. Nevertheless, a variety of plants and animals are under threat. Animal species are in the gravest condition, with two apparent extinctions having occurred (e.g., the desert leopard and the scaly woodpecker). Other species threatened with extinction are the Asiatic wild ass (*kulan*), Bukhara deer, desert gazelle (*dzheyran*), desert sparrow, and bustard (Pryde, 1987). A number of other animal species are becoming rare, including several lizards (e.g. gray baran), the cobra, a number of predatory birds, some types of jerboa, the Turkestan polecat, the steppe cat, and the honey badger. To help forestall additional extinctions, several other natural preserves known as *zakazniki* have been created in Turkmenistan (Table 17.1).

Population growth and the related question of human health are formidable problems for Turkmenistan. The population is small at 3.7 million, and the average density is low at 7.6 persons/km^2 (1990 figures). But being mainly desert, the areas that can support dense human habitation must have access to large freshwater supplies and are therefore limited to several locations along the Amu Darya, Kara-Kum Canal, and places away from these that receive water by pipeline. In light of a limited water supply and the extensive manner in which water is used for irrigation, meeting the needs of a slowly growing population would be difficult. But population is burgeoning

Table 17.1   Preserved Areas in Turkmenistan

Type of Preserve(a)	Number	Total area(b)	Average size(b)	% of Re-public(c)
Nature Reserves (<u>zapovedniki</u>)	8	11114.16	1389.27	2.28
Zapovedniki that are Biosphere Reserves	1	346.00	346.00	0.07
National Parks	0	0.00		0.00
Natural Preserves (<u>zakazniki</u>)	12	6070.00	505.83	1.24
Total	21	17184.16	818.29	3.52

Zapovedniki (date created)	Hectares
Amu-Dar'ya (1982)	50506
Badkhyz (1941)	87680
Kaplankyr (1979)	570000
Kopetdag (1976)	49793
Krasnovodsk (1968; 1932)	262037
Kugitan (1986)	27100
Repetek (1928)	34600
Syunt-Khasardag (1979)	29700
Total	1111416

(a) For the definition of each type of preserve, see Appendix 1.2.

(b) In square kilometers.

(c) Area of Turkmenistan equals 488,100 sq. km.

Source: Pryde, 1991.

here. In 1990, the rate of natural increase was 2.7%, up from 2.6% in 1980, commensurate with the more rapidly growing developing countries of the world. If this rate continues, population would double every 26 years. Fertility is evidently dropping (although slowly) in Turkmenistan as in the rest of former Soviet Central Asia, which means an eventual slowing of population growth. Nevertheless, barring some catastrophe, Turkmenistan's population will become much larger in the next century before stabilizing.

In terms of human health, Turkmenistan is in the worst condition of any republic of the former USSR. It ranks at the bottom in two important health measures: infant mortality (in 1990, 45.2 per 1,000; the USSR average was 21.8) and life expectancy (in 1990, 66.4 years; the USSR average was 69.3) (Goskomstat SSSR, 1991a, pp. 92, 94). It is second lowest in the number of physicians per capita and second highest in cases of typhoid and brucellosis (Feshbach and Friendly, 1992, p. 280).

The health of mothers and children is particularly poor. This is a result of frequent pregnancies, widespread poverty, malnutrition, poor prenatal care, and poor general health conditions, particularly in the rural areas, where the majority of the population lives. Conditions are particularly bad in Dash-howuz (Tashauz) Oblast, where only 23% of the population has running water, infant mortality rates are 75 per 1,000, every third child and fourth mother dies in labor, and 70% of the population suffers from one or more chronic illnesses (Micklin, 1991a). Drinking water here contains 30 times the acceptable levels of pesticides, nitrates, and other pollutants, primarily owing to heavy applications of these chemicals on the region's cotton fields.

Problems of Water Management

The interrelated issues of irrigated agriculture and water management are paramount for Turkmenistan. The republic withdrew 22.6 km^3 in 1990 for all uses, and irrigation accounted for 77% of this total. Turkmenistan has access to around 70 km^3 of surface flow and about 2 km^3 of replenishable ground-water, which, at first glance, implies a significant reserve in this resource. But most of this "reserve" is in the Amu Darya, whose waters are shared with Tajikistan and Uzbekistan. Both Turkmenistan (via the Kara-Kum Canal) and Uzbekistan make huge withdrawals from this river. In truth, the waters of the Amu Darya are already overused, resulting in a variety of adverse environmental consequences, particularly the desiccation of the Aral Sea (see sections on the Aral Sea in Chapters 16 and 18). Thus, Turkmenistan's water situation is poor. Increases in diversion from the Amu Darya, the only source from which large new amounts of freshwater might be taken, have been and continue to be opposed by downstream Uzbekistan and Karakalpakstan. Not only may it be impossible for Turkmenistan to increase water withdrawals from the Amu Darya, but, conceivably, the country may have to reduce them (Micklin, 1991b, pp. 42–82).

There are ways for Turkmenistan to cope with this problem. The first priority is to improve delivery efficiency, a measure of the ratio of water arriving at the field to water withdrawn at the source. In 1990 transportation losses in irrigation here were around 7.5 km^3, or 43% (Goskomstat SSSR, 1991b, p. 81). Lining the larger earthen irrigation canals (with concrete, clay, or plastic) could cut these losses significantly (perhaps to as low as 10–15%) and save considerable water. However, the savings would not be as great as one might think since gross savings must be corrected for diminished return irrigation flows. Also, the cost of lining the huge length of earthen canals in Turkmenistan would be enormous. Improvements in irrigation efficiency at the field through such measures as better leveling, use of advanced technologies such as drip and subsurface, and more precise application control would also be of great benefit but, again, costly. These measures would also improve yields and diminish the widespread problems of secondary soil salinization and waterlogging of irrigated lands.

The most controversial water management issue for Turkmenistan is the Kara-Kum Canal. Begun in 1954, this canal now stretches 1,100 km westward from the Amu Darya at Kerki to Gazanjyk (Kazandzhik) (Figure 17.4). A pipeline carries drinking water from here to Krasnovodsk on the Caspian. In the mid-1980s, withdrawals into the canal were 10–12 km^3/yr, accounting

Figure 17.4   The Kara-Kum Canal near the capital city of Ashgabat, with concrete sides being installed to limit water loss. Photo by P. P. Micklin.

for around 50% of all water withdrawn in the republic (Kirsta, 1989). The original intent was to extend the canal southward from Gazanjyk to the Atrek River, with an increase of headworks diversion to 17 km³/yr. Most of the water is used to irrigate some 800,000 hectares, two-thirds of the republic total (Marchenkov, 1990). The canal also provides municipal and industrial water for settlements along its route. The canal mainly has been under attack because of its contribution to the desiccation of the Aral Sea, although a water management expert from Turkmenistan has pointed out it accounted for only 15% of the water "lost" to the Aral from the 1960s to the mid-1980s (Kirsta, 1989). The canal is unlined along almost all of its course and loses considerable water through infiltration. This has led to the formation of a zone of lakes and wetlands adjacent to the Kara-Kum from which huge amounts of water evaporate and transpire. Lining of the canal would go far to reduce water losses, but given its length and cross-section, the cost would be immense.

Turkmenistan has two other water-related environmental management problems that need mention. First is the problem of the Garabogazkol (Kara-Bogaz-Gol), a large, very saline gulf off the Caspian in the northwest part of the republic. Formerly, it was connected to the Caspian by a narrow channel and, as noted earlier, has been a source of mineral salts. But in 1980, a dam was built across the channel to block flow to the gulf as a means to help stabilize the level of the Caspian (the level of which had been falling for decades but already was rising again by this time). The gulf went from 10,000 km² to 2,000 km² in two years, with adverse effects on the commercial salt industry based upon its brines. The dried bottom also became a source of dust/salt storms that harmed surrounding areas. The gulf would have dried completely, but in the mid-1980s a pipeline was built from the Caspian to partially restore inflow (Shabad, 1985). Since then its area has increased somewhat but still is much less than in 1980.

The second issue is Lake Sarykamysh. This large lake (3,000 km²) has formed from irrigation drainage water since the early 1960s. It is saline (around 12 grams/liter) but nevertheless has become home for a variety of fishes, many of which used to be endemic to the Aral Sea. It also serves as a haven for migratory birds. The major problems of Sarykamysh are high levels of toxic chemicals contained in the irrigation inflow, which have contaminated the fish and birds (thus ending a significant commercial fishery in 1987), and rising salinity. A plan to divert a large share of its inflow to the Aral Sea would likely mean rapid desiccation and salinization of the lake, as well as possible pollution of the Aral Sea (Micklin, 1991a, 1991b, pp. 57–58).

Resource Management and the Future of Turkmenistan

Turkmenistan, like the other former republics, faces an uncertain future. There have been more stability and continuity here since the dissolution of the Soviet Union than in any other republic. Ethnic troubles have been minor, and the old Communist regime and management system remains in place, albeit under a nationalist guise. For resource and environmental management, this has meant continuance of business as usual. The basic resource management agencies (e.g., Ministry of Water Management, Ministry of Water Resources, and the State Committee for Nature Protection [Goskompriroda]) continue their work as before and with the same leadership. Grassroots environmentalism exists but has a low profile, and there are no prominent citizen environmental groups. Opposition to governmental positions and policies is still strongly discouraged and suppressed; it would be difficult for an environmental group to arise unless it had clear governmental approval.

Nevertheless, an independent Turkmenistan must forge a new set of resource and environmental management policies and strategies. Continuance of the old ways, appropriate in a situation with strong central management from Moscow, does not have long-term viability. Turkmenistan has signed the CIS Agreement on Interaction in the Field of Ecology and Environmental Protection. This commits the republic to be ecologically responsible, cooperate with other CIS republics in environmental matters, and abide by international agreements to which the former Soviet Union is a party. The republic is also in the process of developing new trade relations within the FSU.

Natural gas is, by far, its most valuable resource. Natural gas production fell substantially after independence as Turkmenistan lost its buyers within the FSU (Sagers, 1992). But after contentious negotiations over pricing, it has signed new and more favorable natural gas delivery agreements with Ukraine, Armenia, and Azerbaijan. Turkmenistan is also looking to sell its gas outside the FSU. One proposal on the table is construction of a gas pipeline for delivery of this fuel to Europe through Iran and Turkey. It also has a contract with an Argentine company to further develop its oil fields. There is intent to build a railroad to Iran as part of the development of economic and other relations with its large Muslim neighbor to the south.

Turkmenistan is fortunate to have an abundance of natural gas, which can command high prices or favorable terms of trade not only in the FSU but also on the world market. Gas can be used with the developed Western nations as it was with Ukraine: to obtain not only money but also critical technical assistance for development of this and other resources. Hence, Turkmenistan, in spite of its Third World social and economic conditions, has an advantage over seemingly much better off republics (e.g., the Baltic states) that must rely on agricultural products and market-deficient manufactured goods, which command low prices in international trade, to obtain much-needed hard currency and foreign technology. Wisely developed and managed, natural gas could provide the means for Turkmenistan to resolve or alleviate its most serious resource and environmental problems. Of course, this requires a commitment by the government to pursue these goals, which cannot be automatically assumed.

If this effort is undertaken, what are the highest priorities? Slowing population growth and raising living standards are essential. These two efforts are interconnected and could be promoted by a variety of programs aimed at improving educational opportunities and health and medical services, particularly for women. The water issue is also critical. Improvements in irrigation efficiency must be pursued both for economic and environmental reasons. Over the longer term, irrigation of cotton should be reduced, with a portion of the freed water relegated to environmental improvement (i.e., left in the Amu Darya) and the balance reserved for appropriate, relatively non-polluting industrial development, food production, and water supply uses. This would be in harmony with existing programs to enhance education and raise living standards.

Reaching agreements with the other states in the basin of the Aral Sea on the management of the shared water resources of the Amu Darya and a joint approach to the human and environmental problems of the region are also critical. Two recent actions indicate a start has been made here. In early 1992, the governments of the Central Asian republics and Kazakhstan entered into discussions to create a "Council of Presidents" to coordinate the management of all resources in the basin of the Aral Sea (Micklin, 1992). And in February 1992, the five republics signed an agreement for the joint management and protection of interstate water resources.

If success can be obtained by Turkmenistan in the efforts to reduce population growth rates, improve public health, rationalize water usage, and judiciously develop its natural gas resources, the nation's future could be more promising than its past. There is little to suggest, however, that any of these goals can be easily accomplished.

Bibliography

Agreement on Interaction in the Field of Ecology and Environmental Protection. 1992. Signed in Moscow, February 8.

Akademiya Nauk Turkmenskoy SSR. 1986. *Institut pustyn'*. Moscow: Nauka.

Alpat'yev, A.M., A.M. Arkhangelskiy, N.Ya. Podoplelov, and A.Ya. Stepanov. 1976. *Fizicheskaya geografiya SSSR*. Moscow: Vyshaya shkola.

Atlas SSSR. 1983. Moscow: GUGK.

Babayev, A.G., I.S. Zonn, N.N. Drozdov, and Z.G. Freykin. 1986. *Deserts*. Moscow, Mysl'.

Feshbach, M., and A. Friendly. 1992. *Ecocide in the USSR.* New York: Basic Books.

Goskomstat SSSR. 1989. *Okhrana okruzhayushchey sredy i ratsional'noye ispol'zovaniye prirodnykh resursov v SSSR.* Statistical Handbook. Moscow: Finansy i Statistika.

———. 1991a. *Narodnoye khozyaystvo SSSR v 1990g.* Moscow: Finansy i Statistika.

———. 1991b. *Okhrana okruzhayushchey sredy i ratsional'noye ispol'zovaniye prirodnykh resursov v SSSR.* Statistical Handbook. Moscow: Finansy i Statistika.

Kirsta, B.T. 1989. "Problema Aral'skogo morya i Karakumskiy canal." *Problemy osvoyeniya pustyn,'* no. 5, pp. 10–17.

Lewis, R.A., ed. 1992. *Geographic Perspectives on Soviet Central Asia.* London: Routledge.

Marchenkov, Dmitri. 1990. "Turkmenia: The Quiet Republic," *Soviet Life* (August); pp. 9–17, 48.

Micklin, P. 1991a. "Touring the Aral: Visit to an Ecologic Disaster Zone." *Soviet Geography,* vol. 32, no. 2, pp. 90–106.

———. 1991b. *The Water Management Crisis in Soviet Central Asia.* Carl Beck Papers in Russian and East European Studies, No. 905. Pittsburgh: Center for Russian and East European Studies, August.

———. 1992. "The Aral Crisis: Introduction to the Special Issue." *Post-Soviet Geography,* vol. 33, no. 5, pp. 269–283.

Mints, A.A., ed. 1969. *Srednaya Aziya.* Moscow: Mysl'.

Mnatsakanian, Ruben. A. 1992. *Environmental Legacy of the Former Soviet Republics.* Edinburgh: Centre for Human Ecology.

Orlovskiy, N.S. 1982. "Desertification: Its Mechanism and Implications." In *Combating Desertification in the USSR: Problems and Experience,* ed. A.G. Babayev, 30–55. Moscow: Centre for International Projects.

Pryde, P.R. 1984. "Soviet Development of Solar Energy." *Soviet Geography,* vol. 25, no. 1, pp. 24–33.

———. 1987. "The Distribution of Endangered Fauna in the USSR." *Biological Conservation,* vol. 42, no. 1 pp. 19–37.

Sagers, M. J. 1990. "News Notes." *Soviet Geography,* vol. 31, no. 5, pp. 278–314.

———. 1992. "News Notes." *Post Soviet-Geography,* vol. 33, no. 9, pp. 606–608.

———. 1994. "Long-Term Program for Turkmenistan's Oil and Gas Sector." *Post-Soviet Geography,* vol. 35, no. 1, pp. 50–62.

Shabad, T. 1985. "News Notes." *Soviet Geography,* vol. 26, no. 1, pp. 59–61.

Washington Post, May 22, 1990, pp. A10–14.

Zatoka, A. 1993. "Animals in the Headlights: The Vanishing Wildlife of Turkmenistan." *Surviving Together,* vol. 11, no. 1 (Spring), pp. 33–35.

Zickel, Raymond E., ed. 1991. *Soviet Union: A Country Study.* Washington, D.C.: Federal Research Division, Library of Congress.

18

Uzbekistan

Nancy Lubin

The end of Soviet rule in Uzbekistan has left a dual legacy. Certainly Uzbekistan today is more developed than some of its immediate neighbors. It enjoys a comparatively high level of literacy and industrial production, and basic education and health care are relatively widespread. But the human and environmental costs of Soviet development in Uzbekistan have been enormous, and in many respects Uzbekistan remains more impoverished and less democratic than many of its lesser developed counterparts in other parts of the world. Uzbekistan possesses more resources than some of its neighbors that it can utilize in dealing with these problems. But effective national development will require concerted political will to ensure that these resources are in fact used to benefit all segments of society in the new country.

Ethnicity, History, and Political Geography

Before the collapse of the USSR, Uzbekistan was the third largest Soviet republic in population and the fifth largest in territory. Today, with a population and level of industrial and agricultural production roughly 3 to 4 times that of Kyrgyzstan, Tajikistan, or Turkmenistan, Uzbekistan is likely to emerge as one of the dominant republics, if not *the* dominant republic, in the Central Asian region. With a 1994 population of over 20 million people, it is the largest in population, comprising more than 40% of the population of the five new Central Asian states that emerged from the former USSR.

But the importance of Uzbekistan as a single entity is relatively new. Before Russian conquest in the 1860s and the 1917 Russian Revolution, there was little sense of an Uzbek nation as such. Instead, life was organized around the tribe or clan, and traditional occupations centered on the sedentary pursuits of the oasis—agriculture, commerce, artisan trades—or nomadic pastoralism. The population of what is today Uzbekistan was ruled by various khans who had conquered the region in the 16th century, the most powerful of whom were based in Bukhoro (Bukhara), Khiva, and Quqon (Kokand).

All of this changed with the onset of Soviet rule. Resistance was strong to the establishment of Russian rule in 1917, and opposition by Basmachi, or guerrilla fighters, lasted well into the mid-1920s. Soviet power, nonetheless, slowly prevailed. In 1918, the new Russian government in Moscow formed the Turkestan Autonomous Republic, which combined most of Central Asia into one administrative unit. In October 1924, this territory was divided into smaller units, and the Republic of Uzbekistan was born.

The new borders of Uzbekistan ultimately not only created a new kind of Uzbek identity, but by deliberately cutting across existing ethnic and linguistic lines in the region, they also served to sow tension and strife among the different Central Asian groups. In particular, the territory of Uzbekistan was drawn to include two of the main Tajik cultural centers, Bukhoro and Samarqand (Samarkand), as well as parts of the Fergana Valley, to which other ethnic groups could lay claim. These borders have caused animosity and territorial claims among Uzbeks, Tajiks, Kyrgyz, and others for many years, but especially since the collapse of central Soviet rule (Rotar, 1992).

Indeed, even before the collapse of the USSR, Uzbekistan began to witness increased displays of tension among its different peoples and ethnic groups. In June of 1989, for example, ethnic conflict erupted between Uzbeks and Meskhetian Turks in the Fergana Valley, claiming about 100 lives. These were followed by other outbreaks of violence in other parts of the Fergana Valley and elsewhere as tensions also increased among Uzbeks, Kyrgyz, Tajiks and Kazakhs, and other national groups living on Uzbekistan's territory (Table 18.1). Many in Uzbekistan today fear the potential spillover of the conflict in Tajikistan into Uzbekistan, and many fear further unrest among ethnic groups within Uzbekistan itself. Thousands of Uzbeks living in Tajikistan have fled the civil war there and migrated back to Uzbekistan, just as tens of thousands of Russians and other Slavs have left Uzbekistan for northern Kazakhstan or Russia. Crimean Tatars, deported to Uzbekistan at the end of World War II, are migrating out of Uzbekistan to return to the Crimea.

During the 1980s, Uzbekistan gained notoriety through wide-ranging corruption scandals. These centered primarily on the embezzlement of funds by falsifying figures on the production and distribution of cotton, and several high ranking Uzbek officials were prosecuted and imprisoned by the Soviet central government. Despite the fact that Uzbekistan initially wavered in its opposition to the August 19, 1991, coup in Moscow, on August 31, 1991, the Supreme Soviet of Uzbekistan declared the republic independent and recognized the sovereignty and right to secession of the Karakalpak Republic. In December 1991, an independence referendum was passed with 98.2 percent of the popular vote, and Islam Karimov, then Communist Party secretary of Uzbekistan, was elected the first president.

One region that today holds an ambiguous position in Uzbekistan is Karakalpakstan. In 1936, as part of Stalin's nationality policy, the Karakalpaks (a Turkic Muslim group related to the Kazakhs whose name literally means "black hat") were given their own territory in western Uzbekistan and the

TABLE 18.1 Nationality Composition of Uzbekistan, 1959, 1970, 1979 and 1989

	Number of given nationality (thousands)				Nationality as Percentage of Total				1970 as percentage of 1959	1979 as percentage of 1970	1989 as percentage of 1979
	1959	1970	1979	1989	1959	1970	1979	1989			
Uzbeks	5038	7724	10569	14142	62.1	65.5	68.7	71.4	153	131	134
Karakalpaks	168	230	298	412	2.1	2.0	1.9	2.1	137	130	138
Russians	1092	1473	1666	1653	13.5	12.5	10.8	8.3	135	113	99
Tatars	398	438	531	468	4.9	3.7	3.5	2.4	110	121	88
Kazakhs	343	476	620	808	4.2	4.0	4.0	4.1	139	130	130
Tajiks	311	449	595	934	3.8	3.8	3.9	4.7	144	133	157
Koreans	138	148	163	183	1.7	1.3	1.1	0.9	107	110	112
Ukrainians	88	112	114	153	1.1	0.9	0.7	0.8	127	102	135
Kyrgyz	93	111	142	175	1.1	0.9	0.9	0.9	120	128	123
Jews	73	93	74	65	0.9	0.8	0.5	0.3	128	79	89
Turkmen	55	71	92	122	0.7	0.6	0.6	0.6	130	130	132
Other*	254	328	381	513	3.0	2.7	2.6	3.0	129	116	135

* Other nationalities include Belorussians, Azerbaijanis, Armenians, Georgians, Bashkir, Uighurs, Moldavians, Chavus, Ocetians, peoples of Dagestan and gypsies

Source: State Committee on Statistics of the Uzbek SSR, *Itogi vsesoiuznoi perepisi naseleniia 1989 goda, chast' I,* Tashkent: 1990, p. 118

administrative delineation of an "autonomous Soviet socialist republic" (ASSR), an administrative division highlighting differences from the rest of Uzbekistan but still located within that republic's borders. It was given continued republic status in 1992, but pressure from Tashkent and continued ties with the Uzbek government have kept it from exerting full independence. Today, the population of Karakalpakstan is about 1.3 million people.

The capital of Uzbekistan is Tashkent, with a population of 2.1 million people. Other major cities include Samarqand, Namangan, Andijon (Andizhan), Bukhoro, Farghona (Fergana) and Quqon (Kokand) (Table 18.2). As of 1989, roughly 72% of Uzbekistan's population was Uzbek, with the remainder largely Tajik (almost 5%), Kazakh (about 4%), Tatar (2.5%), Karakalpak (a little over 2%), and Russian (8%) (see Table 18.1). Some would contend that the Tajik/Persian ethnic population is almost certainly understated in these figures. Today, Uzbekistan is becoming increasingly homogeneous as Russians and others continue to out-migrate in increasing numbers and as Uzbeks return to Uzbekistan from other parts of the former USSR. With a per capita income estimated at 2,714 rubles in 1991, it ranks as among the poorest of the former Soviet republics.

Physical Environment and Constraints to Development

With a territory of approximately 447,000 square kilometers (roughly the size of Sweden), Uzbekistan is one of the larger Central Asian states. Bordering on Turkmenistan to the southwest, Afghanistan to the south, Kazakhstan to the west and north, and Tajikistan and Kyrgyzstan to the east, the physical envi-

Table 18.2   Largest Cities in Uzbekistan

City (Russian spelling)	Population (1000s) 1970	1989	1970-89 % increase
Tashkent (same)	1,385	2,073	49.7
Samarqand (Samarkand)	267	366	37.1
Namangan (same)	175	308	76.0
Andijon (Andizhan)	188	294	56.6
Bukhoro (Bukhara)	112	224	100.0
Farghona (Fergana)	148	200	35.1
Quqon (Kokand)	133	182	36.8
Nukus (same)	74	169	128.4
Chirchiq (Chirchik)	107	156	45.8
Qarshi (Karshi)	71	156	119.7

Source: Soviet Geography, May 1989.
Placename changes: Office of the Geographer, U.S. Dept. of State.

ronment of Uzbekistan is quite diverse. The southeast portion of Uzbekistan is characterized by the westernmost extensions of the Tien Shan Mountains; the highest peak is 4,643 meters. The vast Qizilkum (Kyzyl Kum Desert) dominates the northcentral portion of Uzbekistan (Figure 18.1).

The most fertile part of Uzbekistan is the Fergana Valley, an area of roughly 20,000 square kilometers lying between two high mountain ranges. The eastern end of the valley abuts against the Tien Shan Mountains in Kyrgyzstan; the western end opens up along the course of the Syr Darya into the Kyzyl Kum Desert. The valley has very low rainfall, roughly 200–300 millimeters (8–12 inches) per year; but only small patches of unirrigated desert remain in the center of the area and along ridges on the periphery. It has a very high density of population.

Uzbekistan's climate is continental, with hot summers and cool winters. In July, the mean temperature is 25°C in Tashkent and 30°C in the desert (77–86°F), while the January average is around −2°C but may fall in places to as low as −20°C. It is also quite arid, with average annual rainfall in most parts of the country between 100–400 millimeters (4–16 inches), falling mostly in winter and spring.

Karakalpakstan, the only autonomous republic in Central Asia under the Soviet system, contains 165,600 square kilometers, or over a third of the entire Uzbek Republic. Located in the lower reaches of the Amu Darya River, it contains part of the Aral Sea and the Kyzyl Kum Desert. Karakalpakstan's economy has always been centered in the very fertile Amu Darya delta, and it had a long history of irrigated agriculture. Today, however, the drying up of the Aral Sea has made Karakalpakstan one of the poorest and most environmentally devastated parts of Uzbekistan, if not the entire former USSR.

The exceedingly arid climate and general scarcity of water in Uzbekistan would be constraints to development anywhere in the world. In Uzbekistan, it has been exacerbated by decades of relentless pursuit of irrigated agriculture, especially cotton, without regard to wastage of water or other natural resources. The cotton monoculture that has destroyed the fertility of much of the soil, the high losses of water due to poorly planned expansion of irrigated lands, the waterlogged soils, the large scale erosion of soil, the vast amounts of secondary salinization of Uzbekistan's soils—all these have had not only a negative environmental impact but also serious public health and economic consequences. After rapid expansion of acreage under irrigation between 1965 and 1986, by 1988 poor water management had actually taken more than 3.4 million hectares out of production in the Aral Sea basin (Feshbach and Friendly, 1992, p. 76). Other reports suggest that more than 400,000 ha of irrigated land were taken out of production in Uzbekistan alone between 1976 and 1985, and almost half (44 percent) of all irrigated land in Uzbekistan today is strongly salinized. The regions of Uzbekistan most seriously affected by salinization are Syr Darya, Dzhizak, Bukhoro, and Khorazm Oblasts and the Karakalpak region. Throughout the 1980s, officials were pumping more investment into farms in Uzbekistan and sustaining greater losses.

Seismic activity is also a potential physical constraint to development. Indeed, much of Uzbekistan's capital city, Tashkent, was destroyed in a major

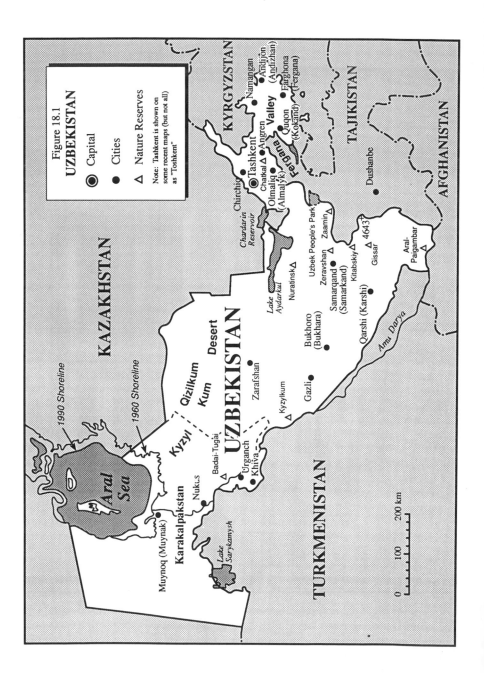

Figure 18.1
UZBEKISTAN

earthquake in 1966. Other earthquakes on a significant scale have occurred both before and since; for example, a very strong earthquake resulted in heavy damage to the Gazli area in 1984. The mountain areas and adjacent foothills are especially prone to earthquakes.

Another major constraint on economic growth is Uzbekistan's exceedingly high rate of population growth. According to estimates by Uzbek demographers, Uzbekistan's population, growing at almost 3 percent per year, is projected to increase by roughly 600,000 people annually through the year 2000. By the year 2005, it is projected that roughly 30 million people will live in Uzbekistan alone, more than the combined populations of Uzbekistan, Tajikistan, Kyrgyzstan and Turkmenistan today. Population density likewise will have almost doubled, to roughly 74 people per square kilometer. "A very great ecological burden will be created on irrigated land in the republic, where already today there are only 0.15 hectares per inhabitant" (Ata-Mirzaev, 1989).

Even at present, five of the eight most densely populated oblasts of the former USSR—Andijon, Farghona (Fergana), Tashkent, Namangan, and Khorazm—are in Uzbekistan, and their populations continue to grow rapidly. Average population density for Uzbekistan is roughly 118 inhabitants per square mile, compared to 16 inhabitants per square mile in Kazakhstan.

Finally, despite the high population growth, the shortage of skilled personnel in Uzbekistan is also a major constraint to future development. Russians and other non-indigenous personnel have long concentrated for a variety of reasons in the industrial sectors of the economy, which include mining and most factory production. With the disintegration of the USSR and the outbreak of violence in Central Asia, many of these skilled personnel have begun to leave.

According to unofficial data, between 1985 and 1991 the number of "nonnatives" in Uzbekistan declined from 2.4 to 1.6 million people, and the number of out-migrants continued to escalate throughout 1992. In the energy sector, half of the power generating units of the Syr Darya electric power station have been shut down because of Russian out-migration, and there are no trained personnel to operate the recently constructed Novoangrenskii power station. In Tashkent, one individual lamented ominously, "Europeans make up more than 90 percent of the personnel of the electric power station and now they are leaving" (Sabov and Cherniak, 1992, p. 2). Efforts are being made to train indigenous cadres, but the shortfall is making itself sorely felt.

Natural Resource Advantages and Existing Industry

Uzbekistan is exceedingly rich in a wide array of natural resources that provide enormous opportunity for future development. These include important mineral and energy resources, cotton and other agricultural crops, and a relatively well-developed industrial processing capacity in these sectors.

Perhaps the most valuable of Uzbekistan's mineral resources is gold. Uzbekistan accounted for about one third of Soviet gold production before the breakup of the USSR. Today, the Muruntau gold mine, located about 250

miles northwest of Tashkent in the Kyzyl Kum Desert near the town of Zarafshan, is estimated to be the largest gold mine in the world (Consolidated
Goldfields, 1979; Sagers, 1992). Other gold reserves have reportedly been located at Oriklisoy and elsewhere. In 1992, a reported 80 tons of gold were
mined in Uzbekistan, making it the eighth largest producer of gold in the
world. Other metals include significant copper deposits, iron ore, lead, zinc,
and silver. Some uranium mining also occurs.

Uzbekistan is also quite rich in energy resources. It was the third largest
producer of natural gas in the Soviet Union after Russia and Turkmenistan,
producing over 10 percent of the natural gas in the former USSR. Gas reserves are tentatively estimated at more than one trillion cubic meters, concentrated mainly in Kashkadarya Oblast, Gazli, Urtabulak, Dengizkul, Shur-
tan, and other locations. The biggest gas deposit, Boyangora-Gadzhak, was
discovered in Surkhandarya Oblast in the 1970s.

Uzbekistan also has small coal reserves, mainly from Angren, and a small
but increasing production of oil. The recent discovery of the Mingbulak (or
"Thousand Springs") oil field in Namangan Oblast may ultimately dwarf
these other energy resources. Some experts suggest this may prove to be one
of the world's best oil fields. The field is on an unfaulted anticline covering
more than 20,000 acres in the central basin of the Fergana Valley (*Oil and Gas
Journal*, 1992). Local sources suggest that Namangan Oblast could soon produce the equivalent of hundreds of millions of dollars worth of oil (Kolbasiuk and Svartsevich, 1992). Western Uzbekistan is also reportedly rich in
oil, with reserves in one deposit, Kokdumalak, reportedly exceeding hundreds of millions of tons.

Uzbekistan's main agricultural resource has long been its "white gold,"
meaning the vast amounts of cotton growing on its territory. Uzbekistan was
long the chief cotton growing region of the USSR, accounting for 61 percent
of total Soviet production, and today it reportedly ranks third in the world.
In 1991, Uzbekistan's cotton yield was more than 4.6 million tons, of which
over 80% was of the first and second grades. In 1987, roughly 40% of Uzbekistan's work force and more than half of all irrigated land in Uzbekistan (over
2 million hectares) were devoted to cotton.

In light of increasing water shortages in Central Asia, and the declines in
food imports to feed an increasingly impoverished population, government
leaders have stated that they would like to reduce the acreage under cotton
cultivation in favor of growing food. But Uzbekistan's short-term needs for
hard currency make dramatic declines in cotton cultivation unrealistic. Likewise, the entire existing agricultural infrastructure (the irrigation system,
layout of the fields, farm machinery, etc.) is geared toward cotton production;
shifting to other crops would require a massive overhaul of the agricultural
system that leaders do not appear to be prepared to risk. The continued commitment to cotton, therefore, is also seen as providing a good base for further
development.

Despite some efforts to diversify the industrial base, Uzbekistan's economy remains dominated by raw materials extraction and processing, mostly
connected with cotton production and mineral extraction. These include extraction of oil and natural gas and oil refining; mining and mineral process-

ing; machine building, especially of equipment for cotton cultivation and the textile industry; cotton ginning and other light and food industries; and, to a lesser extent, the iron and steel, chemical, power and coal industries. Uzbekistan is also home to several major defense industries including aviation factories, from the Soviet era.

The capital city of Tashkent accounts for about one third of all industrial output in Uzbekistan, largely in textiles and agricultural machinery. Electricity for these industries comes from small hydroelectric stations along the Chirchiq River and from a gas-fired thermal power station. Two refineries in Uzbekistan, in Farghona (Fergana) and Amtiari, have a combined capacity of over 173,000 barrels per day. Other centers of processing industries include Angren (coal), Bekabad (steel), Olmaliq (Almalyk) (copper, zinc, and molybdenum), Zarafshan (gold), and Yangiabad (uranium).

In the agricultural sector, there has been little conversion to private enterprise as yet. Uzbekistan has been reluctant to begin the process of breaking up the collective farms and privatizing agricultural land for fear of the political ramifications and destabilizing impact it might have on Uzbekistan's power structure.

Major Environmental Problems

The major environmental problem facing Uzbekistan is the tragedy of the Aral Sea, which has been reduced to about a third of its normal size (see Figure 16.4). Some of the impacts of this disaster include serious salinization of the land under crops, salt and dust storms, increased desertification and consequent loss of plant and animal life as well as arable land, change in climate conditions of the region, lower cotton yields, destruction of historical and cultural monuments, and decreases in public health indices. Irrigation diversions have reduced flow in the lower Amu Darya to almost zero in some years, yet about half the diverted water is not beneficially used on crops (Figure 18.2) (Micklin, 1988, 1991).

The newly exposed bed of the Aral Sea is creating serious downwind problems. Each year up to 150 million tons of salts are reportedly carried distances of as much as 800 kilometers; Karakalpak Ministry of Health experts assert that salt and dust storms from the Aral Sea have raised the level of particulate matter in the earth's atmosphere by more than 5%. Likewise, the continental climate in the Aral region has become more severe: the number of frost-free days has diminished; summers are on average 2–3 degrees hotter, and winters two degrees colder, than they were two decades ago.

The human problem is particularly acute in Karakalpakstan, where public health has deteriorated significantly in recent years. Drinking water is contaminated, and diseases such as typhoid, cancer, and hepatitis are rampant (Feshbach and Friendly, 1992, pp. 73–75). Muynoq (Muynak), once a thriving Aral Sea port, is now many kilometers from the sea and must process imported fish. Other problems in this minority region are noted elsewhere in this chapter, and the nature of the Aral Sea tragedy is discussed further in Chapter 16 on Kazakhstan.

But the Aral Sea disaster is only the tip of the iceberg. Decades of poor

Figure 18.2   The huge Amu-Bukhoro Canal brings irrigation water from the Amu Darya to the extensive cropland around Bukhoro. Because the canal is unlined, large losses of water due to seepage occur.

water management and a lack of water or sewage treatment facilities; inordinately heavy use of pesticides, herbicides, defoliants and fertilizers in the fields; and construction of industrial enterprises without regard to human or environmental impact have led to massive environmental challenges throughout the territory of Uzbekistan.

As but one example of the magnitude of these problems, throughout Central Asia an average of 20–25 kg of various toxic chemicals are applied per hectare, as against a former Soviet average of 3 kg. In some parts of Uzbekistan, upward of 20 times the Soviet average of fertilizer is applied per acre; that is, upward of 230 kilograms of fertilizer per acre, as opposed to a Soviet average of 11 to 12 kg. Pesticide usage per hectare of arable land in places exceeds the safe level of 1.3 kilograms per hectare by 40–50-fold and the USSR average by 26 times (Yablokov, 1992). According to some reports, the concentration of chemical poisons in the atmosphere of population centers during the period of crop cultivation exceeds the maximum permissible concentration by 30–50 times (Torianikova and Karaseva, 1991).

In the words of one local environmental specialist, "Unfortunately, the gratis extensive use of the important natural resources of the republic, and the spontaneous distribution of productive forces undertaken without any consideration of the recommendations of scientific and authoritative specialists, has led to the brink of ecological catastrophe of the natural resources of our republic" (Alikhanov, 1990). Uzbekistan's water, air and land are polluted to dramatic proportions. These various environmental assaults are also adversely affecting wildlife and the nation's network of nature reserves (Table 18.3).

According to one report, practically all of the large underground freshwater supplies in Uzbekistan today are polluted by industrial and chemical

Table 18.3   Preserved Areas in Uzbekistan

Type of Preserve(a)	Number	Total area(b)	Average size(b)	% of Re-public(c)
Zapovedniki (Nature Reserves)	1 0	2162.69	216.27	0.48
Above that are Biosphere Reserves	1	356.86		0.08
National Parks	1	315.03	315.03	0.07
Zakazniki (Nature Preserves)	5	786.00	157.20	0.18
Total	1 6	3263.72	203.98	0.73

Zapovedniki (date created)	Hectares
Aral-Paigambar (1971; 1960)	3094
Badai-Tugai (1971)	5929
Chatkal (1947)	35686
Gissar (1983; 1975)	87538
Kitabskiy (1979)	5378
Kyzylkum (1971)	10141
Nuratinsk (1973)	22537
Suzkhansk (1986)	28014
Zaamin (1959)	15600
Zeravshan (1975)	2352
Total	216269

National Parks	Hectares
Uzbek People's Park (1978)	31503

(a) For the definition of each type of preserve, see Appendix 1.2.
(b) In square kilometers.
(c) Area of Uzbekistan equals 447,400 square kilometers.

Source: Pryde (1991).

wastes (Koniukhov, 1990). Currently, Koniukhov estimates, roughly 6 million people live in regions where the level of water pollution is merely "dangerous," and more than 3.5 million live in areas where the level of water pollution is deemed "critical." In other words, about half the population lives in regions where the water is severely polluted. Only 60% of the farms have a piped water system, and in many rural regions of Karakalpakstan, as well as in Khorazm, Bukhoro, and other oblasts, the population is forced to drink water directly from polluted reservoirs, rivers, and canals.

According to Koniukhov, out of 124 cities and villages in Uzbekistan, Tashkent has the best quality drinking water, but even here heavy pollution of the Chirchiq River and other industrial pollution have made Tashkent's drinking water unacceptable. According to an investigation by the Uzbekgidrogeologia Association, much of the surface waters and groundwater in Tashkent is saturated with heavy metals, phenols, and petroleum products along with other pollutants, giving enormous "cause for alarm" ("They Investigated," 1992).

Air pollution presents just as bleak a picture. Uzbekistan may account for 60% of industrial production among the four Central Asian states, but it also accounts for 60 percent of air pollutants in Central Asia (Zav'ialova and Agafonova, 1991). In 1988, emissions of pollutants into the republic's atmosphere reached 4.1 million tons per year, including 336,000 tons of nitric oxide. High levels of heavy metals (lead, nickel, zinc, copper, mercury, manganese, and the like) have been found in Uzbekistan's atmosphere, mainly from the burning of fossil fuels, utilization of wastes, and ferrous and non-ferrous metallurgy (Zav'ialova et al., 1991). Especially high concentrations of heavy metals are reportedly found in the southern part of Tashkent Oblast near the Olmaliq (Almalyk) metallurgical combine.

Combined with the soil pollution described previously, the environmental situation of Uzbekistan has already had serious health effects. Although it is always difficult to prove a direct cause and effect, the cumulative impact of these problems appears to have been devastating. Frequently cited in the press are increasing occurrences of typhoid, paratyphoid, and hepatitis due to contaminated drinking water; rising rates of intestinal disease and cancers; and increased frequency of anemia, dystrophy, cholera, dysentery, and a host of other illnesses, including, according to one Russian specialist, a "lag in physical development," especially among children (Volkhov, 1988). According to one estimate, 69 out of every 100 adults in the Aral Sea region are deemed to be "incurably ill." The average lifespan in some villages in Karakalpakstan is roughly 38 years.

Infant mortality—perhaps the best measure of the health of a population—has increased dramatically over the past twenty years, by as much as 49 percent in Uzbekistan between 1970 and 1986, or from 31 deaths before the age of one per 1,000 births to 46.2 deaths (TsSU, 1987). Today, official data put the level of infant mortality in parts of Karakalpakstan at roughly 110 per 1,000 children born, meaning that more than one out of every ten children born do not live until their first birthday (Bohr, 1989). Unofficial estimates put the level at twice that figure.

Governmental Structure

President Karimov, and the government of Uzbekistan, has acknowledged the extent of these environmental problems and has stated a commitment to address them. But the governmental structures to deal with these problems remain confused and ill-defined. Old agencies and organizations have been expanded to address these questions and new ones created, resulting in a range of agencies caught in a bureaucratic web with seemingly no real commitment to attack environmental problems head-on.

The key institution for addressing environmental problems in Uzbekistan is the State Committee for Environmental Protection, an outgrowth of the former branch of the all-Union State Committee for Environmental Protection in Moscow, which is currently under Minister Askhad Khabibulaev. It shares overlapping responsibilities with the State Committee on Hydrometeorology and a host of other institutions that play a key role in environmental protection, such as the Ministry of Land Reclamation and Water Resources, the State Committee for Water Resources Construction, the Institute of Irrigation, and the new Institute for Nature Protection. These institutions also work with a plethora of other sectoral ministries and committees. In the energy sector, for example, Uzbekneftegaz, a new Uzbek State Oil and Gas Industry concern, was formed in May of 1992 to develop more effectively and comprehensively Uzbekistan's oil and gas deposits and energy production capabilities ("Ukase," 1992). Its responsibilities directly overlap those of the Sredazgasprom Production Association, the State Committee on Geology, and others.

Various non-governmental environmental organizations and grass-roots organizations have also begun to form, some closely tied to the current government and others assuming more of an opposition stance. Environmental issues were among the first points in the original platform of Birlik, the first major opposition movement to emerge in Uzbekistan. They are a key concern of all opposition groups today and the cause of growing concern, if not discontent, among the population as a whole. The Committee to Save the Aral Sea, formed by Permat Shermukhamedov, held its first congress as a Green Party in June 1992. In November 1992, a new group was formed, the Foundation for Ecology and Health, headed by Shadimetov; the foundation is touted as being "completely autonomous," although Shadimetov himself is a major government figure, heading the Department of Social Issues of Uzbekistan's Council of Ministers. Other groups, such as smaller Committees to Save the Aral Sea and the Union to Defend the Aral and the Amu Darya, remain more grass-roots activist, very much created and supported from below.

To be sure, a wide array of measures have been endorsed to address some of these problems. Plans to introduce payments for resources, especially water; to collect fines from heavy polluters; and to address the Aral Sea crisis head-on have been discussed for some time. But the multitude of government agencies has created administrative confusion. A lack of law enforcement in these areas, a kind of capriciousness in government economic and environmental planning, and heavy centralization in the hands of the Uzbek president with little tolerance of grass-roots groups have greatly hindered addressing these problems. "Basically there are a lot of organizations doing the same tasks and having the same goals and orientation," says one Uzbek geologist, hindering an effective response to Uzbekistan's problem (Polatov, 1992).

And all of this has been exacerbated by a high degree of corruption throughout the Uzbek system. A spate of accusations have appeared in the local press concerning misuse of funds, including allegations of squandering and embezzlement of several million rubles from the "Aral Fund" created under Shermukhamedov's Committee to Save the Aral Sea. In this case, funds allegedly were used illegally for the funding of private businesses and a commercial center, for the construction of a bath house, for the production of a documentary film previously vetoed by the committee as a whole, and for direct personal gain (Mirzaev and Kovalev, 1992). Other alleged cases of widespread "abuse, waste, theft, embezzlement, and sabotage" have been attacked in the sale of Uzbekistan's petroleum products and other sectors ("On Measures," 1992).

Uzbekistan is rich in resources and potential. The country's environmental problems are at heart a result of abuse and mismanagement of Uzbekistan's natural resources, economic wealth, and political power. Until the political will emerges to regard environmental problems as a threat not only to the existing government in power but also to the very survival of Uzbekistan, little will be done by way of effectively addressing these increasingly serious challenges.

External Ties and Economic Potential

Having had independence thrust upon them in 1991, Uzbekistan and the other Central Asian states pressed to become "founding members" of the Commonwealth of Independent States on December 21, 1991. Economically unstable and politically shaky, Uzbekistan has found perpetuating existing links with the former Soviet republics its best hope for the short term. Economic and trade treaties have been signed with Russia, Ukraine, Moldova, Azerbaijan, Kyrgyzstan, and Kazakhstan, and collective security and/or military agreements have been signed with Russia, Armenia, and other Central Asian states. In the environmental area, a protocol among most of the CIS governments was signed in January 1992 that emphasized the Aral Sea problem as a priority for CIS cooperation. A mechanism has been set up for regular meetings to address this problem.

In general, however, little has come of direct CIS cooperation in addressing Uzbekistan's environmental ills. As the other CIS states have focused mainly on their own problems at home, Uzbekistan has begun to look in other directions for cooperation and assistance.

One natural direction for Uzbekistan to look is to its immediate neighbors to the south—Iran, Pakistan, Turkey—and to the wider Middle Eastern and Asian worlds. Uzbekistan's relations with its southern neighbors have greatly increased: Turkey and Iran have been especially active in pursuing economic projects and social, cultural, and diplomatic initiatives in Uzbekistan. For example, Uzbekistan early on was the recipient of most of the U.S.$700 million in credits that Turkey gave the new Central Asian states; Pakistan has followed suit, with particular commercial interest in hydroelectric power, gas pipelines, and other projects. Although initially nervous about the spread of Iranian fundamentalism in Central Asia, Uzbekistan has found mutual economic interests with Iran, and the two have pursued overland links and other joint ventures. During 1992, trade and cooperation agreements were signed with China, Saudi Arabia, Jordan, Pakistan, Iran, and others.

One forum that has emerged as a potentially important structure for cooperation with these countries in environmental issues, as well as other areas, has been the Economic Cooperation Organization (ECO). Although during its almost two decades of existence ECO has achieved very little in the way of economic cooperation, with the inclusion in November 1992 of the five former Soviet Central Asian states plus Afghanistan and Azerbaijan, there have been significant efforts to reinvigorate the organization. At a meeting in February 1993, an ambitious plan was announced to create a new interlinked regional economic bloc among ECO's members by the year 2000. The plan calls for expanding ties in all economic sectors, including tourism; setting up an effective transportation infrastructure to do so; and ultimately abolishing restrictions on the free flow of people and commodities. Energy trade is also to be expanded through the building of oil and gas pipelines and power transmission lines throughout the entire region. Given ECO's track record, it is unclear the extent to which these goals may be reached.

With Uzbekistan now a member of the United Nations, the World Bank, the IMF, the CSCE, the North Atlantic Cooperation Council, and other Western and international organizations, Uzbekistan has also begun to look beyond its immediate neighbors or the Islamic world for cooperation and assistance. The World Bank, for example, has scheduled a preparation mission for a $150 million cotton sub-sector development program to increase on-farm productivity and improve the international marketing of cotton, and more recently began a major effort to address the Aral Sea problem, calling for an investment of over $200 million. On a smaller scale, the European Bank for Reconstruction and Development has approved ECU $155,000 to investigate the economic and technical feasibility of setting up a waste lubricants refining plant in Uzbekistan (Environmental Cooperation Bulletin, 1993).

The bilateral role of the United States has not been negligible. The U.S. recognized Uzbekistan as an independent state on December 25, 1991; diplomatic relations were established in February 1992 following a visit by Secretary of State James Baker to the republic; and an embassy was opened in March. As of December, 1993, the U.S. had provided about $17 million in humanitarian assistance, and $13 million in technical assistance to Uzbekistan. This assistance has included programs in democratization, market reform, health, education, and a range of other areas. U.S. government assistance in the environmental area has tended to focus on the Aral Sea problem, although a number of non-governmental organizations have been exploring and working on a range of environmental issues throughout Uzbekistan.

On the commercial side, U.S. companies have also been making inroads to help exploit Uzbekistan's rich natural resources. The U.S. firm Stan Cornelius Enterprises, for example, helped cap the oil well blowout at Mingbulak in March 1992 and has subsequently established a joint venture with Uzbekneft to develop the oil field and explore and develop other oil reserves in the country. The joint venture expects Mingbulak field to produce for 12–20 years ("CIS Petroleum," 1992).

Likewise, the Colorado-based Newmont Mining Company has established a roughly $75 million joint venture with the Navoi Mining and Metallurgical Combine and the State Committee for Geology and Mineral Resources of Uzbekistan to produce gold at the Muruntau mine near Zarafshan. The venture is expected to cost $100 million in start-up costs, start producing in 1994, and yield an output of about 270,000 ounces of gold per year (Sagers, 1992). Since these efforts began, a trade agreement guaranteeing most favored status to the products of each country was signed in November, 1993, and a bilateral assistance agreement was signed four months later. Other U.S. companies are exploring or already investing in such sectors as power generation, the agrarian-industrial complex, transportation, communications, tourism and ecology, as well as the financial sector.

In July 1992, President Karimov issued a decree establishing a national company called Uzbekturism to build a viable tourist industry; i.e., to develop the infrastructural, educational and organizational basis for all types of tourism and to construct modern tourist facilities with the help of foreign investment. Turkish firms have become involved in building hotels, motels and camping facilities, and several Western firms are exploring possibilities as well.

All of these efforts, however, remain in their infancy, and problems and complications abound. Despite relatively liberal laws regarding tax holidays, repatriation of profits, and tax incentives to reinvest profits in scientific research, the investment climate for foreign companies remains weak. Political instability, highly bureaucratic and centralized control, lack of infrastructure, corruption, and other problems remain major impediments, inhibiting many joint ventures from getting off the ground.

In regard to environmental questions of such immediate importance, perhaps one of the biggest challenges for Uzbekistan will be to establish a greater degree of cooperation with its neighbors. Few of the environmental challenges facing Uzbekistan today, and hence few of the major constraints on their own future development, can be addressed in isolation from the other former Central Asian republics. Water management, air and soil pollution, climate change, the Aral Sea catastrophe, and the like can be handled effectively only if addressed multi-nationally.

For some time, conferences and declarations by leaders in Central Asia have called for more cooperation and collaboration among the five new Central Asian states to resolve the problem of the Aral Sea and regional use of water resources. In December 1992, President Karimov took the lead in proposing the creation of a strong, unified interstate organization to resolve the problems of the Aral Sea. But so far, these new countries have acted far more competitively than cooperatively in their economic policies, and the prospect of interstate cooperation to resolve environmental problems remains a glimmer of hope for the future.

These are the kinds of challenges that face Uzbekistan in its new period of independence, as it strives to reverse a legacy of unbalanced economic development and environmental devastation from roughly seventy years of Soviet rule. One indication of Uzbekistan's desire to show its independence from Moscow was its decision in 1993 to change its native written language from the Cyrillic to the Latin alphabet so as to more easily interact with the non-Russian world. If Uzbekistan chooses to institute democratic domestic reforms, work effectively with its direct neighbors, and judiciously attract foreign investment, it may be able to move along the path to political pluralism, environmental cleanup, and an improved economic infrastructure. Alternatively, if it becomes mired in conflicts, authoritarianism, and local rivalries that leave it caught in a web of infighting, indifference and despair, it may be unable to address adequately an environmental crisis that could ultimately threaten its very survival. Thus, the 1990s will be a defining decade in the history of the Uzbek people.

Acknowledgments

The author would like to thank the National Council for Soviet and East European Research, the MacArthur Foundation, and the Wilson Center for International Scholars for the financial and other support to complete this chapter; and Laurie Boke, research assistant at the U.S. Institute of Peace, for her invaluable assistance and support.

Bibliography

Alikhanov, B. B., and S. S. Tursunov. 1990. "Ekonomicheskiie problemy okhrany okruzhaiiushchei sredy v usloviiakh Uzbekistana." State Committee on Hydrometeorology, November. Unpublished paper.

Allworth, E.A. 1990. *The Modern Uzbeks: A Cultural History*. Stanford, CA: Hoover Institution Press.

Ata-Mirzaev, O. B. 1989. "Prognoz rosta chislennosti naseleniia Uzbekistana i ekologicheskaia situatsiia." Unpublished paper.

Bohr, A. 1989. "Health Catastrophe in Karakalpakstan." *Report on the USSR*, July 21, p. 37, quoting Ponarina, E. "Aral ugrozhaet planetu." *Sotsialisticheskaia Industrilia*, June 20.

"CIS Petroleum Joint Ventures Proceed at Fast Clip." 1992. *Oil and Gas Journal*, August 3, p. 21.

Feshbach, M., and Alfred Friendly Jr. 1992. *Ecocide in the USSR*. New York: Basic Books.

Kolbasiuk, V., and V. Svartsevich. 1992. "Taming a Golden Fountain: American Specialists Help Uzbek Oil Men to Cope with a Sensational Oil Field." April 24, pp. 1, 6, in FBIS-USR, May 4.

Koniukhov, Vladimir Grigorievich. 1990."Ekologicheskaia obstanovka v Uzbekskoi SSR i mery po ee uluchsheniiu." State Committee on Environmental Protection of Uzbekistan. Unpublished paper.

Lewis, R.A., ed. 1992. *Geographic Perspectives on Soviet Central Asia.* London: Routledge.
Lubin, N. 1989. "Uzbekistan: The Challenges Ahead." *Middle East Journal,* vol. 43, no. 4, Autumn.
————. 1993. "Dangers and Dilemmas: The Need for Prudent Policy Toward Central Asia." *Harvard International Review,* Spring, pp. 6–9.
Micklin, P. P. 1991. "The Water Crisis in Soviet Central Asia." In P. R. Pryde, *Environmental Management in the Soviet Union.* Cambridge, Cambridge University Press, pp. 213–232.
————. 1992. "The Aral Sea Crisis: Introduction to the Special Issue." *Post-Soviet Geography,* vol. 33, no. 5, pp. 269–282.
Ministry of Health, Karakalpakstan. 1991. *Mediko-ekologicheskie problemy Priaral'ia i zdopov'e naseleniia.* Nukus.
Mirzaev, S., and Iu. Kovalev. 1992. "Forced Decision: Why We Left the Committee to Save the Aral Sea." *Pravda Vostoka,* February 13, p. 3, in JPRS-TEN, May 22, p. 86.
"On Measures to Regulate the Sale of Petroleum Products and Improve the System of Branch Administration." 1992. Ukase issued by the President of Uzbekistan, *Pravda Vostoka,* September 8, p. 1, as translated in FBIS-USR-92-131, October 16.
Peterson, D.J. 1993. *Troubled Lands: The Legacy of Soviet Environmental Destruction.* Boulder: Westview Press.
Polatov, S. 1992. "Reserves Larger Than Those in the Urals." Interview with Eshim Iskandarov, *Ozbekiston Ovozi,* August 1, p. 3, in FBIS, October 17, p. 120.
Potts, David. 1980. *Gold, 1980.* Report for Consolidated Gold Fields Ltd. London: Westerham Press, Ltd.
Pryde, P. R. 1991. *Environmental Management in the Soviet Union.* Cambridge: Cambridge University Press.
Rotar, I. 1992. "A Mine Laid by the Kremlin's Mapmaker." *Nezavisimaya gazeta,* December 25, p. 1, as translated in *Current Digest of the Post-Soviet Press,* vol. 45, no. 1 (February 3, 1993), pp. 6–8.
Sabov, D., and I. Cherniak. 1992. "Russians Against the Background of Mosques." *Komsomolskaia Pravda,* February 4, p. 2, in FBIS-USR, February 18.
Sagers, Matthew J. 1992. "News Notes." *Post Soviet Geography,* vol. 33, no. 3, p. 190.
"Spotlight on Uzbekistan" (4 articles). 1993. *Surviving Together,* vol. 11, no. 2, Summer, pp. 28–34.
"They Investigated . . . and Became Irritated." 1992. *Pravda Vostoka,* May 30, in FBIS-USR-92-078, June 26, p. 94.
Torianikova, R.V., and T.A. Karaseva. 1991. "Soderzhanie i povedenie pestitsidov v poverkhnostnykh vodakh Uzbekistana." State Committee on Hydrometeorology, March. Unpublished paper.
Tsentral'noe statisticheskoe upravlenie (TsSU). 1987. *Narodnoe khoziaistvo SSSR za 70 let.* Moscow: Finansy i Statistika, p. 408.
"Ukase of the President of the Uzbekistan Republic on the Formation of the Uzbekneftegaz Uzbek State Oil and Gas Industry Concern." 1992. *Pravda Vostoka,* May 5, p. 1, as translated in FBIS-USR, June 1, p. 105.
Volkhov, M. 1988. "Khlopkovyi molokh prodolzhaet poshirat' vremia, sily, zdorov'e detei." *Pravda,* November 24, p. 2.
Yablokov, A. 1992. "Notes on the Environmental Situation in Russia." *Environmental Policy Review,* vol. 6, no. 2, Autumn, pp. 1–20.
Zav'ialova, L.V., and O. A. Agafonova. 1991. "Obzor fonovogo sostoianiia prirodnoi sredy sredneaziatskogo regiona za 1986–88." State Committee on Hydrometeorology, March. Unpublished paper.
Zav'ialova, L. V., O.A. Agafonova, and L.A. Semakina. 1991. "Zagriaznenie atmosfery srednei azii tiazhelymi metallami." State Committee on Hydrometeorology, March. Unpublished paper.

19

Kyrgyzstan

Kathleen Braden

Kyrgyzstan, with only five percent of Central Asia's land area and nine percent of its population, is often the forgotten republic of the former USSR; yet ironically, it may actually serve as a benchmark for all of the region's young countries. The problems of environmental despoliation, economic impoverishment, and ethnic clashes found in Kyrgyzstan mirror difficulties prevalent throughout the area. At the same time, subtle movement toward democratic institutions and economic development efforts may represent viable pathways for all of newly independent Central Asia.

The very isolation and underdevelopment that have allowed much of Kyrgyzstan's natural environment to remain intact have, on the other hand, encouraged ill-advised agricultural and metallurgical activities. Colonial-style economic relationships, which Central Asians accused the Soviet Union of fostering in years past, are very much evident in Kyrgyzstan: irrigated cotton fields, strip mining activities, and low-paying industrial jobs. Now the republic can independently make its own choices for balancing economic development and the health of both its natural ecosystems and human population, but it will be forced to make such crucial decisions against a backdrop of ethnic rivalry, scarcity of investment, and a rising tide of pan-Islamic revivalism. In this region of "Celestial Mountains," where the snow leopard and Pallas cat still find some of their last natural refuges on the planet, the Kyrgyz people must confront the task of deciding not only their own identity as a nation, but also what the future will be for the landscape and biotic resources of Kyrgyzstan.

Profile of the People of Kyrgyzstan

The journalist Igor Rotar wrote in *Nezavisimaya gazeta* that the "problem of the land" in Central Asia was most acute in Kyrgyzstan, where people who for centuries had earned their living by herding in the mountains ended up giving their name to an artificially created state in which they are a minority in its most productive regions. He noted that among the titular nations of Central Asia, the Kyrgyz have the lowest standards of living in their "own" country. (Rotar, 1993, p. 5)

Of Turko-Mongol origin, the Kyrgyz people are closely related to Kazakhs, and in fact, Russian colonial rulers in the 19th century referred to the Kazakhs as Kirghiz and today's Kyrgyz as Kara-Kirghiz. The exact nationality divisions that emerged in the early twentieth century in Central Asia were actually quite blurred in previous times as Turkic, Mongol, and Persian influences pervaded the region. The arrival of Islam in the 8th and 9th centuries provided a unifying force for the various tribal and ethnic groups several centuries before the nomadic peoples believed to form the ancestors of the Kyrgyz arrived from the Yenisey area. By 1884 Russia had conquered most of Turkestan and had begun introducing the social and economic changes that were to continue in the Soviet period, most predominantly the settlement of people who were pastoral nomads into sedentary agriculture, often based on cotton production for the Russian empire.

But dreams of Pan-Islamic or Pan-Turkic unity were revived after the 1917 Bolshevik Revolution. War between local groups, often created under the banner of Islamic nationalism and Bolshevism, ravaged the area. Osh and Jalal-Abad were the scene of some bitter fighting, and the resulting famines of the period took over half a million Kyrgyz lives. Finally subdued as an Autonomous Republic, Kirgizia became a Union republic (SSR) of the Soviet Union in 1936. The Stalin period brought in a policy of crushing any sense of nationalism or resistance to collectivization. Chingiz Aitmatov, the celebrated Kyrgyz writer, argued that the stigma created by Stalin toward native languages and culture was still denying his fellow Kyrgyz a sense of their own history as late as the 1980s. From 1927 to 1932, Kirgizia experienced forced collectivization, destruction of herds, famine, and periodic rebellion and loss of a generation of intellectual elites (Nahaylo and Swoboda, 1990, pp. 70, 76–77).

Kyrgyzstan has existed as an independent country since the December 1991 dissolution of the USSR and creation of the Commonwealth of Independent States. The country's 4.4 million people are only 38 percent urban, with more than half a million in the capital city of Bishkek (renamed from Frunze) and the rest spread throughout six oblasts, or provinces (Table 19.1). But the population is not homogeneous in ethnicity. Second only to Kazakhstan in Russian population, Kyrgyzstan is 21 percent Russian and only 52 percent Kyrgyz, although the latter group was able to attain majority status in their republic between 1979 and 1989. Uzbeks make up an additional 12 percent of the population (Table 19.2).

The standard of living for people in Kyrgyzstan suggests a profile typical of an underdeveloped country: high birthrate, moderately high infant mortality (fourth highest in former USSR), and wages significantly lower than the USSR average. Material well-being is also lower than for many other regions of the former USSR. Kyrgyz observers complained of underinvestment

Table 19.1   Territory and Population of Kyrgyzstan

Region	Territory (sq. km.)	Population (as of 1/1/91)	Urban (%)	Rural (%)	Density per sq. km.
City of Bishkek	n/a	642,000	99.4	0.6	?
Dzhal-Abad Oblast	39,500	782,000	29.5	70.5	19.8
Issyk-Kul Oblast	43,500	427,000	32.6	67.4	9.8
Naryn Oblast	47,300	260,000	21.0	79.0	5.5
Osh Oblast	38,100	1,322,000	27.5	72.5	34.7
Talas Oblast	11,400	198,000	16.5	83.5	17.4
Chu Oblast	18,700	791,000	28.6	71.4	42.3
Kyrgyzstan (total)	198,500	4,422,000	38.1	61.9	22.3
as % of Central Asia*	4.97	8.67			
as % of USSR (1991)	0.89	1.52			

Source: Goskomstat USSR, Nar. khoz. SSSR 1990, pp. 68-73; data are as of 1-1
* Central Asia here refers to five republics, including Kazakhstan.

and inequities during the Soviet period, but central planners in Moscow seemed to regard Central Asia as a type of sinkhole in the national economy, plagued by low labor productivity and tribal control of the local communist parties. The fact that employment was largely agricultural or in low value-added raw materials sectors did little to enhance the economic indicators for Kyrgyzstan.

Physical Geography of Kyrgyzstan

Kyrgyzstan is a high country, with an average elevation of 2,750 meters above sea level. In the 1850s, Russian explorer Peter Semyonov finally reached his goal of visiting the Tien Shan Mountains and wrote of the over-whelming beauty of the region. A later explorer, Nikolai Przhevalsky (for whom the wild horse is named), loved the land so much, he asked that his grave be placed along the shores of Lake Issyk-kul (in Kyrgyz, Yzyk-kol). The parallel-running ranges of the Tien Shan system include 28 peaks reaching over 4,500 m each, with Victory Peak (Pobedy) the highest at 7,439 m (Figure 19.1). The high elevations create a rich group of glaciers, with the largest (Inyl'chek on the Khan-Tengri Massif) forming an area of 583 square kilometers. From the ice and snow of the mountains flow a number of rivers that have significance for the Kyrgyz economy and for agriculture beyond the Kyrgyzstan borders. These include the Naryn (616 kilometers long; drainage

Table 19.2   Major Ethnic Groups in Kyrgyzstan (1979 and 1989)

Ethnic Group	Number, 1979	% of Total	Number, 1989	% of Total	Change, 1979-89
Kyrgyz	1,687,382	47.90	2,228,482	52.34	32%
Russian	911,703	25.88	916,543	21.53	1%
Uzbek	426,194	12.10	550,095	12.92	29%
Ukrainian	109,324	3.10	108,027	2.54	-1%
German	101,057	2.87	101,198	2.38	0%
Tatar	71,744	2.04	70,068	1.65	-2%
Dungan	26,661	0.76	36,925	0.87	38%
Uighur	29,817	0.85	36,779	0.86	23%
Tajik	23,209	0.66	33,842	0.79	46%
Korean	14,481	0.41	18,341	0.43	27%
Azeri	17,207	0.49	15,775	0.37	-8%
Jew	6,312	0.18	5,604	0.13	-11
Other	97,741	2.77	136,076	3.20	39%
Total	3,522,832	100	4,257,755	100	

Source: Goskomstat, Nationality Composition of the Population, 1989, pp. 87-89.

area, 50,000 sq km), Talas (294 km; drainage area, 10,800 sq km), and Chu (221 km; drainage area, 22,550 sq km). The Naryn, which becomes the Syr Darya in Uzbekistan, is supposed to feed into the Aral Sea, but water withdrawn for irrigation along its length has contributed to the Aral Sea environmental disaster (see Chapters 16 and 18). Thus, the June 23, 1990, agreement pledging mutual cooperation to save the Aral Sea was signed by the president of the Kirghiz SSR along with representatives of the other Central Asian republics.

The climate of Kyrgyzstan is arid steppe in lowland areas and cooler and variably wetter in the mountainous regions. A continental climate regime, with great variation of temperatures, is found throughout. Winter average daily temperatures range from a low of −28°C (at Ak-Sai in the Tien Shan range) to a high of −1.5°C (Jalal-Abad). July average daily temperatures reach 27.5°C at Lenin-Dzhol in western Kyrgyzstan.

Natural vegetation includes desert and semi-desert; shrub-steppe; broadleaf forests of maple, birch, and aspen on mid-elevation mountain slopes; coniferous forests higher in the mountains; and alpine meadows and alpine tundra at still higher elevations. Over 120 species of trees and bushes are found in Kyrgyzstan, including spruce and fir, mountain ash, cottonwood, juniper, honeysuckle, and sweetbrier. In all, 633,000 hectares of the country are forest covered, with a total estimated volume of 18.9 million cubic meters of wood (Anuchin et al., 1985, pp. 420–421). Numerous wild nut and fruit trees are a particular feature of central-western Kyrgyzstan, and Lake Issyk-kul, which takes up 12 percent of Kyrgyzstan's territory, contains 346 species of aquatic plants (Sokolov and Syroechevskiy, 1990, p. 366).

Constraints on Development

The high mountains that cover much of Kyrgyzstan have made infrastructure development expensive and limited population to areas of lower elevations, such as the main cities of Bishkek (Frunze), Osh, Naryn, and Jalal-Abad. At the same time, they have provided Kyrgyzstan with an exploitable mineral base, good hydroelectric potential, and rich habitat for flora and fauna. Kyrgyzstan in 1990 had less than ten percent of the paved roads in Central Asia and remains particularly disadvantaged in railroad development, with less than two percent of the total rail lines of Central Asia.

Aridity is another limiting factor for economic development; most crop production in Kyrgyzstan is irrigated, and the process is not done efficiently. Salinization of soils and further reduction of water flow to the Aral Sea may result if Kyrgyzstan attempts to expand its agriculture on irrigated land. Low investment rates in industry and a low standard of living, both legacies of the past, will also constrain future economic development efforts as Kyrgyzstan endeavors to improve the well-being of a population that is still essentially rural and young. Growth pressure caused by high birthrates and large family size means that the need for jobs will increase, while at the same time demand for land reform and limited housing availability will cause more pressures to mount among competing ethnic groups. Indications are that the economy of Kyrgyzstan will continue to be agriculture-dependent for some years ahead. From 1970 to 1988, the share of national product in current rubles attributable to industry fell by nine percent, while agriculture grew by four percent (Goskomstat, 1988, p. 9).

Like other portions of Central Asia, Kyrgyzstan is subject to strong seismic activity. The region from Bishkek eastward through Lake Issyk-Kul to the Chinese border is especially vulnerable, as is the area south and west of the Toktogul Reservoir. A severe earthquake struck the latter region in 1946.

Kyrgyzstan's Economy and Resources

The republic's domestic product has derived from four main sources: irrigated cotton and grain agriculture, livestock raising, mining, and some machine-building for the textile and energy industries. However, Kyrgyzstan has not traditionally created a large share of output even within Central Asia for most of these categories, let alone any significant portion of USSR production, with the exception of a few selected areas in which Kyrgyzstan has concentrated: wool production, horse-raising, refined sugar (from sugar beets), machinery for the meat industry, and electric motors.

Overall, agriculture is still the mainstay of the Kyrgyz economy: the republic produced in 1990 about 8.6 percent of Central Asia's grain (although only one percent of its cotton). Over one million hectares of arable land are irri-

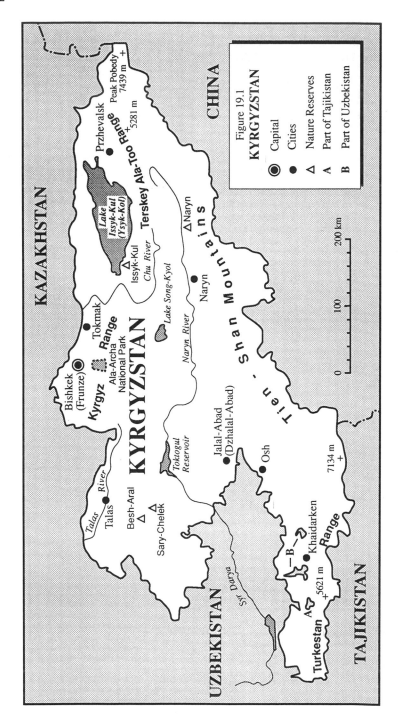

Figure 19.1
KYRGYZSTAN

◉ Capital
● Cities
△ Nature Reserves
A Part of Tajikistan
B Part of Uzbekistan

gated in Kyrgyzstan (Table 19.3), and water projects date back to 1939 with the construction of the Great Fergana Canal. The Naryn and Chu Rivers are the prime sources of water today, but Lake Issyk-kul has also been drawn down for local farming, causing a drop in the lake level and giving rise to the early environmental movement in Kyrgyzstan (Jancar, 1987, pp. 174–175).

In addition to cotton, winter and spring wheat, corn, barley, and oats are grown, as well as vegetables and tobacco. Kyrgyzstan has a large share of the goat, sheep, cattle, and horse herds of Central Asia. The crossing of Kurdish sheep with the Tien Shan breed has produced a high-yielding wool with fine texture. Cattle raising now accounts for 18 percent of Kyrgyzstan's agricultural output and 34 percent of the value of all livestock. Horses are bred not only as workers for shepherds, but also for production of *khymys* (a national drink of fermented mare's milk) and for horsemeat, and in higher elevations, yaks provide milk, hair, hides, and meat (notably yak sausage).

The steep mountains and numerous rivers of Kyrgyzstan create good conditions for hydroelectric development. From the 1960's through the present time, major dam projects have been completed on the Naryn River (Toktogul is the largest, with 1.2 million KW capacity), in Osh Oblast, and along the Chu River. These projects have allowed Kyrgyzstan to become an exporter of electricity to other regions of Central Asia.

The landscape also provides Kyrgyzstan with a number of exploitable mineral deposits, although oil and gas have never been significant in the republic and therefore must be imported. Some lignite deposits are worked, but non-ferrous metals have been the most important source of mining in-

Table 19.3   Agricultural Environmental Indices in Kyrgyzstan (1986-88)

Indicator	Kyrgyzstan	Percent of figure for USSR	Percent of figure for Central Asia
Arable land, 1987 (million ha.)	1.4	0.6	3.2
Irrigated land, 1987 (million ha.)	1.03	5.0	11
Irrigated land as a % of arable	73.4%		
Agri. water use, 1987 (million cu. m.)	8,765	5.8	8.5
Water lost in transport (% of 1988 total)	23%	127.0	87(a)
Water lost in transport (% of 1986 total)	20%	125.0	80(a)
Total fertilizer used, 1987 (1,000 tons)	296	1.0	8.5
Fertilizer used (kg/ha. of arable land)	211	172.0	263(b)

(a) Average weighted by 1987 agricultural water use.
(b) Without Kazakhstan, 74%.

Sources: Goskomstat SSSR, 1989;   Goskomstat SSSR, 1990;   Goskomstat USSR, Material Technical Security of USSR National Economy, 1988, pp. 57-8.

come to the republic. Kyrgyzstan has been the major contributor of mercury and antimony within the USSR, and since the USSR traditionally ranked as one of the major producers of mercury in the world, Kyrgyzstan's output of this material has been significant.

Antimony is a white metallic element used to add hardness to alloys and is important for production of semiconductors, explosives, and batteries. The Kadamdzhaiskiy Antimony Combine in southwest Kyrgyzstan is a center of production and in the 1930s was the first industrial site for antimony in the USSR (Bond, 1993). Found in association with antimony in the Álaiskiy Ridge, mercury is also mined in Kyrgyzstan and processed at the Khaidarken site (Figure 19.1). The nearby towns of Frunze Village, Khaidarken, Sovietskiy, and Chuvai are all based on antimony and mercury mining. New enterprises for production of these two metals were opened in the 1980s and again as recently as January 1993.

Lead, zinc, and tungsten are also mined in Kyrgyzstan, as well as sulfur, arsenic, asbestos, and salts, with sites often dating back to the 1930s. The Talas River valley and the Togoz-Too site along the Naryn River near Kazarman have deep lode gold deposits. Finally, Kyrgyzstan has apparently served as a major uranium producer for the former USSR. The ore is mined at Min-Kush and concentrates shipped to the Chu Valley processing plant. Kadzhi-Say on the south shore of Lake Issyk-kul was also an early uranium mining center (Dienes and Shabad, 1979, pp. 175–176). While some metallurgical processing occurs in Kyrgyzstan, most of the activities are extraction and production of ore concentrates, which are then sent elsewhere for finished production, thus perpetuating the colonial nature of the economic base. Kyrgyzstan has announced that it is exploring ways to establish diplomatic ties with South Africa in order to share mining technology, as South Africa is another major antimony and uranium producer (*Nezavisimaya gazeta*, January 29, 1993, p. 3).

Dangers to the Kyrgyzstan Environment

Just as the republic's raw materials–based economy reflects the situation throughout Central Asia, the litany of environmental damage to Kyrgyzstan may seem familiar: land degradation from improper irrigation; poisoning of air and water with pesticides, herbicides, and fertilizers; air pollution in urban areas; loss of habitat and wildlife due to expansion of domestic herds; and probable damage to local ecosystems from mining and livestock waste.

Problems Related to Agriculture

Crop production has been pried out of the arid environment only through heavy use of chemicals and diverted irrigation water. Kyrgyzstan has about 3.2 percent of the arable land in Central Asia but 11 percent of the irrigated land of the region. The share of arable land that is under irrigation in the republic is about 74 percent. Typical of Central Asia, irrigation canals are merely dug in the earth and a furrow system used to deliver water; thus, evaporation and seepage cause a large loss of water. The situation worsened from 1986 to 1988, as official data reported that water lost in transportation grew from 20 to 23 percent of total water use (Table 19.3). The result is not only water loss, but also salt deposits left on soils. Goskomstat reported that 15.6 percent of the arable land in the Kirgiz SSR had become salinized by 1985. On the whole, Central Asia uses from 5.7 to 10 cubic meters of water to produce a kilogram of raw cotton, much higher than for many other cotton-producing areas of the world (Rumer, 1989, p. 67; Wolfson, 1990, p. 31).

Also associated with cotton production has been large scale use of chemicals. In Kyrgyzstan, the average amount of fertilizer per hectare of arable land is 211 kilograms, less than other Central Asian republics, except for Kazakhstan, but much higher than the USSR average use. Application of mineral fertilizers is particularly high in Osh Oblast, where cotton creates 33% of the regional value of agriculture. One Kyrgyz source states that in 1982, for each hectare of cotton in Osh Oblast, 500–700 kg of nitrogen fertilizers, 1,000 kg. of phosphorous, and 300–400 of potassium were used, a rate far above Kyrgyzstan national averages, which include usage on other types of crops (Oruzbaev, 1982, p. 225).

Because of the prevalence of weeds in cotton fields, herbicides began to be used in Kyrgyzstan in 1963. The chemical Butifos, which defoliated cotton fields, was banned in 1987, but exceptions are still allowed for its use (Bond, 1990, p. 434; Pryde, 1991, p. 104). Oruzbaev notes that forty types of disease and pests are prevalent in Kyrgyzstan, particularly affecting cotton, sugar beets, and tobacco crops, and necessitated the use of sixty different pesticides over an area in excess of 900,000 hectares. Despite the fact that DDT was banned in the USSR in 1972, residues remain in the soil: in Osh Oblast, concentrations of DDT in the soil reached five times maximum permissible levels (Goskompriroda, 1989, p. 83), and 32 percent of soil in the Chu Valley is contaminated with DDT. As late as 1989, other pesticide use was still averaging 3.6 kilogram per hectare on arable land in Kyrgyzstan (Mnatsakanian, 1992, p. 92).

According to the United Nations Environmental Program, more than 99 percent of pesticides usually move into local ecosystems, while only 1 percent of the chemicals actually reach the target pests. Not surprisingly, water in Kyrgyzstan has shown some level of contamination, with most water bodies there containing 4 to 6 times the maximum permitted concentration of toxics (Komarov, 1978, p. 36). Food has been affected as well, with almost 2 percent of food tested in 1988 showing pesticide residue (Goskomstat, 1989, p. 101).

Air and Water Pollution

Bishkek and Osh are both included on the list of the most polluted cities in the former USSR, but Kara-Balta and Tokmak were also noted in 1989 as exceeding maximum permissible concentrations of air pollutants. In addition to typical air pollutants of particulates, sulfur dioxide, carbon monoxide, nitrous oxide, and hydrocarbons, local impacts of mercury pollutants associated with metallurgical operations also occur. In the vicinity of the Khaidarken smelter, 15,700 tons of smoke contaminated with mercury polluted the atmosphere, sometimes with concentrations up to 55 times the maximum permissible amount. Benz(a)pirenes from coal burning in urban areas caused pollution in Bishkek and Tokmak, although in all, automotive emissions accounted for half the pollutants in the capital city (Mnatsakanian, 1992, p. 88).

As noted, agricultural pursuits appear to be the source of much water pollution in Kyrgyzstan, but some wastewater from industrial activities affects the environment as well. Industrial activities in Bishkek, Dzhalal-Abad, and Osh produced the most water pollution, and Goskomstat reported that the major rivers of Kyrgyzstan (the Chu and Naryn) experienced increasing levels of pollutants each year, particularly with oil, copper, ammonia, and nitrites (Mnatsakanian, 1992, p. 91). The type of industry pursued in Kyrgyzstan (metallurgical, heavy machinery, meatpacking) suggests that placement of anti-pollution technologies will be an expensive prospect for the republic.

Problems Related to Mineral Exploitation

The types of non-ferrous substances mined or processed in Kyrgyzstan are particularly dangerous to the environment. Four of these (mercury, arsenic, lead, and antimony) are extremely toxic substances to humans. Many of these metals have carcinogenic effects or impacts on the human central nervous system, as well as on brain and kidney functions.

Use of these substances creates environmental damage in several ways. In the mining phase, there is surface destruction of soils (especially harmful with open-pit mining, as is the case for coal output in Kyrgyzstan), land subsidence, and contamination of lake-water and groundwater with metals and acids. In the second stage of ore concentration (which also occurs in Kyrgyzstan), slag heaps and tailings are produced, in addition to chemical residues released into the atmosphere or water supply. The mercury smelter at Khaidarken has created levels of mercury 100 times the maximum permissible amount in the ground near the smelting operation (Goskompriroda, 1989, p. 89). Gold and lead, which are both mined in Kyrgyzstan, are particularly conducive to waste material creation. Average grade gold ore (.00033%) produces an amount of waste almost equal to the weight of ore excavated, and average grade lead (2.5%) produces 96 tons of waste (including overburden) for every ton of ore mined to obtain lead.

Andrew Bond has estimated that the USSR republics were experiencing a declining rate of recovery from mining ores in the 1980s, as the best reserves were depleted (Bond, 1990, p. 427). This argument may be confirmed by the 1989 Goskompriroda report that stated that there has been a yearly increase in mining waste throughout the USSR. Restoration of mined land is also badly lagging. In Kyrgyzstan, only 6 percent of the disturbed land was reclaimed as of 1988, a lower figure than the unimpressive USSR average of 8 percent (Goskompriroda, 1989, p. 98).

Problems of Habitat Loss and Decreases in Wildlife

While many mining activities exist in the mountains of Kyrgyzstan not far from pristine alpine areas, the major source of habitat loss is expansion of domestic livestock herds. The republic has traditionally enjoyed a wealth of highland plant and animal species representative of Himalayan biotypes.

Many of these are now endangered and some may already be extinct. The 1985 Kirghiz SSR Red Book (*Krasnaya kniga*) of endangered and threatened species listed thirteen species of mammals, 3 reptiles, 1 fish, 5 insects, 20 birds, and 65 plants. The USSR Red Book of 1985 listed 15 species of endangered flora in the Kirghiz Republic, including pomegranate, Semenov pine, Olga mountain ash, and several species of wild tulip.

The amount of land under protected status in Kyrgyzstan totals about 3 percent of the republic's land base (Table 19.4). Although Kyrgyzstan has only 5 percent of the land area of Central Asia (including Kazakhstan), it contributes 8 percent of the region's land in reserve and national park status. The largest reserve is the Besh-Aral, and the Sary-Chelek Reserve is accorded U.N. biosphere status. Additionally, there is one national park, Ala-Archa, created in 1976 in the mountains immediately south of Bishkek (Figure 19.2).

Table 19.4   Preserved Areas in Kyrgyzstan

Type of Preserve(a)	Number	Total area(b)	Average size(b)	% of Republic(c)
Nature Reserves (zapovedniki)	4	2195.53	548.88	1.11
Zapovedniki that are Biosphere Reserves	1	238.68		0.12
Biosphere Reserves, non-zapovedniki	1	118.46	118.46	0.06
National Parks	1	194.00	194.00	0.10
Natural Preserves (zakazniki)	66	3092.00	46.85	1.56
Total	72	5599.99	77.78	2.82

Nature Reserves (date created)	Hectares
Besh-Aralskiy (1979)	116732
Issyk-Kul (1976; 1948)	34753
Naryn (1983)	44200
Sary-Chelek (1959)	23868
Total	219553

National Parks	Hectares
Ala-Archa (1976)	19400

(a) For the definition of each type of preserve, see Appendix 1.2.
(b) In square kilometers.
(c) Area of Kyrgyzstan equals 198,500 square kilometers.

Source: Pryde (1991).

Figure 19.2   Entrance to the Ala-Archa National Park, a few kilometers south of Bishkek. This alpine park is apt to be impacted by increasing visitor use in the future.

Illegal hunting of animals for skin and capture of larger mammals for the zoo trade have reduced the numbers of fauna, but loss of habitat from commercial herding has been the most serious threat. In the case of one endangered species, the snow leopard (Figure 19.3), which sits at the top of the food chain in the Tien Shan Mountains and depends on wild ungulates such as argali for its main prey, reduction of grazing lands for wild species has had significant adverse repercussions (Braden, 1986, p. 228). Geographers from the Kyrgyz Academy of Sciences reported that there has been a decline of 20–30 percent of wild pasturage since the 1970s, with wild grasses being replaced by poorer quality flora as domestic sheep and goat herds are increased and moved further up in elevation. Academy of Sciences members have argued for creation of a new nature preserve in the valley of the Sary-chat-Irtash Rivers, and in October 1989, delegates at the Sixth International Symposium on Preservation of Snow Leopards in Alma-Ata passed a resolution calling for establishment of a new reserve in Kyrgyzstan in the Tien-Shan range adjoining the Tomur reserve of western China.

Social and Political Change in Kyrgyzstan

Until its recent declaration of independence, the Kirghiz SSR managed its environmental affairs at the local level through various ministries (such as agriculture or water supply), through the Kirghiz State Committee on Forestry, through the Commission for Protection of Nature under the Kirghiz branch

Figure 19.3   A young snow leopard (*Uncia uncia*), rare and decreasing in numbers in the mountains of Kyrgyzstan, even though it is protected.

of the Academy of Sciences, and through central organs in Moscow such as Goskompriroda (the State Committee on Nature Protection). The Kyrgyzstan Embassy in Washington reports that environmental matters are now governed from Bishkek via the Kyrgyzstan State Committee on the Environment, chaired in 1993 by Iskander Muratalin. With the entry of Kyrgyzstan into the United Nations in March 1992, the republic takes on new responsibilities via the various environmental programs of the U.N. and may begin to endorse international environmental agreements previously pledged by the USSR government.

Additionally, non-governmental organizations dealing with environmental protection have arisen in Kyrgyzstan, as elsewhere in the former USSR. In addition to the existing Academy of Sciences Commission noted previously, which was originally formed to combat the decline in the water level of Lake Issyk-kul, in 1989 the Club of Ecologists was founded in Bishkek. One issue that may prove of concern is the post-independence migration of Russian and Ukrainian scientists out of Kyrgyzstan. The scientific community in Kyrgyzstan included many non-Kyrgyz and has been quite active in calling for preservation of lake and alpine areas. Increasingly, the burden of pressuring for environmental amelioration will need to be carried by indigenous interest groups and scientists.

The Soviet Republic of Kirghizia did not have a large budget for environmental concerns. Rubles spent on environmental improvement by the republic in 1988 totaled less than three percent of such investment for Central Asia, and only 0.4 percent for the USSR. The question now is whether an independent Kyrgyzstan will be able to afford to improve its environmental record. Ze'ev Wolfson noted, "Environmental protection is among the first victims of inflation and anarchy. . . . The task of creating an ecological infrastructure is as dependent on the progress in the country's overall economy as the development of industry" (Wolfson, 1990, p. 39).

The initial effects of the devolution of the USSR have been devastating for the Kyrgyzstan economy. In 1992, overall production fell by 21 percent, and the harvest declined by 25 percent (Lantsman, 1992, p. 7). Deliveries of fertilizers from other republics have decreased, and market ties are now uncertain. For President Askar Akaev, the idea of breaking loose economically from the CIS may seem remote, since Kyrgyzstan may for a long time remain dependent on old networks. But these gloomy scenarios may be mitigated by the aggressiveness with which Akaev seems to be pursuing new economic linkages. In addition to strengthened agreements signed in 1992 with former USSR republics, Kyrgyzstan joined ECO in November of 1992 (the Economic Cooperation Organization, formed in 1964 by Iran, Pakistan, and Turkey). ECO's plans call for lowering tariffs among member states, creating an investment bank and a joint airline, and allowing movement of goods through Karachi ports. The agreement (signed by four other Muslim republics formerly within the USSR as well) may signal the revival of the pan-Turkic notions popular just after the Bolshevik Revolution. Kyrgyzstan has also looked east to China and created two free economic zones—in Naryn and Osh Oblasts—to encourage movement of goods in and out of China (Savenkov, 1992).

President Akaev may be planning to make up for the scarcity of capital at home, but the issue for the environmental health of the republic centers on the kinds of investment that should be encouraged. Further expansion of agriculture with imported technology from China may not be benign if it requires increased irrigation under inefficient but cheap conditions. A mining agreement with South Africa may open up further areas of the Tien Shan system to exploration and development, and if one looks at the materials that Kygyzstan could sell at highest profit to the outside world, gold, uranium, and opium seem to command the highest profit margin. The newspaper *Moskovskiye novosti* reported in October of 1991 that some factions in Kyrgyzstan were calling for the establishment of new poppy plantations for legal opium production. When this was tried last in the 1960s, 40 percent of the crop was stolen regularly for narcotics smuggling into Russia (*CDSP,* November 13, 1991, p. 29).

Development of environmentally benign forms of tourism (ecotourism) may yet occur to take advantage of the Kyrgyzstan mountains and alpinism opportunities, but an infrastructure that caters to foreign tourists will need to be created. The potential for international tourism is greatest in the northeastern portion of the republic, from Bishkek and Ala-Archa National Park to Lake Issyk-kul and Peak Pobedy. Kyrgyzstan will have to be wary of the experience of Nepal and other Himalayan locales, however, where visitors have severely affected the landscape and culture.

But Kyrgyzstan has shown some signs of positive independent thinking: Akaev was elected with more than 95% of the vote, and the republic is the only one in Central Asia in which the old Communist Party hierarchy does not maintain some control (in fact, the party was disbanded in Kyrgyzstan after the August 1991 coup attempt in Moscow). Land reform and privatization have been referred to many times by Akaev as priorities and may lead to more efficient use of agricultural resources, especially when coupled with a realistic charge for water use. The pace of land redistribution will be intentionally slow; Akaev stated that land reform will occur over a five year period, experimentally at first on 20 percent of former state land, with local decisions made about the system of allocation (*CDSP*, June 24, 1992, p. 27). However, while the president envisions a future in which thousands of peasant-owned farms operate efficiently and form the basis for a new "civil society," accomplishing the new tenure will not be easy due to emerging ethnic tensions.

As one example of the latter, Kyrgyzstan has thus far resisted the temptation to pass land laws favorable to the titular ethnic group; the new Land Code of the republic states that the land belongs to "Kyrgyz and citizens of other ethnic origins" (Olcott, 1992). But the government may have trouble convincing the other nationalities in Kyrgyzstan, notably the Uzbeks, who make up 13 percent of the population nationally (but 26 percent in Osh Oblast, just across the border from Uzbekistan). In May 1990, an Uzbek-language newspaper in Osh published a story that the government was about to make a land and housing allocation that would favor ethnic Kyrgyz and disenfranchise Uzbeks. The resulting violence between the two groups necessitated the intervention of Soviet troops and resulted in hundreds of deaths (Razgulyayev, 1990). The mixture of Kyrgyz and Uzbeks both in Osh Oblast and across the now-international border in Uzbekistan's Andizhan Oblast demonstrates that the unfortunate heritage of Soviet imposed boundaries and the resultant division of endemic ethnic groups will haunt the Central Asian republics for years to come.

Political turmoil, coupled with rising Islamic fervor, old tribal enmities, and new political parties under formation in Kyrgyzstan, means that the climate for stable economic reform and the opportunity to develop environmentally sound growth paths could remain only a distant goal. Yet Kyrgyzstan may eventually find both economic and spiritual benefits from maintaining the character of its ancient landscapes. The mythology of the Kyrgyz tells that the king of the mountain spirits created Lake Issyk-Kul as a place for his bride to gaze and admire her own beauty. Thus, the lake is called "The Mirror in the Sky" by local people, an apt symbol for a republic that reflects all that is both promising and portentous for the future environment of Central Asia.

Bibliography

(Note: CDSP = Current Digest of the Soviet Press.)

Anuchin, N.P. et al. 1985. *Lesnaya entsiklopediya*. Vol. 1. Moscow: Sovetskaya Entsiklopediya.

Bond, Andrew, chair. 1990. "Panel on the State of the Soviet Environment at the Start of the Nineties." *Soviet Geography*, vol. 31, no. 6, pp. 401–468.

———. 1993. "Antimony and Mercury Processing in Russia and Tajikistan." *Post-Soviet Geography*, vol. 34, no. 7, pp. 467–474.

Borodin, A.M., and Syroechevskiy, E.E. 1983. *Zapovedniki SSSR*. Moscow: Lesnaya Promyshlennost'.

Braden, Kathleen E. 1986. "Economic Development in Six Regions of Snow Leopard Habitat in the USSR." In *Proceedings of the Fifth International Snow Leopard Symposium*, Helen Freeman, ed. International Snow Leopard Trust and Wildlife Institute of India, Bombay: Conway Printing, pp. 227–246.

Dienes, L. and Shabad, T. 1979. *The Soviet Energy System*. New York: John Wiley.

Goskompriroda. 1989. *Doklad: Sostoyaniye prirodnoy sredy v SSSR v 1988 godu*. Moscow.

Goskomstat Kirgizskoy SSR. 1989. *Narodnoye khozyaystvo Kirgizskoy SSR v 1988 g*. Frunze: "Kyrgyzstan."

Goskomstat, SSSR. 1989. *Okhrana okruzhayushchey sredy i ratsional'noye ispol'zovaniye prirodnykh resursov v SSSR*. Moscow.

———. 1991. *Narodnoye khozyaystvo SSSR v 1990 g*. Moscow: Finansy i Statistika.

Jancar, Barbara. 1987. *Environmental Management in the Soviet Union and Yugoslavia*. Durham, NC: Duke University Press.

Komarov, Boris. 1980. *The Destruction of Nature in the Soviet Union*. White Plains, NY: M.E. Sharpe.

Koshkarev E.P. 1989. *Snezhniy bars v Kirgizii*. Frunze: Ilim.

Lantsman, M. 1992. In *Nezavisimaya gazeta*, October 13, p. 3, on Bishkek summit, reported in *CDSP*, vol. 44, no. 41, November 11, p. 7.

Lewis, R.A., ed. 1992. *Geographic Perspectives on Soviet Central Asia*. London: Routledge.

Ministerstvo sel'skogo khozyaystva SSSR. 1985. *Krasnaya kniga SSSR*. Moscow: Lesnaya Promyshlennost.

Mnatsakanian, Ruben. 1992. *Environmental Legacy of the Former Soviet Republics*. Edinburgh: Centre for Human Ecology.

Nahaylo, Bohan, and Swoboda, Victor. 1990. *Soviet Disunion: A History of the Nationalities Problem in the USSR*. New York: The Free Press.

Olcott, Martha Brill. 1992. "Spotlight on Kygyzstan." *Surviving Together*, ISAR, Winter, pp. 14–16.

Oruzbaev, B.O. 1982. *Kirgizskaya sovetskaya sotsialisticheskaya respublika* (Kyrgyzskoy sovetskoy entskilopediya). Frunze.

Otobraev, E.O., and Ryazanetsev, S.N. 1970. *Kirgiziya*. Moscow: Mysl'.

Pryde, Philip R. 1991. *Environmental Management in the Soviet Union*. Cambridge: Cambridge University Press.

Razgulyayev, Yu. 1990. "In an Emergency Situation" (Kirgiz-Uzbek Riots). *Pravda*, June 19, p. 2, as reported in *CDSP*, vol. 42, no. 25, July 25, pp. 14–15.

———. 1991. "Politics Abhors a Vacuum." *Pravda*, November 5, p. 2, as reported in *CDSP*, vol. 43, no. 44, December 4, pp. 18–19.

Rotar, Igor. 1993. "Vzorvetsya li Srednyaya Aziya?" *Nezavisimaya gazeta*, January 21, p. 5.

Rumer, Boris Z. 1989. *Soviet Central Asia: A Tragic Experiment*. Boston: Unwin Hyman.

Savenkov, Y. 1992. "Bishkek and Beijing: Ties That Go Back 2,000 Years." *Izvestia,* May 15, p. 5, as reported in *CDSP,* vol. 44, no. 20, June 17, p. 18.

Sokolov, V.E., and Syroechevskiy E.E. 1990. *Zapovedniki SSSR* (Zapovedniki Sredney Azii i Kazakhstana). Moscow: Mysl'.

Wolfson, Zeev. 1990. "Central Asian Environment: A Dead End." *Environmental Policy Review,* vol. 4, no. 1, January, pp. 29–46.

20

Tajikistan

Sharon Eicher

Tajikistan is a small, underdeveloped, but resource-rich country of 5.1 million persons and 143,100 square kilometers. It is mostly mountainous, with developed irrigation and agriculture in the inter-montane valleys. Environmental problems in the country are legacies of poor Soviet management of the natural world and the USSR's compulsion to transform nature. The Soviet government established a conservation ministry but was unsupportive of local requests to close down polluting industries. Today, problems of air and water pollution are directly impacting the human population, and illnesses are increasing. Overuse of agricultural chemicals and secondary salinization are making the land unfit for crops.

Tajikistan inherits a situation in which it is financially burdened and must choose between keeping industries open that pollute heavily or losing much-needed income. Resolving this problem, however, was not even under discussion in 1993, as political stability had not yet been achieved.

Ethnicity and History

Of Tajikistan's total population, 3.2 million are ethnically Tajik. Its population is ethnically mixed, consisting of 62% Tajik, 24% Uzbek, 8% Russian, and 6% other nationalities (Table 20.1). It is bordered by the former Uzbek and Kyrgyz Republics and by China and Afghanistan.

The ethnonym Tojik identifies descendants of Indo-European Iranian tribes who settled throughout the Middle Asian regions of Turkestan, Afghanistan, and India. The Iranian tribes first came to this region from 2000–1000 B.C. Pre-Tajik human habitation dates back as far as the Lower Paleolithic Period, 200,000 to 400,000 years B.C. (*Bolshaya*, 1983).

Alexander the Great, known as Iskander in Central Asia, conquered this area in 329 B.C. His wife Roxanne was reputedly a Bactrian and is claimed by

Table 20.1   Ethnic Diversity of Tajikistan

Ethnic Group	Population (1000s) 1959	1989	% Change, 1959-89	% of Total in 1989
Tajiks	1,051	3,172	201.8	62.3
Uzbeks	454	1,198	163.9	23.5
Russians	263	388	47.5	7.6
Tatars	57	72	26.3	1.4
Kyrgyz	26	64	146.1	1.3
Ukrainians	27	41	51.9	.8
Germans	33	33	.1	.6
Others	70	125	78.6	2.5
Total	1,981	5,093		

Source: Data adapted from Schwartz, 1991, p. 246.

the Tajiks. One of the most significant events for Central Asia was its conversion to Islam, which was introduced in the 8th century. Sunni Islam of the Hanifi School was officially adopted, replacing Zoroastrianism, Buddhism, Manichaeism, and Nestorian Christianity. A minority of the Islamic population today practices Shiism. Later came the Mongol-Tatar invasion of 1219–21. The Tajik-populated cities of Bukhoro, Samarqand and Khujand fell to Chingiz Khan (Ghengiz Khan) in 1220.

The reign of Timur, or Tamerlane, (1336–1405), was a prosperous period based on wealth acquired from commerce along the Silk Route. Tamerlane's empire was centered in Samarqand, and his court was served by Persian, or Tajik, scribes. Both Alexander and Timur became ancestral heroes of the Tajiks.

Russia became interested in expansion into this region in the 18th century, but the real conquest of Turkestan began after 1847. Territorial disputes made the khanates vulnerable to colonialism, and Russia was able to quickly subjugate the small Central Asian states. In 1868 Samarqand and Bukhoro became vassal states; Khiva followed in 1873, and Quqon (Kokand) fell in 1876 (Holdsworth, 1959).

In 1875 Russia and Britain established borders between Turkestan, a colony of Russia, and Afghanistan, which was controlled by the British. This artificial border drawn by Imperial Britain and Russia left Tajik-speaking people in both countries. The territory of the Tajiks in the 1880s was further subdivided; parts lay in the Eastern Bokharan Khanate and in what are now Syr Darya and Farghona (Fergana) Oblasts of Uzbekistan.

Following the Russian Revolution, Turkestan became nominally Soviet. By late 1918, Tajikistan was included in the Turkestan Autonomous Soviet Socialist Republic (ASSR). The small village of Dushanbe became the political center.

Central Asian armed resistance to the Soviet takeover took place through the Basmachi Revolt. Much of the rebellion was located in southern and central Tajikistan, and the area was not fully brought under Soviet control until 1926.

The Law on National Demarcation of Central Asia was passed by the Executive Central Committee of the USSR on October 27, 1924. The existence of the Tadzhik Soviet Socialist Republic was ratified in February, 1931. Unfortunately, its boundaries did not have a close correlation to where most Tajiks actually lived. At the time, 52% of all Tajiks in Turkestan lived in the Bukhoro area, which became part of Uzbekistan (*Bolshaya, 1983*). Similarly, a great many Uzbeks lived within the Tajik SSR boundaries.

Following the USSR's dissolution in 1991, the Central Asian republics retained the territories assigned to them in the 1930s by the Nationalities Commissariat. The former Tajik Republic joined the Commonwealth of Independent States on December 30, 1991. For the first time, this was an independent country with an emerging national identity. In seeking recognition as an autonomous state, Tajikistan emphasized its membership in the CIS; adherence to international law; loyalty to the U.N. Charter, the Helsinki Act, and the Paris Charter; and the inviolability of its borders.

Tajikistan is the only non-Turkic Central Asian state. All the others are more closely tied to the Turkic and Mongolian tribes that entered the region after the Indo-European, Iranian (Persian) steppe tribes. Tajiks are the only Persian speakers in the Commonwealth of Independent States. Dari, spoken in North Afghanistan; Farsi, spoken in Iran; Pashto; and Tajik make up the Iranian family of languages spoken in Central and South Asia. While sharing the same linguistic family with the Iranians, Tajiks are religiously more closely tied to their Turkic neighbors, who are also Sunni; most Iranians are Shiite.

Geographical Characteristics

The dominant geographic characteristics of Tajikistan are aridity, mountainous topography, great diversity of landscapes, and remoteness. The country is subdivided into five oblasts, or provinces. These are Badakhshoni Kuhi (Gorno-Badakhshan) in the east, Khujand (Leninabad) to the north, Qurghonteppa (Kurgan Tyube) and Kulob (Kulyab) to the southwest, and the Karotegin region in central Tajikistan around the capital city of Dushanbe. Much of the country is drained by the Vakhsh and Panj (Pyandzh) Rivers, which become the Amu-Darya in Uzbekistan (Figure 20.1).

The Khujand region extends deep into Uzbekistan and makes up part of the Fergana Valley. Khujand (formerly Leninabad) is the administrative center and predates Alexander the Great's visit in the 4th century B.C. It lies due north of Dushanbe, but the two cities are separated by the Zeravzhan Mountains. It is the country's second largest city, with a 1989 population of 160,000.

The upper portion of the Syr Darya runs through Khujand Province, providing irrigation water. The largest Uzbek population in Tajikistan lives in Khujand and the surrounding lowlands.

Below Khujand is the central Karotegin Province. Dushanbe, the national capital, lies in the western part of this region in a mountain rift between the Zeravshan Mountains and the foothills of the Peter the First (Petra Pervogo) Mountains. Dushanbe is situated in a valley drained by the Kofarnihon (Kafirnagan) River, at about 900 meters elevation. It had a population in 1989 of 595,000. Fifty kilometers away, the Hissar Mountains reach 4,000 meters, and farther to the east the Pamirs rise to over 7,000 meters.

In the southwestern portion of Tajikistan is Qurghonteppa (Kurgan Tyube) Province. The Vakhsh River lowland extends from the Nurek Reservoir southward to Qurghonteppa and is heavily irrigated. Much of the water pollution in Tajikistan flows to this area, delivered by the Panj (Pyandzh) and Vakhsh Rivers. Qurghonteppa's proximity to Afghanistan has made it a convenient crossing point for smugglers, and much of the unrest in the early 1990s occurred in this part of the country.

Kulob (Kulyab) is a small oblast to the east of Qurghonteppa. Kulob, its capital, is Tajikistan's third largest city, with about 77,000 persons. The oblast's southern border is the Panj River, and it lies within steppe and mountain-steppe regions. It is one of the economically least developed and poorest provinces of Tajikistan and is where in the early 1990s local warlords were opposing the pro-Communist leadership.

The autonomous republic of Badakhshoni Kuhi (Gorno-Badakhshan) accounts for almost half of the territory of Tajikistan. This region is little developed. Its mountains are home to various indigenous populations, collectively referred to as Pamiris, or Mountain Tajiks. The groups live in isolation from western Tajiks and may speak unrelated languages. The former USSR's highest peak, which rises to 7,495 meters (24,590 feet), is on its western border. The easternmost portion is mainly a high, arid plateau containing many lakes.

Tajikistan is arid with a continental climate that produces extreme temperature variations. The warmest areas are in the western temperate zone, specifically near Khujand, Qurghonteppa, and Kulob. Average daily temperatures here reach a summer high of 30°C, and they receive on average 230 to 240 frost-free days a year. The coldest region is in the southeast Pamirs, where winter temperatures can drop to −25°C (Mamadjonova, 1968).

Other climatic features are hot, desiccating winds and glaciation. Glaciers cover 8,470 km² of the land. The occasional hot, dry winds blow in the Fergana Valley and in southwestern Tajikistan and in extreme cases can cause dust storms and damage crops.

Natural Resources and Constraints to Development

There are 81 species of mammals in Tajikistan, including unique animals such as the Tibetan wolf, Eurasian otter, stone marten, lynx, jungle cat, snow leopard, Bokharan deer, Asiatic sheep, Argali sheep, Siberian ibex, and many small rodent species, such as Turkestan rat, jerboa, pika, and the Pamir vole (Mamadjonova, 1968). The republic also has 365 types of birds, 49 species of reptiles, and 40 species of fish. Its plant species exceed 5,000, although only 0.8 percent of the republic is forested. In order to help protect this biotic diversity, Tajikistan has created 16 nature preserves (Table 20.2).

Good agricultural land is a limited asset but has been turned into a liability in Tajikistan through poor management. Although irrigated farming has been extensively developed, much of Tajikistan's land is not arable and cannot be put into crops, leaving the country with a deficit of fertile lands. What little land is arable lies in the river valleys or intermontane basins and is subject to erosion and pollution.

Irrigated lands total about 945,000 hectares. These produce cotton, grapes, and silk or are in orchards. Cereals are grown on non-irrigated land. The irrigated land in Tajikistan, as elsewhere in Central Asia, is subject to salinization.

Tajikistan has a variety of mineral resources, which include lead, zinc, silver, and tungsten in the north; antimony, gold, salt, and fluorspar in the west; and gold in the east (Shabad, 1969). Much of its economy is based on mining these minerals.

The republic has a mixture of energy resources, including small amounts

Table 20.2   Preserved Areas in Tajikistan

Type of Preserve(a)	Number	Total area(b)	Average size(b)	% of Re- public(c)
Nature Reserves (zapovedniki)	3	855.68	285.23	0.60
Biosphere Reserves	0	0.00	0.00	0.00
National Parks	0	0.00	0.00	0.00
Natural Preserves (zakazniki)	13	8006.00	615.85	5.59
Total	16	8861.68	553.86	6.19

Nature Reserves (date created)	Hectares
Dashti-Dzhum (1983)	19700
Ramit (1959)	16168
Tigrovaya Balka (1938)	49700
Total	85568

(a) For the definition of each type of preserve, see Appendix 1.2.
(b) In square kilometers.
(c) The total area of Tajikistan is 143,100 square kilometers.

Source: Pryde (1991).

of coal, gas, oil and uranium and considerable hydroelectricity. The three fossil fuels are extracted only in small (and declining) amounts, production in all three being only about a third of what it was in 1970. Tajikistan extracts uranium but does not have the technology to enrich it. The country is now considering joint ventures for uranium enrichment with Middle Eastern states (FBIS, January 2, 1992).

Sixty percent of Soviet Central Asia's hydroelectric resources came from Tajikistan. Its energy production in 1990 totaled 18.1 billion kilowatt hours. The largest electricity producer at that time was the Nurek dam, which generated 80% of Tajikistan's electrical power (Figure 20.2). This power is used, in part, to refine aluminum. The Soviet Union had planned to expand hydropower by constructing twenty-one additional hydroelectric stations on the Vakhsh and Panj Rivers, but these plans now appear optimistic. Tajikistan's hydroelectric potential, which might be as high as 85 billion kWh, may be one of its major assets.

The republic sits in a seismically active area (Figure 20.3). The Nurek and other dams often experience tremors. Pressure from the weight of the dam and water places additional stress on what may be sensitive areas, making them more unstable. Tajikistan's worst recent earthquakes occurred in 1949 and 1989. The 1989 quake, in which 274 people died, registered 6.0 on the Richter Scale. The earthquake apparently undermined the integrity of a mountainside and loosened a landslide upon a village that was only 20 miles

Figure 20.2   The Nurek Dam on the Vakhsh River while under construction. This is the largest earthfill dam in the world. Photo by James Brune.

Figure 20.3 Fault scarp near the Vakhsh River in central Tajikistan. This area has strong tectonic activity. Photo by James Brune.

from Dushanbe (*Washington Post,* January 24 and 26, 1989). The 1949 earthquake was much worse; in that disaster, 12,000 persons died.

Population size will influence the effectiveness of Tajikistan's economic development and may become a burden upon the country's natural and economic resources. Population in Tajikistan increased by one-third in the ten year period from 1979 to 1989. Because of the high birthrate, the dependency ratio is very high, meaning that the working-age population must support an unusually high number of dependents. Family size averaged 6.5 persons, and the country must create jobs for today's children. Tajikistan has high unemployment now; if this situation doesn't change, then the forecast for the future is a further decrease in the standard of living.

Russians make up a significant portion of Tajikistan's professionals, skilled laborers, and doctors, even though they are only about 8% of the population. In the 1990s they began emigrating to other parts of Central Russia and Siberia, fleeing from perceived prejudice against non-Tajiks, social unrest, and implementation of the 1989 Tajik Language Law. Likewise, some better educated Tajiks have also fled from the political unrest of the early 1990s.

The employment situation in Tajikistan is unusual in that, while it is losing its specialists, it has an overabundance of labor. According to *Soviet Sociology,* (no. 4, 1991), only 13% of the working-age population is fully employed. Tajikistan must create an indigenous work force, both to create jobs for the current and future unemployed masses and to fill the void left by the specialized workers who have left the country.

The Environmental Situation

Tajikistan's environmental problems include salinized and overcultivated farmland, erosion, water supplies that are overconsumed or wasted through evaporation, inadequate purification of effluents, air pollution, and endangered wildlife species. The effects of many of these problems are not only damaging to natural communities; they are also directly harming the human population.

Water Resources

Tajikistan is in the headwaters of the Syr Darya and Amu Darya Rivers, which flow to the Aral Sea. Tajikistan's runoff is 51.7 km^3, or 44% of the runoff of Tajikistan, Uzbekistan, Kyrgyzstan, and Turkmenistan combined (Mnatsakanian, 1992). Chapters 16 and 18 have reported on the problem of the drying up of the Aral Sea. This problem doesn't affect Tajikistan directly, although the Tajiks contribute to the causes of the problem.

Water consumption in Tajikistan is 90.81% agricultural, 4.67% evaporation, 4.33% industry, and .14% residential and other uses. Most water goes to irrigating crops, but this agricultural usage harms water quality as salts are leeched out of fields. These flow into downstream water supplies or into newly created lakes that store used irrigation water.

The most significant chemical contamination of water in Tajikistan comes from industry. Reputedly, up to 50% of industrial purification systems are malfunctioning. This affects populations in Dushanbe, Khujand, Qurghon-teppa, and Tursunzade; that is, almost all the major cities. An example given by Goskompriroda is the Vakhsh Nitrogen Fertilizer Plant, which is 13 miles north of Qurghonteppa. There are no safeguards against pollution from this plant, and canal collectors do not work properly. As a result, sewage, chlorine, and nitrogen pollutants are absorbed into the subsoil and enter the underground drinking water supply. Among the other primary polluters in Tajikistan are the Kolkhozabad Cotton Combine, Tajik Aluminum Factory, and Dushanbe Cement Factory (Goskompriroda, 1989).

The Land

In addition to water pollution, cotton production has promoted weed infestation, the wilt virus, and cotton parasites and insects. Much of Tajikistan's available agricultural land is in cotton; it is second in production only to Uzbekistan. Although of great economic value, the present cotton monoculture has weakened the land. It has robbed it of microorganisms and nitrogen and left it salinized and laden with chemical pesticides. One report indicated that 123,700 hectares in Tajikistan were salinized (13% of all irrigated land). Of this area, 113,800 hectares were plowed fields; the rest was not in use as it was too salinized for agriculture (Goskompriroda, 1989).

Among the defoliants (agricultural herbicides) used, Butifos was the most popular. It was likened to Agent Orange in its effect by nationalist environmentalists. Butifos was banned in 1987 after being applied for 23 years, but some may still be used (Pryde, 1991, p. 104). The total amount of pesticides used in Tajikistan in 1987 was 17,359 metric tons. This averaged to 3.4 kg per person, but among the rural (agricultural) population, 6.3 kg per person (Goskompriroda, 1989). In terms of kilograms of pesticides per hectare used in 1986, Tajikistan, at 19.8, was the highest ranked republic and was many times higher than the USSR average of 2.1 (Yablokov, 1992, p. 15).

Pasture lands are overgrazed. Traditional herding was semi-nomadic, but when herding became collectivized, animal husbandry became a much-larger-scale operation. Landslides and erosion are two results of the land being overworked. There are 3.1 million hectares liable to erosion in the country, which is equal to 70% of agricultural lands (Goskompriroda, 1989).

Air Quality

The most serious forms of air pollution in Tajikistan consist of particulates, fluoride compounds, and motor vehicle emissions. Particulates originating from stationary sources in 1988 and 1989 equaled 53,300 and 42,700 tons, respectively (Mnatsakanian, 1992). On average, the concentrations of polluting substances are 1.2–1.9 times maximum health norms (Goskompriroda, 1989), and Dushanbe was on the list of the "most polluted Soviet cities" in 1989. There has been a small reduction in the amount of air pollutants in recent years, possibly resulting in part from the economic slowdown.

The source of the hydrogen fluoride emission is the Tajik aluminum smelter at Tursunzade, one of the largest stationary sources of pollution in the republic. Near the plant, congenital development defects were reportedly eight times as high as in a cleaner nearby region (Feshbach and Friendly, 1992, p. 109).

Health Effects on the Human Population

Other harmful effects of pollutants on humans in Tajikistan have been documented. Illnesses, infant mortality, and unsuccessful pregnancies are all believed to be linked to pollution, primarily to agricultural chemicals. "Results of the analyses of the sickness rate testify to the direct correlation between pesticide use and the sickness rates of bronchial asthma among adults, nervous disorders and psychoses among conscription age youth and congenital anomalies of children" (Goskompriroda, 1989, p. 5).

Infant mortality in the 1989 census was strikingly high, especially when compared with Soviet averages and neighboring republics. The infant mortality rate per 1,000 births was for the USSR, 22.7; for Tajikistan, 43.2; for Uzbekistan, 32.0; and for Kyrgyzstan, 25.9 (*Demograficheskii*, 1990). Infant mortality in Tajikistan ranged locally from 26.1 to 60.8 per 1,000 births. The highest risk areas are in the Panj River region.

Studies in the 1970s and 1980s pertaining to female cotton production workers showed increased occurrences of respiratory illnesses, gastro-intestinal disease, miscarriage and stillbirth, extraruterine pregnancy and birth defects (*Ogonyok*, no. 13, 1988). In addition, the studies found traces of pesticides in the women's blood and milk. Other studies on pregnancy risks demonstrated that working in cotton production increases a woman's chances of miscarriage by 51%; of spontaneous abortion, by 24.5 %; and of premature delivery, by 18.9% (*Zdravookhranenie Tadzhikistana*, vol. 4, no. 229, 1990). Due to chemical exposure to pesticides and defoliants used in growing cotton, this work was often found to suppress immune systems and alter normal oxidation processes in workers.

Significantly higher numbers of deaths due to respiratory illness occur in the country. Rates of tuberculosis, pneumonia, and bronchial asthma in Tajikistan are high. The occurrence of typhoid, viral hepatitis and malaria is either highest, or second highest, in Tajikistan among all fifteen of the former Soviet republics (Feshbach and Friendly, 1992, pp. 279–280).

Environmental Activities

In 1988 the USSR Goskompriroda was created to act as an environmental protection agency. Its aims were primarily utilitarian: to maximize uses of air, water, land, timber and other resources; to include costs for natural resources into overall production costs; and to fine polluting industries. It had a semi-autonomous regional affiliate in each of the fifteen Union republics.

At that time, Tajik Goskompriroda was confused on how to organize itself and develop policy. It was, however, aggressively determined to stop industrial pollution of air and water. Industries it publicly criticized and fined were the Vakhsh Fertilizer Plant, the Tursunzade Tajik Aluminum Plant, the Dushanbe Cement Factory, and the Yavan Union Factory.

At the time of independence, there were at least 31 non-governmental environmental protection committees: 3 at the oblast (province) level, 23 at the district level, and 5 special inspection groups. Since independence in 1991, the environmental movement has not made any apparent progress. The most visible organization has been the Socio-Ecological Union. It is the largest nongovernmental, environmentally active organization in the country and in 1992 had a staff of about 300 persons throughout the former Soviet Union. Goals for the Socio-Ecological Union in Tajikistan for the 1990s are to create a national park system; block further construction of the Rogun Hydroelectric Station; promote ecotourism, traditional agricultural methods, and ecologically clean small businesses; promote population control; and conduct educational programming.

Tajikistan's future environmental goals require both a monetary and a political commitment. An effective governmental agency whose function is solely to set norms, preserve natural resources, and coordinate conservation efforts is necessary. Research to improve methods of agriculture must be carried out. All this requires funding and a public commitment to work toward long-term environmental and social improvements regardless of short-term costs.

Environmental law must be developed further, but more important, the Tajik state needs to support it in a way that the Soviet government did not. Remnants of Soviet orthodoxy in the legal system and in its departmentalist control over resource consumption must be eradicated. State agencies need more than just the ability to levy fines; they must have the power to halt the construction, or output, of industries when environmental standards are not met. Tajikistan needs a means of enforcing conservation and industrial norms other than by fining polluters; fines do not halt the pollution. Planning and policy problems include a lack of environmental philosophy (including a land ethic, population control, and environmental ethics), insufficient legislation and conservation norms, lack of regional planning among Central Asian states and cooperative environmental compacts, the existence in 1993 of civil unrest, and a lack of adequate funding for environmental goals.

Future Prospects

Tajikistan is in a period of crisis, politically and environmentally. It has made one of the least tranquil transitions following the dissolution of the USSR, resulting in civil war throughout 1992 and repression of democratic leadership in 1993. It lacks the resources to pursue economic goals, as well as the political stability, democratic traditions, and national unity needed to enact effective environmental policies.

Before a forced resignation, President Nabiyev in 1992 lifted most foreign trade and investment obstacles in order to encourage joint ventures. Fortunately, Central Asian states have had long experience with market systems. Cities have always had bazaars, artisan shops, and small factories, and these people did not lose all of their market and entrepreneurial skills during the Soviet period. Unfortunately, Tajikistan, like the rest of the former Soviet Union, lacks institutions to manage a private economy and will have to develop its own. This is not only a matter of currency and banking; insurance firms, legal structure, land reform mechanisms, transfers of technology, and commercial structures are also lacking.

Tajikistan has serious economic problems. Its gross domestic product was the lowest in the former USSR. The budget deficit has approached 40% of the GDP by some calculations (*The Economist*, August 1, 1992). The country is now a debtor nation. These factors, together with a lack of political stability, ineffectual guidance of the economy, and desire to reduce cotton production, will make being a new country with old debt even more difficult.

Ties appear to be quickly developing between Tajikistan and its nearby Soviet successor states, as well as with Iran, Pakistan, India, Turkey, and the United States. The first foreign embassy to open in Dushanbe was Iran's. Linguistically related to Iran and Afghanistan, Tajiks historically had close cultural ties with these two countries. An Islamic common market has been created, of which Tajikistan is a member. Called the Economic Cooperative Organization, its members include the four Central Asian republics, Iran, Azerbaijan, Turkey, and Pakistan. Bilateral trade agreements are also being made; Turkey is setting up banks in Tajikistan, and Iran has sponsored trade exhibits. Cuba also signed a five-year trade agreement to develop health care and a sugar trade. Developing trade between Central and South Asian states may help to foster stability in Tajikistan, and a Central Asian consortium might be able to produce efficacious environmental compacts and agreements.

The development of environmental agreements between Tajikistan and its neighbors is essential. These countries must apply uniform conservation strategies; for example, each country along the Amu Darya and the Syr Darya should adopt uniform pollution norms, water consumption procedures, etc. These will be difficult to plan and implement, especially since Tajikistan is economically poorer.

Unless new export industries can be quickly developed, Tajikistan may have to acquire hard currencies by selling raw materials. There may also be a market for surplus hydroelectricity in neighboring republics, although it should again be noted that the Rogun dam is being opposed by environmentalists. If foreign investors can be enticed to come to Tajikistan, its lead, zinc, silver, gold, tungsten, antimony, fluorspar, and uranium reserves could be developed. It especially needs technology in refining these raw materials. An obvious danger in this approach is that, given present political realities, foreign firms may be able to avoid sound environmental practices in order to quickly recoup their investment.

Tajik farmers were producing 900,000 tons of cotton in the late 1980s, a third of which was valuable long fiber Egyptian cotton. Although more could theoretically be grown, many believe that an excessive amount of Tajikistan's agricultural land is currently sown in cotton. It would be possible to decrease the overall scale of cotton growing while maintaining the more valuable Egyptian cotton. A goal might be to gradually revert farming back to earlier practices, growing one part lucerne alfalfa to two parts cotton, soy, corn, fruit and vegetables and rotating fields.

A critical issue is the dynamics of the Tajik population. How will it provide work for its youth, particularly in rural areas, who will soon be entering the labor force? How will a rapidly increasing population impact the land? A related question involves whether large state-run farms will be retained. If not, a transition must be planned for reducing large state farms to efficient sizes or, if desired, for converting them back to family farm operations.

Tajikistan in the mid-1990s finds itself in a crisis situation. It cannot be blamed for the environmental conditions that it inherited as a Soviet successor state. It is, however, now saddled with the problems that Soviet industrial and agricultural planning caused. In order to resolve these, the development of a coordinated economic and environmental improvement program, within a context of peace and political stability, is essential.

Bibliography

Azimov, V. 1987. *Tajikistan*. Moscow: Novosti.

Barthold, V.V. 1956. *Four Studies on the History of Central Asia*. Vol. 1. Leiden: Brill.

Bolshaya Sovetskaya Entsiklopediya (Great Soviet Encyclopedia). 1983. Vols. 17, 25. New York: Macmillan.

Central Asia. 1991. Journal of the Area Studies Centre, Peshawar, University of Peshawar, no. 28.

Cunha, S.F. 1994. "The Global Applicability of the Biosphere Reserve Model: A Case Study from the High Pamirs, Tajikistan." Paper presented to the Association of American Geographers, April.

Demograficheskii Ezhegodnik. 1990. Moscow: Financy i Statistika.

Feshbach, M., and Friendly, A. 1992. *Ecocide in the USSR*. New York: Basic Books.

Foreign Broadcast Information Service (FBIS) reports. 1992. FBIS-SOV-92-003, January 2, and January 17; and FBIS-USR-92-076, June 22.

Goskompriroda Tajikistan. 1989. *Ecological Aspects of Development*. Dushanbe: Tajik Scientific Research Institute.

Hambly, G. 1966. *Central Asia*. London: Weidenfeld and Nicolson.

Holdsworth, M. 1959. *Turkestan in the 19th Century*. Oxford: Central Asian Research Centre.

Lewis, R.A. 1992. *Geographic Perspectives on Soviet Central Asia*. London: Routledge.

Mamadjonova, A. et al. 1968. *Sovietskii Soyuz: Tadzhikistana*. Moscow: Misl'.

Mnatsakanian, R. 1992. *Environmental Legacy of the Former Soviet Republics*. Edinburgh: Centre for Human Ecology.

Pryde, P. R. 1991. *Environmental Management in the Soviet Union*. Cambridge: Cambridge University Press.

Rakowska-Harmstone, T. 1970. *Russia and Nationalism in Central Asia: The Case Study of Tajikistan*. Baltimore: Johns Hopkins University Press.

Schwartz, L. 1991. "USSR Nationality Redistribution by Republic, 1979–1989." *Soviet Geography*, vol. 32, no. 4, pp. 209–248.

Shabad, T. 1969. *Basic Industrial Resources of the USSR*. New York: Columbia University Press.

Soviet Sociology. 1991. vol. 30, nos. 3 and 4.

Wixman, R. 1984. *The Peoples of the USSR: An Ethnographic Handbook*. New York: M.E. Sharpe.

Yablokov, A. 1992. "Notes on the Environmental Situation in Russia." *Environmental Policy Review*, vol. 6, no. 2 (Autumn), pp. 1–20.

Zdravookhraneniye Tadzhikistana (Nigakhdorii Tandurustii Tojikiston). 1983, vol. 6, no. 189; 1990, vol. 3, no. 228; 1990, vol. 4, no. 229; 1990, vol. 6, no. 231; and 1991, vol. 5, no. 236.

21

Conclusion: The View to the Future

Philip R. Pryde

The familiar saying that "today is the first day of the rest of your life" is very apt for the fifteen former Soviet republics. For them, that first day was December 6, 1991, the day that the USSR was first declared to be abolished. For each of the republics, a new era began, one ushered in with both great hope and even more abundant problems. Given the unexpected abruptness of the transformation, it is not surprising that few, if any, of the republics were ready to make a smooth transition to independence.

The preceding chapters have identified a number of recurring themes among the array of contemporary political, economic, and environmental problems that these new nations must address. Among the most common of these recurring themes are the following:

- Internal peace and stability are lacking in many republics, and this situation is retarding both economic and environmental improvement.
- In some republics, ethnic tensions are a primary reason that internal stability is difficult to achieve, and Stalinist political boundaries are a key part of this problem.
- The ongoing economic crisis is a major deterrent to the funding needed for environmental improvements.
- Outmoded, inefficient, and polluting industrial enterprises exist almost everywhere, but shutting them down frequently exacerbates economic problems.
- The waste and inefficient use of both natural and human resources during the Soviet period were staggering.
- For some republics, particularly those in Central Asia, excessive birthrates pose a dilemma, particularly with regard to future employment opportunities.

- Previous supply channels and markets for energy and other natural resources that previously existed in many of the republics are no longer assured.
- The (over)use of harmful chemicals and processes in industry and agriculture is causing human health problems as well as environmental disruption.
- Biotic resources are not being carefully managed; poaching and other causes of depletion are apparently on the increase.
- Both public and administrative understanding of, and support for, environmental enhancement is generally low, especially in times of economic hardship.

Specific examples of these various categories of problems have been given throughout the previous twenty chapters and do not need to be repeated here. The more important question is, What lessons can be learned from the seventy year experience of the command economy, centralized planning, and free-resource practices of the Soviet Union?

Lessons of the Soviet Era
for the Economy and the Environment

The foregoing examination of the Soviet-era experience, and of the current situation in the post-Soviet republics, seems to suggest that certain lessons can be inferred from the economic and environmental deterioration that characterized the USSR on the eve of its demise. Among the clearest of these lessons are the following.

Maximizing production levels is a poor model for a national economic plan. In the Soviet Union, meeting ever-higher output quotas was virtually the only yardstick of managerial success. As a result, not only did quality tend to become subservient to quantity, not only was the natural environment sacrificed in the interests of output maximization, not only does such a system stifle innovation and the introduction of improved technologies and products, but in the long run this type of system is also inherently doomed to failure. Putting additional fertilizer or pesticides on cropland to increase yields, for example, will only work up to a certain point; then it becomes counterproductive. Building huge hydroelectric dams in every feasible location eventually encourages energy waste and irreparably damages biotic resource stocks. Increasing oil production every year encourages its faster consumption and wastage and hastens the inevitable onset of field depletion. But in all these cases, advocating conservation and annual decreases in levels of production would have been heretical to orthodox Soviet planners. As a result, waste and environmental pollution became institutionalized. This leads immediately to lesson number two.

A healthy economy cannot be built on top of an unhealthy natural environment. Another way to phrase this might be that environmental expenditures deferred are environmental expenditures increased. Postponing (or simply ignoring) environmental safeguards is economically foolhardy. Not only does this practice lead to environmental and human health problems; but also it forces a much higher economic hardship on future generations, which must pay the costs of cleaning up the mess, paying increased health care costs, and installing the preferred infrastructure that should have been built in the first place. Today, every one of the newly independent states faces billions of dollars in environmental cleanup, and this cannot help but have a depressing effect on other components of the economy. Two specific large-scale examples of this are the losses produced by diverting water from the Aral Sea and the cleaning up of the mess from the poorly designed Chernobyl reactor. In the long run, the costs associated with environmental cleanup become far higher than if the economic project had been done correctly to begin with.

Out of sight is not out of mind. All ecologists (and probably all economic planners) understand the old adage that "everything has to go somewhere." Soviet planners, however, for seventy years seemed to feel that "somewhere" could be adequately defined as lakes, rivers, oceans, the atmosphere, or anywhere else that was, in the short run, cheap and convenient. Eventually, the foolishness of this approach became clear, first to the intelligentsia and only much later to political leaders—and then not to the latter until public health indices showed that a human crisis had been created by their shortsightedness (Feshbach and Friendly, 1992). Today, the environment of the former Soviet Union is so polluted that only the most uneducable of the bureaucrats believe it can be ignored any longer.

Technical fixes and huge projects often don't work. The same "gigantomania" that characterized industrial and agricultural output also often could be seen in the Soviet approach to nature. Nature was typically viewed by Stalinist planners as a harmful force that needed to be subdued, and therefore large-scale projects to "transform nature" and to "improve" marshes, deserts, and rivers were seen as the way to accomplish this. The Leningrad dike idea (see Chapter 3) is a good example of the giant project approach to handling an environmental problem that in reality required a much more sophisticated and multi-faceted solution. The long-standing dream of some planners to build huge reservoirs and divert vast quantities of water from western Siberia to Central Asia is now widely viewed as a questionable idea. And, of course, the mass production of large nuclear power plant assemblies, rather than greater efficiency in energy use and the development of renewable sources, was seen as the answer to energy needs.

A press release does not constitute an effective program. Russians and the other former Soviet peoples must learn the difference between adopting a program and actually having an effective program. They have frequently passed environmental laws, resolutions, even specific directives, all of which sound excellent—on paper. Rarely, though, have these laws and resolutions been carried out in practice so as to actually cure (or even improve) an environmental problem; in a word, they have rarely been effective. Perhaps the best example of this is Lake Baikal, which was the subject of anti-pollution resolutions in 1969, 1971, 1977, and 1987. As noted in Chapter 4, however, none of these has yet effectively stopped the pollution of this most unique lake.

A more recent example is the program in several republics to test automobiles for excessive exhaust emissions. If the car fails the test, however, the punishment is merely a fine (in July of 1992 in Minsk it was only 35 rubles, at that time the equivalent of about twenty-five U.S. cents). Assuming one is not stopped and tested too often, it is clearly more economical to pay the fine than to have the car repaired, with the result that there is no significant improvement in the quality of urban air. Again, a program exists, but not an efficacious one. A better strategy might be one similar to that used in California, where a car failing an emissions test cannot be legally registered until the problem has been corrected and the car has subsequently passed the test.

The standard Soviet practice of setting very strict (but unachievable) pollution standards was probably also counterproductive. No one bothered trying to comply, and "fines" for non-compliance were usually absurdly low. A new, more realistic system is needed.

The foregoing discussions, taken together, strongly suggest the following conclusion.

There are fundamental problems in the Marxist-Leninist-Stalinist system of economic/environmental management. Although Marx and Engels talked about the need to protect nature, those who described themselves as implementing Marxism were unable to achieve this goal. Part of the reason might be inherent problems in the economic model. These include a lack of value for in situ natural resources, an erroneous assumption that governmental economic planners would necessarily be more conservationist than private ones, and a kind of blind faith that a centrally planned economy would inherently be kinder to nature than one based on private enterprise. Unfortunately, all these assumptions turned out to be wrong. Part of the flaw in the latter assumption is that those who suffer most from environmental deterioration, the general public and especially workers, were cut off in the Soviet system from any effective way to foster changes in the system. It seems clear today that of all the possible checks and balances on both private and governmental abuse of the environment, citizen (or worker) activism may be the most important.

It is to be hoped that the foregoing lessons are being taken to heart in all of the former Soviet republics, for in their future planning efforts they are now on their own. Based on the genesis and nature of the problems that have been discussed in this volume, several remedial courses of action suggest themselves.

What Needs to Be Done?

Some of the actions that need to be taken are programmatic in nature, whereas others involve changes in the basic philosophical approaches used. Some of the most important changes of both types that are needed are as follows.

The economy and the environment must be viewed as a single symbiotic organism. A healthy economy is critical for funding environmental improvements, but the economy cannot be allowed to run rampant over the environment, for, as noted, a healthy economy has never been built on top of a polluted and degraded environment. It is axiomatic that optimal conditions for resolving environmental problems include a stable and healthy economic situation; a weak economy generally means that little money will be available for environmental improvement.

A detailed assessment of the economic needs of the former Soviet republics is beyond the scope of this volume, but it is clear that one essential component of achieving both economic and environmental improvement is the establishment of a viable inter-republic planning mechanism within the Commonwealth of Independent States. Industrial, agricultural, and environmental concerns in all of the former Soviet republics have historically relied on the existence of coordinated programs and material trade among all of the fifteen republics. Barriers to inter-republic cooperation, trade, and environmental planning among the CIS states must be eliminated.

Foreign involvement will be needed in the short run. At present, the CIS nations can't accomplish their most pressing economic and environmental goals by themselves; the necessary capital simply is not available from internal sources. Foreign aid and investment will be essential. Capital investment and construction, however, are not the only form of foreign assistance that is needed. The CIS nations are also in need of appropriate state-of-the-art natural resource management techniques from any foreign countries having effective programs in this area. But foreign concerns can't be allowed to run rampant; foreign investment and development must have a high level of effective environmental review and control by the host country.

Economic "new thinking" must be adopted quickly. Many of the economic tenets of Marxism-Leninism have proven in practice to be counter-productive and need to be replaced. Three instructive examples follow.

1. It must be recognized that natural resources have value in situ. The Marxist labor theory of value held that only human labor imparted value to goods; hence raw materials, water, etc., were deemed to have no economic value until exploited. Indeed, water use was rarely even metered. The inevitable result was the waste of a huge portion of all raw materials, which was equally detrimental to both environmental values and economic efficiency. The in-place value of free-flowing streams, forests, marshes, wildlife, and whole ecosystems must be appreciated and their loss calculated as a negative economic factor when evaluating the net benefits of any proposed new project.

2. Methods need to be developed to internalize the cost of environmental controls into the price of goods and services, preferably at the level of the direct consumer. Deferring environmental costs has proven disastrous in the past, and there is no reason to believe it would be any different in the future.

3. To the extent that Russia or other republics may choose to use the United States as an economic model, they need to understand much more than they do at present about the vast array of control mechanisms, both public and private, that exist in the United States to make private enterprise and a market economy work. What exists in Russia in 1994 is much too reminiscent of laissez-faire capitalism, discredited in the U.S. since at least the 1930s. Federal regulatory agencies, better business bureaus, strictly enforced anti-trust and anti-price fixing laws, and

watchdog consumer organizations and consumer boycotts are all essential components of making the American system work. Few, if any, of these exist in Russia or other republics at present.

The nuclear energy dilemma must be addressed in a more comprehensive manner. Russia's plans to expand its nuclear output (see Chapter 2) should be viewed at this point as merely the short-run expedient selection of the lesser of two evils, assuming the alternative is to build more polluting fossil fuel power plants. A case can be made to support the decision to go ahead with a revised nuclear program, with the major caveat that there must be better control and safety programs. But a long-range energy plan needs to be decided upon now, because many early nuclear facilities are near the end of their useful life. Their output will therefore need to be replaced (or made unnecessary) in some manner. This long-range plan, however, ought to embrace a more environmentally sensitive energy strategy than either nuclear or fossil fuel power plants. The comprehensive plan must also address the huge problem of cleaning up areas that are now radioactively contaminated, as reviewed in Chapters 4, 9, and 16.

Environmental education must be improved. A considerable amount of environmental education exists at present, but it seems to be of low efficacy. Why? A possible explanation is that this education often consists only of exhortations to "cherish nature"; there is rarely an adequate explanation to the general public of *why* it is imperative to protect nature or what the average citizen should be doing.

To the average ex-Soviet citizen, "I love nature" means "I love to go into the woods and fish, hunt, or pick mushrooms and flowers." But this, in essence, is a smaller-scale manifestation of the same nature-exploiting philosophy as is held by the managers of logging, mining, agricultural, and hydrotechnical enterprises. Changing the economic system from state exploitation to private exploitation won't necessarily solve this near-sightedness unless there is a high level of environmental understanding by enterprise managers and government administrators. At present this is a very distant goal.

A more sophisticated approach to environmental education—including such concepts as genetic preservation, sustained yield, in situ value of resources, the health of home and workplace environments, intergenerational responsibilities, and the "spaceship earth" concept—must be adopted. More important, such education must be targeted not only at the general public but also, with even more resolve, at the re-education of all government regulators and administrators.

Public and non-governmental organization (NGO) involvement is important. This is a critical component of implementing the education goal outlined in the previous paragraphs. Here, foreign assistance is already very strong, with numerous Western environmental NGOs actively involved with their fledgling Russian (and other national) counterparts. It has become clear that government agencies by themselves cannot be relied upon in *any* country to automatically implement environmentally sound management practices. Citizen review and empowerment are essential. Yet creating broad-based NGOs is particularly difficult in the former Soviet Union, where people have been told for generations that the government will resolve all their problems in the best possible way and where individual initiative has long been strongly discouraged. Even the clear bankruptcy of this philosophy at the present time is inadequate to motivate many older Soviet citizens who remember full well the penalties for "volunteerism" under the old system. In the former USSR, even more than elsewhere, the younger generation is the key to environmental reform.

Non-governmental organizations as of 1994 have a good record of inter-republic coordination. The most impressive organization at present is the Socio-Ecological Union headquartered in Moscow. It was founded prior to the breakup of the Soviet Union, retains good ties to environmental groups in almost all of the former USSR republics, and is one of the most reliable sources of environmental information about them. In the spring of 1991 the SEU and the Institute for Soviet-American Relations (ISAR) hosted the first USSR-U.S. conference of non-governmental environmental organizations in Moscow, at which dozens of such groups from both countries were represented by delegates (Klose et al., 1991). Other similar organizations exist, such as Ekologiya i Mir, but none appears to be as extensive in its operations as the SEU. An interesting development in 1993 was a report that former USSR president Mikhail Gorbachev was the founding head of a new environmental NGO called the International Green Cross (*Los Angeles Times*, April 27, 1993, p. H2).

An emphasis on efficiency of resource use is essential. The poor efficiency of natural resource use in the Soviet Union has been stressed in every work put out on this subject in the past several years. This is especially true in the areas of water resources development, agriculture, and energy use. One Soviet observer was quoted to the effect that "we don't need any additional energy production, since we spend 1.5 times more energy per unit of GNP than is spent in most western countries" (Wolfson, 1988, p. 21). Many feel the correct number is closer to two times. The same 1.5 ratio probably applies to the efficiency of irrigation water use as well. It is, one hopes, obvious to planners in all the former Soviet republics that an increase in the efficiency of water and energy utilization could preclude the need for additional expensive development of these types of resources, with huge environmental benefits. But efficiency improvements also cost money, presently in short supply. This is another area where foreign assistance might be very beneficial.

Being independent countries, but still being reliant on the old economic system that was put in place under the aegis of the USSR, the former republics will need to sit down with one another and craft new agreements that will allow them to specialize, coordinate, trade, and prosper. Some objectives of such an exercise might be as follows.

The New Post-USSR
Order: Inter-Republic Coordination

A high level of inter-republic cooperation will be essential if environmental concerns are to be adequately addressed in the post-Soviet period. This cooperation should ideally occur at both the official governmental level and the citizen (non-governmental environmental organization) level.

At the governmental level, coordination could be effected by umbrella organizations established under the Commonwealth of Independent States. However, as of 1993 the CIS (which includes all former Soviet republics except the three Baltic states) had not yet demonstrated itself to be a strong coordinating body. It had put together in 1992 an agreement on Cooperation in the Field of Ecology and Environmental Protection among its member states, but this document is more in the nature of a goals statement than a list of specific actions to be undertaken. It did, however, create a coordinating council of the republics' environmental ministers to help bring about effective multi-state policies and programs. The CIS is still young, and it might yet be able to be the agent by which strong bilateral and multi-lateral agreements can be forged.

The most obviously needed multi-lateral compact, noted in previous chapters, would be one to manage the water resources of Central Asia. The Colorado River Compact among the southwestern states of the United States could in some ways serve as a model (although admittedly a less than perfect one). The most preferable form of such a compact would be a five-republic accord encompassing the entire Aral Sea basin, which ideally might be expanded to also include Afghanistan and its portion of the upper Amu Darya (Pyandzh) basin. Less ideal would be separate compacts for the Amu Darya and Syr Darya basins. The latter approach might prove faster to achieve but would respond poorly to the problem of resolving the Aral Sea dessication crisis. A start in this direction occurred when the five Aral basin republics signed an initial agreement on the joint management and protection of the basin's water supplies in February of 1992. It creates a joint commission to regulate and conserve inter-republic rivers and lakes and is made up of the head of the water resources agency in each republic (P. Micklin, personal communication).

A number of other bilateral or multi-lateral river basin compacts might be useful. Among them would be agreements among Russia, Belarus and Ukraine concerning the Dnepr River and its tributaries; between Ukraine and Moldova concerning the Dnestr; among Russia, Belarus, and Latvia concerning the Western Dvina (Daugava); between Russia and Ukraine concerning the Donets; between Russia and Kazakhstan concerning the Irtysh (and Tobol and Ishim); between Georgia and Azerbaijan concerning the Kura; and between Russia and Estonia concerning Lake Peipsi (Peipus) and related drainages. In a more peaceful world, an agreement concerning the Araks River among Armenia, Azerbaijan, Turkey and Iran might even be envisioned, as well as one between Russia and China concerning the Amur.

Unfortunately, several early attempts at multi-lateral cooperation between and among the republics were not successful. A proposal for an agreement among the republics bordering the Caspian Sea to protect that water body was unsuccessful, and the Baltic republics are reluctant to enter into any unnecessary agreements with the Russian Federation or any that suggest that the old Moscow-dominated Soviet Union structure still exists. Significantly, the local Krasnoyarsk government has indicated a reluctance to accept more radioactive wastes from Ukrainian nuclear power stations. The maintenance of long-distance gas and oil pipelines, many of which are known to be in poor condition, will likewise require inter-republic accords in many instances. Early experience in this area indicates that the Russian Federation, as the main provider of oil and natural gas, is adept at extracting favorable quid pro quos in the course of constructing these inter-republic accords.

There is a huge array of economic and environmental coordination that was formerly accomplished relatively easily (though not always wisely) at the Council of Ministers level within the USSR government. Now, all of this coordination requires formal diplomatic agreements. These will be slow and complicated to hammer out but under current circumstances are absolutely essential.

Today, Russia and the other fourteen former Soviet republics are at the most critical point in their history since the 1917 October Revolution. In most of them, the final form of their future economic system is not yet certain, the extent to which they will embrace Western-style democracy is unclear, and the role of the individual citizen and of private organizations, as opposed to continued state control, is still to be determined. Also unclear is the future role of the Russian Federation, as the successor state to the USSR, in providing leadership (or perhaps hegemony) in the new Commonwealth of the Independent States. What *is* clear is that the environment in all of the former Soviet republics is seriously degraded, and that the interests of both the biosphere and human health demand immediate remediation. Unfortunately, the depressed economy in most of the former republics will constrain environmental improvements for some time to come, and the short-term environmental prognosis in all the republics, like the economic one, is not encouraging.

The foregoing chapters have indicated the close relationship among economic development, environmental vitality, and human health and well-being in these newly independent republics. The extent to which the new governments of these republics are able to put in place mechanisms to optimize the state of all three of these considerations will go far toward determining the future stability and prosperity of each of these new nations, and of the former Soviet Union as a whole.

Bibliography

Cole, J. P. 1991. "Republics of the Former USSR in the context of a unified Europe and the new world order." *Soviet Geography*, vol. 32, no. 9 (Nov.), pp. 587–603.

Feshbach, M. and Friendly, A. 1992. *Ecocide in the USSR*. New York: Basic Books.

Klose, E., Lubin, N., Rubin, A, and Cook, J., eds. 1991. *Joint US-USSR NGO Conference on the Environment*. Washington: ISAR.

LeVine, S. and Elliott, D. 1993. "Greater Russia?" *Newsweek*, June 21, pp. 16–18.

Marples, D. R. 1993. "The post-Soviet nuclear power program." *Post-Soviet Geography*, vol. 34, no. 3, March. pp. 172–184.

"Panel on social dimensions of interdependence in the former USSR," 1993. *Post-Soviet Geography*, vol. 34, no. 1 (January), pp. 29–51.

Peterson, D. J. 1993. *Troubled Lands: The Legacy of Soviet Environmental Destruction*. Boulder: Westview Press.

Pryde, P. R. 1991. *Environmental Management in the Soviet Union*. Cambridge: Cambridge University Press.

The Former Soviet Union in Transition, 2 vols. 1993. Joint Economic Committee of the Congress of the United States, Washington: U.S. Government Printing Office.

Wolfson, Z. 1988. "Non-waste technologies in the USSR." *Environmental Policy Review*, vol. 2 no. 2, pp. 17–22.

Glossary

All-Union: Under the USSR, a ministry (or other governmental entity) that supervised all activities under its jurisdiction throughout the entire USSR from a central office in Moscow, with a vertical organizational structure.

AO: Autonomous oblast; under Soviet regionalization, an ethnic region usually containing 10,000–100,000 persons. Less important than an ASSR.

ASSR: Under the USSR, an Autonomous Soviet Socialist Republic, often shortened to autonomous republic. An ethnic region, variable in size, of lesser importance than the 15 union republics (SSRs).

BAM: The Baikial-Amur Mainline; a new railway from Siberia to the Pacific coast built north of the earlier Trans-Siberian Railway.

C: Celsius; a change in temperature of 10°C. equals a change of 18° Fahrenheit. 0°C equals 32°F, 20°C equals 68°F, and 100°C equals 212°F.

CDSP: The weekly translation journal *Current Digest of the (Post-)Soviet Press.*

Central Asia: This term is used in two ways—to refer to the four republics of Uzbekistan, Turkmenistan, Kyrgyzstan and Tajikistan (Soviet practice); or to refer to the foregoing plus Kazakhstan (Western practice).

chernozem: A soil found in steppe regions, characterized by high fertility and a dark brown color.

CIS: Commonwealth of Independent States; successor organization when the USSR was terminated. All former republics except the three Baltic states are members.

continental climate: A climatic region characterized by extreme variation in both daily and seasonal temperatures, typically found in the interior of continents.

cu: Curies; a unit of measurement used to quantify radioactive emissions.

Donbas: Donets basin (Ukraine), largest coal producing area in the former Soviet Union.

ECO: Economic Cooperation Organization; formed in 1964 by Iran, Pakistan, and Turkey, to which the former Soviet republics in Central Asia now belong.

EIS: Environmental impact statement, an analysis of the environmental effects of a development project.

eutrophication: The process by which water bodies accumulate too many nutrients, usually resulting in algae blooms and loss of oxygen in the water.

Far East: Regions of eastern Russia fronting on the Okhotsk, Japan and Bering Seas. Generally also includes Yakutia (now called Sakha).

FBIS: Foreign Broadcast Information Service; a source of current information on happenings within the former Soviet Union.

FSU: Acronym for former Soviet Union.

glasnost: Russian for "openness," Gorbachev's policy of candor in discussing Soviet problems.

GNP: Gross national product; the measure of the value of all the goods and services that an economy produces.

Goskompriroda: Russian acronym for the State Committee on Environment (1988–1991).

Goskomstat: Russian acronym for the State Committee on Statistics (statistical compilation).

GPL: The Great Principality of Lithuania, Russia and Zhamoytiya (a major nation-state in the 14th century).

ha: Hectare; metric unit of area equal to 2.47 acres.

inversion, or atmospheric temperature inversion: An atmospheric condition (warm air on top of cooler air) that traps air pollution near the surface of the land.

km: kilometer; 1 kilometer equals about 0.6 miles.

KMA: Kursk Magnetic Anomaly; a large iron ore deposit near the city of Kursk.

krai: A political sub-division within the Russian Federation, equivalent in importance to an oblast.

Kuzbas: The Kuznets basin, a major coal basin in western Siberia extending roughly between the cities of Tomsk and Novokuznetsk.

kWh: Kilowatt-hour: The standard unit of electric energy output, equal to one kilowatt (1,000 watts) of electricity produced for a period of one hour.

m: Meters; 1 meter equals 3.28 feet, and a 1,000 m mountain is 3,280 feet high.

mm: Millimeters (1/1000 of a meter); 100 mm of precipitation equal about 3.9 inches.

MEP: The Ukrainian Ministry of Environmental Protection.

MPC: Maximum permissible concentration; used in measuring contaminant levels in air, water, soils, etc.

MPD: Maximum permissible discharge (into water bodies)

MPE: Maximum permissible emission (into the atmosphere)

NGO: Non-governmental organization; here NGO usually refers to a private conservation organization.

NIS: Newly independent states; term sometimes applied to the 15 former Soviet republics.

non-point source: Expansive land areas (agricultural fields, parking lots, etc.) from which pollutants escape into the environment from over a large area. See "point source."

NO_x: Oxides of nitrogen; a key atmospheric pollutant that is a component of both photochemical smog and acid rain.

oblast: Province; the main political sub-division in most former Soviet republics.

perestroika: Under Gorbachev, a policy of "restructuring" the Soviet economy and management system in the interest of greater efficiency.

podzols: A soil group found in northernly forested regions (such as taiga) characterized by depleted nutrient levels and only moderate fertility.

point source: A specific, highly localized source of pollution into the environment, such as a smokestack or a storm drain.

Red Book: In many countries, the popular name of the book in which endangered and threatened species are listed (in Russian, Krasnaya kniga).

RSFSR: The Russian Soviet Federated Socialist Republic; the Soviet name for what is now called the Russian Federation.

Sakha: New name for Yakutia (the former Yakut ASSR)

salinization (or, secondary salinization): The buildup of salt at or near the surface of agricultural fields in areas of heavy irrigation.

SO_x: Oxides of sulfur (usually sulfur dioxide), which combine with water vapor in the atmosphere to form acid rain.

SSR: Soviet Socialist Republic; under the USSR, any of the fifteen "Union republics" that are now independent countries.

steppe: A natural landscape zone characterized by grasslands and rich soils, found in areas where precipitation and evaporation are approximately equal.

sukhovey (Ukrainian: *sukhovii*) Hot, dry desiccating wind that occasionally occurs in the steppe regions of the former Soviet Union.

taiga: A natural landscape zone characterized by continuous conifer forests, which cover large areas of Russia and Canada.

tectonic: Refers to the internal forces that transform the earth's surface, most commonly used to refer to earthquake potential.

zakaznik: A natural preserve in the USSR, used to protect some feature of the landscape or significant habitat; see Appendix 1.2.

zapovednik (zapovidnyk): The most important type of nature reserve in the former Soviet Union, used for biotic preservation and scientific research; see Appendix 1.2. The first spelling is used in Russia, the second in Ukraine.

Note: For the new names of cities, see Appendix 1.3, Table 16.2, and the maps that accompany each chapter.

About the Book

The rapid changes in the former Soviet Union have rendered most pre-1992 works on its environment obsolete. A more specifically geographic approach that highlights the particular situation in each republic and region is offered by Philip R. Pryde's new work, *Environmental Resources and Constraints in the Former Soviet Republics*.

Focusing broadly on environmental systems, infrastructures, and problems, the book also surveys each republic's physical geography, ethnography, resources, history, economic bases, and future needs and potential. The environmental legacies of the Soviet period are outlined, and current trends are explored. The volume is well illustrated and includes many maps reflecting the most recent changes in place-names.

For its concise overview of the geographic environment in the post-Soviet republics, this book will be valued as a guide and reference by scholars, students, and professionals.

About the Editor
and Contributors

Kathleen Braden is an associate professor at Seattle Pacific University. She has traveled widely in Central Asia and written extensively on Soviet forestry, Soviet nature reserves, and efforts to preserve the snow leopard.

Oleg Cherp, a native of Belarus, has an M.A. in environmental science from the University of Manchester. He conducts research and works as a consultant on environmental planning in Russia and Belarus. He is the author of several articles in Belarusian environmental periodicals.

Zia Daniell has a degree from Dartmouth College and wide international experience in environmental planning in Germany, France, Hungary, Israel, the United States, and other countries. She has authored environmental articles for several periodicals.

Adriana Dinu works as a biologist at the University of Bucharest, specializing in ecological studies of the lower Danube and its estuary. She is also project facilitator for IUCN's East European Programme in Bucharest.

Juris Dreifelds, born in Latvia and a frequent visitor there, is an associate professor of political science at Brock University, Ontario. His first degree is in forestry, and he has written frequently on Latvian economic, environmental and demographic issues.

Sharon Eicher is an area specialist on the Tajik people and culture and has traveled widely within Tajikistan. She is currently a graduate student in the Department of Slavic Languages at the University of Wisconsin.

William E. Freeman is a specialist on environmental problems in the republics of the former Soviet Union, especially Russia and Ukraine, within the international division of the U.S. Environmental Protection Agency.

Boris I. Kochurov, born in the Volyn region of Ukraine, is deputy head of the Laboratory of Environmental Management in the Institute of Geography, Russian Academy of Sciences, Moscow, where he is responsible for preparing maps that delineate critical ecological areas.

Nadezhda Kovaleva has a degree from Moscow State University in soil science and an M.S. in environmental science from the University of Manchester. Her publications include articles on soil chemistry and acidification in Russia.

Randy Kritkausky is associate professor of social and behavioral sciences at Keystone Junior College in LaPlume, Pennsylvania. He is president of Ekologia, an international environmental organization with a primary focus in the Baltic republics. He has co-authored a Peace Corps manual on the Baltic republics.

Nancy Lubin is a fellow at the U.S. Institute of Peace and a consultant on projects within the FSU, especially Central Asia. Prior to joining USIP, she was associate professor at Carnegie Mellon University. She has lived and traveled in Central Asia and published widely on environmental topics there.

Philip Micklin is a professor of geography at Western Michigan University. He is one of the leading Western experts on water development and management problems in Central Asia and has been published and cited widely on this topic both in the United States and abroad.

Scott Monroe is presently a presidential management intern at the U.S. Environmental Protection Agency. He is a specialist and author on questions of radioactive materials management and nuclear safety in the former Soviet Union.

Philip R. Pryde is professor of geography at San Diego State University. He has written on environmental problems in the Soviet Union for the past twenty-five years and is author of *Conservation in the Soviet Union* and *Environmental Management in the Soviet Union*.

Lynn Richards works for ISAR (formerly the Institute for Soviet-American Relations) in Washington, D.C. She has traveled and carried out research in Georgia and is currently working at the ISAR field office in Almaty, Kazakhstan.

Matthew Rowntree is a postgraduate student in conservation policy and a member of the World Conservation Union's Commission on National Parks and Protected Areas and on Communication and Education, with a specialty in sustainable development.

Anna Scherbakova was born in Chita Oblast and has taught at Irkutsk State University. She is now assistant professor at the Monterey Institute for International Studies, where she specializes in the environmental issues of Siberia and the Far East.

David R. Smith is a postdoctoral fellow at the National Center for Atmospheric Research. He is a specialist on Kazakhstan and the Aral Sea basin and has written on atmospheric change in the Aral Sea basin and its consequent shoreline effects.

Siim Sööt, an ethnic Estonian, lived in Estonia as a child and has traveled there fifteen times in the past two decades. He is professor of geography at the University of Illinois in Chicago and has also taught at Tallinn Technical University.

Holly Strand is a doctoral student at San Diego State University. Fluent in Russian, she has lived and worked in Moscow and has professionally led tours to numerous parts of the former USSR, including the Russian Far East.

Ihor Stebelsky, a native of northwestern Ukraine, is professor of geography at the University of Windsor, Ontario. He is editor of the geography entries in the *Encyclopedia of Ukraine* and co-authored the Ukraine section of *The New Encyclopedia Britannica*.

Armen L. Valesyan, an Armenian citizen who lives in Yerevan and specializes in environmental issues, is currently in Moscow working on his doctoral degree in geography at Moscow State University.

Ze'ev Wolfson is editor in chief of *Environmental Policy Review*, published by the Margorie Mayrock Center at the Hebrew University, Jerusalem. He is well known as the author, under the pseudonym Boris Komarov, of *The Destruction of Nature in the Soviet Union*.

Index

Note: As a convenience to the reader, placenames in the index are alphabetized according to the more familiar Soviet name or Russian transliteration, with recent spelling or name changes listed in parentheses (exceptions: Bishkek, St. Petersburg).